4/5/17

D0408191

THE
SPIDER NETWORK

THE
SPIDER NETWORK

The Wild Story of a Math Genius, a Gang of Backstabbing Bankers, and One of the Greatest Scams in Financial History

DAVID ENRICH

CUSTOM HOUSE

An Imprint of WILLIAM MORROW

Photograph of Tom Hayes on page ix used with permission from Andrew Cowie/ AFP/Getty Images.
Photograph of brokers on page xi used with permission from BBC Motion Gallery/ Getty Images.

HarperCollins books may be purchased for educational, business, or sales promotional use. For information please e-mail the Special Markets Department at SP-sales@harpercollins.com.

FIRST EDITION

Designed by William Ruoto

Library of Congress Cataloging-in-Publication Data has been applied for.

ISBN 978-0-06-245298-6

17 18 19 20 21   LSC   10 9 8 7 6 5 4 3 2 1

FOR KIRSTEN, HENRY, AND JASPER

CONTENTS

CONTENTS

The Family

Tom Hayes

TOM HAYES: Star trader at a succession of banks

NICK: Hayes's father

SANDY: Hayes's mother

ROBIN: Hayes's younger brother

PETER AND BEN O'LEARY: Hayes's stepbrothers

SARAH TIGHE: Lawyer who eventually marries Hayes

The Traders and Bankers

Royal Bank of Scotland (RBS)

BRENT DAVIES: Hayes's mentor, later an ICAP broker

PAUL WHITE: Libor submitter

NEIL DANZIGER: Party-loving trader

SARAH AINSWORTH: Trader; Hayes's girlfriend; later, Crédit Agricole trader

UBS

MIKE PIERI: Trader and manager who hires Hayes in Tokyo

MIRHAT ALYKULOV: Junior trader, nicknamed "Derka Derka"

ROGER DARIN: Trader and Libor submitter who becomes Hayes's nemesis

YVAN DUCROT: Executive aligned with Darin

NAOMICHI TAMURA: Trader and manager

SASCHA PRINZ: Risk-loving trader and executive

CARSTEN KENGETER: Co-head of investment banking division

ALEX WILMOT-SITWELL: Co-head of investment banking division

PANAGIOTIS KOUTSOGIANNIS: Trader known as "Pete the Greek"

HOLGER SEGER: Manager

ANDREW SMITH: Trader and Libor submitter

Citigroup

CHRIS CECERE: Trader, Hayes's boss

BRIAN MCCAPPIN: Karaoke-loving CEO of Japanese investment bank

HAYATO HOSHINO: Trader in London tasked with helping Hayes

ANDREW MORTON: Senior investment banking executive

ANDREW THURSFIELD: Libor submitter and manager in London

LAURENCE PORTER: Libor submitter, Thursfield's underling

BURAK CELTIK: Libor submitter, Porter's underling

Deutsche Bank

GUILLAUME ADOLPH: Trader, nicknamed "Gollum"

DAVID NICHOLLS: Trading manager

MARK LEWIS: Executive who talks with Hayes about possible job

Other Banks

ALEXIS STENFORS: Hotshot trader at Bank of America Merrill Lynch

PAUL ROBSON: Rabobank trader and Libor submitter, nicknamed "Pooks"

STUART WILEY: J.P. Morgan trader

LUKE MADDEN: HSBC trader

MILES STOREY: Barclays Libor official

PAUL ELLIS: Credit Suisse trader

The Brokers

Darrell Read, Noel Cryan, Colin Goodman, Terry Farr, Danny Wilkinson, and Jim Gilmour

ICAP

DARRELL READ: Broker renowned for his university degree and large nose

COLIN GOODMAN: Broker who sends out influential Libor "run-throughs"

DANNY WILKINSON: Red-faced broker and manager

FRITS VOGELS: Manager in London

MICHAEL SPENCER: Founder and CEO

DAVID CASTERTON: Spencer's right-hand man, nicknamed "Clumpy"

ANTHONY HAYES: Broker at Tokyo affiliate, nicknamed "Abbo"

RP Martin

TERRY FARR: Happy-go-lucky, motorcycle-crashing broker

JIM GILMOUR: Down-on-his-luck broker

LEE AARON: Broker, nicknamed "Village"

CLIFF KING: The three brokers' manager

DAVID CAPLIN: CEO, nicknamed "Mustard"

Tullett Prebon

NOEL CRYAN: Amateur boxer, broker

MARK JONES: Party animal, broker

NIGEL DELMAR: Broker, Hayes's best friend in Tokyo

DANNY BRAND: Broker in Hong Kong

ANGUS WINK: Senior executive

The Authorities

Bank of England

MERVYN KING: Governor

CHRIS SALMON: Senior official

British Bankers' Association (BBA)

ANGELA KNIGHT: CEO

JOHN EWAN: Official in charge of Libor

U.S. Commodity Futures Trading Commission (CFTC)

GARY GENSLER: Chairman

DAVID MEISTER: Head of enforcement division

STEPHEN OBIE: Enforcement official

VINCENT MCGONAGLE: Enforcement official

GRETCHEN LOWE: McGonagle's deputy

U.S. Justice Department

DENIS MCINERNEY: Head of fraud division

ROBERTSON PARK: Lawyer in fraud division

WILLIAM STELLMACH: Lawyer in fraud division

SCOTT HAMMOND: Lawyer in antitrust division

U.K. Financial Services Authority (FSA)

MARGARET COLE: Head of enforcement

PATRICK MEANEY: Investigator

U.K. Serious Fraud Office (SFO)

DAVID GREEN: Director

MATT BALL: Investigator

The Lawyers

LYDIA JONSON: Hayes's lawyer, from Fulcrum Chambers

IVAN PEARCE: Hayes's lawyer, from Fulcrum Chambers

STEVEN TYRRELL: Hayes's U.S. lawyer (previously at Justice Department)

GEORGE CARTER-STEPHENSON: Hayes's barrister before his trial

NEIL HAWES: Hayes's barrister during his trial

MUKUL CHAWLA: Barrister representing the SFO

JEREMY COOKE: Judge presiding over Hayes's trial

GREGORY MOCEK: Barclays lawyer (previously at CFTC)

GARY SPRATLING: UBS lawyer (previously at Justice Department)

The small ski resort town, nestled in the mountains outside the city of Karuizawa, was a popular destination for day trips for Japanese families. Bustling during the day, it was mostly quiet this Saturday night. Clouds cloaked the moon.

A chartered bus pulled up outside a bar, its windows aglow. A light snow was falling. Out into the peaceful evening stumbled dozens of rowdy bankers, some toting tall cans of Asahi and Kirin. Most of them were drunk. They quickly took over the small bar.

The drinkers were employees of the American bank Citigroup, one of the world's largest and most troubled financial institutions. A year earlier, at the beginning of 2009, American taxpayers had finished pumping a staggering $45 billion into Citigroup to bail out the collapsing behemoth. Now the transfused recipient was treating dozens of its investment banking employees to a weekend getaway. The bankers were housed nearby in a sprawling luxury hotel, each employee's room designed in Japan's typical spare style.

These festivities weren't so spartan. The point was to foster camaraderie, and that was happening in spades. The party had begun on the hundred-mile ride on the bullet train out from Tokyo. After a day of hitting the slopes, Citigroup ferried the bankers to a bowling alley, where they drank and bowled and drank some more. Their bus had then deposited the intoxicated crew at this bar, before leaving the partiers behind to fend for themselves.

One of the fiesta's ringleaders was a wiry, curly-haired American named Chris Cecere. You wouldn't know it from his behavior

1

now, but he was one of the sharpest people in Tokyo's cutthroat financial markets. A foul-mouthed veteran of the doomed Wall Street firm Lehman Brothers, Cecere (pronounced CHECK-er-ay) had only worked in Japan for a year or so, but he had quickly assembled a team of rock-star traders. His mandate was to push the already risk-hungry Citigroup into brave new financial frontiers.

That wasn't all Cecere was pushing. This snowy night, he was practically pouring shots down the throat of his subordinate, a disheveled British thirty-year-old named Tom Hayes. Slim and nearly six feet tall, Hayes was a brilliant mathematician, one of the most prolific, aggressive traders in Tokyo, if not the world. As with Cecere, he didn't look or act the part. Bespoke suits and expensive shoes were found nowhere in his wardrobe. Specks of dandruff dusted his shoulders. He was far happier with a glass of orange juice or a mug of hot chocolate than a pint of beer, a preference that once earned him the nickname "Tommy Chocolate."

Hayes found social situations uncomfortable to the point of painful—this one included. Before departing for the ski weekend, he had grumbled to his fiancée that he didn't want to go. She told him he didn't have a choice. Hayes's life revolved around work, and Citigroup was his new family. He had only started there a couple of months earlier, and it was important that he make a good impression on his colleagues. So far, he was off to a promising start in that regard. His new bosses bathed him in praise, introducing him around Citigroup's global organization as their newest trophy asset. Only hours before they showed up at the bar, a top Citigroup executive, Brian Mccappin, had described Hayes as "a star" who represented the future of the firm's enormous business in Tokyo. Mccappin proclaimed that their division would further shift its trading approach to take advantage of their new hire's extraordinary talent. Hayes was certainly being paid like a star. After years of feeling like he was getting stiffed by six-figure payouts at his former employer, the Swiss bank UBS, he had pocketed a roughly $3 million cash signing bonus when he joined Citigroup.

Mccappin, the CEO of Citigroup's investment bank in Japan, came along to the bar that night, along with Cecere and Hayes. A native of the gritty English city of Birmingham, Mccappin was tall, with a chubby, dimpled face. A talented singer at thirteen, he and a friend had formed a band called Deadline that sometimes performed at a pub frequented by workers, including Mccappin's father, emptying out of a nearby Rolls-Royce plant. After Deadline split, some of its members went on, years later, to form Ocean Colour Scene, which briefly rose to fame touring with Oasis. By then Mccappin had moved on to other things, but that didn't stop him from occasionally claiming that he'd been a founding member of the infinitely more familiar band.

At the time Hayes arrived at Citigroup, the main outlet for Mccappin's stymied musical ambitions was karaoke, and he was a frequent and enthusiastic practitioner. As Mccappin belted out tunes this night, Hayes grudgingly accepted shot after shot of Jägermeister from Cecere. He struggled to swallow the sweet herbal concoction, fighting an increasingly powerful gag reflex. But he kept throwing the shots back, unwilling or unable to withstand Cecere's schoolboy pressure. Hayes didn't want to disappoint his boss. The earlier part of the day had been easier: Hayes was an expert skier, who embraced risk as eagerly on a black-diamond trail as he did on a frenzied trading floor, and he thrived in the deep powder of the Karuizawa resort. Now, though, beads of sweat started tingling on his scalp. The room began to spin. Hayes staggered to the bathroom and vomited. Then he rejoined the party.

. . . .

Three years later, in January 2013, I was sitting on a sofa in my cramped apartment in London's Clerkenwell neighborhood. Centuries earlier, the area had been the stomping ground of knights who were about to embark on crusades to the Holy Land. In a nod to that history, the narrow alleyway that my wife and I shared with a Belgian beer hall was named Jerusalem Passage. The neighborhood had been repopulated by trendy design studios, sushi bars, and art galleries.

It was just after 8 P.M. when my iPhone buzzed with a text message from a number I didn't recognize. "I'll meet you tomorrow but I need to be certain I can trust you," the text read. "This goes much much higher than me and a lot of what I know even the DOJ [Justice Department] is in the dark."

The message was from a terrified, and very sober, Tom Hayes.

. . . .

Less than two months before Hayes contacted me, the attorney general of the United States had stood at a lectern in Washington, D.C., and announced criminal fraud charges against Hayes, branding him as a greedy, deceitful trader who had ripped off countless innocent victims in order to enrich himself. Here, the planet's most powerful cop declared, was the mastermind of a sprawling, multibillion-dollar scam.

Spread out across time zones and continents, a group of bankers, brokers, and traders had tried to skew interest rates that served not only as the foundation of trillions of dollars of loans, but also as an essential vertebra of the financial system itself. It all boiled down to something called Libor: an acronym for the London interbank offered rate, it's often known as the world's most important number. Financial instruments all over the globe—a volume so awesome, well into the tens of trillions of dollars, that it is hard to accurately quantify—hinge on tiny movements in Libor. In the United States, the interest rates on most variable-rate mortgages are based on Libor. So are many auto loans, student loans, credit card loans, and on and on—almost anything that doesn't have a fixed interest rate. The amounts that big companies pay on multibillion-dollar loans are often determined by Libor. Trillions of dollars of exotic-sounding instruments called derivatives are linked to the ubiquitous rate, and they have the ability to touch virtually everyone: Pension funds, university endowments, cities and towns, small businesses and giant companies all use them to speculate on or protect themselves against swings in interest rates. If you bought this book with a credit card, you quite possibly brought Libor into it. So, too, if you drove to the bookstore in a car not yet paid off—or if you're carrying a mortgage or student loans, or if your town borrowed money to pave its roads, or if you work for a company that issues debt. So if something was wrong with Libor, the pool of potential victims would be vast. As it turned out, *something* wasn't wrong with Libor, *everything* was.

Hayes didn't come up with the idea of manipulating Libor to turbocharge his profits. But during the course of his career, he took the practice to fantastic new heights, oblivious to or uninterested in the fact that he was engaging in unethical activity with the real potential to harm unsuspecting victims. That initially helped catapult the nerdy trader into the upper echelon of the most profitable industry on earth. By the time I met him, it had thrust him into the crosshairs of regulators and prosecutors on three continents, who were yearning to find someone to hold accountable for the mass destruction that the banking industry recently had inflicted on Western economies.

I had spent nearly a decade writing about banks and their misadventures for the *Wall Street Journal* and other publications. But this was a misadventure like none other. On the surface, it wasn't the most eye-catching scandal—which is the very reason it was so easy to pull off. The conspirators were fiddling on the margins with something that few people paid much attention to. But the stakes were so high that even small-scale tinkering had the capacity to spawn fat profits—to the tune of tens if not hundreds of millions of dollars—with commensurate losses afflicting the often-unsophisticated victims.

But the hunt to nab Hayes and his confederates—a group that one participant dubbed the "spider network"—exposed far more than a scheme to manipulate the underpinnings of modern banking. I began to see the saga as rooted in a corrupt, broken financial system, as well as the minimalist, see-no-evil regulatory infrastructure that theoretically was supposed to keep the industry in check. Hayes's moral compass certainly was skewed—perhaps in part due to the mild case of autism he was eventually diagnosed with, which helped explain his incompetence at human relations and his affinity for numbers over people. But just about everyone I encountered suffered from a version of the same defect: obsessed with numbers and profits, eager to use other people as tools for self-advancement, convinced that anyone on the losing end wasn't so much a victim as a sucker who deserved whatever mistreatment he got. And the more I dug, the more it seemed that, at least in some ways, Hayes himself was that sucker, the hapless guy positioned to take the fall for an entire industry's era of anarchic, reckless behavior. His odyssey, as well as the institutions and individuals that goaded him along, reveals a lot about why the banking industry has become synonymous with scandal—and why, even today, its awful reputation remains firmly intact.

PART I

The Scam

CHAPTER 1

Watching the Coronation

The Brackenbury Primary School, in the dumpy west London neighborhood of Shepherd's Bush, was in a three-story, redbrick Victorian-era building. From outside, the school looked grand. Inside, it was a different matter: High ceilings created a cavernous, intimidating vibe, paint was peeling from the walls, and cold air drafted in through ragged insulation. The small campus, just down the street from the Goldhawk Road Underground station, was in a part of London marked by tracts of similar-looking, century-old houses and down-on-their-luck convenience stores, pubs, and Laundromats. Brackenbury's student body, drawn from the surrounding neighborhoods, was primarily working class.

In 1990, one of the school's students was Tom Hayes. The ten-year-old was big for his age, with a mop of sandy blond hair and small dark eyes. He was burning with anger. It was hard to pinpoint the exact reason. His parents had split up six years ago after his mother, Sandy, caught his father, Nick, cheating. Hayes detested Nick's absence from his life. Nor was he thrilled that upon his father's remarrying in 1989, Tom and his younger brother, Robin, had inherited two stepsisters from Nick's new wife, as well as a baby half sister. But Nick wasn't the only issue. Hayes resented what he saw as Sandy's cold, controlling nature and the fact that she seemed more devoted to her job than to mothering her two sons.

Money was tight. Once, before his parents divorced, angry debt collectors showed up at their small, two-floor brick house in Shepherd's Bush after Nick, a ponytailed television journalist, fell behind on the utility bills. Hayes told himself that when he grew up, he'd make enough to ensure that the bailiffs never returned. Every day, he counted his money, which he had earned doing odd jobs around the neighborhood. He stacked the coins by denomination. He memorized the quantities. The rituals made him feel safe. He started carting around all his essential belongings in his backpack, as if ready to flee if the need suddenly arrived.

Sandy worked as a researcher for Gordon Brown, a jowly, Scottish politician in Britain's Labour Party. She toiled long hours, delegating child-rearing duties to a series of au pairs. Hayes perceived her as anxious, angry, and strict. Among her rules: Hayes was only allowed to drink water. To say their relationship was contentious would have been an understatement. Once, in a fit of rage, she hurled a hot baked potato at Hayes. After another fight, Hayes locked his mother in the cellar. Another time, he flung a saucepan at her head. He threw violent tantrums. (Sandy was not his only target. He once assaulted his stepbrother, who came along with Sandy's new husband, Tim, with a pool cue.) "The au pairs couldn't cope," she would later tell a psychiatrist.

Hayes was desperate to win his mother's favor. The only way to do that, as far as he could tell, was to excel at school, so that's what he set out to do. By the time he was six, he was already emerging as a standout math pupil. (Once, he badgered Sandy to buy him a math workbook as a gift.) "Tom is a mature and sensitive boy who gets emotionally upset at times due to family problems," a teacher wrote in a 1987 review that was sent to his parents. "His anger and frustration, and particularly his aggressive will to win, have frequently got him into trouble in the playground and with his peers, though he has calmed down recently."

As confident as Hayes was when it came to math, that's how dysfunctional he was interacting with his peers, especially girls. He could hardly work up the guts to talk to them. He kept track of his number of friends at any given time; he rarely counted more than three and almost never saw them outside of school. Part of the problem might have been his demeanor. Endlessly teased for his attire (Brackenbury didn't have a strict dress code, but Hayes nonetheless routinely showed up wearing a blazer), he won a dubious award from his peers for "best uniform" of the year. "Tom can sometimes come across as arrogant about his abilities," a teacher wrote in 1992. "He should appreciate the value of diplomacy!" his English teacher said on another occasion. Hayes acknowledged the problem: "I need to improve my attitude in that I respect ideas I disagree with," he wrote in a self-assessment.

Buffeted by strife at home and unpopular at school, it wasn't surprising that Hayes sought refuge in things he could easily understand. From his bedroom window, he could see the floodlights over Loftus Road, the stadium that was home to the Queens Park Rangers professional soccer team. When QPR scored, Hayes could hear the crowd roar. The sport became a lifelong passion, and for years he attended every home and road game that the Rangers played. He saw QPR as a second family.

And Hayes became obsessed with collecting things. He stockpiled used train tickets. He built a vast army of metal toy soldiers. He amassed dozens and dozens of soccer stickers, which he arranged in particular orders. His purest love, though, was mathematics. He cherished the simplicity, the objectivity of numbers. They never lied, they never disappointed you, unlike so many people in his life. You couldn't misinterpret numbers—a valuable quality for a literal-minded boy like Hayes. Equations were beautiful, not to mention reliable: Marriages could fail, friends could fight, girls could ignore you, and QPR could (and often did) lose, but the square root of nine was always three, the angles of a triangle always added up to 180 degrees.

That fed a budding interest in finance. It was partly because Hayes had an intuitive understanding for numbers; he wasn't scared of them the way many kids were. Another factor was his paternal grandfather. Raymond Hayes had been a stockbroker for an old firm, Mullens & Company, in the City of London, as the capital's financial district is known. Raymond's nickname at work had been "Talkie" because he was such a blabbermouth, and he loved gabbing to his attentive grandson. Raymond trained Hayes to read the tiny newspaper columns of daily stock price movements, instructing him to search for patterns, and he entertained Hayes with colorful stories, some of which might have been apocryphal, about his days of traipsing into the City wearing a shiny, black top hat. A favorite tale involved Queen Elizabeth II's coronation in 1953. Raymond wanted to watch the ceremony, but he didn't own a TV or have the money to buy one. He told his boss, who advised him to buy shares of a specific company. Raymond bought the shares. They immediately rallied. The next day, he unloaded the shares, pocketing enough money to buy his TV and watch the coronation. (Insider trading didn't become a crime in England until 1985.

During Raymond's heyday, the practice was rife.) Decades later, a watercolor painting of the ornate Mullens headquarters would hang in Hayes's living room—a gift from Raymond before he died in 2000.

. . . .

Just as Hayes was getting into a groove at school, Sandy and Tim, a management consultant, decided it was time to escape dirty urban living in favor of Winchester, a town in the English countryside best known for its medieval cathedral. Hayes was fifteen. The hardest part wasn't moving away from his few friends; it was his newspaper route. He earned £20 (roughly $40) a week, and it was easy money—his route consisted of a single luxury apartment building. He barely had to venture outside.

At his new school, Hayes remained an academic star. "Tom is a talented mathematician," his annual assessment said. Newspaper delivery no longer an option, he sought out other means of pulling in some cash. At lunchtime, his classmates were always desperate for a little extra money to buy more food, generally a supplemental portion of dessert. It was a ripe opportunity for someone to make a nice profit, Hayes realized, so he skipped eating and instead loaned out his lunch money to classmates. He charged usurious 50 percent daily interest rates—in other words, someone who borrowed $5 would owe $7.50 the next day. Hayes reckoned he had to charge so much because his borrowers tended to default at an alarming rate. The venture was profitable, keeping Hayes flush with pocket money.

Other moneymaking opportunities beckoned. British high school students tend to hang out in pubs. Once, sitting in a Winchester watering hole, his friend David Brown noticed Hayes staring at a row of slot machines. Brown thought Hayes was just zoned out. He wasn't. The slot machines had signs on them advertising how often they paid out—for example, that an average of one in ten wagers would be a winner. Hayes was watching people robotically feed coins into the machines and calculating which machine was due to deliver the next jackpot. Then he would put his money in. The tactic worked.

Hayes didn't plan to build a life around math. Though his interest in finance remained, he realized that his argumentative streak could be enjoyably put to use and decided that he wanted to be a lawyer. In college, preferably at Oxford University, he hoped to major in history and then pursue postgraduate legal studies. But his interview with an Oxford admissions officer went poorly. Given his outstanding academic performance, the point of the interview was more social than scholarly. But Hayes had developed a deep aversion to eye contact, finding it easier to concentrate if he fixed his gaze on an inanimate object rather than a human face. The resulting conversation was labored. The admissions officer tried to let Hayes down gently, telling him he just wouldn't enjoy himself at Oxford—British code for him not seeming like the right stock. Hayes was stunned. It was the first time he'd failed for what he assumed were academic reasons.

So it was that an eighteen-year-old Hayes ended up at the University of Nottingham. Nottingham wasn't especially strong in history, but it boasted excellent math and engineering departments. Falling back on his acknowledged strengths, Hayes abandoned the social sciences to become an expert in partial differential equations, advanced calculus, and fluid mechanics.

Freed from his mother's disciplined home—Hayes had a strict 9:30 P.M. bedtime until he left for Nottingham—he went a bit wild, vigorously transitioning from water to much harder stuff. At 3 A.M. one night, Hayes was belting out QPR soccer anthems in his dorm. A professor was awoken and nearly had him kicked out. Still, by the rambunctious standards of most college kids, Hayes seemed normal, more or less. And, for perhaps the first time in his life, he was happy.

．．．．

By then, Sandy's career, attached to that of Gordon Brown, was soaring. Brown had become chancellor of the Exchequer, the British equivalent of the U.S. Treasury secretary and the second-most-powerful post, behind the prime minister, in Tony Blair's Labour government. (It wasn't Hayes's only connection to the British establishment. Sandy's sister was married to a Bank of England official named Chris Salmon, whose career also would soon take off.) After Hayes's first year in college, Brown told Sandy that her son could have a summer job working in the Treasury. She turned down the offer on Hayes's behalf, without asking him. Sandy felt her son was too conservative to fit into Blair and Brown's center-left government. She described Hayes to acquaintances as a Thatcherite, a reference to the 1980s Conservative prime minister Margaret Thatcher. Coming from Sandy, the label was derogatory.

It's hard to imagine how Hayes's life might have ended up differently if he had gotten that summer job. Working in finance in a powerful government department, under the watchful eye of his mother and a supportive boss, might have opened up a world of different possibilities for someone with prodigy-like math skills. Hayes didn't even learn of the job offer until years later.

Instead, he spent that summer and the next working behind the bar at the Winchester tennis and squash club near where Sandy and Tim lived.* He worked eighty hours a week, earning about £3.75 an hour, for a weekly haul of £300, not bad for a summer job. But he chafed as patrons condescended and belittled him, regarding Hayes as lower-class even though his family was a member of the club. Come the end of the summer, he could hardly wait to return to school.

One day in the fall of 1999, Hayes was in the computer lab at the University of Nottingham when he overheard two older students talking about internships they planned to apply for in the London offices of the Swiss bank UBS. The internships paid about £500 a week, though what they actually entailed was a bit unclear to Hayes; they involved something about "operations." That sounded sufficiently vague that Hayes figured he probably could do it—whatever *it* was. He didn't know much about investment banking, aside from vague notions he'd picked up from his grandfather's stories, but the money sounded great.

That December, he showed up for an interview at UBS's London offices. He was running a high fever, felt awful, and didn't think he performed well. He figured he was heading for a repeat of the Oxford rejection, but a few days later, UBS offered him a summer job. The pay was even better than Hayes had expected: £600 a week, or on track to be £27,000 a year. That was more than most adults in Britain earned at the time—and double what he'd earned the prior summer for what he guessed would be less strenuous, more rewarding work. Back to London he would go.

---

* Hayes's boss at the club gave him good marks, but the teenager did exhibit some odd behavior. Once, instructed to gather stray tennis balls, Hayes collected roughly 150 balls and squirreled them away at his home.

. . . .

The internship ran from July to September. Hayes rented a place in London and commuted into UBS's offices, right around the corner from the old Mullens building where his top-hatted grandfather once worked. (In fact, S. G. Warburg, which had been purchased by UBS, had itself purchased Mullens in the 1930s.) Hayes found the job boring. He worked behind the scenes, helping UBS manage its technology and computerized trading systems. At the end of the summer, the bank offered him a permanent job. It wasn't even conditioned on Hayes graduating—that's how much they wanted him. But in his few months at UBS, Hayes had learned about the investment banking pecking order. Back-office roles, such as the one he'd been offered, were close to the bottom. At or near the top were traders.

For most people, the notion of a trader is based largely on movies depicting Wall Street's wild ethos. Bellicose traders, their sleeves rolled up, shout profanities into multiple phone lines simultaneously, while gawking at a half-dozen computer screens and, in their spare time, abusing subordinates, harassing the few women in their midst, and casually cheating anyone they can. The caricature isn't too far from the truth, but it doesn't explain what a trader actually does.

In fact, there were different types of traders, Hayes learned that summer. One common variety was called a market maker. A market maker's defining trait was that he fielded queries from other banks, asset managers, hedge funds, insurance companies, and other institutions that wanted to buy or sell financial products in the market maker's area of specialization, say Mexican government bonds. If a trader at a hedge fund called up and said he wanted to sell $10 million of those bonds, the market maker's job (as an expert in Mexican bonds) was to quickly assess the characteristics of the proposed transaction and then offer the hedge fund a price at which he would be willing to execute the transaction. To be good at the job, the market maker needed a hearty appetite for risk, because if he agreed to do the deal, he then became the proud owner of those Mexican bonds. Sometimes that would be only for a period of a few minutes, before he sold them to another trader at a different institution, but other times it could be much longer. When someone else came along looking to buy Mexican bonds, the market maker would try to eke out a profit by selling the bonds for at least slightly more than he had paid for them.

As long as he was holding on to the securities, the market maker also needed to make sure that the bonds weren't vulnerable to big swings in value. One way to accomplish that was to buy instruments whose values were likely to move in the *opposite* direction of the original Mexican bonds—such as a type of insurance contract that gained in value as the risk of the Mexican bonds defaulting rose. That tactic of protecting himself through offsetting positions was known as "hedging." It was similar to a die-hard Red Sox fan placing a bet that the Yankees would beat his team in the playoffs—that way, even if the fan's heart was broken, he would at least win a little money as a consolation prize.

Pulling off profitable transactions on behalf of clients wasn't the only way that traders made money. They also were expected to place their own separate bets on the direction of markets and to amass positions so that they profited if their bets turned out to be correct. This was fundamentally different from market making, but market makers were among those plying this type of trade in addition to their main jobs. By the time Hayes arrived on the scene, this had become standard operating procedure, but it represented a seismic shift in the traditional role played by a bank.

No longer was the bank serving mainly as an intermediary whose trading was designed to lubricate the financial system or assist clients in managing their finances; this type of trading was an end in itself, designed to benefit nobody other than the bank and its employees.

There were many reasons for this transformation. One was that regulators in the United States, Britain, and elsewhere, lulled by the lack of a recent financial crisis and swayed by the industry's enormous political clout, had taken a hands-off approach to overseeing this sort of speculative activity. In the United States, a law imposed in the wake of the Great Depression that prohibited commercial banks from partaking in investment banking activity was repealed, paving the way for the creation of megabanks like Citigroup whose trillion-dollar balance sheets allowed the placement of massive wagers with the banks' (or, more precisely, its investors' and customers') own money. Another factor was that, over the past couple of decades, many old Wall Street partnerships— firms like Goldman Sachs, Bear Stearns, Lehman Brothers, and Morgan Stanley, which had been owned by a small group of their uppermost, longest-serving employees—had converted into publicly traded companies. That allowed the firms' partners to cash in on their ownership stakes, catapulting some of them to near-billionaire status. But it also meant that the companies became accountable to a new class of owners, many of whom demanded to see profits grow quarter after quarter, year after year. Unleashing their traders to roll the dice more aggressively was one way for the Wall Street banks to achieve that—assuming, of course, that their bets paid off.

Whatever the causes of the shift, it didn't take long for traders—often paid a portion of the profits they generated—to rise to the top of the banking totem pole, to churn out ever-greater profits (and the occasional catastrophic loss) for their institutions,* and, with a little help from Hollywood, to capture the public's imagination. And the interests of a trader whose performance was measured based on how much he helped clients versus one who was rewarded based on how much money he raked in through his own trading—well, they were very different. So were the interests of a bank that mainly focused on its clients' needs and one that profited in large part from trading that was divorced from—and sometimes diametrically opposed to—what its customers wanted.

The art of making money through this so-called proprietary trading was partly in the timing: Bet on something that's cheaply priced, protect yourself with an offsetting position, get rid of the original asset just as it reaches its peak value, extricate yourself from the offsetting hedge position, and pocket the proceeds. In the ideal scenario, savvy traders managed to construct enough over-lapping hedges that they virtually eliminated any downside risk and guaranteed themselves a small profit, regardless of which way markets moved. Traders with advanced math skills, able to swiftly calculate and recalculate the ever-changing odds of a wide range of bets and to craft computer programs to identify opportunities for profits, enjoyed an enormous advantage. And you didn't need to win consistently: Billionaire Ken Griffin once said that he expected the stock market bets of his employees at hedge fund Citadel to pay off just 52 percent of the time. The great news for the trader was that, if his positions gained in value, he would share in the spoils. And if his bets didn't pan out, the worst-case scenario was that he lost his job. That rarely happened and, when it did, it tended to

---

* Trading profits and losses aren't zero-sum among banks. In many cases, nonbank institutions are on the opposite side of a bank's trade, meaning that for every winning trade, there doesn't need to be an offsetting loser at another bank.

be pretty easy to find a new gig, without having to explain much about the reasons for his sudden departure from the prior job. As a result, traders were basically in a no-lose situation.

Hayes cannily accepted the UBS operations gig, but when he returned to Nottingham in the fall, he started applying for trading jobs at other banks: the Royal Bank of Scotland, J.P. Morgan, Goldman Sachs, and Deutsche Bank. He landed interviews everywhere other than at Goldman. When the Scottish bank offered him an entry-level position as part of the bank's training program, he accepted and informed UBS that he no longer wanted the back-office assignment.

Hayes told his mother about his newfound career ambitions. She was opposed in principle to the idea of her son working for an investment bank and spent hours trying to talk him out of it. Hayes's father wasn't thrilled, either. Hayes shrugged off their concerns.

He was hardly alone in being tempted by the potential riches of a career in finance. All over the Western world, promising students, especially those with math and engineering backgrounds, were flocking to banks, seduced by the chance to put their technical skills to use in creative ways, while hauling in fat paychecks. The shift accelerated amid the moribund U.S. economy of the early 1990s, when aspiring engineers realized that jobs in their hoped-for fields, such as aerospace, weren't nearly as plentiful or remunerative as they had expected. At Caltech, one of the country's premier engineering schools, banks were showing up in droves at campus job fairs. "The bottom line is, it pays really well," a Caltech engineering major, headed for a bond-trading job at investment bank Salomon Brothers, explained to the *Los Angeles Times* in 1993. It didn't matter that much of what the industry was doing served little purpose beyond enriching itself. Larry Summers, the Treasury secretary in the Clinton administration, noted that starting in the 1970s, the finance industry was "transformed from a field that was dominated by people who were good at meeting clients at the nineteenth hole to people who were good at solving very difficult mathematical problems that were involved in pricing derivative securities."

One of Hayes's classmates at the University of Nottingham was a young man named Kweku Adoboli. The Ghana-born son of a United Nations peacekeeping official, Adoboli grew up in the Middle East and then England. At Nottingham, he majored in computer science. Afterward, he got a summer internship at UBS and then was offered a full-time operations job. Unfortunately for both men, their lives would continue to follow parallel trajectories.

. . . .

After graduating from Nottingham in July 2001 with honors in math and engineering, Hayes flew to the United States. It was his second trip there, following a 1998 visit to South Carolina to visit his father's relatives. This time, he had stops in Miami and New York City before heading to Washington, D.C. His uncle, Chris Salmon, had been sent on a temporary assignment by the Bank of England to work at the International Monetary Fund, just down Pennsylvania Avenue from the White House. Hayes wasn't terribly close to Salmon, but they had shared interests in economics and finance, and Hayes spent the brief visit talking with him about how he envisioned building a career as a bank trader.

Hayes started at the Royal Bank of Scotland that fall. RBS's office was on the bustling eastern edge of the City, just across a busy street from the Bishopsgate Police Station. Hayes's starting salary was about £35,000, along with an expected £15,000 bonus—a substantial take for someone just out of university.

Hayes was in a training program that sent its aspiring million-aires cycling through various trading desks to get a taste of the different flavors of the bank's businesses. Hayes spent most of his time doing menial tasks. There was a lot of data entry. He learned to use Microsoft Excel, whose spreadsheets served as the backbone for many of RBS's trading models. He also scurried around doing personal favors for established traders—he got their keys cut, fetched their coffee, delivered their clothes to the dry cleaner, purchased gifts for their parents and girlfriends. Hayes, like plenty of grunts on trading desks, endured merciless mockery. One subject of harassment was his clothes—he still dressed too well. He wore a jacket and tie to work while most colleagues opted for a business-casual look of slacks and a light-colored button-down. One trader threatened to cut off his necktie if he wore it again.

There were no classes where wannabe traders were taught the ropes. They were supposed to learn through osmosis, by watching veterans do their jobs. And the lessons Hayes picked up were similar to those absorbed by a generation of traders across Wall Street and the City of London: Make money at all costs. Traders' performances were evaluated based on two factors: their ability to manage risks and their ability to maximize revenue. There were really no other criteria. Traders were encouraged to go the extra mile to wring out extra profits, trained like bloodhounds to sniff out that edge. It could be in the form of unique information, or unique relationships with huge clients, or unique access to naïve and gullible customers, or a unique way to massage indexes or benchmarks to make trades more profitable. Whatever the edge was, you had to find one. The way you dressed, the way you behaved—those might make you a target for teasing, but they were irrelevant when it came to how much you got paid. And that was the ultimate yardstick of success. When it came to obeying the rules, the only check was the bank's legal and compliance department, which was supposed to make sure employees knew the rules—statutory, not moral—that they had to follow. That department—a sort of internal affairs bureau—wasn't exactly a force to be reckoned with. During compliance training sessions at RBS, traders hunched over their BlackBerrys playing the addictive "Brick Breaker" game. The goal was to knock out each layer of tiles, brick by brick, the high score the only measure that mattered.

CHAPTER 2

The Hall of Mirrors

Mohammad Reza Pahlavi needed cash. In fact, he needed $80 million of it.

Two years earlier, in October 1967, dressed in full military regalia and wielding a scepter, Pahlavi had anointed himself Iran's Shahanshah, or King of Kings; he would henceforth be known as the Shah for short. His coronation ceremony was held at Tehran's mosaic-and-mirror-covered Golestan Palace. The Shah marked the occasion, which also happened to be his forty-eighth birthday, by donning a large, jewel-encrusted crown over his graying hair. He also placed a sparkling platinum crown on the bowed head of his third wife, Empress Farah. His golden throne glittered with 26,733 jewels. "I feel closer than ever before to my noble and patriotic people," he declared to his subjects.

The Shah had inherited the title from his father, Riza. Riza Shah the Great, as he liked to be called, was a military general who deposed the previous ruling dynasty and changed the country's name to Iran from Persia. After taking over from his father, Shah Pahlavi briefly lost power when a democratically elected government, Iran's first, came to power in the early 1950s. That government, led by socialist prime minister Mohammad Mossaddegh, nationalized Iran's vast petroleum industry. Believing his politics smacked of communism, in 1953 the CIA orchestrated a coup and reestablished the Shah's supremacy. If that wasn't enough to leave the Shah in the West's debt, the massive amount of American military and economic aid pouring into his country surely did the trick.

Now the Shah was looking for an $80 million loan to finance a new government agency. To facilitate the deal, one of the Shah's emissaries got in touch with a tall, mouse-faced man named Minos Zombanakis. Born in 1926 in a poor town on the Greek island of Crete, Zombanakis endured the German occupation of his country during World War II and then, without a college diploma, worked his way up through the Greek banking system, including a stint at the central bank. As a twenty-nine-year-old, he showed up in Cambridge, Massachusetts, and talked his way into a Harvard University graduate program, where one of his classmates was Henry Kissinger. Afterward, he returned to banking, working in Rome and the Middle East, fostering connections in Iran, before settling in London with his wife and son. By the 1960s, he had emerged as a pillar of the city's banking industry, someone with a reputation for innovating and taking risks. In 1969, when the Shah was seeking the loan, Zombanakis had just opened the London outpost of Manufacturers Hanover, a large New York bank that would later become part of the J.P. Morgan Chase empire.

The $80 million that the Shah wanted was too much for one bank to just fork over, even if the would-be borrower happened to be a government leader backed by a superpower. So Zombanakis lined up a couple dozen Western and Middle Eastern lenders to make the loan as a group.

Now the question became what interest rate to charge the Shah. This was the type of problem that was increasingly vexing London's banking industry. The City, whose labyrinth of narrow, windy streets largely dated back to Roman times nearly two millennia ago, had always played a leading role in global finance, thanks to London's status as an imperial capital. But globalization was accelerating the transcontinental flow of cash and cementing London's role as a global financial crossroads. As business boomed, bankers like Zombanakis came up with creative ways to meet customers' diverse financial needs and, in the process, to make a lot of money for themselves. One invention was the use of a group of banks, known as a syndicate, to jointly make loans. That had the advantage not only of reducing the amount that any individual bank had to kick in, but also of sidestepping rules that capped the amount of risk that banks were allowed to take with individual clients.

Normally, a big loan would carry a fixed interest rate, one that didn't change at all over the life of the loan. That had the benefit of simplicity, but it left the banks vulnerable to changes in prevailing market interest rates in the years before the loan was repaid. If, for example, a central bank had set its base interest rates at 3 percent, the banks might charge their customer a fixed 5 percent interest rate for the duration of the loan. That would be enough for the banks to pocket a tidy sum. Even if the central bank then hiked interest rates to 4 percent, the banks would still manage at least a small profit. But if rates rose further still, their profits would be wiped out. If the loan was small, the loss was small, too. But when the amount was massive—and that's what the Shah was looking for—well, that was different.

One way to address the risk would be to have the interest rate that the banks charged fluctuate in tandem with base interest rates.

That seemed easy enough; after all, central banks generally adjusted their rates only on occasion. But in London's increasingly busy financial markets, that still left the banks exposed to changing market conditions. Most banks financed themselves by borrowing money from a variety of sources, including short-term loans from rival banks, part of the financial merry-go-round that kept the banking world spinning. These interest rates that the banks charged each other fluctuated much more frequently. The changes tended to be small, but even minuscule moves could have big impacts when applied to multimillion-dollar loans.

Zombanakis came up with a novel idea. What if the banks that were part of the Shah's loan syndicate regularly reported what it cost them to borrow money? Those figures could be averaged out and, every few months, the interest rate on the Shah's loan could be adjusted to reflect the changes in the banks' average funding costs. That would insulate individual banks from the risks of a loan becoming unprofitable due to changes in interest rates. Of course, the banks would tack on a bit of a supplemental charge above their funding costs to ensure that the loan was even more lucrative. Zombanakis convinced the other banks it was worth a try.

This sort of rate-setting mechanism had never been tried before. As a result, the Shah got his money, a bunch of banks profited from sizable interest payments, and Zombanakis got credit for what the *Economist* at the time praised as a "very cunning" new financing arrangement. In Manufacturers Hanover's newly opened London offices, the bankers celebrated the milestone with flutes of champagne and trays of Iranian caviar.

Zombanakis and his colleagues couldn't have imagined it at the time, but their brainchild would soon become a crucial piece of the world's financial plumbing, an interest rate woven into countless financial contracts.

. . . .

On the trading floor at RBS, Hayes noticed that it wasn't the biggest clients who elicited enthusiastic laughter and applause when they called. Instead, it was small pension funds and other unsophisticated investors—so-called dumb money. They lacked access to high-quality financial data and generally weren't as sensitive to tiny differences in the prices that banks would offer them. In other words, they were ripe for being duped, and RBS traders fought to get access to them. Shouting matches on the trading floor over who had the right to the clients were routine. Nobody thought about it in moral terms. It was just part of the game, just the way things worked: Get your TV and watch the coronation.

Years later, as Wall Street scandals piled up, one trader after another who cut his teeth at the same time as Hayes would offer a similar description of the era's amoral culture. "I remember that if I voiced an opinion based on moral considerations, I'd get looked at as if I were an alien," a former investment banker explained to Dutch journalist Joris Luyendijk.

Hayes's promise quickly became evident. He breezed through a series of regulatory and trade group exams in late 2001 and early 2002, earning him the right to work in jobs where he interacted with clients. Because those jobs entailed responsibility for looking after clients' finances, they were subject to extra doses of supervision from bank compliance departments and financial regulators—or at least that was the idea. In reality, London was in the midst of a revolutionary free-market experiment. The City was selling itself as something of a regulation-free zone, especially compared to its chief competitor, New York, in a bid to attract banks and other financial institutions. The laissez-faire approach was christened "light touch." The United Kingdom's understaffed Financial Services Authority only had a small handful of employees assigned to oversee some of the world's biggest banks—and was mocked by a satirical magazine as the Fundamentally Supine Authority. Sandy Hayes's boss, Gordon Brown, would become one of the idea's loudest cheerleaders. "Not just a light touch but a limited touch," he would declare in a 2005 speech. The approach, Brown said, "helps move us a million miles away from the old assumption—the assumption since the first legislation of Victorian times—that business, unregulated, will invariably act irresponsibly. The better view is that businesses want to act responsibly. Reputation with customers and investors is more important to behavior than regulation, and transparency—backed up by the light touch—can be more effective than the heavy hand." It would turn out to be a disastrous misreading of capitalism.

. . . .

One of Hayes's peers in his training program had been a young woman named Sarah Ainsworth. She was a pretty brunette with a nice smile, pronounced cheeks, and a controlling personality. Like Hayes—who still couldn't seem to make eye contact—Ainsworth was not only brainy but also a bit odd. The pair hit it off, became friends, and eventually started dating.

Hayes forged other friendships through his job. On a rotation through one of RBS's trading departments, he sat next to a veteran named Brent Davies. A tall, hulking man with a mane of wild blondish hair, Davies was eleven years older than Hayes. At age twenty, he had joined the banking industry, working as a clerk at a bank that one day would be folded into RBS. He slowly clawed his way up through the ranks and became a trader. By the time Hayes arrived, Davies had been there thirteen years. Davies liked the bright, quirky young man and took him under his enormous wing. He would buy Hayes beers after work if he'd endured a tough day. When Hayes and Ainsworth had problems (which was often), he listened and sometimes dispensed advice. Hayes embraced Davies as a father figure. Of course, traders being traders, Davies teased Hayes about the fact that his mother still cut his hair and that he was still sleeping under a duvet cover decorated with superheroes. He suggested that his mentee read *The Curious Incident of the Dog in the Night-Time,* a novel whose autistic main character reminded Davies of Hayes. (Behind his back, Davies nicknamed him "Kid Asperger." Other colleagues christened him "Rain Man.") Notwithstanding the sometimes nasty edge of Davies's ribbing, Hayes always smiled, seeming not to notice.

Hayes soon landed a permanent gig among a fast-growing cluster of RBS traders who specialized in products called derivatives. Derivatives came in many flavors, but they all shared a common characteristic: They were instruments whose values *derived from* something else. What you were buying or selling was not the thing itself (widgets, bushels, gold bars) but something related to that thing, maybe its future value, or how it compared to something totally different. If you wanted to buy ten gold bars, that was straightforward; if you wanted to place a bet that nine months from now the price difference between ten gold bars and fifty bushels of wheat would be twice the difference between five bushels of wheat and sixteen widgets, then you were playing with derivatives.

Derivatives had been around, in various forms, for a very long time. In the twelfth century, English merchants at medieval fairs signed contracts guaranteeing to deliver their wares at a set price at a future date—a primitive type of futures contract. Five hundred years later, Japanese feudal lords used a similar practice to lock in rice prices to protect themselves from bad weather or war. The famous Dutch tulip bubble largely involved the frenzied trading of options to buy or sell the bulbs—a precursor to modern-day stock options—rather than transactions involving the actual flowers.

Derivatives really exploded in popularity in the 1970s, in large part due to unprecedented volatility that hit financial markets. Oil prices ricocheted up and down. Governments delinked their currencies from the gold standard, causing exchange rates to swing wildly. Rapid inflation spurred central banks to jack up interest rates. Companies and individuals needed ways to protect their fortunes from these new risks—and banks and brokerages were there to help, peddling a growing array of derivatives. A company that offered hot-air-balloon rides might purchase derivatives whose value rose the more rainy days there were in a season, thereby shielding the company from the adverse effects of bad weather. The banks or other companies that sold those instruments would charge a fee and then would try to balance out their positions by offering the opposite positions—say, a derivative whose value climbed based on the number of sunny days—to other customers, such as umbrella manufacturers. Boiled down to their essence, derivatives were designed to help people or institutions protect themselves from future circumstances. And no matter the sunshine or the clouds, one party in the transaction always came out ahead—that was the bank that, for a fee, engineered the derivative.

Derivatives were uniquely suited for speculation, because traders could dabble without actually having to own a product. Someone who bought or sold pork belly futures, for example, was unlikely to actually own, now or ever, any actual pig parts. But future swings in the price of pork bellies might be a good gauge of expectations about the weather or a harvest or a disease's severity or just basic macroeconomic trends. And so investors might buy or sell pork belly futures to get a piece of that action.

The increasing popularity of derivatives as a speculative vehicle unnerved many experts. After the 1987 market crash, a White House report blamed derivatives for worsening the crisis by intensifying the snowball-like nature of panicked selling. In April 1994, derivatives landed on the cover of *Time* under the headline "Risky Business on Wall Street." (The magazine's cover illustration was of an evil-looking nerd staring at a computer screen.) And in 1998, the chaotic collapse of the giant, derivatives-investing hedge fund Long-Term Capital Management, run by mathematicians and Nobel Prize–winning economists, further underscored the instruments' risks. "Every time there's been a fire, these guys [derivative traders] have been around it," the former U.S. Treasury secretary Nicholas Brady noted in response. But derivatives were not going anywhere.

. . . .

IBM had a problem. The company, with operations all over the world, had issued debt to finance its European businesses in Swiss francs and German marks. But IBM preferred to have all its debts denominated in American dollars—otherwise its finances were tethered to volatile and unpredictable international exchange rates. In 1981, IBM turned to Salomon Brothers for help. The Wall Street firm approached the World Bank—one of the leading issuers of debt anywhere, and an entity with a tolerance for bonds denominated in a variety of currencies—and convinced it to sell a slug of bonds that were identical to the IBM debt except for one crucial difference: They were in dollars. Then IBM and the World Bank simply swapped responsibility for making interest payments and eventually repaying the principal on their respective bonds. It was the birth of a new financial derivative: the swap.

Derivatives tied specifically to interest rates became common as Hayes came of age in the banking industry. Say that ABC Corp. borrowed $100 from First National Bank. The loan had a floating interest rate tethered to the Federal Reserve's base rate,* which currently stood at 2 percent. That carried risks. If the Fed subsequently hiked rates, ABC Corp. would see its interest payments shoot higher. So investment banks concocted a derivative product, known as an interest-rate swap, that would help protect ABC Corp. from the possibility of being burned. ABC Corp. and Giantbank would enter into a derivative contract that simulated a pair of similar $100 loan transactions. First, ABC Corp. would agree to borrow $100 from Giantbank with a fixed 2 percent rate. Then Giantbank would agree to borrow $100 from ABC Corp. with a floating rate tied to the Fed's base rate or another metric. At the end of the loan period, whichever party—ABC Corp. or Giantbank—owed more money on their side of the contract would pay the other party. (The $100, called the derivative's notional amount, wouldn't change hands.) Under this construction, ABC Corp. would stand to make money on the swap if the floating rates jumped above 2 percent, which would make up for the higher interest rates it would owe First National on the original loan. If floating rates declined, ABC Corp. would owe money to Giantbank, but that would be offset by its savings from the declining rates on the First National loan. In other words, the derivative neutralized the interest-rate risks ABC Corp. faced in its original loan. (Got it?) Providing interest-rate swaps was a valuable service, involving not only complex calculations but also the assumption of large risks, and banks charged their clients handsomely.

---

* The Fed's base rate, or federal funds rate, represents how much banks charge each other to borrow money that's on deposit at the Fed. It serves as the basis for the interest rates that banks charge to lend that money out to their customers.

If that setup sounds terrifyingly complicated, keep in mind that like so many instruments in the hall of mirrors that is modern finance, there might not even be an "ABC Corp." The swaps were simply another vehicle with which banks could bet on the future direction of interest rates. That meant a particular interest rate—and this is where Libor would eventually come into the equation—could have massive effects when it came to a bank's bottom line: If it moved in an advantageous direction, a particular swap could become extremely lucrative. By 2010, some $1.28 *trillion* of these interest-rate swaps would change hands on a daily basis, up from $63 *billion* fifteen years earlier. As always, the advantage went to the trader who found an edge—whether that edge was a gullible client, a superior product, a more sophisticated computer model, whatever. Sometimes the edge was simply pushing the envelope just a little bit further than anyone else.

Hayes landed in a subgroup of the interest-rate team that specialized in products derived from Japanese rates. At first, one of his main tasks was to rewrite the computer models that RBS used to figure out how much its derivatives were worth. It was a monstrously complex task. Hayes needed to come up with intricate models to predict not only the future direction of Japanese interest rates, but also the prices of a variety of instruments that were underpinned by those interest rates, as well as their likely interactions with interest rates elsewhere in the world. The process was made all the more grueling by the archaic state of RBS's computer and software systems.

In 2002, Hayes was handed partial responsibility for a small segment of his team's trading. Under his boss's supervision, he was allowed to start buying and selling limited quantities of low-risk derivatives tied to Japanese rates. Hayes had arrived; he was a trader, near the top of the Wall Street food chain. But it was an unglamorous assignment. He was squeezed on RBS's teeming trading floor, surrounded by row after row of loud, cocky colleagues, with only a stack of computer monitors to act as a buffer between the awkward young man and his rowdy deskmates. The real problem, though, was that the Bank of Japan had kept interest rates at zero for nearly ten years, trying in vain to resuscitate the country's moribund economy, a period that would come to be known as Japan's "Lost Decade." With interest rates flatlined, the derivatives Hayes was responsible for were pretty dull. Another downside: He needed to be at his desk for a large portion of the period each day that Japanese financial markets were open. That meant arriving at RBS's offices as early as 4 A.M., which in turn meant going to bed by 7:30 P.M. Unlike most traders, Hayes was far from social, and so he didn't mind the early bedtime. In the summer, he loved strolling through the City's ancient, deserted streets as predawn daylight emerged over seventeenth-century church steeples and twentieth-century skyscrapers. But during the winter, the sun didn't rise until after 8 A.M. Then, having to drag himself out of bed at 3 A.M. was torture.

Because many of the clients looking to buy or sell Japanese derivatives were based in Japan, Hayes got to travel to Tokyo. One trip happened to overlap with a visit by Fred Goodwin, RBS's hard-charging CEO. Goodwin was staying at the luxurious Four Seasons; Hayes was in a crummy hotel down the street from RBS's offices. Misreading the cues, Hayes ribbed the CEO about his posh digs and jokingly complained that he wasn't permitted to stay there. The attempt at humor fell flat with the ill-tempered Goodwin.

RBS had a small office in Tokyo, and most of its trading business involved proprietary trading, in which traders made large bets simply using the bank's money; there was no ancillary business of making markets for or otherwise helping clients. Goodwin was introduced to a group of traders. He looked at each of them, asking what they did for the bank. "Prop trading," came the proud response. The CEO looked queasy. After all, what business did a Scottish bank really have employing high-stakes gamblers on the opposite side of the globe? Years later, Hayes would recall that Goodwin appeared to be "a bit nervous that there was some Nick Leeson waiting in the wings in Tokyo." Leeson was the Singapore-based trader whose unauthorized, money-losing gambles caused the 1995 collapse of Barings Bank, what had been the United Kingdom's oldest investment house. But Goodwin wanted growth. That meant taking risks—by the company and by its legions of ambitious young traders. And Goodwin would get what he wanted.

CHAPTER 3

Classy People

The eight-year-old boy left Ethiopia in search of a better education and a brighter future.

It was 1963, a time of considerable change in the country where the boy had lived with his parents. Thousands of Western tourists were venturing there, hoping to enjoy Ethiopia's sunny weather and its ancient history. In the capital, Addis Ababa, new buildings designed by prominent European architects were sprouting up as a gusher of foreign aid—and a boom in the export of Ethiopian coffee—lifted the economy. And the city was the home of the new Organisation of African Unity, a confederation of dozens of African countries. At its inaugural summit that May, the two-thousand-plus delegates—which included thirty-one heads of state—pledged to devote themselves to decolonizing the rest of the continent. Ethiopia's autocratic emperor, Haile Selassie, tried to refashion himself as a beacon for independence and self-determination. "May this convention of union last 1,000 years," the seventy-one-year-old emperor declared at the summit, before inviting the delegates to a sumptuous banquet.

The optimistic mood didn't temper the reality on the ground. Selassie was a brutal, absolutist ruler. Most Ethiopians were impoverished peasants. Even the affluent couldn't avoid the sight of things like leprosy and widespread destitution. While the Western world had grown accustomed to viewing coronations and other events on live TV, very few people in Ethiopia could afford to buy a television set and, even if they could, there were no broadcasts to actually watch.

And so the eight-year-old, named Michael Spencer, decamped to England. His parents, diplomats in the British civil service, had enrolled him in a Catholic boarding school in the rolling green hills and farmland south of London. The young Spencer was a strong student and was later admitted to Oxford University, where he studied astrophysics. But his goal, ever since he'd been fifteen, was to work in finance. He was fascinated by the Rockefeller and Morgan dynasties in the United States. Most important, he craved money. His father, back in Addis Ababa, didn't discourage the obsession. "Money can't make you happy, but it does allow you to be miserable in comfort," he counseled his son.

After graduating from Oxford, the twenty-one-year-old Spencer, with a hippie haircut and beard, landed his first job in the City of London in 1976 at stockbroker Simon & Coates. He was fired in 1979 after losing gobs of money on a bet that the price of gold would go down; instead, the price had soared after the Soviet Union invaded Afghanistan. Spencer seemed to blame the mishap on his absorption of the industry's prevailing culture. "I rather naively believed one could get rich quick, and the whole idea of working in the City was to get rich quick," he would tell an interviewer in 2005. Spencer soon bounced back and secured a new gig in London at the American bond-trading firm Drexel Burnham

Lambert. Once again, he was fired after three years, this time not only for making bad trades but also for trying to conceal them.

In many industries, that would have been the final straw, but London's financial arena in the 1980s was a wild, reckless place. The City was about to undergo the violent tremors of Margaret Thatcher's deregulatory revolution, and hungry young traders and brokers were in high demand. Spencer resurfaced at a smaller brokerage firm called Charles Fulton. By now, despite his money-losing ways, he was developing an expertise in a fast-growing corner of the markets called interest-rate derivatives. When Charles Fulton converted into a publicly traded company in 1985, Spencer took his earnings—about $200,000—and with a few colleagues decided to create a new brokerage firm that would specialize in matching up buyers and sellers of interest-rate swaps and other derivatives. They launched Intercapital in May 1986. Its name would later be shortened to ICAP.

· · · ·

One of the pieces of sage counsel that Brent Davies pounded into his impressionable mentee's head, over and over again, was the following: "Never trust a broker." Brokers, he explained to Tom Hayes, were like the hyenas of the investment banking world, wild, clownish figures who feasted on the carcasses left behind by stronger, more cunning predators—namely, traders. These weren't run-of-the-mill stockbrokers, the types who handled many grandparents' portfolios of blue-chip stocks. These particular middlemen—known in the industry as "interdealer brokers"—solely interacted with people at big banks and other financial institutions. Say that a trader at RBS wanted to buy a bundle of interest-rate derivatives. To avoid tipping his hand to rivals, the trader would tell one of his favorite brokers that he wanted the derivatives and was willing to pay a certain price, say $1,000 per contract. The broker would tell his colleagues. Then those brokers—generally keeping the identity of their client secret—would fan out to their trader contacts at other banks and see if there was anyone willing to sell that product at something resembling the price the RBS trader was willing to pay. If so, the match was made and the trade got done. For his efforts, the broker's firm was rewarded with a tiny percentage of the transaction's value as a commission. Because the trades regularly ran into the millions of dollars, and lots of them occurred every day, such commissions quickly stacked up. The brokers personally received a big chunk of their commissions.

But the brokers also played another, less tangible role in the shadows of London's financial markets, as purveyors of gossip and other often-questionable information. When a trader wanted to get a sense of where a market was heading, he might call a broker to get a feel for where rival traders were putting their money. The brokers—few of them university educated, but most of them with street smarts—also were infamous for spoon-feeding traders bogus information that had no purpose other than tricking them into doing trades that weren't really worthwhile to anyone but the brokers themselves. Similarly, if a *trader* wanted to spread misinformation in the market—for example, nudging the price of a thinly traded instrument higher based on a hazy rumor about pent-up demand for that particular product—a broker could be an ideal conduit. One illustration of the industry's culture was that brokers used the word *broking* to mean "tricking" or "misleading"—as in, *I was broking him to believe something that wasn't true.*

For a good trader, however, brokers were indispensable as

sources of trading opportunities and information. As a result, when Hayes gained responsibility for a small amount of trading, his colleagues started introducing him to brokers—and warning him about the hazards they posed, especially to someone who was gullible and prone to social confusion. One of the first brokers Hayes met was Noel Cryan, an amateur boxer who worked at one of London's biggest brokerages, Tullett Prebon. The son of Irish immigrants—his dad was a construction worker, his mother a nurse—Cryan attended Catholic school, where he struggled with disciplinary issues. He dropped out at age seventeen and spent the next couple of years working odd construction jobs. One miserably cold winter morning, Cryan stood outside at a construction site and decided that perhaps it was time to start a career. Despite his lack of interest in school, he was good at math, and he found an apprenticeship at a local gambling company. He enjoyed the job and figured he could earn a better living putting his skills to work in finance. A broker he knew said he'd be a good fit in that industry, and so, at age twenty-one, Cryan joined the profession in which he would spend the next quarter century.

Cryan—with a bulbous nose and hangdog cheeks, he had a slight resemblance to Kevin Spacey—was married with two sons. An avid sports fan, he'd taken a liking to the New England Patriots, but his biggest passion was soccer; he supported a third-rate London club called Millwall, whose fans were renowned, even in England's bare-knuckled hooligan culture, for their pugilistic tendencies.

Hayes regarded Cryan as bright and likable, especially because he, like Hayes, was loyal to a mediocre soccer team. (In Hayes's linear mind, fidelity to a downtrodden squad was a sign of strong moral fiber and therefore meant the person could be trusted under virtually all circumstances.) The feeling wasn't mutual. Cryan, a bit of a party animal, thought Hayes was basically a loser, shy and antisocial, and seemed to suffer from some sort of obsessive-compulsive disorder. (That Cryan's wife was a special-needs teacher probably made him more attuned to this sort of thing than the average broker.) When they went out for a drink, it was hard to get Hayes to talk about anything other than financial markets or soccer, and he still refused to make eye contact. Hanging out with him was exhausting.

Like Hayes's teachers from a decade earlier, Cryan found that the young trader could be combustible. The slightest provocation—a real or perceived slight, for example—would set him off. Cryan quickly learned that there was no point trying to argue with Hayes about the wisdom of trades or the accuracy of data. When Hayes was in one of his moods, Cryan would let him rant and rave, turning down the volume on his phone so he didn't have to listen. He would wait out the storm and call him out on his bad behavior the next day after he'd calmed down. Hayes typically would apologize and promise to make it up to the broker.

Despite his qualms about Hayes's personality, Cryan respected his chops as a trader, albeit a relatively green one. His ability to spot patterns was stunning. His grasp of tricky market phenomena was equally impressive. And for all his flaws, he seemed trustworthy. He was just very, very intense.

Hayes also was introduced to a parade of brokers at a much smaller London firm, RP Martin. RP Martin was an insular, tightknit outfit. Its CEO, David Caplin, ran the place with close attention to details large and small. He was universally known as "Mustard," a nickname that stemmed from his early days as a broker. (Back in the 1980s, senior colleagues had described his eager attitude as "keen as mustard.") Balding, with blue eyes and an impish smile, he often retired to the local pub with his workers to engage in foul-mouthed banter and name-calling. Such was the culture Mustard instilled at his firm.

One of the first people Hayes met at RP Martin was Lee Aaron. His nickname was "Village," shorthand for "Village Idiot." Aaron, who had started as a broker in 1998, relished his goofball reputation, which appealed to some traders who were more interested in having a relationship with a chatty, fun-loving guy than with a financially literate broker. Hayes was not one of those traders. He had little time or patience for those he deemed less intelligent than himself—a cohort that encompassed most of the world's population. Over and over, Hayes demanded that RP Martin, if it valued its relationship with RBS's derivatives traders, find him a new broker. After burning through his third or fourth unsatisfactory RP Martin broker, Hayes told the company that he wanted someone young, someone whom he could mold. Behind closed doors, the RP Martin brokers fumed. One dubbed Hayes "the most rude person" he "had ever had the misfortune to meet." Nobody, it was agreed, wanted to work with this guy.

Then along came Terry Farr. Farr was about eight years older than Hayes. His mother worked for the government; his father sold shrubs and plants at a local market. Farr had dropped out of school at age fifteen. He had always wanted to work with dogs; he figured maybe he could become a canine handler in the military. That turned out to be impractical, so instead he followed his sister into banking. His first job, two days after he turned sixteen, was as an entry-level clerk at Lloyds Bank. Four years later, not long after getting laid off, he had a son with his teenage crush, Clare, a short, pretty redhead; they eventually married and settled in a house on the English coast. Farr, blond and with a ruddy, boyish face, cherished the freedom of being able to race his motorcycle—he had a particular fondness for Ducati bikes—along the hilly, windy countryside roads. Once, a wasp stung him on his chin while he was on his motorcycle. His neck and chin swelled up so much that the normally pudgy Farr look like he had suddenly become morbidly obese. He was also prone to crashes.

After a long stretch of unemployment, in which he worked with his father at their market stall, Farr became a broker. He got the job through one of Clare's ex-boyfriends, whose father was the chairman of a brokerage firm. Farr's inability to do math beyond simple addition and subtraction didn't prove problematic. Five years later, in 1999, Mustard personally recruited him over beers at a London pub, nearly doubling Farr's salary to £60,000. Farr came to love Caplin and the casual culture he presided over. In the summer, Farr showed up to work wearing Bermuda shorts and flip-flops—fine by Mustard.

By the time Hayes appeared on his radar, Farr was a veteran. But he had never mastered the technical side of things. His boss regarded him as hardworking but "not the sharpest person in the box." (More than a decade later, Farr would remain confused about the defining characteristics of the instruments, such as interest-rate swaps, that he was helping clients trade.) Farr's expertise was as a social creature. Beer in one hand, cigarette in the other, he was a focal point in the pub, charismatic and friendly, able to make strangers feel at ease with a casual wink and a knowing smile. When Farr heard that the notoriously prickly Hayes was looking for someone malleable to be his broker, he raised his hand. Farr knew he could easily play the part of the clueless newbie. He was good at handling difficult people, and he sensed an opportunity to get in at the ground floor with a promising young trader. "I can put up with being shouted at a bit," Farr thought to himself.

The relationship got off to a turbulent start. Hayes wasn't interested in the broker's excuses about not understanding basic financial concepts. He regularly screamed at Farr, who would turn the other cheek, and the abuse would gradually subside. Once, however, Farr, embarrassed that his colleagues had overheard him getting chewed out by the young trader, felt compelled to stand up for himself. To the broker's surprise, Hayes immediately backed down and apologized. After that, he was easier to deal with.

The two men spoke daily, and before long they were on the phone a dozen or more times each day. Farr worked overtime, arriving at 5 A.M. and staying till 6 P.M., to keep Hayes happy with a steady stream of chatter about what his rival traders were up to. Gradually, to reward Farr for his patience and scraps of information, Hayes routed an increasing number of lucrative transactions through Farr.

One final broker rounded out Hayes's squad: ICAP's Darrell Read.

. . . .

Slim and well dressed with close-cropped dark hair and dark, scowling eyebrows so pronounced that they seemed to cast shadows over his deep-set eyes, Read wasn't like most other brokers. The son of a carpenter, he had graduated from Liverpool University in 1986 with a degree in geography and zoology—the first member of his family to earn a college diploma and an achievement uncommon among his professional peers. A passionate rugby player and fan, he once turned down a job in Zurich because of Switzerland's lack of a rugby culture. One of his teammates on his local rugby squad was an ICAP broker, and he suggested that Read apply for a job there. Read declined. But, years later, stuck in a dead-end job as a clerk at a small bank, he ran into his rugby friend again. This time, Read took him up on the idea.

After getting the job, Read continued to tell friends that he'd like one day to become a geography teacher. But he and his wife, Joanna—the two had known each other since college and had two young sons—soon grew accustomed to his six-figure income. In an industry where creative nicknames were prized above almost all else, Read's original moniker was "Beryl," a nod to the British actress Beryl Reid, who had spent a career depicting eccentric characters. That proved too harmless to be much fun. Read's long, pointy nose offered greater inspiration: Among his subsequent nicknames were "Noggin," "Nogs," "Nez," and "Big Nose."

Read liked Hayes. He could tell the guy was razor-sharp. But it was also clear that he was in way over his head. He was shy and socially maladroit—the first three months of their relationship, Hayes didn't want to meet in person—and Read felt a bit bad for him. RBS had thrown him into a market-making job where his success would hinge in large part on his ability to come up with precise prices so that he would know at exactly what levels to buy and sell the derivatives he was trafficking in. It didn't take the technically oriented Read long to notice that some of the prices Hayes was relying on were at best imprecise. Other brokers pounced at the chance to exploit the youngster's errors; Read offered him some pointers instead.

Like Hayes, finance and markets intuitively made sense to Read. He had a spongelike memory, especially for numbers and data. He was the rare broker who could come up with sophisticated trading strategies rather than simply executing them. Hayes, therefore, respected him. Read, fifteen years Hayes's senior, also appealed to the young trader as a father figure. He encouraged that sentiment by coaching Hayes on the markets and trying to help the emotionally volatile young man remain on something resembling an even keel.

. . . .

From its roots as a four-man shop, ICAP had quickly become a powerful force. It benefited from impeccable timing, coinciding with London's growth as a crucial trading and broking hub. Michael Spencer, as CEO, had gobbled up smaller competitors and steered the firm into new markets, although interest-rate derivatives remained one of the company's core focal points and profit sources. He had recruited similarly ambitious brokers from other London firms, men like David Casterton, who would come to form his inner circle. Before long, ICAP had a hand in a substantial fraction of all interest-rate derivatives transactions and employed nearly three thousand people in dozens of countries.

Dressed as a City dandy in red suspenders, gold cuff links, and colorful Hermès ties, Spencer had spawned the world's biggest interdealer brokerage. But even as his thriving company became part of the British establishment, the CEO prevailed over a retrograde culture. For years, he had refused to hire women. "It was a private club," he would explain years later. (His paternalistic concern, apparently, was whether women would put up with all the scatological language.) Spencer had a hot, unpredictable temper, and colleagues noted how his large brown eyes sometimes would go from warm and welcoming to narrow and cold, his face twisting into a grimace, when things didn't go his way. A framed picture of the *Austin Powers* villain Dr. Evil graced his office wall.

Spencer's company was rich, and so was he. He decorated ICAP's headquarters with pieces by his favorite modern artists, including Lucian Freud. He loved wine and big parties, and ICAP soon boasted a world-class cellar. Spencer once staggered into work with such a hangover that, after he passed out on an office sofa, his employees scrawled a message on his forehead with a felt-tip pen.

By the mid-2000s, Spencer was a billionaire. He bought a ranch in Kenya, replete with black rhinos, elephants, lions, and leopards. Secure in his station, he adopted a more casual wardrobe, eschewing neckties and leaving his designer dress shirts sufficiently unbuttoned to expose an ample portion of his chest. He waded into politics, seeking to use his money to advance a tax-cutting, deregulatory agenda. He donated millions of pounds to the opposition Conservative Party and befriended its young leader, David Cameron.

None of that changed the fact that the company Spencer had built was at the center of the wildest galaxy in an out-of-control financial universe.

. . . .

At the heart of the brokerage industry were a series of simple equations. The first was that for every trade a broker arranged, his firm pocketed a commission—generally ranging from a few hundred dollars to several thousand, depending on the size of the trade. Of that, the broker personally stood to pocket up to 30 percent in the form of his quarterly bonus payment. As a result, the brokers were perfectly positioned to benefit from the banking industry's evolution from a for-client business into a self-serving profit generator, characterized by frenzied short-term trading. The key to becoming a successful broker was cultivating cozy relationships with big traders. How did brokers manage that? By doing whatever it took—with virtually no exceptions—to please important clients.

The resulting madness was rooted in another simple equation: For every $100 that a trader generated for a broker in commissions, the broker recycled $5 or $10 of that back to the trader in the form of "entertainment." It was meant to cement the broker's relationship with his client and, more important, to create a direct causal connection between the amount of business a trader transacted through his broker and the amount of all-expenses-paid fun that the trader enjoyed. If that sounds like a kickback, well, that's basically what it was. In an earlier era, this might have meant taking clients out to drinks or expensive meals. But as investment-banking businesses grew, and trading volumes soared, and competition among brokers intensified, the practices metastasized. A prolific trader could rack up $1 million a year—and sometimes two or three times that—in commissions for his favored broker. Try as the brokers might, and they would try hard, it wasn't easy to burn $100,000 on a single trader's steaks and cocktails.

And so practices evolved. Dinners at Michelin-starred restaurants and thousand-dollar bottles of champagne at clubs were just the tip of the iceberg. All-expenses-paid jaunts to the Mediterranean resort destinations of St. Tropez and Monaco became the norm. So were boozy ski trips to the Alps; the Alpine resort town of Chamonix became something resembling an off-site campus for ICAP and Tullett. Private jets and helicopters ferried traders to the MTV European music awards. Some brokers picked up $10,000 golf club membership fees for their favored traders. One dinner hosted by the brokerage firm BGC Partners at the trendy London NYC hotel in midtown Manhattan became celebrated among brokers for the $27,500 bill that they ran up on booze alone as they plied their clients. Legend had it that over the course of the evening, the brokers and their guests managed to exhaust the hotel's entire supply of champagne before moving on to bottles of 1970s vintage red wine. There were wild weekend trips to Las Vegas, with all (from felt tables to G-strings) that implied. When brokers got really desperate to show their prized clients some love, they would simply pick up the traders' hotel or restaurant tabs—even if the brokers themselves weren't there.

But leaving your credit card number on file at a restaurant or hotel was easy. One night at a club in London, an ICAP derivatives broker asked a colleague to please shut the door to the bathroom because the trader he had brought as a guest was getting out of control as he snorted line after line of cocaine. Where did the drugs come from? The broker, of course. Another ICAP broker had a standing arrangement with a lucrative trader to hire a prostitute for him a few times a month. "The next day, there would be a line of trades for me," that broker recounted.

Of course, the brokers officially weren't supposed to be spending company money on go-go bars, much less prostitutes or cocaine. But the industry's efforts to police the practices were halfhearted at best. Some brokerage firms' compliance departments maintained "banned lists" of strip clubs and other establishments that were supposed to be off-limits. So brokers would pay cash out of their own pockets, then submit inflated expenses for car services and taxis.

If there was an award for the most over-the-top entertainment, it might have gone to the brokers at Tradition Financial Services, some of whom became regular customers of a service called Lady Marmalade Adult Parties, housed in a private four-bedroom apartment near London's Paddington Station. When the brokers and their clients showed up, they were greeted by scantily clad women and an "erotic love swing." It got more libidinous from there (Lady Marmalade's website promised customers "an orgasmic time"). For really high-end clients, the Tradition brokers took things a few steps further via a luxury villa they rented in the Moroccan desert.

During the day, they lounged poolside; at night, they went out to clubs in Marrakesh. The brokers and their middle-aged guests often returned to the villa with prostitutes in tow. One guest referred to the occasional Marrakesh jaunts as his "week [of] joy in the NSL zone." That stood for "no sperm left." Once, laughing so hard that they nearly cried, the brokers offered to pay a Moroccan prostitute the equivalent of two dollars to be defecated upon. "Yup," one of those brokers reflected, "we are classy people."

. . . .

It was a good time to be a young trader at RBS. The bank's CEO, Goodwin, was determined to transform RBS from a provincial Scottish bank into a global powerhouse—part of a trend at the time of once-sleepy banks chasing riches through breakneck international expansion. Between 2001 and 2008, the Edinburgh-based institution would see its assets grow to about £2.4 trillion, compared to £369 billion when Goodwin had become CEO. Much of that growth came from outbidding rival banks to buy weaker competitors; Goodwin proudly described his company as a "supreme predator." He would eventually be knighted for his services to the British banking industry.*

In the early 2000s, an essential element of Goodwin's expansion strategy was building an army of traders and salesmen to establish RBS as a vital, everyday presence in global markets, helping hedge funds, pensions, insurance companies, and other clients buy and sell a wide variety of securities, currencies, and other assets. The plan worked. By 2003, Hayes and the rest of his team of interest-rate derivatives traders were hitting their strides. They

---

* The honor would be stripped away, years later, after the financial crisis.

had amassed gargantuan positions; RBS's books that year were jammed with £5.3 trillion of interest-rate derivatives, compared to £3.7 trillion two years earlier. Worldwide, there were more than one hundred traders in the squad—in London, Tokyo, New York, Singapore, and elsewhere—and as the profits poured in, RBS's management pulled out the stops to impress them. The company paid for weekend trips for the team to gather in sunny destinations like Rome and Barcelona. They put the traders up in five-star hotels. In Monaco, they were flown to their hotel by helicopter. Senior bank managers came along, too, lavishing the traders with praise and alcohol.

One chilly evening in December 2003, RBS rented out a portion of Finsbury Square, a large grass-and-gravel gathering place nestled among the skyscrapers of central London. A decade later, the square would be home to London's iteration of the Occupy movement, whose camped-out protesters spent months denouncing banking's excesses. This night, RBS was throwing a big Christmas bash for its traders. With the winter sun setting in midafternoon, dozens of traders had ducked out of work early to get a head start on the revelry. The bank erected a large, white marquee tent stocked with free food and booze. By evening, the square was overrun with hundreds of inebriated bankers and traders.

Hayes was among those still crowded into the tent. He was wearing his new, casual getup of sneakers and a ratty sweater. As the party raged around him, the twenty-four-year-old sat in a corner by himself. He found loud music disorienting. Instead of socializing, he was immersed in a novel, *We Need to Talk About Kevin*, a disturbing psychological thriller about a damaged, detached mother trying to come to terms with her son's unspeakable crime. Hayes couldn't put the book down.

· · · ·

As 2004 got under way, Hayes was beginning to look like the full package as a trader. His math and computer savvy allowed him to craft sophisticated pricing models that gave him an edge over rivals, helping him eke out at least small profits on most of his trades as a market maker. He possessed an intuitive grasp of markets and finance, which helped him, more often than not, position his portfolio to take advantage of future changes in the price of the assets he was trading. And—a fringe benefit of not having much of a social life—he was an exceptionally hard worker who enjoyed poring through dense statistical databases and research reports, hunting for clues about the future direction of markets. Many traders had at least one of those skill sets; some had two; few had all three. Hayes's success bred confidence, which in turn encouraged him to take greater risks, which ultimately, notwithstanding the occasional money-losing trade, produced even more profits.

Rival banks were starting to get wind of RBS's hot young thing. One such competitor was the Royal Bank of Canada. (Its name, like RBS's, derived from its roots as a royally chartered bank.) A manager there named Andy Scott had heard about Hayes through a broker. Scott put out feelers to see if Hayes would be interested in joining the Canadian bank's London office. Hayes told his bosses at RBS about the approach, and they responded by kicking Hayes's pay into the six figures, to £105,000. He said no to the Canadians.

Ainsworth had by then become a saleswoman specializing in derivatives. She and Hayes lived together in a rented house in London's Limehouse neighborhood, an up-and-coming area on the north bank of the River Thames. The district's old warehouses and tenements, which for centuries swarmed with sailors and dockworkers, had been converted into single-family homes, apartment buildings, and art galleries. A recently introduced elevated light-rail line and proximity to the gleaming Canary Wharf financial district meant Limehouse was increasingly filled with the Mercedes and fancy sports cars belonging to the rising banking caste.

The couple squabbled—a lot. Among the issues: Ainsworth didn't think Hayes went on enough vacations. She wanted them to spend some of their hard-earned money on weekend getaways, but Hayes didn't like the distraction from his job. Plus, he told her, the ratio of travel time to leisure time would be suboptimal and the unit cost of a short vacation would be much higher than a longer break where the costs of airfare could be amortized over a greater number of days, and . . . Yet he had no misgivings about attending every home and away Queens Park Rangers game, which under a similar "cost-benefit" analysis would suggest the best course of action was to make sure the TV remote was working. But Hayes saw things only from where he stood; he had little ability to empathize. He knew what he felt, and everything else was erratic and unreliable. Ainsworth found Hayes's brand of logic to be exhausting and hypocritical. On a couple of occasions she stormed out, saying she was dumping Hayes, only to return hours later.

One night, Hayes went home after work and decided he would cook dinner for them. Ainsworth, stuck at work on a conference call, was running late. When she finally got home, dinner was nearly ready, but Ainsworth was wiped out and declared that she wanted to decompress in a bath. "Give me ten minutes," she said. After a while, Hayes went upstairs to the bathroom to see what was taking so long. Ainsworth was still soaking in the tub. Hayes was hungry. He'd prepared a shepherd's pie, a casserole-style combination of ground beef, mashed potatoes, and peas, and he wanted to eat it before it got cold. Ainsworth asked for a few more minutes. Ten minutes passed. Hayes marched back upstairs and dumped the pie into the water. Ainsworth, stunned, sat in the bath, peas bobbing around her.

At work the next day, Davies asked Hayes how his night had been. Hayes took the casual question literally, and without reserve or the slightest sense of faux pas told Davies what had happened. Within days, the pie-in-the-bath story had bounced all over the City's trading and brokerage floors. It would continue to circulate for more than a decade.

．．．．

In 2004, Bank of America expressed interest in hiring Hayes. Scott tried again, too; the Royal Bank of Canada offered him a modest raise—and, more important, the fascinating challenge of overhauling its antiquated trading systems so that they could handle the type of derivatives that Hayes was starting to develop a specialty in. This wasn't the province of an IT department; whoever designed the systems needed an intimate knowledge of how derivatives were structured and how financial markets worked. Scott argued that this was Hayes's chance to make a real name for himself. He also told Hayes that the Canadian company was a kinder, gentler bank, where his "career will be nurtured and looked after."

Indeed, Hayes had started feeling distinctly unloved at RBS. That summer, a batch of his trades had gone wrong. He had been up about £600,000 for the year. Suddenly, he was down £100,000. The £700,000 swing was a pittance for a bank of RBS's size, but it meant that managers needed to be informed. That turned out to be a problem: Hayes had started trading a new type of instrument without getting the proper authorization inside the bank. It hadn't seemed like a big deal, but now that he had lost money, that decision was going to get someone in trouble. Hayes's boss didn't intend for that person to be him. He instructed Hayes to write an e-mail to a manager a couple of rungs higher, acknowledging that he had been trading when he wasn't supposed to. Within a few months, Hayes was told to fall on his sword and hand in his resignation. With an offer from the Royal Bank of Canada in his pocket, Hayes followed orders. The voluntary resignation didn't leave any blemish on his records and was undetectable for future employers. Indeed, when the Canadian bank asked the investigative firm Kroll to perform a standard background check on Hayes before his contract was signed, RBS informed Kroll that "we have no reason to doubt the individual's honesty and integrity."

. . . .

Hayes joined the Royal Bank of Canada (RBC) in November 2004, after a month of mandatory downtime that he used to score brownie points with Ainsworth, taking her on a vacation to the sunshine-and-shopping destination of Dubai. For his first year, RBC had agreed to pay him £80,000, plus a guaranteed £40,000 bonus (a total of about $216,000). The bank didn't have formal training programs in place. In fact, Hayes, despite being the junior man, was the one expected to provide training to his new colleagues about how to trade derivatives. Aside from being in a new part of the City—RBC occupied a squat building alongside a busy London thoroughfare, a mile or so from Hayes's previous office—the work environment was more or less the same: row after row of desks, personal space only demarcated by computer monitors and phone lines. Hayes got to work digging into the bank's interest-rate and currencies trading systems. Once again, he had to figure out how to price the different derivatives. He wrote the models and consulted with an American software company, Sun-

Gard, to develop constantly updating risk management systems. Pleased with the outcome, Hayes's managers recommended he be made a full member of staff after his six-month probation ended in May 2005.

By early 2006, Hayes was already elevating RBC's stature among competing institutions. Using some of the same panache for gambling that he'd showcased when gaming pub slot machines and his classmates' need for short-term lunchtime loans, he studied the odds closely, compiling huge caches of historical market data to identify patterns and to isolate variables that could affect the odds, even at the margins. He devoured financial figures and reports— and then he bet big. Trying to win his burgeoning trading business, ICAP brokers wooed him with a ski weekend in Chamonix, but it was too boozy for Hayes's taste. When the brokerage invited him and a couple dozen other leading interest-rate traders to a golf tournament, he said no.

. . . .

Even for an elite trader, luck plays a big role in determining success. Something with a 90 percent probability of happening will go the other way one out of every ten times, and in those cases, just because the trade went wrong, it doesn't mean it was a bad idea. Hayes, despite his mastery of statistics, didn't seem to grasp that. A bad week of trading would put him in a surly, dark mood. Farr tended not to be very helpful. "It's Monopoly money, don't worry about it!" he counseled on one occasion. Read was better. He had a way of reassuring a struggling Hayes, who drew comfort because he knew that Read also was a market expert. He could feel his pain. "Keep positive, mate," Read commiserated. "Your luck will turn."

Read was right. That spring, the Bank of Japan had raised interest rates to 0.25 percent, abandoning its long-standing zero-interest-rate policy. Virtually overnight, trading products linked to Japanese interest rates went from an obscure backwater to a major moneymaker—gambling on future volatility no longer looked like a fool's errand. Hayes found himself at the center of that small, exciting world; he had dutifully learned everything there was to learn about the dull Japanese market. That made him a rare commodity at an aggressive Western investment bank. His only competitors were traders at stodgy Japanese banks who lacked the carnivorous instincts of a London-trained trader. By early summer, he was making millions of dollars for RBC.

Other banks hustled to bulk up their teams in the area. Pretty quickly, rivals started knocking on Hayes's door. J.P. Morgan considered hiring him, before being turned off by Hayes's bizarre behavior, in particular his tendency to blab to anyone who would listen—including his competitors—about what positions he was holding. UBS also had its eyes on Hayes. In Tokyo, an Australian named Mike Pieri was looking to deepen his team's expertise. He also was desperate to do something drastic about the bank's dilapidated derivatives-pricing models, which thanks to the market turbulence were frequently getting overwhelmed and crashing. A headhunter working for UBS came upon Hayes. The bank's pitch, in addition to added money and a loftier title, was that it would be good for Hayes's career to work in Tokyo. Hayes, intrigued, was introduced to a UBS executive in London and then to Pieri. Pieri was impressed: Hayes seemed sharp and to be brimming with good trading ideas.

UBS was practically salivating in anticipation of landing its former intern. The Bank of Japan's rate hike meant the derivatives market "has come alive again," executives wrote in an internal form to get authorization to make Hayes an offer. "We need some-one to . . . focus on the opportunities that have been created due to the lack of experience of other traders in the market." Hayes inter-viewed with a half-dozen UBS executives before receiving an offer of $138,000 per year of salary, plus a guaranteed first-year bonus of nearly $500,000 and free housing in Tokyo.* UBS executives told him he could expect his salary and bonus to balloon higher if he produced as expected.

Hayes's boss, Andy Scott, happened to go on vacation as the flirtations intensified. When he returned, Hayes told him that he was thinking of jumping to UBS, and Scott scrambled to retain his young prodigy. RBC offered more money. But Hayes wasn't swayed—moving to Tokyo seemed like an adventure and, more important, UBS enjoyed much greater stature and career opportu-nities than a Canadian bank.

On June 6, Hayes told Scott that he had made his final decision: He was resigning. He walked Scott through his outstanding trades. What Scott saw floored him. The portfolio was much, much larger than he had realized. RBC at the time had few internal checks to prevent unsupervised traders from essentially going wild. It turned out that while Scott was on vacation, Hayes had gone on a bit of a binge. Since it was now clear that during that stretch Hayes was already in talks with UBS, at least from Scott's perspective the fre-netic trading activity over those couple of weeks seemed designed to curry favor with brokers who were getting Hayes's name out in the job market—not an unheard-of tactic among highly competi-tive traders, but nonetheless unsavory.

That day, RBC marched Hayes out of the building.

---

* Bonuses historically made up the vast majority of traders' and investment bankers' total compensation.

. . . .

RBC got to work untangling Hayes's trades. (With him no longer around, it would be far riskier to hang on to his bets than to quickly exit the positions.) The process took several days, and it was ugly, as rival banks took advantage of RBC's need to sell. The positions were so big that the losses piled up quickly. A few weeks later, adding insult to injury, RBC got the bills for about $500,000 from the brokers Hayes had used to execute his transactions over the past month. The total tab for cleaning up Hayes's mess reached about $7 million.

RBC opened an internal review to figure out what exactly had gone wrong. The first discovery was that Hayes had provided confidential information to an outside party. After he agreed to join UBS, but before he actually left RBC, the Swiss bank's headhunter had requested data about his annual profits and losses, known as his P&L, which the headhunter assured him was routine. Hayes, without much thought, handed the data over. "The proprietary information contained material that Royal Bank of Canada considers to be confidential and sensitive," the bank wrote in a report about the matter. Hayes's actions "were in breach of his employment contract and RBC's Code of Conduct."

The bigger problem, though, was what the bank found next. As RBC employees dug into Hayes's trading positions, they realized that the computer models he'd built to price derivatives—and that his managers had praised as best-in-class—weren't working as well as advertised. In fact, they were spitting out false numbers—and they were false in a way that exaggerated the profitability of Hayes's trading. "This action misled the firm regarding the value of the trades and strategies employed," the bank's report said. That, and the huge payments to brokers, raised "questions regarding the integrity" of Hayes.

The saga came at an awful time for Scott. His marriage was on the rocks, and dealing with the Hayes mess doubled the stress. He ended up keeping his job, but he would harbor resentments toward Hayes for most of the next decade. Despite his fury, though, he doubted that Hayes had actually done anything deliberately wrong; it looked to him to have been more likely a case of sloppiness and bad luck.

Scott's managers weren't so sure. The bank reported its discoveries to its regulators at the Financial Services Authority. An RBC compliance official also phoned UBS to warn them about what it had uncovered. The alert quickly went up UBS's chain of command.

Soon after arriving in Tokyo, Hayes received an e-mail from an RBC employee back in London who wanted to arrange an "exit interview." Hayes was confused. Why were they doing this now, a month after he left RBC? He nonetheless agreed to talk by phone a couple of nights later. As Hayes paced the small living room of his apartment in Tokyo's Roppongi neighborhood, the RBC officials told him that they had reviewed his trading patterns and Excel models and found a number of anomalies. They suspected that he had misled the bank. It was important that Hayes come clean, now, if he had done anything untoward, they said. Hayes "appeared distracted and may not have been focusing clearly on the issues," an RBC official later reported to a counterpart at UBS. Hayes responded that he had no clue what the RBC man was talking about.

Given his resignation from his first employer, the Royal Bank of Scotland, this threatened to be the second time he left a bank under a cloud. Angry and stressed, he called Scott to ask what was happening. Scott lied that he had no idea. Hayes then turned to Read. "They want to talk to me about the trades I did before I left," he told the broker. "But [I] can't think of anything." He told

Read that RBC had decided to withhold its reference—an important step in the process of jumping from bank to bank, one that normally was the equivalent of a rubber stamp—until their review was complete. "Not sure whether they are going to try to imply I behaved badly. Am very nervous about it."

"The trades you did? That's complete rubbish," Read said. "You did absolutely nothing wrong."

"They are looking to cover their backs internally by implying I was up to something, I reckon," Hayes told Read. "I am nervous because I am in the dark." Ainsworth also grew anxious.

Read told them to chill. "You are both worriers, which is not the best combination in times like this," he said.

Once again, Read's counsel turned out to be savvy. Having rung loud alarm bells, in a late-August phone call the Canadian bank's head of compliance in London adopted a softer tone with his UBS counterpart. "I also had the clear impression that RBC . . . was, if not backtracking, at least playing down the severity of the seriousness of the issues," a UBS employee wrote in a file note about the matter. The RBC man "confirmed that they would probably not have fired TH. One surmises that if UBS were to take significant action this may place RBC . . . in an uncomfortable position." In other words, if UBS were to fire Hayes, RBC could end up with egg on its face. While Hayes hired a lawyer to represent him before the FSA, that turned out to be unnecessary: The regulator, living up to its light-touch reputation, took no action, opting to let the matter be handled internally by the banks.

In a follow-up phone call a few weeks later with UBS, the RBC compliance executive concluded that Hayes "had not been openly underhand, but was in some respects perhaps young and naïve. RBC would have given him 'a good bollocking' and subjected him to enhanced supervision with the aim of making a better human being of him." The RBC executive added that "they had no proof that this was down to deliberate dishonesty. It may have been that it was simply a poorly constructed model or even the result of inadvertent error." RBC recommended that UBS subject Hayes to three to six months of enhanced oversight.

After weeks of discussion within its legal and compliance departments, UBS decided to let Hayes start trading. The only condition: For three months, he would be on probation and would have to get his supervisor to sign off on his books at the end of each day. Most new employees were automatically subjected to similar trial periods. This barely amounted to a slap on the wrist, not even the "good bollocking" that RBC had recommended as it sought to minimize the problem.

Based on Hayes's experiences at the royal banks of both Scotland and Canada, this seemed to be the way banks dealt with mishaps: Rinse them away in the least disruptive manner possible. The lesson was hard not to internalize.

CHAPTER 4

Peak Performance

John Ewan was born five years after Minos Zombanakis fathered his interest-rate mechanism. But by 2005, his professional life revolved around Zombanakis's creation. Ewan didn't have any particular interest in finance or banking. Raised in a family of quasi-socialists, he aspired to be a scientist, majoring in biology at the University of Bath in southwestern England. Tall and with muttonchop sideburns, Ewan played the guitar and loved the theater. But his real passion was traveling. While classmates and then colleagues hewed to the well-beaten path, Ewan trekked to Borneo and Costa Rica for vacations where he could hone his scuba-diving skills. But he had to find a way to pay the bills. His first job out of college was working in the call center of a large investment firm near his hometown, answering the phones as customers rang with questions and complaints. A year later, in 1998, he joined the Financial Times Stock Exchange group, a London provider of financial indices known in the finance industry as FTSE (pronounced FOOT-see). After five years there, working as an administrator, Ewan quit in 2003 to fulfill a lifelong dream of traveling around the world. When he reached Rio de Janeiro, he fell in love with the city and settled in. Then, after fourteen months of adventure, he ran out of money. It was time to return to reality.

Back in England, the twenty-nine-year-old Ewan applied for a bunch of jobs. He eventually accepted one at the British Bankers' Association and started working there in April 2005. Founded in 1919, the BBA was mainly devoted to lobbying for lax regulations on the banking sector. The group occupied the third floor and the basement of a modern stone building (complete with a waterfall splashing through its atrium) smack in the middle of the City. The Bank of England's colonnaded headquarters was a short walk down the street. At the time Ewan joined, the group was representing more than two hundred banks, from sixty countries, and was enjoying remarkable success, thanks to the traditionally anti-bank Labour Party's embrace of a staunchly pro-bank regulatory philosophy.

The BBA wasn't a bank. It wasn't a government agency. It wasn't even a company. It certainly wasn't regulated. But it was probably one of the financial world's most powerful institutions. And that was because the BBA controlled something called Libor.

Zombanakis's innovative method of calculating interest rates on large loans had quickly become popular, but for more than a decade, it had remained an informal mechanism. Whenever a group of banks teamed up on a loan, they essentially would arrange their own version of the benchmark. There was nothing etched in stone, no way to easily replicate the rate for day-to-day use.

By the 1980s, this piecemeal setup was increasingly seen as problematic by some in the industry and regulatory community. Banks in London had begun dabbling in a wild array of derivatives and other financial instruments—things like interest-rate swaps—that were designed not only to meet customers' needs but also to create new playgrounds for the growing teams of avaricious traders. But, to the consternation of British politicians and financiers, London was at risk of lagging behind. The era of bowler hats, starched collars, and my-word-is-my-bond gentlemen's agreements among the City's privileged caste refused to give way to the frenzied international competition that was taking place in rival financial centers like New York. At the same time, the armies of midlevel bank employees and brokers continued to relish their long, beer-soaked lunches of fish and chips, oblivious to the speed of change and dealmaking occurring around them.

It wasn't just restless traders who were scowling at established antiquity and lassitude. Even the tradition-bound Bank of England governor—whose office continued to be guarded by tailcoated attendants and whose wooden desk was adorned with crystal pots of red and black ink—wanted the City to remain in the game. One impediment to accommodating these nascent markets was the lack of uniformity in how banks calculated interest rates that fed into swaps and other instruments; negotiating interest rates on a contract-by-contract basis was hardly efficient. At the request of the Bank of England, in October 1984 the BBA set up a committee of commercial bankers and powerful central bank officials to contemplate the issue. After extensive deliberations, the group hatched an idea: Each day, the BBA would collect from a group of banks—not just British ones, but also American and European lenders—data about how much it cost each of them to borrow money from each other, on a percentage basis down to two decimal places. Around lunchtime, after knocking out the highest and lowest estimates, the BBA would disseminate the average to the banks and others for use in various financial instruments. The number was dubbed "the BBA standard for interest rate swaps." That didn't exactly roll off the tongue, so the group decided on a marginally catchier acronym:

BBAIRS. That name didn't last long. On New Year's Day in 1986, the BBA for the first time published something called the London interbank offered rate—Libor, for short. Pronounced LIE-bore, it would soon be the basis for much of the modern financial world.

That same year, Margaret Thatcher ignited what came to be known as the "Big Bang." It was her attempt to make London a vital financial capital by loosening restrictive, antiforeigner rules that had long governed the London Stock Exchange, and freeing the country's banks from curbs on their growth and consolidation. The reforms unleashed a frenzied period of expansion and consolidation in the financial industry. They also precipitated an invasion of American financiers, who appeared poised to stampede the City's gentlemanly culture. Before long, more than five hundred foreign banks were operating there, and a new class of workers—those who saw an opportunity for riches and had, by dint of background and pedigree, been locked out of the elitist, insular institutions that historically dominated the City—began gravitating to the industry.

While the Americans were exporting their bankers to London, the Brits were exporting their benchmark around the world. In the United States, the interest rates on most home mortgages historically had been based on the Federal Reserve's rarely changing base rate. Libor, by contrast, had the potential to move daily, in tandem with market conditions, or at least in tandem with what banks reported market conditions to be. Now bankers could set interest rates on mortgages or credit cards or other loans at Libor plus a certain amount—and that certain amount was essentially the bank's profit, which they would pocket regardless of where interest rates moved. That was enticing for customers—they'd no longer worry about missing out on savings if interest rates dropped in the future—and it was attractive for the banks—the variable rate would encourage customers to borrow more, while locking in profits for banks above what it cost them to borrow money. By the 1990s, the phrase "London interbank offered rate" was buried in the fine print of an increasing number of American loan agreements. Before long, the fortunes of just about anyone who borrowed money in the United States and, to a slightly lesser extent, elsewhere in the Western world hinged on Libor.

Libor's spread was part of a much broader trend: the globalization of finance. No longer were banks confined to specific regions or even individual countries. Increasingly, they spanned the planet, collecting deposits in one part of the world and loaning out the money in another. Similarly, a mortgage that got issued to a family in Michigan might be packaged into a complex financial instrument that would end up, after cycling through several intermediaries, being purchased by a German pension fund or a Japanese bank. In the 1990s and early 2000s, the phenomenon made it easier for people and companies to borrow money at affordable rates. How? By better matching up would-be lenders— anyone who had deposits stashed in a bank account, or money they were looking to invest in a mortgage security, to name just two examples—with would-be borrowers—such as credit card customers, students who needed help paying their tuition, or governments that wanted to finance military spending or entitlement programs. For the first time in history, it seemed possible to distribute capital almost instantly and with perfect efficiency worldwide.

Not surprisingly, things turned out to be considerably more complex. The trend enabled many borrowers—not just Americans who wanted to buy a house, but also acquisition-hungry corporations and free-spending governments—to gorge on levels of debt that would later become crippling. And, when markets inevitably turned, the increased interconnectedness meant that the resulting financial crisis would prove deeper, longer lasting, and further reaching than it otherwise would have been. But few people saw that coming. And for now, the fact that an interest rate set by banks in London and overseen by a British trade group was determining what a family in Kalamazoo was paying on its mortgage was hailed as a manifestation of a laudatory global trend.

From the start, though, Libor was prone to problems. Chief among those was the potential for banks to manipulate it for their own benefit. Doing that was alarmingly easy. In the 1990s, junior bank employees would simply pick up the phone and call in their submissions to financial data company Thomson Reuters every morning around eleven o'clock. A low-level Reuters employee punched all the banks' data into a computer and calculated the averages. Nobody of any seniority monitored the process. Virtually all it took for a bank to skew Libor was for it to skew its own submission. As long as the bank's figures weren't the very highest or the very lowest of all that day's submissions, a change in its data would ripple through the average.

In 1991, a young Morgan Stanley trader in London named Douglas Keenan was placing bets on interest-rate futures. Their value was calculated based on where Libor moved. After the market moved against him one day, Keenan came to suspect that someone—he wasn't sure who—was somehow manipulating the instruments to suit his or her own trading positions. He shared his suspicions with his colleagues. They laughed at his naïveté. It was common knowledge that banks tweaked Libor to benefit their own trading positions. It seemed that everyone other than Keenan already knew it was happening.

Banks had multiple incentives to push or pull Libor. One was that, because each bank's submission was made public, investors scoured the data for indicators about the bank's financial health.

A bank that reported a spike in its borrowing costs might be in trouble—after all, why else would rival institutions suddenly be charging it more to borrow money? That gave banks a reason to keep their submissions low, especially during periods of market unease. Another enticement for banks to tinker with Libor was to increase the value of the vast portfolios of derivatives that the banks' traders were sitting on at any given time. Those positions could incentivize a bank to move Libor higher or lower—or both, in the frequent event that different traders at the same bank had amassed different positions. It all depended on what their traders had recently bought or sold.

The implications of this were potentially enormous. It meant that there was a possibility that the interest rates on everything from mortgages and credit card bills to enormous corporate loans could be based on flawed data. If banks pushed Libor higher, it meant that ordinary people all over the world collectively were getting ripped off to the tune of billions of dollars in excess interest payments. Even if Libor was moved artificially lower, there were losers aplenty. Many American cities and pension funds, for example, had purchased interest-rate swaps to protect themselves against the risk of rising rates. If Libor declined artificially, those municipalities and pensions would be stiffed out of money that was rightfully theirs. Normal people would be the victims.

. . . .

Going back to the years leading up to the Civil War, the Chicago Mercantile Exchange had been the trading hub for contracts to buy and sell things like corn and livestock at a set price at a future date. The exchange bustled with traders who wore color-coded jackets to identify their roles. They communicated over the trading floor's din using hand signals. (The system worked partly because trading was clustered around "pits," where the floor was angled slightly downhill, like the seats of a stadium, to facilitate communication.) In the 1960s, the Merc (as it was fondly known by traders) diversified into futures contracts on things like pork bellies. Futures contracts allowed businesses and farmers to lock in future prices for essential products and thereby to make long-term investment and strategic decisions.

By the 1980s, the Merc was branching into a growing menu of financial products that traders could buy and sell, among them instruments linked to U.S. dollars parked in European bank accounts. The Merc wasn't offering to let traders buy or sell these so-called Eurodollars. Instead, it was offering contracts that essentially gave traders the *theoretical* right to buy or sell the Eurodollars elsewhere in the future at a set price. That future price was determined based on interest rates. (In essence, a Eurodollar's future value was derived from how much someone could expect to earn by stashing it in an interest-bearing bank account.) As with the trader of pork belly futures who has no interest in owning any actual pork bellies, the entire purpose of these derivatives was to allow traders to roll the dice about future fluctuations in interest rates.

To determine the value of the derivatives, the Merc had to build a benchmark interest rate into the contracts. For years, the Merc calculated that rate by conducting a random survey of what it cost an ever-changing group of banks to borrow from one another. But in 1996, the exchange wanted to simplify the process of calculating rates. Libor was by now widely accepted around the world as a trustworthy proxy for interest rates. Why not just incorporate Libor into the Merc's increasingly popular derivatives?

The decision wasn't entirely up to the Merc. An obscure U.S. government agency, the Commodity Futures Trading Commission, had the power to approve or veto changes to the design of certain futures contracts. So the Merc applied to the CFTC for permission. Using Libor, the exchange argued in its application, "will make our Eurodollar futures an even more attractive risk management tool."

Not everyone agreed. When the CFTC invited the public to comment on the Merc's proposal, Marcy Engel jumped at the opportunity. Engel was a lawyer for Salomon Brothers, then firmly established as one of Wall Street's most aggressive bond-trading houses (it soon would become part of Citigroup). She worried that linking Libor to the Eurodollar futures would provide banks, which had huge businesses trading those contracts, "an opportunity for manipulation . . . to benefit its own positions." Richard Robb, at the time a thirty-six-year-old trader at a small Japanese financial company, DKB Financial Products Inc., also wrote to the commission to caution that Libor was vulnerable to manipulation and therefore shouldn't be embedded in the contracts. "If two banks worked together, they could raise the average" substantially, he warned.

During Bill Clinton's presidency, the CFTC had earned a reputation as a hands-off, probusiness regulator. In December 1996, staffers wrote a memo to the agency's leaders saying that Libor "does not appear to be readily susceptible to manipulation." The commission approved the Merc's application. The next month, Libor officially became an integral component of the fast-growing derivatives market.

. . . .

When Ewan arrived at the BBA, his job duties were largely administrative—befitting someone whose only professional experience was clerical and who seemed to have little interest in finance. He worked for Alex Merriman, a bedraggled-looking man with stringy blond hair and a droopy mustache. Merriman wasn't the easiest guy to work for. He sometimes nodded off during meetings and, when awake, tended to have a short fuse. Merriman had a number of responsibilities, one of which was running Libor. At the time, this was a pretty simple task. It consisted of making sure that the drones at Thomson Reuters did their job of compiling the data, and, once a year, embarking on a series of meetings around London to make sure that the banks contributing data to Libor were satisfied with the process. When Ewan came on board, Merriman immediately handed him responsibility for handling Libor-related paperwork. Before long, Merriman had delegated basically all of his Libor responsibilities to his underling.

Ewan's colleagues liked him. He seemed like a friendly, normal guy. He loved Formula 1 auto racing and made frequent trips to European cities to catch the action. Once, when the BBA was looking for a volunteer to go on a business trip to Mongolia, Ewan was the only one to raise his hand. Nobody else had any interest in flying halfway around the world to a barren country with few tourist attractions. Ewan saw it differently, noting Mongolia's rich reserves of useful minerals. "That's not a country," the onetime aspiring scientist told bemused colleagues, "it's a chemistry lab." But Ewan found this to be a confusing period. Nobody actually explained to him how the markets worked. He was on his own to figure things out.

To bankroll the organization, the BBA relied on annual dues paid by its members, as well as the occasional conference the group hosted. Those membership payments varied by the size of the bank, but generally they were several thousand pounds a year. The BBA also made money off Libor by selling licenses to companies that allowed them to incorporate the benchmark into their products. If the group was going to keep growing and gaining power, it was going to need new sources of money.

One way for the BBA to wring more revenue out of Libor was to create new versions of the benchmark. The most prominent versions of Libor were the British pound and the U.S. dollar varieties, but by 2005 Libor came in ten flavors: The pound and dollar were joined by the Australian dollar, the Canadian dollar, the Swiss franc, the Danish krone, the euro, the Japanese yen, the New Zealand dollar, and the Swedish krona. And within each of those, there were fifteen subcategories, broken down by time periods. For example, a three-month U.S. dollar Libor was supposed to measure how much it would cost a bank to borrow dollars in London for a three-month period. Other time periods included one month, six months, one year, and so on.

Big providers of financial data were among the entities paying licensing fees to use Libor. So were banks. But the largest, most lucrative clients were those (like the Merc) that were spending lots of time creating new types of derivatives. Those derivatives needed to be based on something, and Libor often seemed like a good bet. Ewan got to work expanding the menu of Libor varieties and licensing out the benchmark for use in what he called an array of "novel derivatives." Within a few years, he would boast that he had managed to quadruple the money that the BBA was making from Libor. Products like interest-rate swaps now increasingly relied on Libor as the basis for the floating-rate segment of the transaction (the one in which Giantbank would agree to pay interest to ABC Corp.).

Ewan, however, didn't see Libor as ultimately being his responsibility. In fact, he didn't see it as even being the BBA's responsibility. That might seem odd, but it was a fiction that had been passed down over the years, long predating Ewan's arrival. The BBA insisted that policing Libor, to the extent that it needed to be policed at all, was the responsibility of an obscure assemblage of midlevel British bankers called the Foreign Exchange and Money Markets Committee. The purpose of the FXMMC, the tongue-tying acronym that its members used as shorthand, was to discuss issues relating to London's foreign-exchange and cash markets. The committee's members worked for dozens of large banks, most wallowing in unglamorous departments that specialized in moving money back and forth among different internal units of their companies.

The committee itself was something of an old boys' club. At its meetings, generally attended by about twenty people seated around a large rectangular conference room in the BBA's underground boardroom, members would politely form a consensus. The committee never actually voted on anything. The sessions rarely lasted more than an hour, partly because the participants weren't thrilled to be there. Attendees didn't win any points within their own institutions for showing up—it was just part of the job, and a dull one at that. Citigroup's representative on the committee, a bald, plump, by-the-books man named Andrew Thursfield, tended to arrive at the very last minute and to rush for the exit as soon as the meetings adjourned. Occasionally, especially around the holiday season, the group would adjourn to a nearby pub. Even those outings were brief; most participants stuck around for only a half hour. Indeed, the committee's members would turn out to be more concerned with minimizing their time commitments and protecting their respective banks than they would be about trying to deal with Libor's increasingly obvious problems.

. . . .

Each spring, Ewan and Merriman or another colleague fanned out across the City of London and Canary Wharf to check in with the banks about how they thought Libor was working. As far back as 2005, around the time that Ewan started his job, the BBA had been hearing scattered complaints about Libor's integrity. That year, Barclays was the main dissenter. Its concern was that Libor was too high; banks seemed to be reporting data that overstated their borrowing costs. (An exaggerated Libor would result in them making more money off their loans to individuals and companies.) Barclays, however, wasn't thrilled with the situation; perhaps its traders had amassed positions that would profit if Libor moved lower. In any case, it was alone in sounding the alarm, though the proud British institution, with its Quaker roots tracing back to 1690, wasn't in a great place to be casting aspersions—some other banks privately had voiced concerns to the BBA that Barclays was itself manipulating Libor to suit its own interests.

By 2006, Barclays's concerns had faded. In fact, the feedback the BBA received that spring was overwhelmingly positive. Everyone seemed happy. "It's not broken. Don't try to fix it" was the concise appraisal from Citigroup's Thursfield. The same was true in the spring of 2007. One bank after another gave Libor an enthusiastic thumbs-up. When Ewan visited Deutsche Bank's offices, in a building across the street from the ruins of the London Wall, which Romans had built two millennia ago, a bombastic Canadian executive named David Nicholls expressed "complete satisfaction" with the benchmark. Officials at France's two biggest banks lauded Libor's accuracy and said it seemed to be getting more reliable over time. J.P. Morgan's representative assured Ewan that there weren't any signs of the rate being manipulated. And when Ewan showed up at Barclays's Canary Wharf skyscraper, adorned with its prominent blue-eagle logo, he was greeted with still more good news. An executive, Miles Storey, told him that the bank thought Libor was "currently at peak performance." Storey also happily noted that the nasty rumors about Barclays manipulating the benchmark "seem to have now subsided." Storey wanted to make one thing abundantly clear: Barclays had not been manipulating anything, ever. In any case, he observed with a smidgen of condescension, there really was no way for the benchmark to be rigged, given the large number of other banks that would have to be involved in such a conspiracy. It just wasn't possible.

. . . .

Some six hundred miles to the southeast of London, Andrew Smith showed up for work at UBS. The bank was headquartered in the center of Zurich, where streetcars glided along cobblestone streets. Smith, however, was based in a satellite office out by the Zurich airport where UBS stashed its fast-growing fleet of traders and math whizzes, as well as the back-office gnomes who processed their transactions and made their systems run. Cows grazed in a field outside. On clear days, the snow-covered Alps could be glimpsed in the distance, peeking above the southern horizon.

For more than a century, UBS—its name an acronym for its predecessor, the Union Bank of Switzerland—was a conservative lender, not aspiring to anything more than being a trustworthy servant of its mostly Swiss clientele. It was considered the premier place to work in Switzerland. Like (of course) clockwork, bankers were rewarded with promotions every two years. When they reached the rank of vice president, managers got to line their new office with their choice of wood: mahogany, walnut, or pine. But the bank had started to stray from tradition during the last decade of the twentieth century. Enviously watching Wall Street firms, Union Bank embraced practices such as hedge fund investing. In 1997, it merged with Swiss Bank Corporation in a $25 billion deal that made UBS the world's biggest bank. Swiss Bank's CEO, Marcel Ospel, had spent years trying to turn the staid institution into a globe-spanning investment bank through acquisitions of derivative firms and investment banks such as Britain's flagship finance house, the merchant bank S. G. Warburg. Now Ospel became CEO of UBS. He kicked the risk-taking into higher gear.

Smith, a Brit, hadn't attended college, having gone straight into banking in 1989, joining a company that would one day be absorbed into UBS. In 2003, he was transferred from London to the Zurich office, where he was a midlevel trader. He was working on what was known in the industry as the cash desk, the part of the trading floor where employees kept their fingers on the pulse of the markets for cash—in other words, the markets that served as one of several outlets for banks like UBS to borrow or loan money from or to other financial institutions. Because of their supposed line of sight into these markets, they were the guys generally responsible for figuring out and then submitting Libor data. That was true not just at UBS but at most banks. Sure enough, one of Smith's duties upon arriving in Zurich, where he would remain for the next five years, was to handle UBS's submissions of the British pound, or sterling, version of Libor. It was viewed as an administrative duty, as drudgework. There was a password-protected Excel spreadsheet into which he was supposed to enter data every morning about how much it cost the bank to borrow money from other banks. Then he would hit a "submit" button embedded in the spreadsheet, and off the data went. The system was an upgrade over the phone-it-in approach that the BBA had used in previous years, but it was still clunky and prone to crashing.

Smith had basically no clue what he was doing. He didn't know how to go about figuring out the bank's borrowing costs, which were supposed to be the entire basis of the bank's Libor data. He didn't even know whom to talk to internally. So Smith did what plenty of his peers at other banks were doing: He took a shortcut and spoke to brokers, in this case those at ICAP, Tullett Prebon, and RP Martin—the same firms with whom Smith's younger colleague, Tom Hayes, was building relationships.

To be more precise, Smith *listened* to the brokers. Atop the desk of just about every trader at any major bank anywhere in the world sat a device known as a squawk box. It was essentially a series of open phone lines, connected to other parts of the bank or to outside brokers, and then broadcast over a small, crackling desktop loudspeaker. It was a version of the old trading pit that accommodated the fact that the "pit" was now spread across floors and buildings and entire cities. Smith's box was linked to brokers who specialized in sterling derivatives, and some of them provided a useful service: In the morning, they would shout over the box where they expected Libor to move that day. So Smith, lacking much other relevant information, would make up his submission based in part on what the brokers were predicting. It was certainly simpler than trying to navigate UBS's internal bureaucracy. And handling the bank's Libor submissions was just one of Smith's duties, not a top priority.

Brokers weren't Smith's only sources. One of the investment bank's priorities at the time was to improve collaboration between different parts of the company. The idea was to transform UBS into a more efficient, collaborative beast, with everyone aware of what his colleagues were up to and pulling in the same direction.

The directive was communicated down the chain of command by a senior manager named Holger Seger, a veteran trader who'd worked at UBS and before that Swiss Bank Corp. since 1990. It might have sounded like a vacuous corporate platitude, but UBS employees, at least some of them, took it seriously. Smith was supposed to co-ordinate with UBS's traders who specialized in buying and selling interest-rate swaps, instruments whose values rose and fell based on movements in Libor. Sometimes the swaps traders would lob a request in his direction about where they wanted him to submit the bank's Libor data that day. Even as a rookie on the desk, he understood what was going on. The traders had big positions whose values hinged in large part on Libor—precisely what Marcy Engel and Richard Ross had warned the CFTC would happen. A lot of money was on the line. So Smith generally followed their requests when it came to what he entered into his spreadsheet. He didn't see any reason not to.

CHAPTER 5

The Lucky Turnstile

The bottles of red were $500 each and yet they kept arriving at the table, one after another. The traders at the Tokyo restaurant on this evening in September 2006 could afford the wine without any difficulty, but it struck Tom Hayes as a gratuitous waste of money. "To be honest," he told a friend the next day, it "felt a bit obscene." He didn't even like the taste of the expensive stuff, but someone—Hayes couldn't remember who, although he suspected it was a particularly over-the-top trader from the French bank BNP Paribas—had felt the need to up the ante.

Excess was everywhere in the heady days before the financial crisis. Similar to UBS, BNP had started out back in 1848 as a run-of-the-mill French lender, but by now it had become a continent-leaping colossus, dabbling in everything from retail banking in Hawaii to lending money to Greek shipping magnates to trading derivatives in Tokyo. Befitting the bank's grandeur, in 2000 its top executives set up shop in a converted Parisian mansion that had been the venue for Napoleon Bonaparte's wedding in 1796. The boom—as well as this boozy evening—would end more squalidly.

Hayes had been in Tokyo a rough couple of months. There was, of course, the lingering ugliness surrounding his trading in his final weeks at the Royal Bank of Canada, but it seemed like nearly everything else had been a mess, too. After he had spent a few days working in UBS's office, the human resources department got around to collecting his documentation and realized he didn't have a work visa, only a tourist one. It therefore was illegal for him to be working in Japan. Hayes was ordered by a distressed HR officer to immediately leave for Seoul, South Korea, and to stay there until his Japanese visa came through. The mix-up didn't inspire much confidence in UBS.

When Hayes returned to Tokyo a couple of weeks later, he was lonely. In a leap of faith, Ainsworth had followed him to Japan. She didn't have a job lined up, but given her expertise in derivatives, she figured she could find a gig at one of the Western banks with big Tokyo offices. First, though, she wanted to get to know Tokyo; before long, she was staying out till five thirty in the morning doing karaoke with her new friends.

If he was honest about it, Hayes wasn't thrilled to have Ainsworth around. Their always volatile relationship had soured, and he had come to resent her. After a month or two, Ainsworth landed a job at French bank Crédit Agricole, so she wasn't going back to England anytime soon. Lacking any circumstantial excuses, his only way to end things would be to break it off himself. But every time he started working up the nerve to have the Talk with her, he was racked with guilt. He couldn't bring himself to abandon her, especially right after she'd moved nearly six thousand miles to be with him. And so they stuck together.

Aside from Ainsworth, Hayes didn't have friends in Tokyo. He didn't speak the language. He didn't like the food. He preferred to just head home after work. "Any excuse not to go out is my mantra," he told a colleague at the time. He met one broker, named Nigel Delmar, who showed him around and helped him find an IKEA and a Western-style burger joint, but that was the extent of his social life. Trying to ease his homesickness, he stocked his kitchen with ground meat, herbs and spices, and a Japanese grain by-product and made his own sausages. He installed a device that allowed him to pipe British and American television shows into his apartment. Now he could watch familiar TV programs while eating his sausages along with baked beans and french fries—a classic, if unhealthy, British meal.

More assistance soon came from his RP Martin broker, Terry Farr, who flew to Tokyo in September. Farr had asked Hayes what he could bring him from England, and the homesick trader had requested cans of Heinz ravioli and a couple of issues of a soccer magazine called *FourFourTwo*. Pal that he was, when Farr got off the plane in Tokyo, his suitcase was bulging with canisters of pre-made beef ravioli.

Not to be outdone by a competitor, ICAP's Darrell Read soon paid Hayes a visit. What could he bring? Hayes requested a supply of black garbage bags—they only seemed to sell transparent ones in Tokyo. There was something about black garbage bags that appealed to Hayes, maybe the fact that he didn't like his trash on display for everyone to see. In any case, Read did as requested.[*]

At least money wasn't a problem: Hayes's compensation that year amounted to more than $600,000. And UBS paid for his

---

[*] Following Read's delivery, Japanese trash collectors sent Hayes a letter telling him he had to stop using the black bags. It was against the rules. Hayes grudgingly complied.

housing expenses—no minor perk in Tokyo's hyperexpensive real estate market. That left plenty of money for Hayes's limited extra-curricular activities.

At his desk on the cavernous fifth floor of UBS's Tokyo sky-scraper, with teams of traders clustered together in a cacophony of shouting, Hayes generally dressed in jeans or wrinkled black slacks and a polo shirt or, in the winter, a thin sweater. His clothes were old and worn—except those that had been given to him as gifts. (His brokers loved presenting him with polo shirts embroidered with their corporate logos. Tullett Prebon had started the trend, but ICAP couldn't bear the thought of its prized client wearing a rival's clothing and so raised the stakes with ICAP-branded polo shirts with Hayes's name stitched on the back.) He didn't always shower and knew he looked like "a tramp." When he was stressed, which was often, he vigorously scratched his head, sending dan-druff flakes fluttering onto his shoulders and desktop and generat-ing an endless series of snow-related jokes from colleagues. Though self-conscious about his appearance, he didn't do anything to im-prove it; instead, to the best of his ability, he avoided being seen. Many UBS traders used a videoconferencing system called Avistar to communicate with each other. It was faster than writing e-mails or even typing into the real-time electronic chat programs that were a preferred mode of communicating for traders and brokers, and calls on the system weren't recorded, unlike the bank's normal phone system. Without a paper trail, you could say whatever you wanted without fear of repercussions. But Hayes refused to use Avistar—the combination of his slovenly appearance and his long-standing aversion to eye contact made him hate it. As a result, most of his communication—in writing and over the phone—would be preserved for posterity.

Hayes's first task was to build the pricing and risk systems that he would use for his trading—the same kinds of models that he'd designed at RBC, preferably without the errors. Once again, he used Microsoft Excel spreadsheets to craft the programs. The resulting files were massive, consuming hundreds of megabytes of disk space, and they could instantly process ridiculously detailed calculations about the interrelationships between hundreds of variables. Punch a proposed trade into one cell, and another cell would automatically spit out a price at which it would be profitable for UBS to do the trade. Hayes lovingly regarded his intricate models as similar to living organisms in their complexity.

Hayes reported to Mike Pieri, a sharp, sociable manager who'd made his name at UBS as a successful trader. Immediately after graduating from small, beachfront Bond University on Australia's Gold Coast, Pieri had started working at a company that would later be merged into the Swiss bank. He hadn't intended to make a lifelong profession out of banking, figuring it would just be a way station on the path to one day running his own small business. But like many people who reckoned they would muck around in finance for a few years, just long enough to pay off student loans and, perhaps, amass a small nest egg, it didn't work out that way. Fourteen years later, after stints in Singapore, Australia, Hong Kong, and Tokyo, Pieri was still at UBS. (Along the way, he had married a tall, blond former flight attendant named Donna, whom he had met years earlier at an Australian soccer tournament.)

In addition to doing some trading himself, Pieri now was responsible for twenty-seven traders and salesmen. Among them was a young trader named Mirhat Alykulov, who had arrived at UBS as a temporary worker before being admitted into its trader training program in April 2006, shortly before Hayes moved to Tokyo. Alykulov had grown up on a chicken farm in Kazakhstan. A promising student, he was admitted into a high school exchange program that sent him to the Pennsylvania village of Quakertown, where he joined the high school wrestling squad and picked up something resembling an American accent. Back in Kazakhstan, he won a coveted scholarship to go to college in Tokyo, where he learned Japanese and was a member of a championship English-language debate team. From there he ended up on UBS's trading floor. Pieri had grabbed him for his interest-rates team as part of the effort to expand after the Bank of Japan hiked rates earlier in the year. Now Alykulov was seated near Hayes, who, with the title of director, was two rungs above him.

Almost immediately upon his arrival at UBS, Alykulov, with his unusual name and hard-to-place Eurasian looks, was bestowed with a series of nicknames. One was "Derka Derka," which derived from a common refrain in the deliberately offensive 2004 movie *Team America: World Police*. (The film was wildly popular among traders and brokers who reveled in their political incorrectness.) The *Team America* puppets depicting Middle Eastern terrorists used the phrase "Derka derka Muhammad jihad" instead of speaking actual Arabic. Alykulov wasn't an Arab, and Kazakhstan isn't in the Middle East. No matter. "Haha, that's great," Pieri said when he learned of his subordinate's nickname.

Alykulov looked up to Hayes, who was a few years older and enjoyed a reputation as a superstar in the making. (Plus, Hayes never called him Derka Derka.) The following summer Hayes would become the Kazakh's supervisor, a relationship that would yield life-changing results for both men. In the meantime, Hayes thought the junior trader, with black hair and a short, slightly pudgy build, was unremarkable. Women, however, found him quite appealing, resulting in a succession of attractive, pouty-lipped Japanese girlfriends.

• • • •

Hayes's first day of trading was September 29, 2006. He was tasked as a market maker responsible for handling derivatives linked to Japanese interest rates—in other words, helping UBS customers fulfill their buy and sell orders by building up an inventory of the products and then managing the associated risks via hedging against unfavorable swings in rates. But, as always, wagering the bank's money on the future directions of interest rates was at least as important. The rapidly expanding universe of swaps, futures, and other derivatives flooding the market allowed financial whiz-zes like Hayes to make massive wagers on the directions of rates in different currencies and over different time periods. It wasn't as simple as predicting the Bank of Japan would hike interest rates at some point in the future. Instead, Hayes organized his bets around derivatives that would deliver profits if, at a specific date, the *difference* between two interest rates—say, those in the United States and those in Japan—narrowed or widened by very precise margins. Hayes might wager that U.S. dollar Libor might fall relative to yen Libor. Other classes of trades tried to profit from predicting the convergence or divergence between different time periods of yen Libor—say, whether one-month Libor would rise relative to three-month Libor—or, even more complicated, whether the difference between one-month and six-month Libor would be greater three months or six months in the future. Hayes loved the challenge; it was like trying to complete a three-dimensional jigsaw puzzle whose pieces constantly changed shape.

The nature of the instruments Hayes was trading meant that his fate was chained to Libor, but it wasn't the only benchmark that mattered. By then, Libor's success and the BBA's marketing efforts had inspired even more local variants all over the world.

In Brussels, there was Euribor, tied to the euro. Hong Kong had Hibor, Singapore had Sibor, Hungary had Bubor, and South Africa had Jibar, to name just a few. Each rate was determined by an association of banks, both homegrown ones and those with substantial local presences. These were all separate from Libor and the BBA and generally were run by the local banking associations in those countries. The Japanese Bankers Association administered Tibor—the Tokyo interbank offered rate—which was an ingredient in many of the derivatives that Hayes and his counterparts were buying and selling. (Whereas yen Libor was supposed to measure what banks would pay to borrow Japanese currency from each other in London, Tibor measured borrowing rates in Tokyo. The bigger difference was that yen Libor and Tibor were based on different groups of banks providing data, and they therefore didn't move in lockstep.) Tibor became one more roulette table for traders.

Hayes started out his UBS trading conservatively. Always prone to anxiety, he had been scarred by the RBC episode. He felt such acute pressure, such paranoia, that he would get nauseous as he squeezed onto Tokyo's crowded subways each morning. He didn't sleep well, waking up multiple times each night to check movements in the U.S. markets. At the end of each day, when he had to assess the profitability of his trades and assign values to the assets he was still holding, he erred on the side of making them seem less profitable than they actually were. (These were just estimates, so Hayes had some wiggle room as he valued the positions.) Each evening, Pieri eyeballed Hayes's summation of that day's profits and losses. But no one looked at Hayes's individual trades. He was struck by the laissez-faire attitude—UBS clearly trusted him to do the right thing.

Hayes's team was on a floor that also included specialists in trading currencies, commodities, and bonds. The entire group would go out for beer-and-bowling nights three or four times a year at the Tokyo Dome Bowling Center, next door to the indoor stadium where the Yomiuri Giants baseball team played. These were among the few work events that Hayes genuinely enjoyed. He grudgingly went along to other such gatherings, but without much enthusiasm or effort. Once, at a dinner some colleagues had organized, he showed up lugging a thick economics textbook, which he spent the meal reading.

With as many as twelve computer screens and two keyboards, Hayes's workstation looked like something out of a sci-fi film. He had several monitors tracking different relationships between different market indices. Numbers whizzed up and down the screen as trades elsewhere in the market were reported. Charts moved. Color-coded, interactive Excel spreadsheets were open in the background. And then there were normal Web browser windows, and a couple of screens running chat programs and e-mail. Two humming computer terminals—and sometimes a third as well—powered the whole setup, with one machine devoted to making his Excel models run lightning-fast. His personal intercom system barked with a constant flow of data from brokers and colleagues. The monitors cast a glow on Hayes's scruffy face as he stooped over his desk, shoulders tense and hunched as he glared at his screens. He reminded a colleague of the Neo character in the *Matrix* trilogy: "He could just see these numbers."

The corner of the trading room in which Hayes, Pieri, and Alykulov sat was laid out in a deliberate fashion. The guys responsible for submitting the bank's daily Tibor data to the Japanese Bankers Association were seated next to the traders, like Hayes, who were making wagers that depended largely on the movements of Tibor and Libor. In some cases, the Tibor submitters themselves were making those trades. It wasn't hard to guess the result. Long before

Hayes arrived in Tokyo, the submitters and the traders had realized they could help each other out. It had been common practice at UBS for traders to ask their deskmates to nudge Tibor in helpful directions, and to ring colleagues in other parts of the UBS empire for help moving Libor. Those colleagues didn't have to comply—they could have reported something resembling the bank's actual borrowing costs—but who wanted to be the martyr, the goody two-shoes, who interfered with traders raking in profits for the bank?

In addition to watching his colleagues interact, Hayes had an unobstructed view of UBS's trading positions and how they intersected with its Libor submissions. Always adept at spotting patterns, he quickly realized that the bank was moving its submissions in ways that benefited its trading positions. That didn't seem like a coincidence—in fact, Hayes had noticed the phenomenon back when he was at the Royal Bank of Canada. At one point, he'd asked an RBC manager about UBS's seemingly odd submissions, which happened to be hurting Hayes's own trades. His manager bluntly told him it was because of the Swiss bank's trading positions. Hayes wasn't the only one who noticed. Eighteen months before he joined UBS, a client had complained to the bank about its self-serving Libor submissions. "It's our natural right," the UBS employee shot back. "Any other bank will do the same."

One afternoon that September, Hayes was chatting electronically with a Tokyo broker named David Perfect. After disappearing for a couple of hours, Hayes returned and explained that he'd just been on an expedition to procure a Japanese cell phone and contract. It had turned into an adventure—unable to understand what the guy at the phone store was saying, he'd ended up just randomly selecting a phone plan.

"Not sure what I've signed up to," Hayes reported. The broker sympathized—communicating with the Japanese, even those who spoke English, could be mind-boggling. Perfect offered advice on how Hayes could save money on his international phone calls. Then their conversation turned to work. Hayes, in the process of building his Excel models, grumbled that he was having trouble figuring out the trajectory of interest rates.

It's "very, very hard to price stuff with the fixes"—trader shorthand for benchmarks like Libor—"being so manipulated and inconsistent," he complained.

"The fixes are manipulated?" Perfect deadpanned.

"Yes, of course they are," Hayes said, not picking up the sarcasm.

"Kidding," Perfect clarified.

"Just give the cash desk"—the guys responsible for the bank's Libor submissions—"a Mars bar, and they'll set wherever you want," Hayes went on, still oblivious. "They are usually staffed by fat people." He was kidding, kind of. For more than a decade, traders and brokers had used the punch line of giving the cash desk a Mars bar as shorthand for the well-established pattern of derivatives traders pleading for favorable Libor submissions.

And so on his first day of trading, as Hayes chatted with Terry Farr, he threw in a casual aside: "Do me a favor today and get Libors right up."*

"I'll do what I can," Farr responded.

. . . .

Many of Hayes's contacts with brokerage firms—guys like Read and Farr—remained in London. Depending on the time of year,

---

* Hayes would later claim that he didn't view it as a genuine request so much as an articulation of his desire to see Libor inch higher.

and whether daylight savings was in effect, Tokyo was either eight or nine hours ahead of the British capital. As a result, it wasn't until Tokyo's evening trading session that most of the London brokers arrived at their offices. Unless, that is, the brokers radically adjusted their schedules to suit their clients' needs. Because his primary clients were focused on the Tokyo markets, Read tended to arrive at ICAP's London offices around 3 A.M. and then work a twelve-hour day before beating the rush-hour commute home. That was far from ideal; most nights, he got less—sometimes much less—than five hours of sleep. But it soon grew worse. With Hayes now in Tokyo, Read started arriving in ICAP's darkened offices shortly before midnight. He would switch on the lights and then spend the next five or six hours in isolation, the only one on the vast brokerage floor, until some of his early-bird colleagues started trickling in. Most days, he stuck around till noon, ensuring that he overlapped for at least a few hours with all his colleagues, before trudging home and grabbing a nap before his sons returned from school around 4 P.M. It wasn't a recipe for a happy family. Joanna, who had given up her career as a court clerk to look after the kids, was feeling more and more like a single parent.

One morning in October 2006, Read was alone in the office when he heard from Hayes. Outside, the London sky was still dark, and a thick mist hung in the air. Hayes had continued his bizarre— and reckless—practice of spilling his guts about whatever he was trading. To brokers, the information was like gold; they cannily shared it with grateful clients, and the smarter, more entrepreneurial brokers—men like Read—were able to anticipate related transactions that might appeal to traders and then pitch them as opportunities that had suddenly popped up in the market. Now Hayes confessed to Read that after trading for less than a month at UBS, he was already encountering trouble. *What he would do for the six-*

month version of yen Libor to go down slightly! Otherwise he stood to lose a bundle of money. Normally, someone in Hayes's shoes might have just asked UBS's own Libor submitters for help. In his previous jobs, it had been second nature for him to talk to the guys on the cash desk. Hayes had sat near them, and they were a valuable source of market intelligence. The problem was that at UBS, the Libor submitters were based in cities all over the world—Zurich, London, Singapore—but not Tokyo. (Only the Tibor submitters were stationed in Tokyo.) As a newbie, Hayes had no one to turn to.

Except for Read. Hayes knew that he and his ICAP colleagues were plugged in when it came to Libor. In fact, Read at times had noted to Hayes that he had an acquaintance at a German bank, WestLB, someone he'd known back in school, who now was involved in that bank's Libor submissions. Now Read had an idea. It involved his ICAP colleague Colin Goodman.

After quitting school at age eighteen, Goodman had started in finance as a bank clerk back when Hayes was a toddler. Bored, he saw a newspaper ad for an entry-level brokerage job at a company that later would become part of ICAP. His application was successful, and he started in 1984 as a trainee. From fetching sandwiches and making coffee, he climbed, very slowly, through the ranks. By the time Read first interviewed for his ICAP job a few years later, Goodman had sat in on the meeting. By now, working in ICAP's yen derivatives team, he was a veteran. Goodman—who had a long, narrow face, a chin so weak it was nearly invisible, and thick brown hair that he carefully parted on his left—was renowned for his drinking. (So well known was his penchant for downing a bottle of Australian Shiraz over a long weekday lunch that a colleague christened him "Lord Luncheon.") Despite his imbibing, Goodman was an early riser. At 5:25 A.M. every day, he caught the first British Rail train going from the suburbs into

London's bustling Waterloo Station. From there he hopped on the Tube to get to ICAP's offices by 6:30 A.M. His first task was to check in with traders and brokers in Tokyo, Hong Kong, and Singapore to get a feel for where transactions were taking place in the market, and at what prices. That knowledge was key to his ability to tell other clients about where markets had been and where they were likely heading. Around 7 A.M., he sent out an e-mail called a "run-through" to a slew of bank traders. The dispatch contained a simple spreadsheet—basically just a box of numbers—pasted into the body of the message. It listed where every tenor—the technical term for time period*—of yen Libor had stood the past day or two and where Goodman expected it to end up that day. He called that last figure "Suggested Libors." Each morning, he prefaced the data with the same simple note: "GOOD MORNING YEN RUN THRU."

The run-throughs had been an ICAP fixture since the late 1990s. Before long, ICAP's marketing team had sensed their commercial potential. Every so often, an executive traipsed around to a bunch of banks and touted the run-throughs as a valuable service ICAP provided important clients. And so the number of recipients on Goodman's run-through list grew. Libor submitters received it. Derivatives traders received it. Even Bank of England officials received it.

Read and Goodman had realized something interesting about the mundane run-throughs. Employees at some banks—including Citigroup, J.P. Morgan, Royal Bank of Scotland, WestLB, and Lloyds in Great Britain—who were in charge of submitting Libor data sometimes appeared to simply copy ICAP's data rather than

---

* Those tenors ranged from overnight—in other words, the rate at which a bank thought it could borrow money for less than a day—to one year. Intervals included one week, one month, two months, three months, and six months.

go through the onerous process of coming up with their own hypothetical estimates of what it would cost to borrow across different currencies and time periods. Relying on the run-throughs represented an enticing shortcut. And because of the inherent subjectivity of the Libor estimates, nobody was likely to notice.

But Read and Goodman did notice. (So, apparently, did Read's manager, Danny Wilkinson, who informed his bosses in 2006 that "banks are becoming dependent on ICAP for Libor calls.") Once, when Goodman's run-through contained a typo, suggesting six-month Libor at 1.10 instead of 1.01, Read noticed that Citigroup and WestLB copied it, even though it represented a huge leap from the previous day's level. When Goodman corrected it the next day, the banks again followed suit. In other words, the laziness of a few bank employees—"sheep," as Read sometimes called them—meant that ICAP's run-throughs had a startling amount of real power. If Goodman's e-mail contained slightly inflated Libor estimates, for example, there was a good chance a few banks also would submit higher data. That would nudge the overall benchmark higher. To traders like Hayes, even a shift of 0.01 percentage points—or one basis point, in the lingo—could be worth hundreds of thousands of dollars. For anyone with a contract whose interest rates or payouts were linked to Libor, significant money was on the line.

So Read told Hayes that October morning that he might be able to help.* He didn't mention the exact plan, only saying that his colleague Goodman would do what he could to spread the word that Libor seemed to be heading lower. That sounded great to Hayes, who mentioned the idea to his boss, Pieri. "That's good news," Pieri affirmed.†

---

* Read would later deny that it was his idea.

† Pieri would later say that he thought such arrangements were standard industry practice.

Still, Hayes was a bit surprised when ICAP actually seemed to succeed in altering banks' Libor submissions. A pattern soon emerged: Read would take a request from Hayes based on his trading positions, then relay it to Goodman via e-mail. Often the messages had subject lines like "Libors!!" (One of the enduring mysteries of the British finance lexicon is its tendency to pluralize random proper names. *Goldman* becomes *Goldmans*. *Lehman* becomes *Lehmans*. *Libor* becomes *Libors*.)

Read told Goodman that he'd get lunch in exchange for his efforts. Read had lost his credit card during a recent drunken night out bowling; once he retrieved it, he promised, he would be "supplying you with copious amounts of curry" as a thank-you—Indian food being the preferred takeout option among London's traders and brokers. After fielding three days of similar requests, and still not having received his promised curry, Goodman raised the stakes. How about taking him to K10, a popular Japanese restaurant, for a nice lunch, presumably one with wine? "Or," Goodman joked, "cash would be preferable."

Sometimes Goodman seemed to comply with Read's requests; other times, apparently feeling that they were too far outside the realm of reality, he balked. Read marveled to colleagues about the strategy's success. "Tom needed them high so our boys sent them out high and it seems people copied them," he boasted.

••••

Roger Darin was a thirty-four-year-old trader in UBS's Singapore office. A Swiss native and a fan of Italian opera, in particular the tenor Luciano Pavarotti, Darin had a reputation in the industry for being aggressive and at times nasty—hardly an unusual personality type on a bank trading floor. Bald and bearded, he suffered from a disorder that had left half of his face looking slack, one of his eyes lazy. (Despite the defect, he still cycled through a number of girlfriends among his UBS colleagues.) One of Darin's duties in Singapore was to handle the daily submissions of the bank's yen Libor data. It was a dull part of his job, but because Darin was himself a trader who specialized in interest-rate derivatives, it imbued him with a certain power. And it would make him indispensable to Hayes.

Hayes at first didn't know who was in charge of UBS's yen Libor submissions. Neither did Pieri, who suggested that Hayes get in touch with Darin to see if he knew.

"Hi Roger, who sets our Libors?" Hayes asked, eschewing any social niceties, one day in November 2006.

"Me," Darin replied. Well, that was easy! Hayes asked if Darin could do him a favor and lift UBS's yen Libor submission as high as possible that day. No problem, Darin responded. "Will get it an extra notch today." He hiked UBS's submission to 0.6 from 0.55 the day before—a big, five-basis-point boost. That helped push the overall yen Libor average up sharply to 0.57938 from 0.545. Traders like Hayes calculated their potential profits based on Libor swinging by a basis point or even less. This was a move of more than three basis points.

Two days later, Hayes again asked Darin to push Libor higher. This time, Darin said he couldn't help—he told Hayes he had his own trades that would benefit from Libor declining. Hayes proposed a solution: He would buy Darin's trading positions so that increasing Libor would be profitable—or at least not detrimental—for both of them. Darin's positions were small enough that Hayes could afford to purchase them without sacrificing the profits he stood to collect if Libor rose. Darin agreed. The following day, Hayes suggested a repeat. "We can try to do what we did yesterday which worked out well for both of us!"

"It did work indeed," Darin agreed.

Over the next two years, Hayes—or Alykulov, who had eagerly accepted a job as Hayes's deputy, hoping some of his brilliance would rub off on him—would ping Darin on hundreds of occasions asking him to move UBS's Libor data in helpful ways. Darin often complied. Neither he nor Alykulov thought much of the requests, partly because it was so clearly common practice on the bank's trading floors. Darin knew that his colleagues in other parts of the world routinely took into account their colleagues' trading positions when deciding where to place their Libor submissions. Plus, Darin had received the same marching orders as Andrew Smith had: Holger Seger had instructed them to cooperate as much as possible with their fellow traders. Darin, like Smith, interpreted this as meaning that they were generally supposed to play ball when it came to Libor-nudging requests.

That's not to say that Darin always acceded to Hayes's entreaties. On occasion, he rejected them as outlandish. "I don't mind helping on your fixings, but I'm not setting Libor seven basis points [0.07 percentage points] away from the truth," Darin responded on one occasion in early 2007. "I'll get UBS banned if I do that, no interest in that."

"Okay, obviously no interest in that happening either," Hayes agreed. "Not asking for it to be seven basis points from reality."

The exchange reflected an important dynamic: There were limits to the extent that traders would tinker with Libor. You could move Libor within a certain plausible band to help yourself, but straying outside that range was at best unwise. Did that principle stem from a sense of propriety, a notion that while the definition of

Libor was a bit amorphous, the submissions needed to have at least some integrity? Or was it simply that traders wanted to avoid detection as they rigged a vital interest rate? Years later, that question would be hotly contested.

In any case, the constructive relationship between Hayes and Darin was doomed. Even before that first friendly trade, Pieri had informed Darin that he and Hayes planned to start making markets in a product called overnight index swaps. These were another flavor of interest-rate derivatives, the rare one that wasn't linked to Libor. Until then, those swaps had been Darin's turf, but Hayes's move to grab this area had received the blessings of UBS executives who wanted to take advantage of their new hotshot trader in Tokyo. "Obviously, it was not well received," Pieri told a colleague. Darin's crew "believe they own the product." Before long, a bitter Darin would start trashing Hayes to anyone who would listen.

. . . .

Every day when Hayes arrived at UBS's building in Tokyo, he was greeted with several sets of turnstiles. He had to choose which one to walk through. Most people wouldn't give the choice any thought; to Hayes, the decision and its effect on his daily routine were of great consequence. One morning in early 2007, he entered through the right turnstile on the cluster of turnstiles farthest to the right. That day, his trades were like gold. He made money everywhere he looked. Superstitious by nature, Hayes decided that his choice of turnstile must have had something to do with his great day. "The lucky turnstile chose me," he would say. From that day on, he used the same gate every single time he entered the building. It wasn't just the turnstile. Hayes also had a lucky pair of black Hugo Boss pants and a preferred pair of yellow Ralph Lauren bumblebee socks given to him by a Hong Kong broker named Danny Brand. He wore the trousers so often that holes started to appear in the crotch area.

Hayes's life revolved around his job. He typically arrived at work around 8 A.M. and stayed till at least 7 P.M. He came in when he was sick. He rarely ate lunch. An assistant fetched him afternoon tea. He only grudgingly went to the bathroom during trading hours. By evening, he was exhausted but didn't want to go home. Instead, he often sat at his computer playing Pac-Man. When his father visited, Nick overheard his son on the phone at odd hours chattering about Libor. The term was familiar to Nick—who by now had reinvented himself as a day trader—but he didn't grasp the extent to which his son's job hinged on interest-rate determinations. When Nick tried to start a conversation about the Queens Park Rangers, Hayes wouldn't engage, preferring instead to remain glued to his BlackBerry. Nick found his son's stoniness, his lack of animation, unsettling.

Though Hayes was obsessed, he was hardly miserable. For the first time in his life, he was popular with women. The fact that he was a well-paid rising star probably didn't hurt. But he also felt more relaxed talking to Japanese women (those who spoke English, that is) than he did Western ones because he didn't find the former to be physically attractive. Japanese women took an immediate liking to him, apparently because he seemed nonpredatory and sweet compared to some of his peers.[*] One woman at UBS found his quirky personality adorable and bought him a pair of panda dolls. Propped up on his desk, they became his lucky pandas.

Panda influenced or not, Hayes's good fortune continued. Hit-

---

[*] While most adults in Japan get a "-san" attached to their names, Hayes was known as "Tom-chan"—a suffix usually reserved for children.

ting his stride, he often earned millions of dollars a week for UBS, establishing a reputation as one of Tokyo's elite traders. This success had little to do with his nascent Libor-massaging efforts; he was just making smart wagers.

To Hayes's surprise, some of his higher-ups started pushing him to step on the gas. It was part of UBS's spectacularly ill-timed strategy to get bigger in risky markets, on the eve of a once-in-a-century financial crisis. One of those bosses was a London-based executive named Sascha Prinz. Prinz had a reputation inside UBS for being loud and combative, known for sometimes ripping people to shreds when he was unhappy with them. Constantly chugging cans of Red Bull, he was an avid risk-taker; some colleagues regarded him as a reckless cowboy. On one visit to Tokyo, Prinz asked Hayes how much risk he had on—in other words, the total amount he stood to gain or lose depending on the outcome of all his bets. Hayes told him the dollar figure. It was a large number, but without missing a beat, or seeming to think it through very carefully, Prinz told him to double it. "Christ, Sascha, you're mental," Hayes thought to himself. "It's a big risk already." But far be it from him to defy an order. He happily doubled down.

Adding to his growing confidence, Hayes came to realize that he didn't need to rely solely on Darin and the ICAP brokers for help with Libor. Thanks to his time in London's tight-knit community of derivatives traders, Hayes had a few contacts at companies other than UBS. And it soon occurred to him that they could help him get his way.

The traders whom Hayes knew at other banks were an unremarkable bunch. Sure, the group was studded with the occasional party animal, but it was not a standout crowd. These were the proletariats of banking, young infantry toiling away for the benefits of their institutions and, in many cases, their institutions' lavishly paid senior executives. Hayes's cohort was hardly poor—he and his peers were pulling in mid-six-figure salaries and bonuses—but by investment-banking standards they weren't worth a second glance. For the most part, they weren't even making creative or otherwise exceptional trades. They were simply marching along a well-trodden path, except for one important wrinkle: Without fully realizing it, they were entering into a partnership that would, a few years hence, be construed as a criminal enterprise that embodied greed, recklessness, and hubris—in essence, everything that made Wall Street evil. At the time, it seemed like business as usual.

CHAPTER 6

The Sycophants

One day in February 2007, Hayes was chatting with a J.P. Morgan trader named Stuart Wiley. The American bank had a thriving trading business in London, an operation so big that it was spread across multiple buildings: one in Canary Wharf, one near the ancient London Wall, and another in an ornate stone building on the north bank of the Thames that sat above one of London's biggest vaults of gold bullion.

Wiley and Hayes had gotten to know each other through brokers back when Hayes worked in London. Though mere acquaintances, Hayes, not the best at grasping social boundaries, thought it appropriate to see if Wiley could lean on whoever handled J.P. Morgan's Libor data to nudge it down slightly. The answer was no, but Wiley hardly faulted Hayes for asking. "Unfortunately," he said, J.P. Morgan's submitters "have gone all 'we need to be independent' on us. So unfortunately nothing much I can do for a while."

"No worries," Hayes said. "My guys are reasonable, so just let me know when you need something." As it happened, Wiley did need something: He was looking for six-month yen Libor to remain low for the following week. Hayes said he'd see what he could do to help.*

Brent Davies, who had mentored Hayes when he joined RBS straight out of college, was still working at the Scottish bank. In 2007, Hayes started pinging him with requests to get RBS's submissions up or down. Davies was skeptical that Hayes's requests would have any effect, but he dutifully passed them on.

There were a few other traders Hayes could turn to. Otherwise, he viewed most competitors as enemies. "You're in a war," he would explain later. "At the end of the day, this is a sort of zero-sum game and you're up against people who are fighting for the same customers, you're up against people who you're trading with on a competitive basis, and there's a winner and a loser. And so, you know, there isn't a lot of time for friendships." What about golfing with rival traders? Did that sound like fun? "Unless you're going to hit them with the club, no."

. . . .

While the ICAP crew seemed to be able to sway Libor by passing slightly skewed data along to banks, Hayes figured that he could amplify the effect by enlisting another trusted broker. He had just the man: Terry Farr. Lots of traders approached him for guidance on where Libor was heading. And the charismatic, happy-go-lucky broker was an expert at fostering goodwill and then calling in favors. That was what Hayes wanted him to do now: call in

---

* Before long, J.P. Morgan would install a new Libor submitter, one whom Wiley viewed as more amenable to requests from traders. "So do you wander over, give him the odd Mars bar and say, you know, 'end of the year, we'll sort you out'?" an ICAP broker asked after Wiley shared the good news. Yes, Wiley replied.

favors. If Hayes needed Libor lower, he would ask Farr to reach out to traders or rate submitters at a few banks. The maneuver required a subtle, deft touch. A bank wouldn't just adhere to a random request, especially one passed on behalf of a trader at a rival bank—unless, that is, it had good reason to do so. But in the backscratching, quid-pro-quo world of traders and brokers, there often were plenty of reasons. Doing a favor on a Libor submission was really no different than doing a favor by taking someone out to a boozy night at the club.

Farr tackled the task with gusto, enlisting his fellow RP Martin brokers to phone their contacts, too. Sometimes Hayes drew up specific suggestions about which traders and banks Farr should target. One thing that made this tricky, Farr told Hayes, was that the Libor submitters at banks like Deutsche Bank and Dutch lender Rabobank were taking instructions from their own interest-rate traders. Why would they field requests from Hayes if someone who worked at their own bank was making a contradictory request? They wouldn't. That was frustrating news for Hayes. But it contributed to his impression about the widespread nature of banks goosing Libor. Everyone seemed to be doing it.

What was less common was the extra mile that Hayes was taking it, enlisting brokers and rival traders in his efforts to influence the Libor submissions of *other* banks. It's not clear that Hayes, twenty-seven years old at the time, detected that distinction—blurry boundaries, like nonverbal cues, often were invisible to him. In any case, Hayes was a pioneer of these aggressive new tactics. He viewed his job as pushing things to the max to make money for his bank. That's what good traders did—they ruthlessly hunted for tiny inefficiencies and loopholes they could exploit to gain a leg up on rivals or the broader market. Nobody ever told him it was inappropriate—legally, ethically, or otherwise—to lobby outsiders for help on Libor. What kept him up at night wasn't that what he was doing was wrong. It was that he wasn't doing it well *enough*.

Hayes was so open about, and preoccupied with, his strategy that he would change the status on his Facebook page to reflect his daily desires for Libor to move up or down, a self-deprecating poke at his nerdy fixation. At night, he dreamed of the rate. When it didn't move in a favorable direction, Hayes often lost his composure, ranting to Alykulov that he didn't understand why rival traders didn't accede to his and his brokers' requests.

While pushing Libor around only took up a few minutes of his frenetic days, his obsession was overpowering. And so Hayes decided to get his younger stepbrother, Peter O'Leary, involved. O'Leary had come into Hayes's life when Hayes was eleven years old and his mother remarried. O'Leary and his brother, Ben, moved in with Hayes and his younger brother, Robin. Hayes liked his new stepfather, Tim, and got along well with Peter and Ben. Now Peter was looking to follow in Hayes's professional footsteps. He landed an entry-level trading gig in the New York office of the British bank HSBC. After six months there, he reluctantly moved back to London with HSBC. As Hayes knew from his own experience several years earlier, traders like O'Leary on a training scheme were just a rung or two above janitors in the pecking order at big international banks. They were there to run errands and, if they were lucky, learn a thing or two through osmosis. The last thing they should do is bother their senior colleagues.

One day in April 2007, after Hayes had wrapped up his trading and played a little Pac-Man, he called O'Leary. After catching up about whether his stepbrother missed New York—he did, badly—Hayes started explaining how his Libor-dependent trading strategy worked. O'Leary eagerly listened, lapping up the knowledge. "I've got a mate at RBS who set it down at 0.64 for me," Hayes said. He noted that a contact at Bank of America had seemingly disregarded his requests. "Can't stand B of A," Hayes said.

"B of A, booooooo," O'Leary parroted.

Then Hayes cut to the chase: Did O'Leary know his HSBC colleague who was in charge of the bank's yen Libor submissions? Yes, kind of. His name was Chris Porter, called "Darcy" because he seemed posh. O'Leary and Darcy had run into each other a few times.

"If you can, have a word with those guys," Hayes started. "Just say, 'if you can set a low yen three-month Libor, you'd really help my brother out.'" O'Leary laughed, but Hayes wasn't joking. "Seriously, man," he continued. "I've got several million-buck fixes." In other words, Hayes explained, for every basis point that Libor declined, UBS stood to nab a roughly $1 million profit. O'Leary was stunned. He had no idea Hayes was rolling the dice so aggressively. Hayes seemed pleased to have an admiring youngster to whom he could trumpet the magnitude of his trades. "The notional is massive," he said, referring to the underlying size of the trade.* "I'm talking about trillions of yen."

O'Leary said he'd see what he could do; nothing happened. Hayes tried again in June. O'Leary said he'd drop his colleague a line. "Just keep it super-casual," Hayes advised.

The next day, Hayes sent O'Leary a reminder, referring to Darcy as O'Leary's "mate."

"Will do," O'Leary responded. "For the record he's definitely not my 'mate'!" O'Leary was feeling a bit sheepish about making the request. "Dunno if he'll do anything on it seeing as he doesn't

---

* The notional value refers to the "headline" size of the instruments that the derivative is referencing—as in the $100 swap that ABC Corp. entered into with Giantbank. The actual amount of money that changes hands in the derivative transaction is much lower than the notional amount.

really know me and is massively more senior than me," he cautioned.

"Well, no harm in asking!" Hayes typed.

O'Leary banged out a quick instant message to his colleague. "high 6m yen libor owuld be gd according to my brother!" The reply came back: "WILL DO MY BEST."

A few hours passed. HSBC kept its Libor submission unchanged from the day before. O'Leary's skepticism had been well founded.

Hayes decided this was pointless. And he had a bout of remorse. He hadn't viewed O'Leary's efforts as likely to actually help, but, based on statistical probabilities, the more people he contacted for help, the greater his odds were of success; it was like buying an extra lottery ticket. Later that day, Hayes told Read that he was done asking O'Leary for favors: "I don't want to get him in trouble." He followed up with an apologetic phone call to O'Leary. "I don't think I'm going to bother asking for your help on the Libors again, because he didn't shift it at all," he said. "But also I don't want to put you in that position, I've decided. . . . In retrospect, he probably thinks 'that cheeky young lad.'" Hayes followed up with an instant message, apologizing a second time. Then the two groused about work; O'Leary had to be in the office the following weekend. "Bit upsetting!" he groaned.

"Sorry mate, welcome to banking," Hayes said. "The bonuses will follow later! Usually about two years or so."

"Yeah, we'll see!" his stepbrother replied.

• • • •

All this might have seemed harmless—or at least only harmful to other major banks that were up to similar tricks—except that there were other people and institutions, far from Wall Street and Tokyo and the City of London, that were also dabbling in financial products linked to Libor and its brethren.

Jeffrey Laydon was a computer geek turned salesman who, after attending a technical college in Milwaukee and spending five years as a consultant at Southwestern Bell, had moved to Florida in the mid-1980s. For the next two decades, he lived outside Orlando and worked at a series of computer and telecommunications companies, keeping mainframes online and helping address big clients' computing needs. Balding, with ruddy cheeks, wire-rimmed glasses, and a sandy mustache, Laydon had a couple of hobbies. One was sailing; he loved taking a boat out on Lake Monroe, where he was a member of the local sailing association. Another passion was investing. From the comfort of his home, he traded stocks, options, and futures via an online brokerage account. He was doing well enough that he toyed with the idea of quitting his job and becoming a full-time day trader, someone who could even help educate other wannabe investors.

By 2006, Laydon had discovered a new area to wager on: Japanese interest rates. He didn't know much about Japan, but derivatives linked to the yen were becoming increasingly popular after the Bank of Japan's rate hike, and he decided to give it a go. He spent thousands of dollars, a considerable gamble for a small-time trader, on futures contracts on the Merc that would pay out if Tibor declined. He had no way of knowing that on the opposite side of the planet, a posse of traders was working to push Tibor in the opposite direction. By the time Laydon's traces matured, his money had vaporized.

Laydon wasn't alone. In the years leading up to the financial crisis, public pension funds had been growing increasingly bold and creative in the gambles they made with their members' money. Markets were booming, and it was hard to resist the temptation to leap for the double-digit annual returns that hedge funds and other professional money managers were attaining. So the Oklahoma Police Pension & Retirement System, a traditionally risk-averse fund, hired a bunch of asset managers to help it amp up its returns. Before long, the OPPRS—exactly the type of dumb-money clients that Hayes and his ilk battled for the right to do business with—was the proud owner of Japanese interest-rate derivatives. Sure enough, the bets soured—a result, the fund would later claim, of manipulation by Hayes and his pals. A similar scenario played out in California. CalSTRS, the giant fund handling the retirement savings of the state's teachers, bought derivatives linked to Libor and Tibor. CalSTRS would realize years later that it had paid inflated prices for those instruments because someone had pushed the benchmarks artificially higher.

Hayes had never heard of Laydon, probably couldn't point to Oklahoma on a map, and most likely didn't know what CalSTRS stood for (California State Teachers' Retirement System). He viewed himself as operating within a closed system, facing off against other predatory professionals who were sufficiently sophisticated, and often avaricious, to deserve whatever they got. The perspective of the financial system as a playing field for these competitors, where amateurs were viewed as fair game if they were thought of at all, had been hammered into Hayes since he first set foot on a trading floor. It was a narrow, self-serving view, and its prevalence helped explain why the finance industry was heading for all sorts of trouble. But this was a game played hard, and if there were corners cut and envelopes pushed—well, that was just business.

· · · ·

Before long, Hayes's tactics were becoming known in the marketplace. One day, a broker named Scott Harris was talking with Roger Darin, the UBS Libor submitter in Singapore. Harris had heard through the grapevine that Hayes had been leaning on Libor submitters. Darin pounced on the opportunity to bad-mouth his nemesis.

"He's been trying that for a while now," Darin explained, neglecting to mention that he had agreed to move Libor on Hayes's behalf at times in the past. "Very embarrassing."

"Hope he gets buried," Harris said. "Mike [Pieri] may not think he's such a 'golden boy' anymore."

"Doubt Mike will learn," Darin lamented, almost sounding sad.

Hayes wasn't venturing out on a limb alone. Pieri knew what his trader was up to, or should have, thanks to Hayes's repeated e-mails, instant messages, and in-person conversations. Every morning at 8:30 and 11:00, Hayes and Pieri gathered with more than a dozen colleagues in a conference room; Hayes tended to perch on a windowsill instead of crowding around the oval table. The participants discussed their plans to get Libor moved. It wasn't a secret; when senior executives cycled through Tokyo for periodic visits, they usually sat in on the meetings, too. And when Libor moved in profitable ways, Hayes sometimes told Pieri that he owed Read and Farr beers for their valuable assistance.

At one point in 2007, Hayes and Ainsworth were preparing to head off on a weeklong trip to Thailand. Hayes had delegated the task of picking the destination and hotel to Ainsworth, a nod to her persnickety standards and Hayes's general lack of interest in vacations. She informed Hayes that they would be staying at the Trisara resort in Phuket, a tropical island off the west coast of the Thai peninsula. "Congratulate Sarah," Read said when Hayes mentioned where they were heading. "Probably the most expensive hotel in Asia."

"Thank God it's just one week," Hayes replied, before adding that Ainsworth would be footing half the bill.

"You have loads of money," Read pointed out.

"Which I should be saving for a house!"

Hayes was so stressed about a big batch of trades that were nearing fruition that he nearly canceled the vacation. Instead, he e-mailed Pieri, Alykulov, and two other UBS colleagues to remind them to ping the ICAP and RP Martin brokers if they needed Libor "pushed one way or other." Read, meanwhile, promised Hayes that he'd work hard to ensure that Goodman tweaked his run-throughs, and, sure enough, he repeatedly asked his London colleague to jack three- and six-month Libor higher. Goodman told Read that the figures didn't reflect what he was seeing in the market—and then he did it anyway. Read, unsatisfied, asked him to send out a revised run-through with the figures higher still, noting that Hayes so far that month had paid ICAP £83,000 in commissions. Goodman grudgingly complied.*

In Phuket, Hayes and Ainsworth stayed in a waterfront villa at the secluded five-star resort. Calm turquoise waters lapped at the private, white-sand beach. Ainsworth relaxed in the sun, sipping champagne and getting spa treatments. There on the beach, it dawned on Hayes that he could now afford this high-rolling

---

* Goodman would later say that the run-through was based on figures he was seeing in the market and wasn't an attempt to manipulate Libor.

lifestyle. The bill at the end of the week was massive. He and Ainsworth usually split the tab. This time, feeling lavish, Hayes picked up the whole thing.

• • • •

By the standards of the brokerage industry, good old RP Martin was tiny. It had fewer than two hundred employees, in five countries, most of them in the firm's headquarters in an unmarked building on a narrow street in the heart of the City of London. The firm's roots traced back more than a century, and over time RP Martin's specialty became helping banks trade currencies and other financial products that weren't available on public exchanges. One of its niches was catering to traders who focused on products linked to Libor. What RP Martin lacked in size, it made up for in scrappy enthusiasm. The firm's brokers were known for crashing parties thrown by rival companies in order to get face time with coveted clients. Some traders liked working with RP Martin because of its familial style and working-class culture, albeit one with six-figure salaries. The culture came straight from the top: David "Mustard" Caplin tried to set his shop apart from larger rivals like ICAP and Tullett Prebon by cultivating a down-home feel. "You're joining part of a family," he would tell new recruits. He incented his staff by giving them equity in the firm.

To survive, RP Martin had to be aggressive, going the extra mile for clients. Until 2010, Mustard resisted even having a compliance department; the basic guiding principle governing employee conduct should be common sense, he thought, not a rigid set of rules. When he finally bowed to reality and created a compliance group, he did what he could to marginalize its employees.

Warning the new department's chief not to inadvertently "desta-bilize" things, Mustard told him not to introduce any initiatives that would affect the brokers. The last thing Mustard needed was an intrusive internal affairs bureau causing his stars to jump to competitors.

That attitude trickled down. Cliff King had joined RP Martin in 1980. In 2006, Mustard tapped him to run a squad of bro-kers responsible for Japanese products, interest-rate derivatives, and the like. King spent the bulk of his time tending to his own clients, which included traders at some giant banks. The way he saw it, his posse—which included Terry Farr, Lee Aaron, and Jim Gilmour—didn't require much supervision. They seemed to take care of themselves.

It was a curious bunch. There was the motorcycle-crashing, flip-flop-wearing, ravioli-toting Farr. There was Aaron, whose nickname was short for "Village Idiot." Gilmour, for his part, had been busted a few times as a teenager for minor offenses, left school at age sixteen, briefly trained to join the army, landed a job as a cabinetmaker, and ultimately became a broker in the late 1980s. Slim with slowly receding brown hair, Gilmour might once have passed for handsome, but when he was stressed or sleep deprived, he developed dark, puffy bags under his eyes. As the years went on, those bags became an almost permanent facial feature. Gil-mour, whose salary was £75,000, was battling multiple scourges. His bank account was perpetually overdrawn. His colleagues an-noyed him. And his wife, Lisa, with whom he had two daughters, seemed to derive great pleasure from calling him at work, either to update him on the squirrels and other mundane wildlife scurrying through their suburban backyard or to harangue him for screwing up their TV-recording device, interrupting her planned daytime viewing of *Law & Order.*

. . . .

Farr didn't have much history of success. Growing up, he was always the last one picked for soccer games—a mark of shame for someone coming up through the British school system. Year after year at RP Martin, his personnel files included paperwork explaining absences caused by an almost comical array of medical problems. In 2002, he was out with a viral infection, followed a few months later by what he described as "blood poisoning caused by an arm infection." In early 2004, he fell victim to food poisoning. That was also the summer of his "severe allergic reaction" to a wasp sting, "causing large swelling and infection and nausea." Later in 2004, he missed work due to "tooth extraction causing severe discomfort." A few years later, he was out due to what he thought was swine flu. (It turned out to be a cold, but it got him to temporarily ditch his pack-a-day smoking habit.)

But business had never been central to his sense of self. Indeed, what really animated Farr was his son Sam. When not riding motorcycles together, Farr enjoyed counseling the teenager on, among other topics, how to get women into bed. "Mate, look," he told Sam on one occasion. "If you want to have a little rub with some bird, you need to lower your sights a bit, go for fat ones."

In the summer of 2007, however, Farr was finally coming into his own at work—thanks to having hitched himself to two successful traders. Hayes was emerging as a star, and the business he kept sending Farr's way was generating buckets of commissions. But Hayes wasn't Farr's biggest client. That distinction belonged to a trader named Alexis Stenfors.

Stenfors grew up in a small town in Finland near the Baltic Sea. Athletic, with high cheekbones, brown sideburns, and deep-set brown eyes, he was the unusual combination of a runner and smoker. As a young man, he thought about going into academia. Instead, he took an internship at a German bank, where he handled the paperwork for derivatives transactions that the bank's traders executed. He became intrigued by the huge sums of money involved in transactions such as interest-rate swaps—often the "ticket" accompanying those trades would run well into the tens of millions of dollars. Another thing that caught his eye was the bizarre, rhyming acronyms that littered the terms of the transactions: names like Libor and Tibor and Fibor and Pibor. A few years later, in 1995, he became an interest-rate trader in a British bank's Stockholm office. Soon he was the one executing big transactions pegged to Scandinavian benchmarks like Stibor, Nibor, Cibor, and Helibor. While trading, he managed to cowrite a paper about European currencies in a Finnish academic journal with a Swedish economics professor—hardly normal fare for his peer group.

Stenfors cycled through some of the world's biggest banks. In September 2001, he was working in London in the investment-banking division of Crédit Agricole when terrorists hijacked planes and crashed them into the World Trade Center in Manhattan. The French bank's New York offices were on the ninety-second floor of the World Trade Center's North Tower—just below where the first plane crashed. (Sixty-nine Crédit Agricole employees perished that day.) Early that afternoon in London, footage of the disaster was broadcast on the wall-mounted TVs around Crédit Agricole's trading floor. Stenfors and his colleagues kept doing business as if nothing had happened. As weeks passed, Stenfors was increasingly chilled by his and his peers' amoral, unemotional reactions—and he wasn't alone. Traders at other banks, many of which had outposts in the twin towers, realized that their first instincts had not been to fret about their colleagues' well-being or the geopolitical implications of the attack, but instead to hunt for profitable trading opportunities. Then again, didn't money make the world go round? Their recollections were tinged with regret, but for most just barely.

Stenfors certainly kept trucking along in his career, eventually landing in the London office of the Wall Street giant Merrill Lynch. In 2007, thirty-six years old, married and with two young daughters, Stenfors—trading currencies and interest-rate derivatives, including those pegged to the Japanese yen—was one of the savviest, most ambitious risk-takers in London's booming markets. His prowess was reflected in the astronomical sum—about $120 million—that he earned for his bank in a single year. Stenfors didn't fully embrace the industry's wild ethos—not a surprise, given his academic tendencies—and jokingly booked squash and tennis courts under the name Patrick Bateman, the fictional investment banker and serial killer in the book and film *American Psycho*. But when it came to earning money, he was as ruthless as anyone. There were no limits, at least none that Stenfors knew of, restricting how much risk he could take with the bank's money. Year after year, the bank gave him "budgets"—industry lingo for the amount of revenue he was expected to generate—that stretched into nine digits.

Stenfors and Farr were tight. Stenfors thought the broker was friendly and honest, and it felt nice to do business with an underdog firm and an up-from-his-bootstraps broker who was making a fraction of what someone at a rival firm would earn.

The tandem rises of Hayes and Stenfors were excellent news for Farr—especially as his two clients got to know each other. In 2007, the pair happened to be seated next to each other at a Christmas party ICAP hosted for traders. The soiree featured treasures carted up from Michael Spencer's wine cellar and a gaggle of beautiful women hired to act as "hostesses." As they milled around the room, sitting on the traders' laps and laughing at their jokes, an uncomfortable Hayes and Stenfors spent the entire evening immersed in an intense conversation about financial markets and trading minutiae. Obsessive and at the top of their games, each could tell that the other derived something approaching pure bliss from the subject. There weren't very many people in the world who could carry on a discussion like this, with such fluency and at such a high level.

After clicking at the ICAP party, Hayes and Stenfors started trading together more and more. Hayes soon became one of Stenfors's biggest trading partners, and they tended to automatically route their transactions through Farr, who pocketed fat commission payments for almost no work.

As the fees added up, Farr's renown grew. Tullett Prebon tried to hire him, dangling a salary of nearly $300,000 plus roughly $200,000 in up-front cash. But Farr loved working at RP Martin, in particular its tight-knit, casual vibe. Mustard eventually convinced him to stay by handing him nearly $100,000 in cash as well as a roughly $100,000 interest-free loan. The loan allowed Farr, who regarded himself as terrible with money, to settle some of his outstanding credit card debts, as well as to cover some of the ballooning costs of a home renovation that had left him without an indoor bathroom for four weeks. And he was promoted to manager. (The elevated status didn't mean much: Farr was managing only one employee, Gilmour, signing off on his expenses and making sure he showed up on time and didn't take too many sick days.) Later, when rival brokerage BGC tried to stage a raid on RP Martin employees, Farr was singled out for a "loyalty bonus" of about $40,000. Before long, his son Sam would join dad at work as a broker-in-training.

. . . .

To the frustration of some of his brokers, Hayes remained uninterested in being lavishly entertained. He preferred to sit at home with a bucket of fried chicken from KFC and a tall glass of orange juice, followed by a hot bath. One evening, a desperate broker showed up outside UBS's Tokyo office and pleaded to let him take Hayes out to dinner; the broker needed to show his bosses he was entertaining the star client. Hayes finally relented—and then led him to a nearby Burger King, where the broker spotted a rat scuttling across the floor.

That's not to say Hayes was uniformly obstinate. In London, after he'd repeatedly rebuffed Noel Cryan's offers of dinner, the broker had come up with an alternative: Hayes could take Ainsworth out for an expensive meal and then get reimbursed by Tullett. Read treated Hayes and Ainsworth to a similar Christmas feast in 2006, leaving his personal credit card details on file at the restaurant and then getting paid back by ICAP. As time went on, and Hayes's stature grew, brokers became more creative about coming up with such goodies. They lined up expensive sports tickets for Hayes's friends and family back in England. Nigel Delmar occasionally stopped by the home of Hayes's brother Robin, delivering expensive booze or other gifts. (Robin told Hayes he thought the practice was weird; Hayes responded that it was just how the industry worked. Robin wasn't convinced—it seemed a little like bribery—but there was no point in arguing with his stubborn older brother.)

Another goodie came in the form of win-win trades. Brokers sometimes were approached about possible trades by pension funds or other long-term investors who weren't sensitive to small price variations. These dumb-money clients, or "muppets," which bought something and then held on to it for months, maybe years, didn't fit into the industry's carnivorous culture and weren't especially good for the trading business. Brokers, face-to-face with one of these sloths, had the distinct pleasure of finding a predator to take the other side of the trade—and Hayes was increasingly hearing the words *I've got a gift for you.* The lucky trader (in this case, him) would be able to do the deal at a favorable price that a more sophisticated institution, such as a fast-moving hedge fund, would never accept.

There was one final way brokers could thank Hayes for all the lucrative commissions. And that was by continuing to help him with Libor.

. . . .

Hayes's move to Tokyo had wreaked havoc on Darrell Read's personal life. He had dropped his other clients in order to cater full-time to the increasingly lucrative—and combustible—Hayes. Read's nocturnal office hours meant that he only rarely saw his family. Eventually, Joanna gave him an ultimatum: He needed to do something—anything—to regain a normal life. Read was inclined to agree; he was feeling like a failure as a husband and a father. The family had already been toying with moving to New Zealand, where Joanna had relatives. The original idea was for ICAP to temporarily keep him on the payroll as a favor, allowing him to get a visa, but not requiring him to set foot in the New Zealand office. But Hayes's ongoing success in Tokyo sparked a new idea: Read could work from the brokerage's small Wellington quarters, now only three time zones ahead of his client, so he could revert to a relatively normal schedule. The plan was for Read to do it for a year and then find something more fulfilling and less stressful to do with his life, perhaps teaching. In the meantime, his office hours would be scaled back to merely 10:30 A.M. to 9:00 P.M.

The Read clan moved to Wellington in April 2007. The transition proved harder than expected. In the Southern Hemisphere, winter was approaching. Read missed the hubbub of ICAP's frenetic London office; the Wellington outpost, staffed by perhaps a dozen people, was a morgue by comparison. Shouting matches—sometimes good-natured, sometimes less so—had been common in London, as were friendships with colleagues. Now heads would turn at any conversation that involved a raised voice.

Read figured the fact that he was working less and in a better mood would help with the transition, but Joanna, home alone without any adult interactions, missed her friends. The winter weather wasn't helping. She found limited distraction by working on the design of a new house they were planning to build.

The irony was that, just as the Reads started to settle down, Hayes was thinking about returning to England. Ainsworth, after getting off to a fast start in Japan, now was entertaining a fantasy of opening a clothing store back home. ("Independent woman," Read remarked sarcastically. "Fantastic.") Hayes, meanwhile, missed the food, his family, the ability to communicate relatively easily, the weather (he hated Tokyo's hot summer days and longed for soggy England), and especially Queens Park Rangers. Maybe he could move back to London, enroll in business school, and pursue a profession less intense than trading. He gave himself at most another couple of years in Tokyo. "I will definitely need a rest," he told Read.

Once Read heard that, he decided that he would throw in the towel whenever Hayes left. If Joanna hadn't acclimated to New Zealand by then, they, too, would return to England. If teaching didn't work out, maybe he'd take up gardening or even become a postman three days a week to break up the monotony of early retirement. In the meantime, Read spent virtually the entire day at work on the phone with his lone client. They had a direct, always-on phone line connecting them, and Read would later estimate that they typically talked between fifty and three hundred times a day.

. . . .

Back in ICAP's London office, Danny Wilkinson oversaw the group of other yen brokers who catered to Hayes and his rivals. Seated in a T-shaped formation near the center of the brokerage floor, the group was surrounded by tall whiteboards on which a junior broker would scrawl all the prices the brokers were seeing so that they didn't have to rely on hearing each other. (They used an elaborate series of hand gestures to communicate.) Wilkinson was fat, his hair buzzed practically to the scalp, with doe-like blue eyes accentuated by long eyelashes and a penchant for wearing button-down shirts that were only barely buttoned. He loved wine, stockpiling vintage bottles at home and happily recommending new varieties for Read to sample in New Zealand. Wilkinson's watermelon-red complexion was the subject of vigorous ribbing. (A crimson-faced emoticon installed on an electronic chat program sometimes was used to make fun of him.) During a London lunch with Hayes and his stepbrother Ben O'Leary, Wilkinson boasted about his wild escapades, among them hosting a crazed party on a yacht in Marbella, Spain. O'Leary dubbed him "Danny the Animal," and it wasn't affectionate. Wilkinson's colleagues didn't impress O'Leary, either. He called the whole group "The Sycophants" because of how the brokers sucked up to Hayes. (The brokers were so offensive to O'Leary that he decided not to pursue a career in finance and to go into medicine instead.)

Wilkinson had not always been so feral. He grew up outside London, the son of a welder. As a child, he was plagued by severe asthma and other ailments, confining him to hospital beds for long stretches. Bored with school, he dropped out when he was seventeen, hoping to go out in the world to earn some money. His first job, in the early 1980s, back when he enjoyed a relatively slim thirty-four-inch waist, was working as a clerk at a retail bank near his hometown. In 1985, some of his buddies had earned enough working in the City to buy themselves flashy cars; Wilkinson wanted one, too. He snagged a paper-pushing job in the London office of an Australian bank, and eventually was promoted to the role of a junior trader. But he was required to take a regulatory exam, which he failed multiple times, precluding him from being a full trader. After taking some time off to work as a DJ on the Spanish island of Majorca, he decided to become a broker, for which there were no test-taking requirements. Wilkinson dashed off dozens of letters to prospective employers. He got a single reply, from a brokerage that would become part of the ICAP empire. He started in November 1989 as a trainee, reporting to Darrell Read. The twenty-three-year-old's annual salary was £8,000—hardly the road to riches or sleek sports cars. But after a year or two, he was promoted to a full-fledged broker. That meant he could do things like speak to real live clients—once he got some. Wilkinson flipped through a financial services directory book and started cold-calling banks. He was gregarious and persistent and had street smarts and eventually landed a small handful of clients. Wilkinson had found his calling. Tethered to some successful traders, his career took off. In the late 1990s, he was promoted to running the yen desk. He managed about a half-dozen employees, including Read. ICAP's hierarchy was so flat that Wilkinson was only a few rungs below Spencer.

Wilkinson, by then married and with two sons, fit right into ICAP's frat-house culture. Brokers were openly rude to each other, even to their bosses. Profanity-dense shouting matches were common. Wilkinson sometimes would slap David Casterton—one of ICAP's top-ranking executives, just below Spencer—on his hairless head and call him "Baldy." (Casterton's more prevalent nickname was "Clumpy." When he went bald, his hair had fallen out in clumps.) Wilkinson's brokers would occasionally, and affectionately, refer to him as a "cunt." On the frequent occasions that he showed up to work with a severe hangover and fell behind on the constant flow of trades and data pouring in, he would lie to clients that ICAP's computer systems were suffering technical problems.

With Hayes, Wilkinson was confronting one of the strangest clients he had ever encountered. He noticed that Hayes would make bids or offers in the market, but would specify that they were only good for certain banks or even individual traders. In other words, he might be willing to do a specific trade at a certain price with a Deutsche Bank trader and the same trade at a less favorable price with a Merrill Lynch trader. At one point, Hayes simply refused to consider any trades with Morgan Stanley. This was basically unheard-of—not to mention financially irrational. (It made sense to Hayes, who didn't see the point in doing business with traders he found objectionable.) Wilkinson came to view Hayes as a brilliant, obsessive nutcase, perhaps the most talented trader he'd ever encountered. He wondered whether Hayes was autistic.

Wilkinson was hardly the only broker perplexed by the star trader's behavior. When Hayes got his mind set on something, he wouldn't let it go. When Tradition was planning to dismiss a broker he liked, Hayes intervened, proclaiming that if the broker wasn't given a generous exit package, Hayes would sever his relationship with Tradition's Tokyo unit. The threat worked. In the eat-what-you-kill finance industry, it was a rare example of some-one using his own leverage to benefit someone else. The broker's mistreatment offended Hayes's sense of justice: There was a differ-ence between right and wrong, and this was wrong, and Hayes had the power to make it right.

But while Hayes was loyal to those he considered to be his friends, others were terrified of his propensity for unpredictable blowups and retribution. One day, Danny Brand, in Tullett's Hong Kong office, tardily responded to one of Hayes's queries. Panicked, Brand explained his absence by claiming he'd been kidnapped. Hayes believed him.

Hayes didn't seem to care what anyone thought about his behavior. Over the squawk box, he would bellow his and other banks' trading positions to anyone within earshot. (He was aware of other banks' positions because, as a market maker, he sometimes had helped them amass those positions.) This was not a good way to make friends. Once, Wilkinson had been on the phone with a client at HSBC when Hayes started shouting about that bank's trades. "Who the fuck is that?" the HSBC trader demanded, hearing Hayes in the background. "Who's telling you what we're doing?" On another occasion, Colin Goodman was strolling around ICAP's brokerage floor. As he walked past the derivatives crew, he overheard a voice booming through a squawk box: "Get those fucking Libors down." It was Hayes. Someone promptly silenced the line. Goodman exchanged awkward glances with a couple of colleagues, then walked away, shaking his head. "He's got to be stupid," Goodman thought to himself.

Still, the whole ICAP crew was pulling for Hayes—the money was just too good not to. In October 2006, Hayes's first full month of trading, the 129 trades he transacted through the brokerage had generated £72,889 in fees. By the end of the year, the fees were flowing so fast that the two companies decided it would be simpler for UBS to automatically pay a flat fee of £70,000 (at the time roughly $140,000) a month to cover his commissions, not an uncommon arrangement for banks and brokerages to strike.

When Read couldn't get his way with Goodman, he often enlisted Wilkinson to lobby on his behalf. Wilkinson generally complied, although he tended to be more subtle than Read in the way he worded his requests.* Other times Read turned to different ICAP colleagues.

"Try to hold it [six-month Libor] please at 0.86," he requested in July 2007.

"Colin says his shoulders are aching holding them up!!!" a colleague replied.

"He's a strong lad, I can smell him from here!!" Read joked.

. . . .

When Read moved to New Zealand, the UBS fee was split four ways. A chunk went to Wilkinson's team in London. Another slice went to ICAP's New Zealand office. A third portion went to ICAP's Japanese affiliate, which shared the relationship with Hayes because he was based in Tokyo. The remainder went to Read himself.

That worked out well for a lot of people, but Colin Goodman, who wasn't part of Wilkinson's team, wasn't one of them. Still, his daily run-throughs were an important part of why ICAP was so valuable to Hayes. And by early 2007, the requests to tinker with the run-throughs were so frequent—from Hayes and other traders—that Goodman christened himself "Lord Libor," replac-

---

* Wilkinson would later say that he never tried to get Goodman to skew his run-throughs inappropriately and that he often was trying to con traders or his colleagues by only appearing to help.

ing his previous sobriquet of Lord Luncheon. (Read played along, deferentially addressing Goodman as "my lord." When Hayes first heard the nickname, he figured maybe Goodman hailed from a line of aristocrats.) Goodman fumed about not getting a cut of Hayes's lucrative commissions. While Read in 2006 pulled in £202,780 in compensation—a figure that would more than double the following year—Goodman's salary was just £80,000. (He received a small bonus, too.) "They were kind of like Formula 1 drivers and I was a little guy in a pedal car," Goodman reflected.

One day in 2007, Read e-mailed his latest Libor request. Goodman had a snappy retort: "Tell Dan, broker number 103"—a reference to Goodman's employee number in ICAP's internal computer system. That system was used, among other purposes, to assign commission payments to specific brokers, and Goodman was instructing Read to instruct Wilkinson to allocate him a cut of the action or risk noncompliance with Hayes's requests. A few days later, Wilkinson gave Goodman commissions on a trade— likely funneling at least a few thousand dollars into the latter's paycheck. But Goodman, who had mentored Wilkinson when he first became a broker, had a nagging feeling that he wasn't getting his fair share—an impression that Hayes reinforced back in London that spring. Out for beers with some ICAP brokers, Hayes and Goodman found themselves talking alone. After a few drinks, the conversation shifted from market trends to money. "Perhaps you ought to get a slice of the action," Hayes suggested.

That sounded about right to Goodman. Over the next several days, he sent a series of increasingly agitated e-mails to Wilkinson. "I get the dribs and drabs," he groused. "Life is tough enough over here without having to double guess the Libors every morning and get zipper-de-do-da." When another big trade from Hayes landed, with no cut for Goodman, the broker finally lost his cool. "Happy days for you," he told Wilkinson. "Fuck all for me again!!" He signed his e-mail: "M'lord no more, Mr. Libor," stripping himself of his noble honorific.

That got Wilkinson's attention, although he detected a pattern of Goodman getting especially worked up after he'd had a couple of lunchtime drinks with his colleagues. "I have been thinking of ways of sorting you out," he said. He proposed lunch. At a high-priced sushi bar in the bottom floor of ICAP's building, Wilkinson agreed to pay Goodman a regular bonus for his efforts.

Wilkinson then shifted his attention to a scheme to wring more revenue out of UBS. The plan was for Read to plant the seed with Hayes that Goodman might pull the plug on the whole Libor-assistance arrangement if UBS didn't agree to fork over even more money to ICAP. The tactic worked. On July 1, UBS agreed to pay ICAP a monthly fixed fee of £75,000 pounds—£5,000 more than the prior arrangement. There was no doubt about whom the agreement was being negotiated for. Goodman was to be "recognized for his help with calling Libor fixes which UBS found invaluable," David Casterton, aka Clumpy, e-mailed a colleague.* Goodman thought the £5,000 payment was nothing more than "a scrap" that amounted to a "bit of a kick in the teeth." To supplement, on a trip back to London, Hayes took him to a vintage wine shop and bought him a couple of bottles of nice champagne.

• • • •

If Hayes had realized what was really going on, he might not have been feeling so magnanimous. While Read at times was genuinely

---

* ICAP would later say that Casterton didn't realize that the payment was related to Libor manipulation.

trying to help him with Libor, he had stumbled upon an enticing shortcut in his efforts to please a crucial client: Read didn't need to tell the truth. Hayes had no way of checking whether Read was, for example, actually passing on his Libor-moving requests to his colleagues or if those requests actually had their desired effects. And even if he did have a way of checking, the gullible, literal-minded Hayes wasn't one to detect dishonesty. So he had no clue that much of the assistance that Read claimed to be providing was illusory. Read was lying to Hayes, and it wasn't just once or twice—he was lying habitually, as a matter of course.

Hayes had been under the mistaken impression that Goodman, like Farr, had an informal, casual way of spreading the Libor misinformation through the market. He hadn't realized that there was actually an e-mail that Goodman sent every morning. Before Hayes and Goodman met, Read instructed Goodman, "please don't tell him too much about your run-throughs you send out as I often lie about what you have sent if it doesn't suit him!" To be extra safe, Read had gotten in touch with Wilkinson with a similar cautionary message. If Hayes phones you about Libor, Read had said, "I have asked you to pull in favors to keep three-month [Libor] up." Read hadn't actually relayed that request; he was just covering himself in case Hayes started asking questions.

So it had gone for a while, and so it would continue. When Read told Hayes that his WestLB buddy was out of town, and that's why the German bank's Libor submission moved the wrong way, it was a lie; the reality was that his old schoolmate just wasn't in a position to help that day. Ditto when he told Hayes that Goodman had exhausted his goodwill with a trader at another bank; Goodman just didn't want to expend his goodwill on Hayes's behalf. When he told Hayes that other ICAP colleagues had convinced an RBS trader to move Libor in a helpful direction, the move was just a lucky coincidence. And when he revealed to Hayes what numbers Goodman was disseminating, sometimes Goodman wasn't even at work. Time after time, Hayes bought the lies, and his friend Read kept churning them out.

. . . .

The MGM Grand Garden Arena, tucked in the bowels of the bright green hotel and casino on the Strip in Las Vegas, was jammed with a capacity crowd of 16,459. Many in the audience on this Saturday night in late 2007 were rowdy Brits. Some were playing trumpets. Others pounded on drums and belted out "God Save the Queen." Thousands of boos rained down on the singer who performed "The Star-Spangled Banner." The fans had flown in for what was being billed as an epic boxing match: Ricky Hatton versus Floyd Mayweather. The Brits were there to cheer on Manchester native Hatton, whose boxing trunks this night had a Union Jack flag splayed on the posterior.

The fight was a hard ticket to come by. Hatton and Mayweather were both undefeated; the winner would be crowned the welterweight champion of the world. The crowd was sprinkled with celebrities, including Angelina Jolie and Brad Pitt. And there, sitting not far from the ring in a roped-off VIP section, was Hayes, flanked by Charlie, his childhood friend, and Nigel Delmar. The tickets were part of a VIP package that included unlimited food and booze as well as the killer seats. The tickets had cost more than $3,000 apiece, but Hayes and his pals hadn't paid: ICAP had picked up the tab.

The weird thing was, no ICAP brokers were at the event with Hayes. Delmar, who worked for Tullett Prebon, had formed a tight bond with Hayes, regularly coming over to his apartment on

Friday nights to watch TV, and Tullett had covered the costs of the three men's hotel and some of their nights out. It hadn't taken much arm-twisting for Delmar to get his boss to sign off, given that Hayes had already raked in $50 million in profits that year. Here was a client they couldn't afford *not* to entertain.

Similar logic explained why ICAP was paying for the VIP tickets. David Casterton had personally okayed the expense after he nailed down the £75,000-a-month UBS deal. "Whilst I do not usually sanction buying expensive tickets for customers," he explained to another executive, "in the unusual case that Tom is, I feel it is worth it."

Las Vegas was an appropriate place for traders and brokers to go for a weekend of debauchery. It wasn't just that the desert city was synonymous with gambling. Through years of rapid, speculative real estate development, Vegas also had become a symbol of the easy credit and ubiquitous home ownership that defined America in the early and mid-2000s. By the time of the Hatton-Mayweather bout, the foundation of that epic boom was starting to crumble. More and more homeowners were falling behind on their mortgage payments. Banks and mortgage brokers that had splurged on reckless loans were going belly up. Soon Las Vegas's outer tracts would be littered with abandoned, boarded-up, and half-built homes. Of course, Hayes and his ilk weren't responsible for that mess—they hadn't doled out the ill-considered loans, even if some of their employers had. But the instrument that Hayes wagered on most voraciously—Libor—was embedded in many of the home loans that had fueled the frenzy and now were at the heart of the Great American Mortgage Bust. Flying into Las Vegas's Mc-Carran International Airport, it would have been hard for Hayes and his pals to miss the impact of the giant bubble: plot after plot of cookie-cutter housing developments, some of them still under construction, stretching for miles into what not long ago had been barren desert.

The fight that night lasted ten rounds. In the final round, Mayweather landed several vicious blows. Hatton staggered back to his feet, but the referee ended the fight, Mayweather the victor by way of TKO. Luckily, Hayes and his disappointed friends had plenty of other fun still to look forward to—the night was young, and it was all, of course, on someone else's dime.

CHAPTER 7

Your Name in Print

On a scorching Sunday afternoon, Hayes decided to go swimming. He went to the InterContinental hotel, nestled among the skyscrapers of the trendy Roppongi neighborhood, to take advantage of the outdoor "garden pool" on its fourth floor. The piano-shaped pool was surrounded by umbrellas and lounge chairs, as well as a small kids' pool. Visitors could pay a hefty fee—nearly $100—for access to the facility. By now, in September 2007, that was pocket change to someone like Hayes. Plus, he respected the supply-and-demand dynamics that clearly were at play in setting the steep price.

No sooner had he sat down poolside than something shiny caught his eye. Sitting on the terrace floor was a tall, pale-skinned, blond woman. She was wearing a pink crocheted bikini. It wasn't just her looks: Even from afar, there was something about her mannerisms that captivated him. He stared at her for the next half hour, wondering if she would notice him. She didn't. Hayes didn't consider trying to talk to her. He was far too shy for that. Plus, he was living with his girlfriend—what point would there be in trying to strike up a conversation with a random woman? Then he noticed that she was reading a book that he had just read himself, *Queen Camilla,* a satire about the British royal family taking up lives as commoners. Hayes took it as a sign. He nervously walked over to the woman. "That was the bravest I've ever been," he would later recall.

Sarah Tighe was a London-based associate at the corporate law firm of Shearman & Sterling. The twenty-seven-year-old had a month of unpaid leave at work as she waited to officially become a lawyer and so had gone on vacation with a friend. After a week in Tokyo, they'd been scheduled to catch a flight to Okinawa, but a typhoon grounded the plane. They got a room at the InterContinental. Then Tighe came down with food poisoning. As she slowly recovered, she parked herself at the hotel pool to read and perhaps take a nap.

Tighe sat poolside, dangling her toes in the cool water. Suddenly a shadow blocked out the sun. Tighe looked up from her barely opened book. Standing above her was a slim, nerdy-looking man wearing a red England soccer jersey and matching shorts. His golden Queens Park Rangers pinky ring glinted in the bright light.

"Alright, good book?" Hayes blurted out.

"Oh my God," Tighe thought to herself, appalled by the man's childish outfit and awkward demeanor. An overeager, oversize boy—this was the last thing she wanted to be dealing with right now. She made her best "bitch face," hoping to scare him away. "I don't know, I'm on the first page," she hissed. As far as she was concerned, the conversation was over.

But it wasn't. Hayes plopped down next to her. He started to talk about *Queen Camilla.* Then his monologue veered into finance. A crisis was brewing, he excitedly told her. In the United States, banks were starting to teeter as borrowers fell behind and then defaulted on their mortgages. In Europe, funds run by BNP

Paribas, which made the mistake of investing in products linked to those American mortgages, were collapsing. In England, customers were lining up to pull their money out of troubled mortgage lender Northern Rock. These were the early tremors in what would soon become an extraordinary, globe-swallowing earthquake. These were crazy times.

Tighe didn't care. Her stomach was unsettled, and she wanted to get back to sunbathing. But Hayes wouldn't leave her alone. He looked at the terrace's tiled floor and the sparkling pool and the hazy blue sky. He didn't make eye contact. Eventually the one-sided conversation meandered to Tighe's line of work. She explained that she was an aspiring lawyer and hoped one day to specialize in oil and gas law.

"What's the price of a barrel of oil?" Hayes demanded.

"I don't know," she said. "I'm on holiday." The reality was she wouldn't have known even if she wasn't on vacation.

"How can you be an oil lawyer if you don't know the price of oil?" Hayes asked, unimpressed.

Tighe was tempted to tell him to scram. But she didn't have the heart—she was beginning to feel a little sorry for the guy. It was obvious how much effort he was pouring into the strained con-versation. She figured she would let him extract himself gradually to save face. But Hayes was just getting started talking about the markets.

Two hours later, the sun was starting to set. The pool would be closing soon. Tighe, still in her bikini, was getting cold. But she was also intrigued. It turned out that she and Hayes had things in common. Both had moved as young teenagers from large urban centers to towns in the Hampshire region, Hayes to Winchester and Tighe to Fleet, where both struggled to acclimate and were picked on because of their lower-class accents. Tighe had a close relationship with Emma, her younger sister; Hayes was similarly close with his younger brother, Robin. Hayes liked that Tighe, loyal to her childhood home, still supported Birmingham-area soccer team Aston Villa. It even turned out that they had both attended a 1994 match when QPR faced off against Aston Villa in London; Hayes recalled the game's exact date and score. Tighe could tell this was an extraordinarily intelligent man. And, come to think of it, he wasn't bad-looking, either.

They walked together into the hotel to the locker rooms. Tighe was in town for a few more days, and she was hoping Hayes would ask for her phone number or e-mail address. But she wasn't going to be the one to make the first move; she had a policy of not asking guys out, and she wasn't about to stray from that now. Granted, the policy hadn't served her very well over the years—aside from a college boyfriend, Tighe hadn't ever had a serious relationship. Finally, before disappearing into the men's locker room, Hayes dug a crumpled business card out of his shorts and shoved it into Tighe's hand. "E-mail me if you want to go out with your friends sometime," he said. He still wasn't making eye contact. His face was flushed with embarrassment. He didn't mention that he was living with his girlfriend.

Two days later, Tighe e-mailed Hayes. The subject line was "Ce soir"—*this evening* in French. "It's Sarah from the Intercontinental pool," she wrote. She invited Hayes out to dinner with her friend that night. Hayes accepted the invitation, then inundated Tighe with detailed instructions about how to explain to a cab-driver where the restaurant was. Tighe responded a few hours later to confirm. She noted in passing that she hoped she had caught him before he left the office. "Caught me in time? I'm usually in the office till 8pm!" he boasted.

It was a fun, boozy, late night. Hayes brought along Nigel

Delmar. The group met at the swanky Oak Door Bar on the sixth floor of the Grand Hyatt hotel. Hayes told Tighe that he'd been flummoxed by the "Ce soir" subject line. He didn't know what it meant, and, after he figured it out, he couldn't understand why an English speaker, communicating with another English speaker, would write something in French. It's not as if they were in France. Then he grilled Tighe with endless questions. Did she want kids? (Perhaps.) Did she smoke? (No, she lied.) Was she a vegetarian? (Hell no.) Did she have a strong work ethic? (Yes.) Was she committed to her career? (Very much so.) What were her political leanings? (Apolitical; Hayes, much to his parents' chagrin a Tory of Thatcherite leanings, was unimpressed.) Did she enjoy reading and, if so, what kind of books did she favor? (Yes; fiction about wars, assassins, and spies.) How much had she read by Michael Lewis, one of his favorite authors? (None.) Tighe was taken aback by the machine-gun nature of Hayes's questions, which seemed designed to gauge their compatibility as mates. She was also charmed.

The next day at work, Hayes was hurting. He wasn't accustomed to drinking on weeknights. He usually was in bed not long after 9 P.M., and now his head was pounding, his mouth cotton-dry. None of that mattered when a note from Tighe arrived in his UBS e-mail account. She told him that she "had an awesome time." Hayes couldn't suppress a smile. He typed an effusive response. "It was really, really nice to meet you . . . Was pretty tired and hungover this A.M. but luckily the market is being kind to me today, so am making some money without doing too much, maybe I should go out more often!" He continued: "I really enjoyed your company and it's a shame we live 6,000 miles apart!" He said he'd be back in England in the next few months. It "would be nice to catch up in London at some point."

. . . .

In 2007, his first full year at UBS, Hayes earned about $48 million for the bank. It was a strong performance, but not a blowout; some traders at rival banks were easily generating twice as much, although many more had been losing money in the now-turbulent markets. UBS itself was suffering mountainous losses, but on top of his roughly $170,000 salary, Hayes got a $1 million bonus. To most people, especially someone in his late twenties, that would be a life-changing windfall. It certainly was the biggest haul of Hayes's career. But he viewed it as too low by at least half given the small fortune he'd generated for the Swiss bank. He was devoting his entire life to an intense, exhausting job, and he didn't feel like he was being adequately valued. The good news, Hayes told Read, was that "they sort of promised me a better one next year, even if I only make half the money."

"Try and get that in writing, mate," Read said, marveling at Hayes's naïveté. "If the bank has a hard time again this year, the same excuses will roll out and you are two years further down the line."

Hayes's trading in those early crisis days had been frenzied. He was executing at least fifty transactions a day, sometimes double or triple that. He was trading products tied to the yen and dollar iterations of Libor. He was trading products linked to Tibor. He was trading currencies. He was trading something called overnight index swaps. Occasionally, he'd squeeze twenty or thirty trades into five minutes. The transactions whizzed across his computer screens faster than he could enter them into his spreadsheets. The risks and interrelationships between positions became dizzying, the three-dimensional puzzle pieces getting jumbled. It wasn't unusual for him to make or lose $10 million in a single day.

Hayes's managers, especially Pieri, were impressed. His 2007 performance review credited him with having "greatly enhanced" UBS's trading profile and helping to build an "outstanding" business, generating revenue "above expectations . . . through some of the most challenging markets." But, Pieri's review added, Hayes had some problems: He was too intense. He yelled too much. Some younger employees were scared of him. "Needs to work on self-control and stress levels," Pieri wrote. "Learn about how to deal and talk to others such that you can achieve your desired result without anger. Learn about emotional intelligence." As he had back in school, Hayes acknowledged his shortcomings in a self-assessment: "I can be snappy and need to stop this." He knew that his tendency to growl "you're useless" at colleagues was not endearing.

The explosive attitude wasn't reserved exclusively for his colleagues. His developing reputation for incivility and pushing the envelope a shade further than anyone else won him fewer and fewer allies. In the testosterone-fueled trading community, rivals weren't shy about calling him out on his tactics. One day in March 2008, a Lehman Brothers trader in Tokyo named Jeremy Martin noticed that Hayes was trying to nudge one part of the market involving short-term interest rates (known as "the short end") in a favorable direction. The prior year, Martin had invited Hayes to a meeting to talk about a possible job offer; Hayes later concluded that Martin had simply been trying to trick him into revealing information about his investments in the hope of pilfering his ideas. Since then, Hayes had been doing whatever he could to make Martin miserable—including offering to buy or sell a certain volume of instruments, then withdrawing or downsizing his offer as soon as Martin took him up on it. Martin didn't realize that Hayes was just messing with him; he thought the UBS trader was trying to influence prices by momentarily appearing to increase demand.

The tactic was common, but it nonetheless struck rivals as manipulative.

"If you want to fuck around in the short end then you should do market size when you are hit," Martin wrote to Hayes in an instant message. In other words, he should honor the amount he was offering to trade if someone accepted his offer. "Everyone is getting pissed off with your shit."

"What is market size please, seeing as you are the short-end expert?" Hayes replied sarcastically.

"I just want to trade," Martin wrote back. "You seem more interested these days in pushing markets rather than trying to trade. It is frustrating for people like me who want to do something in the market because half the time it is not real."

"Yes, clearly I am not a big player and you are, that really bothers me!" Hayes sneered.

"It's not about big or small, it's about being professional."

"It's about making money, I thought?" Hayes said.

. . . .

In December 2007, UBS's CEO, Marcel Rohner, gave a presentation to investors in London. Projected on a screen in front of the audience, the presentation cited "structured Libor" as one of the bank's "core strengths" and as a "high growth/high margin business." This was the business that Hayes, along with his counterparts trading variations of Libor linked to currencies other than the yen, had helped turbocharge.

A relatively small chunk of Hayes's profits for UBS—he would later estimate at most $5 million a year—came from his attempts to get the benchmarks moved in favorable directions, the rest deriving from some combination of luck and skill. Moving Libor was a team effort at UBS. Rank-and-file traders received help from their managers, who in turn sought support from their bosses. Pieri sometimes lobbed in his own requests to Hayes's brokers. The same month that Rohner delivered his presentation, Hayes's group had a huge position about to mature: For every basis point, or 0.01 percentage points, that three-month yen Libor rose, Hayes's portfolio stood to gain $2 million in value. He had been trying to get UBS to hike its Libor submissions in order to help push the overall average higher. But he was running into resistance. So Hayes turned to Pieri.

"We have been riding a wave on this trade, but everyone will be trying to influence the fixing next Monday reflecting their position," Pieri e-mailed Sascha Prinz. Prinz said he would talk to another executive. A few days passed. Pieri checked back in on December 14. "I need some assurance they will put their rate up please," Pieri pleaded. "Our rate input can make a significant difference." Pieri was successful. The trade would notch roughly $500,000.

A week later, a similar thing happened. Hayes was back in England for a three-week vacation. Naomichi Tamura, a Tokyo trader a rung above him, sent an e-mail to Hayes's personal account asking for help shifting Libor up. Hayes deferred dealing with Tamura's request, and more pleas, increasingly urgent, soon followed. After opening presents with his family on Christmas morning, Hayes and Robin drove more than three hours to the southwestern city of Plymouth to see Queens Park Rangers lose, 2–1. The game didn't end until around 5 P.M., but with Tamura frantic about Hayes not managing to get Libor higher, Hayes glumly decided they needed to drive back to London so that he could show up at UBS's offices by the time Japanese markets opened for business in the middle of the British night. There was work to do. He could nap at his desk if he really needed to. Hayes stayed up all night at work while Robin dozed in a hotel.

• • • •

As he and his brother had driven back to London, Hayes had been in a foul mood. It wasn't just because QPR had lost again. He wondered what he was doing in this job—and he wasn't the only trader harboring such misgivings. Not many of those who filed into trading floors around Wall Street or in Canary Wharf really enjoyed the work. Sure, plenty—probably most—felt that aspects of what they were doing were worthwhile. Some found satisfaction in solving the mathematical riddles that financial markets presented. Others enjoyed the frat-house atmosphere. Still others basked in the social and professional glory of being near the top of the great investment banking totem pole. And just about all of them liked the money: The sturdy six-figure pay-check, the anticipation of ever-greater riches in the form of your annual bonus, the prospect of being lured to a rival bank or hedge fund in exchange for a massive payday. There were also the pleasures that all that money could buy: Luxury vacations, first-class plane tickets, fast cars, penthouse apartments, great seats at marquee sporting events and concerts, top-of-the-line watches and jewelry, access to the most exclusive clubs and the best Michelin-starred restaurants.

But ask most traders if they were happy with their professional lives, if they found their jobs fun, if they intended to do it forever. The answer was almost always an unequivocal "no."

Part of it was that the jobs were stressful. The hours were long, the competition relentless, the pressure—to not only perform well but also perform better than your rivals and even your colleagues—never-ending. The lifestyle was rarely healthy. Traders ate bad foods and drank too much. They didn't get enough sleep. Anger flowed freely on trading floors. Shouting matches were encouraged as a sign of machismo. Friendships among traders were often mirages. And the job itself just wasn't all that enjoyable, especially when you worked at a global bank. Once you got the hang of trading, it became monotonous. Hour after hour, day after day, month after month, the trader sought to exploit tiny price differentials to make small amounts of money in the hopes that it would add up to a sizable profit for the bank and therefore a bigger bonus for himself. But aside from money for the sake of money, there was no purpose. You weren't building anything of value, other than more trading opportunities for your colleagues and rivals. Around and around it went. Behind their cocky facades, many traders wallowed in self-doubt and wrestled with existential questions. They were dispirited. And so it was that in the world's major financial districts, discretely signposted mental health clinics peddling treatments for depression and anxiety were competing with gyms, coffee shops, and steak houses for scarce real estate.

· · · ·

Despite UBS's best vacation-ruining efforts, Hayes's trip back to England wasn't a total bust. He managed to catch five QPR matches, and his team eked out three victories—an impressive feat for the beleaguered squad. But that wasn't the best part. Before he had returned from Tokyo, Hayes and Tighe had become friends on Facebook and talked on the phone a couple of times. In London, he spent time with her and her friends, and on Christmas Eve the two of them went to Basingstoke—a town so dull it was nicknamed "Roundabout City" for its large number of traffic circles—where they browsed a bookshop's bargain rack and went out for burgers. Hayes spent several nights in Tighe's one-bedroom flat in London's Islington neighborhood. (Ever ignorant about appropriate behavior, he spent the time complaining about the fact that she didn't have a TV and that her supply of hot water was inadequate.) The pair fantasized about Hayes returning to London or Tighe moving to Tokyo. Hayes was still with Ainsworth, but he was beginning to brainstorm about ways to finally extricate himself. In an attempt to express his hard-to-articulate emotions, Hayes offered to pay Tighe's credit card bills. She politely declined.

When Hayes returned to Tokyo in January, he was already stressed. For a change, it wasn't related to work—it was the two Sarahs. "We've been together a long time," he told Read. "I met someone else who I really like. I haven't cheated on her, but it's made me doubt the whole thing. Like whether she is the person for me for the rest of my life. I've never been in this position before."

Read patiently listened to Hayes's dilemma, and then shared his own sad story. He had spent the holidays with his family in a national park in New Zealand. Despite the tranquil setting, he couldn't get Libor or his lone client—his livelihood—out of his head. Hayes had several big trades riding on three-month Libor but, preoccupied with his courtship of Tighe, uncharacteristically wasn't pestering Read. But the broker had a job to do; he tried to call Goodman in London to remind him to help. In the middle of the national park, however, Read's cell phone couldn't pick up a signal. Abandoning the holiday, he got in his car and started heading toward civilization. By the time the phone was back in range, Read had been driving for ninety minutes. The trip was pointless—it turned out that Goodman already knew about

Hayes's positions. "He told me to go away, he had it covered," Read told Hayes.[*]

It wasn't hard to see why Goodman would want the Wellington-based broker to go away. Traders from banks including BNP Paribas, J.P. Morgan, and elsewhere also were pelting him with requests to move Libor. But Read was the most relentless. Goodman hated putting his credibility on the line for the sake of a broker in New Zealand and some obnoxious trader in Tokyo whom he hardly knew. And the requests kept pouring in, the buzz of his iPhone disrupting the tranquillity of his predawn train rides into Waterloo Station. Goodman occasionally tried to get Read off his back. Early one morning in March 2008, his train ride was interrupted by a text message from Read requesting slightly lower Libor. After seventeen minutes and no response, Read repeated his request.

Goodman waited another twenty minutes before answering Read's two texts. "Have compliance asking about various things, i.e. Libors," he wrote, trying to get Read to shut up.[†] But the text-messaged requests kept coming and coming. Read's appeals remained so dogged that when Goodman forgot to bring his cell phone to work one day, he e-mailed Read to let him know. "No mobile today."

"Bugger," Read responded. Then he e-mailed over his daily request.

. . . .

On February 27, UBS convened a special meeting of its shareholders on the outskirts of the medieval Swiss city of Basel. For the

---

[*] Read would later claim that he never made that phone call to Goodman and that he fabricated the whole tale in order to impress Hayes.

[†] Goodman would later insist that nobody in compliance had ever spoken to him about Libor. He couldn't even recall writing that message to Read.

event, the bank rented out a venue called St. Jakobshalle, which was usually used for concerts and small sporting events. Investors were to cast their votes on whether the bank should be permitted to sell about $13 billion worth of its shares to Singaporean and Middle Eastern institutions. The goal was to fortify UBS's rapidly deteriorating finances.

Shareholders were grumpy. Over the past six months, the bank's stock price had tumbled nearly 40 percent, thanks to UBS's awful bets on securities made up of risky American mortgages. The situation was all the more galling because of the bank's history as a reliable, risk-averse Swiss institution. The proposed creation of the new stock meant that the already-ravaged existing shares would be worth even less.

More than six thousand investors packed into St. Jakobshalle that morning. They grudgingly approved the proposal—and then took the opportunity to vent their rage. One after another, they marched up to the lectern and lashed out at the bank's executives and board members.

"As a good housewife, I know you shouldn't put all your eggs in one basket," one shareholder scolded. "A bank is not a casino." "Put an end to the Americanization of the Swiss economy!" another shouted, before charging the podium and being dragged away by security guards. Some shareholders demanded the resignations of the bank's chairman and fellow board members. Others called for UBS to recoup the bonuses it had just finished handing out to its investment bankers and executives.

Sitting at their desks in London, two UBS traders, Andrew Walsh and Panagiotis Koutsogiannis, watched a live video feed of the meeting. The traders were disgusted, especially by the suggestion by "some tosser," as Walsh put it, that UBS should rescind the bonuses.

"As if," fumed Koutsogiannis, universally known within the bank as Pete the Greek.

"Morons," Walsh said.

"People don't realize that the value of the firm is its people," Pete said. He felt that the penny-pinching bank was already stiffing its star performers—a group, incidentally, that he considered himself to be an important part of. The Greek citizen had joined UBS straight out of college and had worked at the bank his entire career. By now he was a midlevel executive who still did some of his own trading. Like Hayes, he specialized in derivatives tied to interest rates. Also like Hayes, he regularly pinged the bank's Libor submitters with requests to move the rate in directions beneficial to his trades. Walsh, who submitted some Libor data for the bank, was sometimes helpful in that regard. And so the two men alternated between plotting to skew Libor and complaining about their woebegone employer.

"Hey mate, we want a really low fixing tomorrow," Pete wrote to Walsh the day after the shareholder meeting.

"That's fine," Walsh responded. For emphasis, Pete added that he had £100,000 riding on the outcome.

A couple of months later, after the two agreed to keep Libor as high as possible, Pete the Greek said sarcastically that maybe UBS should form a committee to discuss where to set the rate—that's how many people, he mused, were involved in the deliberations.

••••

Hayes's family sometimes turned to him for financial advice. Once, Robin was looking to buy a house and phoned his older brother in Tokyo to talk about getting a mortgage. Robin said the interest rate on the proposed loan was based on something called "lee-bore."

Hayes perked up, correcting his younger brother's pronunciation. "That's my whole job!" he exclaimed, before rattling off his projections for future changes in interest rates. It was a rare moment of recognition by Hayes of his job's connection to the real world of ordinary people and their bank accounts.

Hayes's father, too, came calling, seeking counsel for his new pastime as an amateur investor. There were few things Tom Hayes was happier to talk about, and he happened to have a bright idea: Hayes had a friend who worked at Bear Stearns. Its longtime CEO, the pot-smoking, bridge-playing Jimmy Cayne, had gambled on instruments linked to the U.S. housing market, and the friend was convinced that his firm was circling the drain. His analysis struck Hayes as persuasive, so he told his dad to place a bet that Bear's shares had further to fall.

This wasn't quite the plain-vanilla type of investing that Nick was comfortable with. After monitoring Bear's shares for a couple days, he decided against the idea. At the time, the shares were trading above $30 each. On March 16, J.P. Morgan agreed to buy the stricken firm for $2 a share. The trade Hayes had suggested could have made his father a killing overnight.

Hayes, meanwhile, eventually worked up the nerve to dump Ainsworth—in the nick of time. He felt guilty, but she needed to be out of the picture before Tighe came to visit Tokyo. By the time she arrived, Hayes realized he was in love. Her visit lasted four days. Hayes introduced her to his local watering hole, a pub called the Windsor. The bar's owners, a Japanese couple, had taken such a liking to their loyal patron that they'd given Hayes keys to the place and let him go behind the bar to pour pints for his friends even when the pub was closed. (He carefully detailed what he and his friends had consumed and paid the tab later.) Hayes was obsessed with Rod Stewart so he and Tighe listened to his songs on repeat. (Fortunately, Tighe had a high tolerance for "Da Ya Think I'm Sexy.") At night, they watched movies and TV. Hayes was a huge *Seinfeld* fan and had memorized numerous episodes, but his favorite thing to watch was the 1997 movie *As Good as It Gets.* He could see shades of his own personality in Jack Nicholson's obsessive-compulsive character. As he and Tighe watched it together, he recited every line of dialogue aloud. Tighe thought it was adorable. Lovestruck, they adopted the Rihanna song "Umbrella" as their personal anthem.

Tighe started considering the logistics of moving to Tokyo. Before she took that leap, though, Hayes felt like he needed to get some things off his chest. He told her he wanted to engage in a "disclosure exercise." In highly organized fashion, he cataloged all his faults to Tighe, among them his obsessive tendencies and awkward demeanor. At times, Hayes had wondered why Tighe was attracted to him. "Are you only with me for my money?" he asked more than once. Tighe assured him that wasn't the case—although his wealth certainly was a nice perk. (He would continue to ask the question for months. Eventually, sick of the refrain, she threatened to break up with him if he asked one more time. He never did.)

Two weeks later, Tighe handed in her resignation at work. "Moving to TOKYO!!!!!!!!!!" she posted on Facebook. She knew it was rash, but she overrode her cautious instincts. "When you know, you know," she said.

"I'm just happy for once," Hayes gushed to Read.

Before Tighe moved, Hayes returned to England. One of his priorities was to meet Tighe's parents. In advance, Hayes familiarized himself with Tighe's mother's favorite TV shows so that he'd have something to discuss with her. "Look, I'm socially awkward," he announced to her mother, Karen, when he caught her alone in the family's kitchen. "It's taken me all day to think of things to talk to you about." Karen arched her eyebrows. He also met Tighe's sister, Emma, who was eighteen months younger. The tall, blond siblings were sometimes mistaken as twins, a misperception they playfully encouraged. Emma, however, viewed anyone tied to London's financial industry as suspect. Her ex-husband had been a broker (at ICAP, no less). Right off the bat, though, it was clear that Hayes wasn't anything like her party animal ex, and she agreed to withhold judgment.

Tighe planned to live in her own apartment in Tokyo, at least at first—after all, she didn't really know Hayes very well. But he persuaded her that this was a waste of money. "Sarah loves Tom," she posted on Facebook on May 12. When she arrived two weeks later, they moved in together.

Now she could witness Hayes's oddball personality up close. She would often return to their apartment in the evenings to find him and Nigel Delmar finishing up watching the same movie, *The Blind Side,* for the umpteenth time. Hayes adored the film, based on a book by his beloved Michael Lewis, and he subjected Delmar to countless repeat viewings. This was how it was with Hayes— when he liked something, he might watch it hundreds of times. It was safe, no surprises, each scene always the same as it had been before. Hayes was not putting Rod Stewart or Jack Nicholson on repeat because, like a critic, he was dissecting, searching for deeper meaning. He was doing it because the repetitive nature brought him an intangible but very real sense of comfort and security.

His moods swung in lockstep with the markets. If he was making money, he was relatively calm and could even be jubilant. But if things weren't going well, a switch would flip and he would become nearly catatonic. Tighe was stunned when she saw him in one of his zombie-like states, staring, refusing to answer questions. There was no middle ground, no moderation. Hayes never told Tighe, but during those money-losing stretches, he sometimes contemplated suicide. The idea would flit through his mind, then vanish just as quickly, but he kept the dark thoughts to himself.

The trader gene in Hayes ran so deep that it extended to his wardrobe. He had more money than he knew what to do with, but he shopped for clothes on eBay—he loved the chase and trying to game rival bidders. He became fixated on Porsche, but he wasn't about to buy a car in Tokyo, so he settled for items made by the company's clothing and accessories arm, Porsche Design. He wouldn't leave the apartment unless he was wearing a Porsche sweater or a Porsche polo shirt or at least was carrying a Porsche key chain in his pocket.

. . . .

During his time at UBS, Hayes executed tens of thousands of trades—all but a few dozen of them with other banks or Wall Street firms. In his capacity as a market maker, he offered prices to prospective customers on nearly a half-million occasions. It was a calling in which he and his peers took smug self-satisfaction. Market makers viewed themselves as responsible for the proper functioning of the markets—a vital duty, albeit one that primarily benefited the banks and other specialized investors that accounted for the overwhelming majority of trading. "We *are* the market" was a common refrain among market makers. Hayes was exceptionally good at his market-making job. He never hesitated to say yes to a trade if he was comfortable with the price that his models spat out. "Of all the things Tom was, he was a force of nature in the market," Danny Wilkinson would recall. "He was like the George Soros of the yen market." In one bit of folklore, Hayes sometimes traded so heavily that he skewed the market in noticeable ways. For example, six-month yen Libor should always be higher than the three-month variety because it costs more—reflecting the higher risk—to borrow for longer time periods. But sometimes that relationship inverted. Brokers attributed the phenomenon to Hayes.

One spring day, a journalist got in touch, looking for expert commentary about the turbulent market. It was the first time Hayes had spoken to a reporter. Hayes proudly shared the resulting e-mail exchange with Read. "I like it, mate," Read said. "Your name in print."

No, Hayes clarified, his comments would be attributed to an anonymous trader. "I don't want my name in print," he said. "Fame has no appeal for me. Nor infamy."

CHAPTER 8

A Yacht in Monaco

Once again, rivals were taking notice of Tom Hayes. One of them was Goldman Sachs, the investment bank that epitomized Wall Street success. Its roots traced back to 1869, when it was founded in a one-room office in lower Manhattan. Over the decades, the firm became the go-to for blue-chip clients and rich individuals seeking reliable, unbiased financial counsel. By the time it converted from a privately held partnership into a publicly traded company in 1999, Goldman was not just dispensing advice but also making a killing selling and trading just about any financial product under the sun. With that success came controversy. Goldman was accused of profiteering off struggling clients and even countries, of providing conflicted, self-serving advice, of distorting public markets for its own profits. "The world's most powerful investment bank is a great vampire squid wrapped around the face of humanity, relentlessly jamming its blood funnel into anything that smells like money," *Rolling Stone* journalist Matt Taibbi would write of Goldman in 2010. The Vampire Squid moniker stuck. Still, if you were in finance, Goldman exerted a gravitational pull like few other bodies.

One day in spring 2008, Hayes got a message from an executive at Goldman: They were interested in hiring him; would he be willing to meet? Hayes felt some loyalty to UBS, which had after all brought him to Japan and put him in a position where he was enjoying professional success that a few years ago would have been unimaginable. Plus, he was grateful that UBS had stood by him when RBC leveled its accusations. But he remained irritated by his pay. That was one thing about Goldman: It had a legendary ethos for earning money not just for its clients but also for its employees. Tighe encouraged her boyfriend to take the meeting, pointing out that the firm was the pinnacle of Wall Street and also happened to be headquartered in Manhattan. Hayes had long wanted to work in New York, where the opportunities for a skilled trader seemed virtually limitless. He agreed to meet.

Goldman's starting point was to offer a $4.5 million package, as well as a 10 percent cut of all his trading profits. Here it was, the life-changing bonanza that Hayes—along with just about every other trader on the planet—had been waiting for. But Hayes worried about how he'd fit into Goldman's buttoned-down culture. As part of their recruitment efforts, the Goldman executives took him out to dinner at an exclusive Japanese restaurant. Hayes showed up in his usual work getup of casual trousers and one of the polo shirts he'd received as a gift from a broker. His dinner companions, a handful of Goldman bigwigs, wore tailored suits. Hayes felt out of place. A picky, parochial eater, whose adventures in ethnic cuisine basically extended as far as a kebab or curry despite having now lived in Japan for nearly two years, he couldn't decipher the menu. He picked at the weird-looking food that arrived at the table, but he hardly ate. Uncomfortable, Hayes made an odd demand: He wanted formal assurances, ideally a provision in his employment contract, that he would be allowed to wear polo shirts to work. It was perhaps the first time in Wall Street history that a hotshot recruit had made a sartorial demand as part of a high-stakes job negotiation. The Goldman executives discussed the bizarre stipulation, then assented.

Even so, Hayes remained torn. "It's like leaving your girlfriend. I'm really happy where I am," Hayes told one of his Goldman suitors, an executive named Edward Eisler.

Eisler, one of Goldman's top trading executives, didn't hesitate. "It's like leaving your girlfriend because you've met your future wife," he replied. Hayes was impressed by the witty retort, but it didn't help him overcome his anxiety.

Hayes told Pieri about the flirtations with Goldman. Moving to retain its young star, Pieri went directly to Tighe, arguing that Hayes was a highly valued member of the team who could look forward to untold riches in the near future if he stuck around. Sascha Prinz e-mailed the head of UBS's investment banking division, Jerker Johansson, to enlist his support, referring to Hayes as "one of my most talented young traders" and noting that as of June he had raked in $45 million in revenue that year—matching his total for all of 2007. Prinz proposed to Johansson that UBS give Hayes a guaranteed 2008 bonus of $2.5 million. That was unorthodox, especially for a bank that was on the ropes, but Prinz reckoned it was the least they would be able to get away with paying to ensure that Hayes didn't accept Goldman's richer offer.

"Approved," came Johansson's one-word reply five minutes later.

The deal wasn't as ironclad as it originally seemed; it hinged on UBS and Hayes achieving their expected performances. But it was good enough for Hayes. He became one of the bank's youngest executive directors and took on a few employees. UBS started flying him around the world to meet with some of the world's biggest hedge funds and asset managers, whom he presented with his best trading ideas.

Hayes extracted one other concession from UBS: He and Pieri wanted to be in charge of a type of interest-rate contract known as forward rate agreements, or FRAs. Those derivatives had been the subject of a turf war between Hayes and Darin. Now Hayes emerged as the undisputed victor.

But the conquest quickly proved pyrrhic. The move enraged Darin, who remained responsible for UBS's Libor submissions, giving him considerable power over Hayes and Pieri. Until now, the daily decision about where UBS would put its Libor numbers had been the product of a collaborative process; the group would discuss who needed what and a consensus would emerge, with Darin the ultimate decision maker. Now, though, Darin would field Hayes's request and then push UBS's Libor submission in the opposite direction. Clients' needs were secondary to the internal battle. The antagonism prompted Hayes to stop speaking in person to Darin, who had moved from Singapore to Tokyo; instead, he relied entirely on typing out instant messages, even though they were sitting next to each other. And so their conversations became part of the permanent written record.

. . . .

That summer, Hayes and Tighe went on a five-day vacation to Bali, their first as a couple. Hayes didn't enjoy the change in routine. Having to string together ill-fitting pieces of an inexact itinerary stressed him out. When they got off the plane in Bali and went to retrieve their luggage, Tighe's suitcase didn't emerge, while Hayes's came off the baggage carousel a bit banged up. Hayes freaked out—not about his girlfriend's missing belongings, about which he seemed uninterested, but because of the scuff marks on his luggage. Already irritated by her misplaced bag, Tighe was further irked by her boyfriend's reaction. When they got to the resort, the pasty-skinned Hayes promptly headed out to sunbathe, refusing to apply sunblock to avoid anything interfering with his absorption of the precious UV rays—that was how he wanted it, and no amount of warning would sway him. The predictable result was that he got severely burnt. That evening, Tighe placed damp cloths over his scarlet arms to ease the pain.

Back in Tokyo, he soon succumbed to one of his periodic bouts of homesickness. "To be honest I want to go home really badly," he told Read. The problem was that Tighe had arrived only a few months earlier. She had landed a job as an associate at the law firm Herbert Smith Freehills and couldn't quit so soon after being hired. Plus, she loved Tokyo. "She won't even discuss going home," Hayes sniffed. She had even figured out how to speak a functional amount of Japanese—a skill that had eluded Hayes during nearly two years in Tokyo, despite eighty-five hours with a Japanese tutor paid for by UBS. Hayes figured the earliest they could return to England without imperiling Tighe's career was June 2010—nearly two years away. He asked Read how old he'd been when he had his first child. Nearly thirty-one, Read replied, and told Hayes to hang in there for a couple of years before returning to England. After all, he was doing pretty well for himself, right? How was 2008 going? Read was floored by the answer: Hayes had made $64 million for UBS so far.

Read had been doing some life planning himself. He'd only expected to work for ICAP in New Zealand for a brief spell; by now he'd been doing it more than a year and had finally had enough. Working in New Zealand, he was isolated. On the other hand, he was continuously bombarded with shouted requests from dozens of brokers in Tokyo and London, not to mention the countless less-than-relaxing hours he spent each day on the phone with Hayes. Sure, he was making good money—he was on track to pocket £254,757 (nearly $500,000) in 2008—but he was only seeing his two sons for an hour each morning. His eldest had started complaining that he was spending less time with his dad than when the family was back in England—defeating the entire purpose of the move.

In mid-July, Read flew to Tokyo. He met Tighe for the first time, at one point taking her aside and telling her to be kind to Hayes because he was fragile. Then Read broke his big news to Hayes and Pieri: He had decided to retire at the end of the year. He planned to buy a house on the beach and spend lots of time with his family. Read's importance to Hayes was hard to overstate; in addition to his Libor help, the broker was handling about half of Hayes's trades, not to mention providing constant emotional support. Now Hayes would have to get along without his favorite broker.

Read's news deepened Hayes's feeling of malaise. "I know it's funny, but I spend so much of my time doubting myself," he confided to Read. "I don't enjoy myself."

"Which is why I thought you would take the megabucks for a couple years at Goldman Sachs and then do whatever pleased you," Read said.

"The pressure at Goldman would have been even worse," Hayes sighed. "That's one reason I turned it down." The conversation meandered for a few minutes. Then Hayes continued. "To be honest, I hate having this 'big' reputation. Makes people really wary of dealing with me."

"A consequence of success," Read said. Then the two men got back to trading.

. . . .

Read's pending retirement meant that Hayes's second preferred broker, Terry Farr, would have to pick up some slack. Farr was having a rough summer. His other main client, Merrill Lynch's Alexis Stenfors, was bleeding money. It didn't help that Libor—whose direction it was Stenfors's job, as an interest-rate trader, to anticipate—was moving in utterly unpredictable ways. Merrill Lynch wasn't among the banks that helped set Libor, so Stenfors was mystified by its movements, but he suspected that someone, or multiple people, were skewing it deliberately. In any case, Stenfors's lousy performance was awful news for Farr. "Don't wanna know, mate," Farr said when Hayes started gossiping about Stenfors's problems. "He goes, I go. That guy looks after me very well, don't need that going pear-shaped. He pays me a fucking lot" of commissions.

"I like him," Hayes said.

"Me too. And of course, there's one other guy that looks after me when he can," Farr replied with a virtual wink.

Farr was preparing to depart on a two-week vacation, hiking in England's Lake District before heading up to Inverness in Scotland. First, though, Hayes was looking for a favor. He had already asked ICAP to get one-month yen Libor down sharply to 0.63. He needed RP Martin to hit up its bank contacts for help, too. One of the keys was persuading Dutch lender Rabobank, a former agricultural cooperative that had developed an unfortunate taste for trading exotic financial products, to lower its submission. That's where RP Martin came in. Farr's colleague Jim Gilmour had a good relationship with Rabobank's Libor submitter, Paul Robson (nickname: Pooks). Farr enlisted Gilmour, who pulled it off: Pooks slashed Rabobank's Libor submission from 0.71 to 0.63.

And HSBC, where Farr and Gilmour had another contact, also moved lower after hearing from the brokers.

For Hayes and his crew, these efforts had become so routine that they hardly merited a raised eyebrow. But they were venturing further and further into the territory of unequivocally improper behavior, not only fiddling with an individual bank's Libor data but reaching out across corporate lines to tweak a widely used benchmark for their own financial gain. It wouldn't be hard to construe the behavior as collusive, as a conspiracy to move Libor in ways that had absolutely nothing to do with a bank's estimated borrowing costs. The thought had certainly occurred to Hayes at times; for comfort, he told himself that Pieri knew exactly what he was doing, which surely would provide him with cover if things ever went wrong.

. . . .

Two months later, Lehman Brothers went bankrupt, the giant insurer American International Group received a record-breaking government bailout, and Merrill Lynch was gobbled up by Bank of America in an emergency deal. Thousands of traders, investment bankers, and other employees—not to mention the secretaries and security guards and janitors and cafeteria workers who populated these firms in the thousands—were about to lose their jobs. And the dominoes were just starting to fall: Over the next few weeks, some of America's biggest banks would be subsumed by stronger rivals. Giants like Citigroup, Bank of America, even the great Goldman Sachs teetered on the brink. Overseas, the carnage was similar. Hayes's former employer the Royal Bank of Scotland needed a huge bailout from the British government. His current employer, UBS, got one courtesy of Swiss taxpayers. Policy makers in the United States and Britain fretted that the entire financial system might collapse. Some experts wondered whether companies would be able to pay their employees and whether cash machines would keep dispensing money. It looked like the onset of another Great Depression. The bill was finally coming due for decades of reckless financial expansion.

The day of Lehman's demise was a public holiday in Japan. At 6 A.M., Pieri called Hayes at home. He broke the news to his sleepy employee: Lehman was filing for bankruptcy and Hayes needed to get to work immediately. In UBS's mostly deserted office (Pieri himself was overseas on vacation), Hayes spent the day trying to identify every outstanding trade that his desk had with Lehman that hadn't been routed through a central clearinghouse. A bankrupt financial institution couldn't be counted on to follow through on its trades, so Hayes had to go through each transaction and figure out where UBS stood after negating all deals with Lehman. He was in the office until 3 A.M. working with a tech guy to complete the task.

Hayes had another challenge that day: He had invested millions of dollars in derivatives that were due to pay off soon if yen Libor inched lower, a speculative bet that banks' overall costs to borrow money in the Japanese currency—or at least what banks reported those borrowing costs to be—would decline. The problem was that, with the world's financial system knocked to its knees, basic supply-and-demand dynamics dictated that banks' borrowing costs would likely spike. That would presumably push Libor higher.

Hayes needed his brokers to do everything they could to ensure that didn't happen. He called RP Martin looking for Farr in London. "He's gone on a motorbike track day with a couple of people," Gilmour grumpily explained. Hayes asked the broker to do whatever he could to push Libor down. Gilmour called Pooks and relayed the request.

Pooks wasn't optimistic. "They might go up because the people aren't going to lend again, are they?" he said. "Who are you going to lend to? Everyone's going to go fucking bust." Not to worry, though: Pooks's colleague at Rabobank also wanted Libor lower, for the same reason that Hayes did. And so Rabobank, at the onset of a vicious crisis, submitted data that indicated its borrowing costs, at least in yen, miraculously had *declined*.

Before long, Hayes realized the global crisis could play to his advantage. Most market makers had simply closed up shop, preferring to sit out the stampede. He was one of the few people still open for business. This allowed him to charge huge spreads on each transaction. Everyone was looking to sell, which meant Hayes had to buy, and he did so with abandon, quickly amassing large positions. The value of his trading portfolios swung wildly—up $12 million one day, down $10 million the next. Sometimes the gyrations were hourly. But the overall trajectory was upward: A week after Lehman's bankruptcy, Hayes was up $70 million for the year. The biggest reason is that he was snapping up assets from desperate sellers at steep discounts; even if markets declined slightly, Hayes's positions were still worth more (at least on paper) than what he'd paid for them. Another helpful factor was that Pieri had leaned on Prinz and others at UBS to get them to cooperate with the bank's Libor submissions. Hayes's trades stood to gain about $4 million for each basis point that Libor fell, and Pieri happily reported to his higher-ups that "we got some concession" from the bank's rate submitters. "We will be a little bit lower. Every bit helps." Amid a once-in-a-century meltdown, Hayes was making bags of money.

That didn't mean he was having fun. Too anxious to sleep, he was pulling outrageously long hours; at times he felt himself coasting onto autopilot and had to remind himself that this was no moment to let down his guard. "Every time I relax, the next day something happens to screw me," he lamented to his old RBS colleague Brent Davies. (The normally easygoing Davies was stressed, too. He had much of his life savings on deposit at the fast-unraveling RBS. He told Hayes that every day he withdrew £500 from the bank and kept the cash at home.)

It was an inopportune time for Tighe's parents to come to Tokyo to stay with the couple. But their trip from England had been scheduled far in advance, and there was no getting around it. Hayes didn't adjust his schedule, and more than once he remained at the office until 3 A.M. Wiped out by the time he staggered home, he would sit in a trancelike state, glaring at his phone and watching CNBC. He hardly spoke to Tighe's parents. "He's always a zombie," Karen told her daughter. "All he ever does is look at his BlackBerry." Hayes was irritated by her parents' lack of appreciation of the depth of the financial crisis.

Tighe had taken it upon herself to try to improve her partner's woeful skills in situations like these. Before going out together, she would walk Hayes through a lengthy list of dos and don'ts: Do make polite small talk. Do comment on how you like the host's apartment and enjoy the meal they prepared. Do ask open-ended questions about how work is going. Don't ask people how much money they earn. Don't interrogate them about their views on politics or economic events. Don't comment on their weight. Don't remark on someone being drunk or having eaten a lot. They would agree to a certain signal—a cough or a gentle nudge—that Tighe would use to indicate to Hayes when someone was getting bored with one of his rants about soccer, financial markets, or the deleterious impact of divorce on families.

It was an uphill battle. In November, the couple went to an

American friend's home for Thanksgiving dinner. A number of UBS colleagues were there, including Alykulov. He brought his latest girlfriend, who was seated across from Hayes. He learned that she worked in L'Oréal's haircare division. As everyone ate turkey, Hayes delved into a detailed and loud explanation about his chronic dandruff problem. (Afterward, the girlfriend sent Alykulov to work with two bottles of L'Oréal antidandruff shampoo to present to Hayes.)

For Read, the crisis was both good and bad. The chaos reinforced his decision to retire. By October, he was excitedly counting down the remaining days. But that enthusiasm was tempered by the fact that his retirement savings, invested in the market, had been chopped in half. "Not a good time to walk out of a job!" he said. The same thought had occurred to Hayes, who entertained a brief moment of optimism that his indispensable ally wouldn't be financially strong enough to quit. ICAP, too, tried to seize on Read's financial problems. A senior manager, Frits Vogels, offered to set up a miniature brokerage floor in Read's new, beachfront house in Tauranga, New Zealand, so that he could work from the comfort of home. Hayes loved that idea, even if it meant the broker's home would be echoing with his client's shouting. "Better sound-proof it!" he said. But Read wasn't interested. If he really needed the cash, he told Hayes, maybe he'd get a job as a bus driver.

· · · ·

One of the many things the financial crisis upended was Terry Farr's livelihood. At least from Hayes's perspective, the RP Martin broker had come to play a vital role helping him get Libor where he needed it. (In reality, even when he didn't have much to do with it, Farr sometimes was taking credit for banks moving their Libor submissions in favorable directions.) But when Lehman collapsed, the volume of trades Farr was handling for clients plummeted, even though Hayes was still doing a brisk business. That inflicted a direct hit upon the commissions Farr was receiving.

Four days after Lehman's bankruptcy, Hayes and Farr came up with a strategy to solve the broker's problem. It involved a squirrelly type of transaction called a "switch trade." Two traders at different banks would execute a pair of mirror-image trades. For example, Trader A would sell 100 shares of Company X to Trader B, and then Trader A would buy 100 shares of Company X from Trader B. The rapid-fire transactions neutralized each other, but they still had value, at least to someone. Standing in the middle was the broker, who would collect a commission on both transactions from one or both of the traders' banks. It was a way of thanking the broker for a big night out or for anything else of value.

Now, Hayes and Farr figured, was the perfect time to deploy switch trades. Move Libor lower, Hayes told his broker, and "I will fucking do one humongous deal with you, alright? Like a 50,000-buck deal. I need you to keep it as low as possible, alright? If you do that, then . . . I'll pay you, you know, $50,000, $100,000, whatever you want. . . . And I'm a man of my word." Later that day, they hammered out the details of a planned switch trade. Farr could hardly contain his enthusiasm when Hayes outlined a deal so large that it would generate more than $30,000 of commissions. "That's excellent," Farr giggled.

But Hayes had been speaking literally when he threw out those very large numbers earlier. "That's only $31,000, so we'll have to do more than that," he declared. He suggested doubling the transaction's size.

Farr laughed again. "We'll see what we can do then, fucking hell!" he said.

The next step was to find traders at other banks to take the opposite side of the switch. After all, a trade needed two parties, and Hayes could only be one of them. Hayes and Farr started canvassing their contacts. Farr approached Stenfors. "I don't know if I can do that," Stenfors responded.

"If it's a bit dodgy that's fair enough," Farr said.

Stenfors interjected: "Yeah, it is actually." Merrill was in the process of being acquired by Bank of America—a deal designed to save the Wall Street firm from bankruptcy—and its managers were trying to get their traders to dial back their risk-taking. This was not a good time to be experimenting with some big switch trades. Farr reported back to Hayes that Stenfors was a no-go. Merrill has to be "squeaky clean," he said.

Hayes then approached Stuart Wiley at J.P. Morgan, asking if he'd take the opposite side of the trade. Hayes emphasized that it was a zero-risk, zero-cost transaction for J.P. Morgan, because only UBS would pay commissions to RP Martin. "What is the reason for it?" Wiley asked.

"I owe Terry a deal," Hayes replied. "He has been letting me have good info."

"Okay fine," Wiley agreed. Farr then called Wiley to nail down the specifics. He proposed a mammoth 400 billion yen (roughly $3.6 billion) transaction—and promised that he'd take Wiley out one night as a reward. But that was way too big for Wiley. They settled on a 50-billion-yen deal instead—enough to generate roughly $10,000 of commissions from Hayes.

The goal was to do as many switches as possible—it was free money, after all! But to make the scheme work, Hayes needed more trading partners. Luckily, Farr's colleague Lee "Village" Aaron had just the man for the job: a Royal Bank of Scotland trader named Neil Danziger. Born in South Africa in 1975, Danziger's parents, opponents of the country's apartheid government, bolted to England when he was young. Dark-haired, with a doughy face and ruddy complexion, he still maintained a trace of his South African accent. In London, Danziger was a member of RBS's interest-rate derivatives team; his main job was executing trades on behalf of his prolific boss in Singapore. Rivals, including Hayes, viewed Danziger as lazy.

Out of the office, though, Danziger was a different man. The thirty-two-year-old was ubiquitous at bars and clubs around London. He had a few brokers on speed dial, including Aaron and Tullett Prebon's Noel Cryan and Mark Jones. All of them loved the nightlife. And while Danziger himself wasn't much of a trader, he was handling an envious amount of traffic that originated with his boss, so the brokers did what it took to impress him. RP Martin was spending roughly $800 a week entertaining him; other brokers took him to Spain and Romania, destinations that generally were popular for British bachelor parties. But there were few places in the world that Danziger liked more than the strip clubs and casinos of Las Vegas. One getaway cost Tullett roughly $20,000. (Such lavish spending caught the attention of a senior Tullett executive, Angus Wink, but when he learned how valuable Danziger was to the firm, Wink told Mark Jones to carry on.)

Danziger was wild, but he was also principled, at least in his own way. When his brokers shelled out for a wild night or weekend, Danziger could be counted on to return the favor, sending a big trade their way. Often, the commissions on that one trade would exceed the cost of whatever extravagant hijinks had occurred the night before. Everyone seemed to win: The brokers personally pocketed about a third of whatever they hauled in through commissions, and Danziger enjoyed the raucous entertainment. He never saw the relationship between the partying and the ensuing trade as a quid pro quo. It was just good manners.

So Danziger was an ideal candidate to participate in the lucrative switch trades. Aaron explained to him that he wouldn't have to pay any fees on the transaction. But Danziger—apparently eager to rack up chits with his fun-loving brokers—surprised him.

"I'll pay one side for you," he offered.

"Sorry?" Aaron said, taken aback.

"I'll pay you on one [side]," repeated Danziger, knowing full well that the gratuitous commission payments would find their way back to him in the form of entertainment.

"Will you?" the incredulous Aaron responded, not believing his good luck. "Fucking hell. He said he can pay us on one side of that," he said to Farr, seated nearby. "Oh mate, that's amazing, mate. Thanks very much." RP Martin promised to send enough lunch over to feed Danziger and all his colleagues. When Aaron called back to finalize the deal, they settled on a 200-billion-yen ($1.8 billion) transaction. "You are beautiful, mate," Aaron cooed. "I love you. Like your style, thank you very much."

At 9:08 A.M. in London, RP Martin executed the first 200-billion-yen trade between UBS and RBS. Thirty seconds later, the brokerage processed another trade, the mirror image of the first. The trades entailed virtually no work by RP Martin. But they generated the tiny firm nearly $60,000 in commissions, most of it from UBS, plus another $10,000 from the transaction Hayes did with J.P. Morgan.

Farr and his colleagues exchanged high-fives. Caplin, the CEO, congratulated them. When told that Danziger voluntarily kicked in more than $16,000 in commissions, he lauded the RBS trader as "a good boy." A bean counter in RP Martin's back office, apparently the only one whose ethical antenna had picked up a signal of potential trouble, noticed the unusually large commissions and asked what had happened. "You really don't want to know" was the response. The back-office guy didn't inquire further.

Hayes walked over to Pieri's desk. "Look, I've done a couple of trades with Terry in and out," he told his boss. "I just need to pay him some brokerage. I just wanted to check is that alright." Pieri said it was fine.*

. . . .

One day in late 2008, Angus Wink summoned Noel Cryan for a meeting. Wink's spikey brown hair and boyish face belied the fact that he'd been in the brokerage industry for more than twenty years. Unlike Tullett's brokers, who worked in an open-plan trading floor, Wink enjoyed the privacy of his own office, albeit one with glass walls and nicknamed "The Box." At the time, he ran Tullett's squad of interest-rate brokers, but he was about to be promoted to run all of the brokerage's business areas in Europe, the Middle East, and Africa. He had heard through the grapevine that RP Martin was tapping a gold mine via its relationship with Hayes. Specifically, Wink had picked up market chatter that the rival brokerage had pulled in roughly $160,000 in a single month through commissions on interest-rate derivatives trades. This was supposed to be Tullett's area of expertise—it was certainly supposed to be Wink's area—and yet they weren't enjoying such riches. Meeting in the Box, Wink instructed Cryan to find out what was going on.

So Cryan asked Mark Jones. Jones asked Danziger. Danziger, of course, knew exactly how RP Martin was making so much money through Hayes, and he told Jones about the switch trades.

---

* Pieri would later deny saying this, telling regulators that he was unaware of the switch trades.

Jones told Cryan, then Cryan told Wink. "We need to get involved in this," Wink said.*

And so Tullett did. One pair of switch trades in September generated a quick $48,000 for Tullett, all of it courtesy of RBS. Cryan wanted Hayes to show some love, too. One Monday afternoon in February 2009, after a round of banter about Cryan's hapless Millwall soccer team, Hayes asked the broker to get his colleagues to help push three-month Libor lower. "I will look after you off the back of it," he promised. "I do that for RP Martin, too."

Cryan didn't see much downside—and there was plenty of opportunity. Cryan said he'd help—and then did nothing. "Just spoke to them [his colleagues] and they are on the case," he lied to Hayes a minute later.

"OK, mate, much appreciated," Hayes said. "If we do this going forward, it will come back to you in spades." Indeed, Hayes promptly agreed to pay Tullett commissions on a big trade at an inflated percentage rate.

The next time Hayes asked, Cryan protested that there wasn't much Tullett could really do to help. Its brokers responsible for the Libor submitters weren't very good. Hayes interpreted this as Cryan refusing to help. A loud argument ensued. Hayes, once again, threatened to stop doing business with Tullett. Cryan defused things by promising to do whatever he could to help. He got off the phone. Everyone in the vicinity had heard the explosive argument. "He wants me to fucking go and start talking to the cash lines and he wants Libors moved," Cryan explained scornfully.

"Are you going to do anything?" a colleague asked.

"No, sod him, he's never going to know," Cryan said. He didn't

---

* Wink would later deny that he had known of the switch trades or had had that conversation with Cryan.

feel any guilt about tricking Hayes; this seemed like what Hayes deserved to pay for being so unpleasant.

The decoy worked: More switch trades soon started flowing in Tullett's direction. Hayes and Danziger paired up on each transaction and both paid commissions to Tullett; some transactions generated more than $80,000 in fees—massive sums considering that Cryan's team normally produced less than $10,000 a day in revenue.

To anyone paying attention to the team's fortunes, the huge daily spikes were impossible to miss. On some occasions, Cryan told his bosses the jackpots were due to the trades with Hayes and Danziger. But he also knew to keep the information as fuzzy as possible. "Have you just done a 35-grand trade today or is that just gone in wrong?" Simon Rogers, who was Cryan and Jones's manager, asked in February 2009.

"We did that, yeah," Cryan responded in a near whisper.

"Holy shit!" Rogers said. He asked Cryan where it came from.

"You don't want to know," Cryan said.

"Oh, don't I?" he said. "Alright, I get you. I don't want to know."

. . . .

Over the next eleven months, UBS and RBS would route another seven switch trades through RP Martin, generating well over $400,000 in commission payments. Five similar transactions went through Tullett, resulting in more than $160,000 in commissions. The brokers—in exchange for attempting to manipulate Libor (or, at least, for tricking Hayes into thinking they were trying)—personally pocketed about 30 percent of the commissions they generated. Partly thanks to trades like this, Farr's total compensation that year would roughly double to the equivalent of nearly $350,000, followed by about $400,000 the next year. Gilmour (whose bank had recently let him know that he had access to a total of less than $30 thanks to an overdrawn checking account) would see his annual income exceed $224,000. Each time one of the trades was booked, Farr ran around the brokerage floor laughing and whooping with delight. He occasionally pulled off a cartwheel. Management came by to congratulate the team. "You've had a great day, lads" was a common refrain. Bottles of champagne were sent around. "This yen desk is going fucking crazy," Aaron gleefully told Danziger after one of the trades. After work, the team—Farr, Aaron, Gilmour, Cliff King—headed down to the pub for celebratory beers.

By paying commissions on meaningless trades, in exchange for receiving help manipulating Libor, Hayes and the brokers were engaging in what most people would regard as fraud for hire. To be sure, there were no specific company policies against the practice nor laws that explicitly forbade using switch trades to compensate for Libor manipulation. But even if the word *fraud* didn't cross their minds, the participants should have been under no illusion that the switches were kosher. Hayes justified the deals to himself by the fact that he had received Pieri's permission, but he sometimes lowered his voice to a whisper when discussing the arrangements with Farr. "Don't fucking put it on chat," he instructed on one occasion. "The point is, I'm not really supposed to do it, am I?"* Danziger took such pains to conceal the transactions that he insisted that Tullett vary their timing, sizes, and terms each time a deal was executed so that it didn't look like a pattern. He asked Aaron to keep the trades out of the normal brokerage

---

* The phone call was recorded, defeating the purpose of not discussing it in a written chat.

software program that would be visible to his RBS colleagues. And he requested that the trades be executed after his boss had left the office for the day.

Farr was deeply indebted to Hayes for the switch trades. In June 2009, Hayes asked him to get six-month Libor higher, going so far as to suggest that he cook up fake data to make it look like that was the direction that other banks were moving in—a signal that could persuade other banks to follow suit. It was a variation on the tactic that had so enraged Jeremy Martin, the Lehman trader, a year earlier, and it was a common if unsavory industry practice. But nobody had previously taken the approach to its logical extreme, and pushing the envelope to create a bogus trail of statistics was duplicity of a higher order. "I'll make a special effort," Farr pledged. Then he added: "Mate, you're getting bloody good at this Libor game. Think of me when you're on your yacht in Monaco, won't you?" It was a joke—the idea of the pasty-skinned, scrubby Hayes on, much less owning, a yacht in Monaco was laughable—but it spoke to a deeper truth: Hayes seemed to have it made. What could possibly go wrong?

PART II

Ascendance

CHAPTER 9

What's a Cabal?

John Ewan was not happy. The past eight months had been stressful for the man in charge of Libor at the British Bankers' Association. Starting the prior fall, he had been on the receiving end of a growing chorus of complaints about the benchmark. Phone calls and e-mails were pouring in from bankers who said the rate was divorced from reality. As the financial crisis intensified, banks' borrowing costs were soaring. Yet Libor wasn't moving. To make matters worse, the Bank of England was sniffing around about the rate's accuracy. At a November 2007 meeting at the central bank's headquarters, regulators and bank executives grumbled about Libor being too low. Ewan reassured participants that the BBA had rigorous quality control measures to prevent any problems.

The reality was different. Ewan knew troubling things were afoot. Banks, terrified about the escalating financial crisis, were hardly lending to each other anymore. Giving money to another bank, even a relatively safe one, seemed to be a reckless act of doubling down on a highly distressed industry. The safer bet was just stashing money in accounts maintained at any number of central banks. That made the Libor estimates little more than guesswork. How could banks figure out how much it cost them to borrow from other banks if such borrowing wasn't taking place? Plus, banks had a powerful incentive to err on the side of understating their borrowing costs. If it seemed like it wasn't expensive for them to borrow, it might look to the outside world that they were more stable than a bank that faced higher borrowing costs, which would represent a bright red flag for jittery investors.

One day, Ewan received a phone call from an acquaintance at Gulf International Bank. The Bahrain-based bank, which had a small London outpost, wasn't on a Libor-setting panel. But the Gulf official had received a phone call from a bank that *was* on a panel, expressing interest in borrowing money from Gulf at a specific interest rate. Later that day, that same bank submitted Libor data that was a tenth of a percentage point—ten basis points—lower than what they'd been willing to pay Gulf to borrow. In other words, the bank had been citing a specific rate and hours later appeared to be understating its borrowing costs by a substantial margin. Something smelled fishy, the Gulf executive complained to Ewan. Before he could divulge the name of the offending bank, Ewan asked him not to. He didn't want to know—such knowledge might force him to act on the allegations.

Ewan had a new boss, named Angela Knight. Trained as a chemist, decades earlier she had run a small company before being elected to Parliament representing the Conservative Party in the mid-1980s. After losing a reelection bid, she decided to put her political connections to work, running a trade association for stockbrokers for the next decade. In April 2007, Knight joined the BBA as its CEO. She was a tough boss and prone to explosions. Ewan wasn't interested in provoking her—and he knew that pushing her into a confrontation with the BBA's members was a surefire way to cause ignition. Instead, Ewan decided to write a letter to the Libor banks, urging them to behave. At the very least, he needed to create a paper trail—"if only to be able to defend myself that I'm taking action if I'm stood up by the FSA or by a journalist or something," he told an acquaintance.

"I do not want the fixings to lose credibility in the market," he pleaded to the FXMMC panel that was supposed to be overseeing Libor. He didn't have any specific request other than for the bankers to think about the situation. Then he apologized for eating up their precious time.

The responses trickled in, with some bankers explicitly stating that rivals were routinely lying about their borrowing costs. More evidence arrived the following spring. A BBA employee got an unsolicited e-mail from Deborah Wallis, who worked in the London office of a midsize German bank, Landesbank Berlin. It was clear to her that many banks' Libor submissions were simply bogus. This was bad news for a bank like hers, because the wild, unpredictable swings in Libor made it much harder for Landesbank Berlin to make money by lending money to individuals and small businesses, its bread-and-butter business. Wallis had come to believe that the phenomenon was more serious than banks simply understating their borrowing costs for fear of appearing financially weak. "The problem is that they have a conflict of interest," Wallis wrote. Many banks had big portfolios of derivatives whose values rose and fell with Libor, and she suspected that banks were basing their Libor submissions at least in part on those positions. "It is of course difficult for me to prove this but surely I'm not the only one to raise this question?"

....

Scott Peng dreamed of becoming an astronaut. He loved the idea of floating weightless above the earth, conducting trailblazing experiments that only a few dozen other humans had ever had the chance to perform. Born in Taiwan, Peng and his family moved to Swaziland when he was a young boy so that his father, a scientist, could teach advanced agricultural techniques to the southern African country's subsistence farmers. After a few years, the family relocated another world away, to College Station, Texas, where the elder Peng took up teaching and research at Texas A&M University. By then, Scott's genius-level brains were on full display. He graduated from high school at the age of fifteen and from Texas A&M, with a degree in nuclear engineering, three years later. The eighteen-year-old then headed to the Massachusetts Institute of Technology to get a Ph.D. in plasma physics. That's when he met Franklin Chang Díaz, a former astronaut who had helped build the International Space Station and then became a part-time researcher at MIT. Chang Díaz dazzled his mentees, commuting up to Boston on a trainer jet—a modified version of an F-5 fighter—supplied by NASA. He and Peng worked together on research, jointly financed by NASA and the U.S. Air Force, into the next generation of rocket propulsion systems, which would rely on cutting-edge fusion technology. The former astronaut coached his protégé on what he would need to do to follow in his footsteps.

Then Chang Díaz learned something devastating about Peng: He was nearsighted. Chang Díaz hadn't realized it earlier because Peng wore contact lenses. The brilliant Peng somehow had neglected to look up the credentials of successful astronauts. Among them: twenty-twenty vision. Peng was crushed. Just like that, his dreams were shattered.

Once he got over the shock, Peng had to figure out, quickly, what he wanted to do with his life. It was 1991, he was about to graduate from MIT, and a recession meant that jobs were scarce in the scientific field in which he had figured he would spend his professional life. While in graduate school, he had taken a few finance classes at MIT's business school, so he put out some feelers to banks. Before he knew it, he had landed a job in New York creating exotic financial instruments at Lehman Brothers, at the time one of the world's most aggressive investment banks. Peng joined the swelling army of engineers, mathematicians, and scientists heading to work on Wall Street.

Notwithstanding the accidental nature of his career, Peng came to love working in banking. The challenges presented by designing and understanding complex financial vehicles like derivatives shared some traits with the challenges of creating newfangled rocket engines. One similarity was that not many people, aside from Peng, really grasped how either type of device worked, certainly not well enough that they could actually take them apart and then put them back together again.

Peng was stimulated, but he didn't like everything he saw among his Lehman colleagues. He was sitting with a group of four other traders who peddled something called structured notes to clients. At the time, in the mid-1990s, structured notes were among Wall Street's hottest fads. A type of bond whose value was partly linked to derivatives, the notes were custom-made by investment banks on behalf of companies that were looking for new ways to entice investors to lend them money. Peng soon realized that most of those investors didn't understand what they were buying or what the products were actually worth. The investment banks were taking advantage of that ignorance, which was a big part of the reason the market was booming.

The practice offended Peng. He'd been taught that properly functioning markets relied on all parties possessing similar levels of information—that was essential if market forces were going to achieve two of their signature goals: coming up with accurate prices and efficiently allocating capital. So in 1995 Peng set out to narrow the information asymmetry between banks and their clients: He wrote a book, *The Structured Note Market: The Definitive Guide for Investors, Traders & Issuers,* a four-hundred-page, decidedly nerdy volume.

A decade later, Peng was still working on Wall Street, but no longer as a trader. He was now a researcher at Citigroup, writing detailed analytical pieces explaining the intricacies of the financial markets to the bank's clients. The job was slower paced than being a trader, and Peng savored the opportunity to dig into and then illuminate the financial system's musty corners. He wasn't afraid of ruffling feathers by exploring topics that put the banking industry in an awkward spotlight. The tendency didn't always endear him to his coworkers, as he learned after writing a piece that warned—presciently, it would turn out—of the perils lurking in a hot segment of the bond markets known as asset-backed commercial paper.

In spring 2008, Peng's latest research interest was Libor, a benchmark that was close to his heart because of its importance in the structured notes market. (Libor helped determine the values of many structured notes.) For the past several months, Peng had been picking up unsettling chatter about problems with the interest-rate benchmark. The financial crisis was intensifying, banks were paying more to borrow money, and yet Libor wasn't budging. That didn't make any sense—those borrowing costs were what the benchmark was supposed to be measuring. At that point, the market gossip was nothing more than hearsay. Then, in March, Bear Stearns collapsed. Central banks in several countries launched aggressive plans to try to stabilize the teetering financial system. One weapon in the Federal Reserve's arsenal was doling out billions of dollars in loans to cash-strapped banks. The banks had to bid for the loans, and the prices they paid were made public. Here, Peng realized, was an easy way to measure banks' approximate funding costs. He compared the data about the prices of the Fed loans with where the banks were reporting Libor. Sure enough, the figures diverged. The banks were paying high interest rates to borrow from the Fed, but Libor remained suspiciously flat—in other words, banks appeared to be understating their actual borrowing costs. Libor was artificially low.

Peng typed up a quick five-page report, titled 'Is Libor Broken?" To jazz it up, he stuck a modified Hamlet quote—"Something is rotten in the state of [Libor]"—at the top. Peng figured his report was going to cause a stir. After all, its clear implication was that banks were fudging their Libor data—an incendiary accusation, given Libor's central place in the financial system. So he summoned his boss, an executive named Michael Schumacher, into a small meeting room. It was important to get his buy-in to ensure there wouldn't be any blowback to Peng.

"I wrote something, and I think it might be a little controversial," Peng said. Then he handed Schumacher the draft.

Schumacher scanned the report and then paused for a moment. "Go for it," he said. The report was sent out to Citigroup's clients, as well as a handful of reporters, on April 10, 2008.

For a few days, nobody seemed to notice.

• • • •

Fleet Street in London used to be swarming with journalists. Starting in the 1700s, more than a dozen newspapers set up shop along the narrow, winding road, vying for proximity to a huge audience of readers as well as the printing presses clustered in the area. Fleet Street soon became the media capital of the English-speaking world. That dominance lasted for a couple of centuries. By 2008, the name "Fleet Street" remained shorthand for the British media establishment. But the actual street bore few traces of its storied past—just a handful of ghostlike signs marking the places where long-dead newspapers like the *People's Journal* once resided. The magnificent art deco headquarters of the *Express* now served as Goldman Sachs's European headquarters, its gilded lobby off-limits to all but a few of the investment bank's lucky visitors.

A stone's throw away from Fleet Street, across a busy intersection and up a steep flight of stairs, was a ten-story building covered in an exoskeleton of black marble and steel. The building's unusual design garnered it architectural awards after it opened in 1993. Fifteen years later, the building was showing signs of its age. Carpets were stained and worn. Toilets regularly flooded. Overworked elevators—"lifts," in the local parlance—often broke down. Nestled in a corner of the fifth floor was the London bureau of the *Wall Street Journal*. The group consisted of about a dozen reporters and editors, who occupied small cubicles divided by flimsy, chest-high dividers. One of the reporters was Carrick Mollenkamp, a lanky, well-dressed, hot-tempered, eccentric southerner. His cubicle and the surrounding floor were blanketed in papers, books, and back issues of *Gray's Sporting Journal,* a hunting and fishing magazine. A textbook workaholic, he often didn't leave the office until the wee hours of the morning, only to return a few hours later. He had a tendency of phoning sources or editors in the middle of the night, demanding that they answer his questions or tweak a headline. He didn't believe in the concept of weekends. He consumed pots of coffee and packs of cigarettes every day. Some of his colleagues were terrified of his tendency to swing abrupt_y from chivalrous mentor to fiery screamer. A reporter in the London bureau jokingly described Mollenkamp as having "a face like a bulldog chewing a wasp." On more than one occasion, he and other reporters had to be physically separated during newsroom altercations.

Notwithstanding his tantrums, nobody questioned Mollenkamp's talent; he churned out scoop after scoop, front-pager after front-pager. He was renowned for being one of the *Journal*'s best-sourced financial reporters. He had moles inside most of the big investment banks, everyone from rank-and-file traders and salesmen to C-suite executives. By the time Peng's report on Libor landed in his inbox on April 10, Mollenkamp was already hard at work on a story examining problems with the benchmark.

Months earlier, Mollenkamp had written a couple stories that mentioned Libor. He realized that he didn't actually understand how Libor worked and, naturally curious, set out to learn all he could about it. One Saturday in March, alone in the *Journal*'s offices, he came across an obscure central bank research report that described Libor's erratic behavior. Mollenkamp was intrigued. For the next couple weeks, he schlepped around London with a highlighted and underlined copy of the report folded in his pocket, showing the dog-eared document to his sources and soliciting their opinions. By then, Libor's problems had become the subject of whispered conversations among banking officials and even regulators. (In early April, for example, a Barclays trader had phoned Fabiola Ravazzolo, an analyst at the New York branch of the Federal Reserve, which was responsible for monitoring big Wall Street banks. "We know that we're not posting an honest Libor," the trader said. Ravazzolo got off the phone and alerted her bosses.) Now such murmurings made their way to Mollenkamp.

Mollenkamp's editor was a longtime economics reporter named

Mark Whitehouse. The rare journalist with an Ivy League business degree, Whitehouse had become the deputy London bureau chief in August 2007, after spending time in New York investigating subprime mortgages before it was cool to investigate subprime mortgages. In addition to being Mollenkamp's boss, he was in many ways his polar opposite. Slightly built with floppy red hair, Whitehouse was so mild-mannered that he was sometimes mistaken as meek. As an editor, he was patient, deliberate, and slow. When Mollenkamp occasionally started kicking Whitehouse's metal filing cabinets in frustration, the editor stared at him, refusing to react. Whitehouse didn't even drink coffee. He sometimes showed up to the office wearing sandals with socks.

A few days before Peng's report was published, Mollenkamp had briefed Whitehouse on the planned story. The editor immediately grasped the potential magnitude. But Mollenkamp hadn't found anyone willing to speak on the record about the problems with Libor. Even though the concerns were widely held, Libor was so ubiquitous, such an ingrained part of the financial system, that publicly raising questions about its integrity seemed to border on blasphemy. Peng's report therefore represented a breakthrough. Finally, someone—and someone affiliated with a major financial institution, no less—had dared to stake his credibility on the widely held critique. But Peng's report also represented a threat to Mollenkamp: It was possible that some other reporter would read it and recognize the significance. Mollenkamp and Whitehouse accelerated their plans. Whitehouse patiently explained, over and over, to New York editors why Libor was so important and, therefore, why the story deserved prominent placement. At the last moment, the *Journal*'s page-one editors decided that they would take it. The story ran April 16, 2008. The above-the-fold headline was a play on London's misty weather: "Libor Fog: Bankers Cast

Doubt on Key Rate Amid Crisis." The story opened: "One of the most important barometers of the world's financial health could be sending false signals. In a development that has implications for borrowers everywhere, from Russian oil producers to home-owners in Detroit, bankers and traders are expressing concerns that the London interbank offered rate, known as Libor, is becoming unreliable."

• • • •

Before Peng even had a chance to sit down at his desk that morning, he was pulled into an urgent meeting. A handful of people were clustered in a conference room, with others piped in over an open phone line. Since publishing his Libor report, Peng hadn't heard a peep from anyone, aside from a phone call with Mollenkamp. Now all hell seemed to be breaking loose. "Your piece has caused a lot of issues," someone barked over the phone. Unbeknownst to Peng, Citigroup's traders previously had amassed positions that stood to profit if Libor fell. Now, with the spotlight suddenly shining on the apparent tendency of banks to understate their borrowing costs, Libor had shot higher. The three-month iteration had leapt by 0.17 percentage points (or 17 basis points), the biggest jump in eight months.

One of Peng's colleagues angrily told him that he had just cost the bank $10 million. Plus, another official chimed in, the BBA was irate. Someone at the trade association had called that morning and was demanding that Citigroup retract Peng's report. His colleagues were inclined to bow to the pressure rather than fight the powerful group. Peng replied that he would be happy to retract the report if anybody could identify inaccuracies in it. Nobody did, so the report stood. But that didn't stop his colleagues from bad-mouthing him. "My personal view is that Scott Peng was rather distant to the whole process and would not really have known about the intricacies of Libor, not being an expert in the money markets," Andrew Thursfield, Citigroup's representative on the Libor oversight committee, would later declare.

A few hours after Peng's dressing-down, Angela Knight dashed off a letter to banks about Libor. She said the BBA planned to accelerate its annual process of reviewing the rate, and she invited any input about ways to improve its credibility. And she noted that recent, negative analyst research by banks like Citigroup was exacerbating the problem.

Later that day, the BBA held a two-hour board meeting in its offices. One attendee was a longtime Deutsche Bank executive named Charles Aldington. A former trader, Aldington was now chairman of the German bank's British operations. In the meeting, he alleged that many banks were not only downplaying their borrowing costs to avoid the harsh glare of publicity, but also were engaged in outright manipulation to enhance the value of their derivatives trades—just as Deborah Wallis had suspected. By now, Ewan had heard several warnings like this, but Aldington's explicit tone surprised him. The next day, Ewan called Deutsche Bank's David Nicholls to discuss Aldington's remark. The fast-talking Canadian managed some of the bank's highest-paid traders. Ewan asked him what Aldington had been referring to. Nicholls hurled the ugliest insult he could think of: Aldington wasn't even really a trader, at least not in any recent decade. "If you're going to be a top trader, you're not going to be making those comments. No bank could manipulate Libor."

"A cabal of them could," Ewan tentatively suggested.

"What's a cabal?"

"A group together could."

"That's an interesting conspiracy theory."

"I'm playing devil's advocate," Ewan clarified.

"Banks do not collude to try to set a Libor rating," Nicholls lectured. He added that he was "very confident" that the media and analysts like Peng simply didn't understand how Libor worked. Then he whipped through a detailed dissertation about derivatives and their relationship to Libor. Ewan was lost. "I must admit, I wouldn't want to try to effectively reconstruct that argument," he sheepishly admitted to Nicholls.

Nicholls wasn't done. "I think I'm just hearing a lot of hysteria," he said. "The talk that some institutions are manipulating Libor . . . is so far from factual."

The BBA embarked on a weeks-long campaign to convince everyone—investors, regulators, the media, the public—that all was well with Libor. Ewan took the lead, producing a flurry of research reports insisting that even in the worst case, Libor only needed very minor adjustments. He also tried to convince the press to stop writing about Libor, meeting with Mollenkamp and his competitors at the *Financial Times* to assure them that there was nothing worth looking into. Ewan struck Mollenkamp as a lightweight. The entire BBA, for that matter, seemed out of its depth with Libor. At times, the frustration boiled over. Screaming matches erupted between the hapless Ewan and Mollenkamp, who perceived the BBA as trying to hide the increasingly obvious problems with its flagship product.

For her part, Knight wrote a typo-strewn e-mail to bank CEOs asking them to "secure specific posative comments" from research analysts and to make sure we "have them on side . . . We need to reinforce Libor." The efforts were not entirely successful. A Barclays researcher named Tim Bond, apparently not having received the marching orders, went on TV and said what he claimed everyone by now knew: Libor had become "a little bit divorced from reality." Bond added that the prior September, Barclays had gotten sick of submitting bogus data and decided "to quote the right rates." The implication was that most of Barclays's competitors were not doing the same. Knight couldn't believe one of her member banks was throwing fuel on the fire. She lodged a complaint with a senior Barclays executive, Gary Hoffman. "In effect," she e-mailed him, "we are in a position whereby some less than helpful actions by some banks and less than helpful comments in a febrile atmosphere has created a serious problem out of a market issue."

"Sorry about that," Hoffman apologized. "Even if what he is saying is true (which it is), I'm not sure what the benefit is to Barclays or the industry."

On April 25, Knight met with senior British bankers and officials from the Bank of England at the central bank's headquarters. She told them she was in the midst of a "charm offensive" in London and New York to convince journalists, hedge funds, and others that Libor wasn't irreparably broken. Then she dropped a bombshell: Maybe, she said, a trade group like the BBA shouldn't be responsible for such an important financial benchmark? Perhaps regulators or central bankers should be involved in administering or at least overseeing it. She was greeted with blank stares. Nobody wanted to be responsible for this mess.

· · · ·

The first weekend in May, the world's most powerful central bankers gathered in Basel, Switzerland, for a regular meeting at the Bank for International Settlements, a sort of central bank for the world's central banks. On Sunday evening, an elite handful peeled off for what one journalist dubbed "the most exclusive regular dinner party on the planet." The gathering was known as the "Informal Dinner for Governors of the Economic Consultative Committee." It took place on the eighteenth floor of the BIS's cylindrical tower, which like the United Nations technically sat on international soil. From the United States, Federal Reserve governor Ben Bernanke and Tim Geithner, at the time the head of the New York Fed, were there, as were the governors of the central banks of Japan, Germany, France, Italy, Canada, and Switzerland. Also in attendance was Mervyn King, the owlish, tradition-bound governor of the Bank of England. At the dinner, Geithner grabbed King for a brief chat to discuss Libor.

Geithner's research staff in New York, including Ravazzolo, had been digging into the benchmark. They were especially fascinated by the sharp move in Libor following the *Journal*'s April 16 story. They euphemistically referred to the spike as a "repricing event."

Geithner told King he had some thoughts on how to improve Libor. King said he would welcome the suggestions and asked the American to write him at a later date to explain his thoughts. The conversation didn't last long. King and Geithner were always in high demand, and King wasn't a big fan of impromptu conversations, especially about sensitive topics.

••••

On May 19, the FXMMC gathered for what was probably its most important meeting ever. Representatives of seven banks attended, as did Ewan and three BBA colleagues. Ewan kicked things off: They needed to address the problems surrounding Libor. The room quickly got an earful from one banker, who said that the fundamental problem was the media and yearned for a return to the days when nobody was looking into the industry. Debate shifted to whether and how to change Libor. One problem was that any change could ripple throughout the financial system because so many financial contracts—everything from mortgages to derivatives—contained language linked to Libor. "We need to adopt a minimal approach," another banker said. "Too big a change would cause an explosive reaction." But the absence of change could be just as damaging, someone else warned. Everyone knew this meeting was taking place; if it ended without any action, what would people think? So, what to do about banks that submit bogus data? The consensus: not much. "Policing should be done by just picking up the phone . . . and have a conversation behind closed doors," a banker said, winning nods of ascent from his colleagues.

The meeting concluded with no progress.

A few days later, the FSA met with the BBA. The regulators pointed out to Ewan and his colleagues that Libor's "accuracy is poor." But the agency wasn't interested in getting involved. Despite the onset of the financial crisis, it was clinging to its light-touch strategy.

• • • •

For their next project, Mollenkamp and Whitehouse set out to *prove* that Libor was broken. They decided to look at an instrument called credit default swaps. These were basically insurance contracts between a bank and another party that paid out if a company defaulted on its debts. Investors used the instruments to protect themselves when they were buying corporate bonds. This way, if the bonds defaulted, the swaps would make up for their losses. The swaps had another interesting feature, which is what appealed to the *Journal* reporters: Their prices fluctuated along with the perceived riskiness of the company whose bonds they insured, and as a result they were a decent proxy for companies' borrowing costs. (As a company became riskier, buying insurance on its bonds became more expensive; similarly, lenders would demand that the company pay higher interest rates on any loans.) Whitehouse, the math whiz of the two, started building a massive Excel spreadsheet that compared banks' CDS prices with their Libor data over a several-month period. The finished spreadsheet showed that many banks' Libor submissions had little resemblance to their CDS prices and, therefore, their apparent funding costs.

The story hit on May 29 with the headline "Study Casts Doubt on Key Rate." Like the April 16 article, it ran on the paper's front page. The story focused on especially suspicious data being submitted by Citigroup, UBS, and a few other banks. It quoted two statistics professors who validated the methodology and significance of the *Journal*'s analysis, as well as a man from Del Mar, California, whose monthly mortgage payments had leapt higher as a result of bizarre movements in Libor. Mollenkamp and Whitehouse further noted that some public-sector entities—hospitals, schools, and governments—that relied on instruments linked to Libor to protect against swings in interest rates were increasingly worried about the benchmark's integrity.

This time, the reaction was swift. The banking industry went into overdrive to destroy the story's credibility. J.P. Morgan took the unusual step of publishing a piece of research specifically aimed at debunking an article, calling the *Journal* story "deeply flawed." "Do I think that Libor is perfect? No," wrote Felix Salmon, one of a number of well-known bloggers to blast the *Journal*'s piece. "In this world, no spread measure is going to be perfect, especially at tenors of longer than a couple weeks. But Libor is not nearly as flawed as the WSJ makes it out to be."

The public broadsides and lack of public affirmations discouraged Whitehouse. With an epic financial crisis brewing, he decided to move on to other topics. Mollenkamp, after six weeks of relentlessly churning out minor and major Libor stories, also soon shifted gears.

Nevertheless, just about everyone with any business trading derivatives linked to Libor read the *Journal* stories. Goodman had forwarded the original April 16 article to Read, who'd been impressed—it was the clearest articulation he'd seen of what was going on with Libor—and passed the story on to Hayes. The trader took solace in the article's focus on the U.S. dollar version of Libor, not the yen one in which he specialized. Besides, the article wasn't focused on traders; it dwelled on banks understating their Libor submissions as a way to project images of financial strength. The next day, Hayes had texted Goodman his latest Libor-moving request.

By the time of the second article, though, the *Journal*'s onslaught grated. "Just trading like a monkey," Hayes told a colleague. "Bit worried about this bloody Libor story." He speculated to a friend that perhaps ICAP, now pushing its own benchmark to rival Libor, was the source of the *Journal* stories.

In London, RBS traders and ICAP brokers bantered about the article. "When they mean dodgy Libors, don't they mean Tom Hayes?" Neil Danziger hollered over a squawk box.

. . . .

Vincent McGonagle plopped down into his leather desk chair in a corner office at the Commodity Futures Trading Commission. Springtime was short in Washington. Not much time separated the chilly, wet winter from the stifling heat, humidity, and mosquitos of summer in the drained swamp that served as the nation's capital. April 16 was one of those all-too-rare spring days, warm but not hot, a few clouds but no threat of rain. Along the Potomac River and the National Mall, delicate pink-and-white cherry blossoms flowered.

The CFTC was in Washington's downtown business district, a tidy grid of modern buildings occupied mostly by law firms and trade organizations whose businesses revolved around lobbying federal policy makers. McGonagle's seventh-floor office, with plush blue carpeting and enough space for a sofa and coffee table, overlooked an adjoining building whose roof was jammed with satellite dishes. He was the second-highest official in the agency's enforcement division, which was supposed to ensure that market practitioners adhered to the rules governing the sales and trading of everything from pork belly futures to interest-rate swaps.

McGonagle, with bushy eyebrows and sandy blond hair, bore a slight resemblance to Robert Redford. Raised in a small Philadelphia suburb, after law school McGonagle had devoted his entire professional life to government service and had been at the CFTC since 1997. Inside the agency, he was known as a low-key and friendly fellow, a straight shooter, a bit cautious, not someone who would bend the rules or push the envelope. At industry conferences, as colleagues sipped complimentary drinks and mingled with finance executives, the socially awkward McGonagle tended to huddle in a corner talking to other CFTC officials. At times, his behavior led colleagues to wonder whether he had Asperger's syndrome, a mild form of autism.

The original mandate of the CFTC, founded in 1975, was to regulate the fast-growing universe of futures and other instruments being traded on exchanges like Chicago's Merc. But the agency never managed to establish a reputation as important, partly due to the efforts of sharp-elbowed rival bodies like the Securities and Exchange Commission to eat away at its turf. When a soon-to-be member of the agency's board was awaiting Senate confirmation, a former agency official gave him a warning: "You're going to need a hobby." The CFTC was so slow-moving, so dull that being one of its five commissioners wasn't considered a full-time job. (One commissioner tended to work from his home in Arkansas, only occasionally showing up at the agency's headquarters.) Staff cycled through the agency on their way to lucrative jobs representing companies that had business before the commission.

The CFTC's technology was embarrassingly antiquated—a problem that dogged plenty of federal agencies, but especially troubling for one charged with overseeing vast, complex financial markets. Up until around 2010, the CFTC still allowed institutions to submit their trading records by fax each evening; staffers then had to manually input the numbers into creaky spreadsheets. By the time the figures were processed, they were obsolete.

The agency's weak reputation was compounded by its seemingly obsessive focus on small-bore cases. McGonagle and a small cadre of other enforcement officials had been trying to overcome that image. Earlier in the decade, alerted by the collapse of Enron to a new class of frauds involving energy companies manipulating markets, the CFTC started homing in on bigger targets. The agency, partnering with the Justice Department, nailed several executives for trying to rig oil price benchmarks that were based on data submitted by energy trading companies. But the cases took forever to put together. McGonagle wanted to find some way to quickly establish the CFTC's street cred.

Each morning, McGonagle received an e-mail from an agency staffer that contained a list of the day's news stories that affected the universe that the CFTC was supposed to be overseeing. On

April 16, he scrolled through the clippings. The synopsis of the *Journal*'s story caught his eye. He clicked on the link and read the full piece. Then he read it again.

• • • •

For the next couple of weeks, McGonagle did some preliminary research on Libor—what it was, how it worked, why it mattered. One day, he walked down the hall to the office of his deputy, Gretchen Lowe. The enforcement division was housed in a warren of narrow passageways lined with tall file cabinets. Little natural light filtered in. Lowe, tall, gangly, and bespectacled, had been at the CFTC even longer than McGonagle. She liked being an underdog, going toe-to-toe with banking lawyers who she knew were taking home in a month what Lowe and her ilk earned in a year.

She and McGonagle discussed the *Journal* story and whether there was more to it. The only way to answer that was to launch an investigation, but that was easier said than done. The agency was constantly battling budget shortages (resources were so tight that employees had to bring their own coffee mugs to work), and investigations were expensive: Agents had to fly all over the world, lawyers had to be hired, depositions recorded. Before going any further, McGonagle and Lowe needed to alert their higher-ups.

Their manager was Stephen Obie, who was running the CFTC's enforcement arm. Raised in the Bronx, Obie was the son of a New York City bus driver. A decade earlier, he had been toiling as an associate at a major law firm, trying to figure out what he wanted to do with his life. A colleague gave him some advice: Lawyers were becoming like doctors—if they didn't develop specialties, they became dispensable. The way to build a specialty, he was convinced, was to work for a government agency, so Obie applied for

201

jobs at the CFTC and at the New York City Transit Authority, the same agency that had employed his father. Both made offers, and he opted for the CFTC gig, partly because of its convenient New York location in the North Tower of the World Trade Center. He joined in 1998 as a trial lawyer. The learning curve was steep, but the transition was made easier by the CFTC's tradition of targeting small fries. For a while, Obie's big get was busting a couple of California taxi drivers for fraud.

On the morning of September 11, 2001, Obie was at work on the thirty-seventh floor of the North Tower when a plane smashed into the skyscraper. He felt the floor buckle; it was like riding a wave. He and his colleagues scrambled down the stairs and escaped, shocked but unhurt.

The brush with death prompted Obie to again reevaluate his professional life. He wanted to go after bigger fish. That fall, he volunteered for a federal task force investigating Enron. The experience proved formative. The CFTC and Justice Department worked closely together, and Obie realized the power that Justice brought to the table. People readily lied to the CFTC—but it was much different when an FBI agent was in the room. And the psychological impact of staging a "perp walk," parading a handcuffed suspect in front of the TV cameras, was not to be underestimated. The CFTC didn't own any handcuffs.

Obie was tall, beefy, and at times sported a crew cut. He looked a bit like a cop. Once, when he accompanied a CFTC commissioner to a speech near the United Nations in midtown Manhattan, passersby mistook him for a Secret Service agent. In April 2008, Obie had just been promoted to become the agency's acting enforcement director. He wasn't shocked by the *Journal*'s first story. Some pension funds had been grumbling to the agency for months about apparent problems with Libor; the funds felt they weren't getting the money they deserved on some of their derivatives contracts as a result of Libor's inaccuracy. But the complaints hadn't prompted the CFTC to do anything.

McGonagle and Lowe told Obie the Libor case looked like it had the potential to be big. Two days later, a Friday, the CFTC commissioners held their weekly closed-door meeting to discuss enforcement matters. The meetings were not known for being exciting. If there were nothing major going on, the commissioners might spend time ruminating about the effects of something like an African civil war on coffee prices, before devoting fifteen minutes to running through a checklist of open investigations. The general rule of thumb was that the enforcement staff would seek approval from—or at least give a heads-up to—the five commissioners before they devoted more than twenty man-hours to an investigation. Obie gave that heads-up. He told them he wanted to open an investigation into Libor. "We don't know much about it, but we're going to take a look," he said. Nobody objected.

• • • •

A few weeks after Geithner chatted with Mervyn King in Switzerland, his staff produced a six-point plan to address Libor's shortcomings. The ideas were predicated on the notion that not only was Libor inaccurate, but also that banks were deliberately skewing their data. At the time, that was a radical accusation: The BBA was still insisting that the rate was sacrosanct; the notion that banks were intentionally distorting it could be interpreted as heresy. Geithner's solutions, e-mailed to King on June 1, mainly involved modest tweaks to make it feasible for someone in an oversight role to double-check Libor's accuracy and, if problems were discovered, to rectify them, either through rewarding accuracy or punishing inaccuracy. Two days later, King's assistant replied on behalf of the governor, notifying his American counterpart that the Bank of England would pass on the suggestions to the BBA.

From late May to early June, dozens of e-mails and phone calls crisscrossed the Atlantic between top officials at the Fed, BBA, Bank of England, and, to a lesser extent, FSA, in an attempt to forge a consensus about what to do with Libor. The process at times was slowed down by King's refusal to use e-mail. He preferred to have his private secretary, Chris Salmon—the same Chris Salmon who years earlier had done a stint at the International Monetary Fund in Washington and helped stoke his nephew Tom Hayes's interest in finance—print out the e-mails, and then King would scrawl his barely legible comments on the top of the pages. The BBA incorporated some of the suggestions into a report it was working on about ways to improve Libor; it wanted to cite the central banks' input, but they wouldn't let their names be included. In any case, despite the increasing concerns about Libor, the Bank of England continued to rely on it. When it unveiled a new emergency lending program for British banks, it used Libor to determine the interest rates and fees banks would pay to participate. There was nothing the Americans could do—which is just how Hayes, his fellow traders, and the BBA liked it.

• • • •

That summer, Lowe assigned a few employees to the investigation—a significant investment of manpower, considering the enforcement unit's entire staff, including secretaries and other low-level employees, barely numbered a hundred. Progress was glacial. By September, five months after the *Journal's* initial story, the investigators hadn't collected a shred of outside information. They hadn't conducted any interviews. This was still nothing more than a hunch. When Obie asked McGonagle about the status, he was alarmed to hear that things had stalled, in part because one of the only staffers on the case had gone on maternity leave. The CFTC, Obie concluded, needed to either do something or move on.

It was clear that they needed outside help; there just wasn't much information available to the public. A natural starting place was the BBA. McGonagle and Lowe drafted an informal letter to the group, figuring it would be just as concerned as they were about the prospect of Libor being manipulated. As a courtesy, Obie got in touch with his counterpart at the FSA in London, a prim former white-collar defense lawyer named Margaret Cole. The two had enjoyed a solid working relationship, dating back to their collaboration on some of the energy-price-manipulation cases earlier in the decade. But to Obie's surprise, Cole didn't seem all that interested in Libor. She hadn't heard anything to suggest there were problems with the rate. Her only request was that the CFTC keep her agency in the loop.

On September 10, less than a week before Lehman Brothers went bankrupt, the BBA received a letter from the CFTC stating that the agency was conducting an investigation into the U.S. dollar version of Libor. The letter asked the BBA to hand over documents and other information. Similar letters went to a half-dozen big banks.

Ewan got to work figuring out how to derail, or at least stall, the investigators. He sent a memo to Knight explaining that it was not clear that the CFTC even had jurisdiction to make such a request about the *London* interbank offered rate. He suggested enlisting the FSA to help fend off the Americans. The BBA's lawyers, from the law firm Clifford Chance, gave similar advice. That sounded good to Knight. Her impression, after talking to the FSA, was that the agency was at best lukewarm about the investigation; on a recent conference call about Libor, all of the agency's top officials had hung up, leaving a lone junior employee representing the agency. So the BBA replied to the CFTC that it would be happy to cooperate, but all requests needed to be routed through the FSA; for now, it wouldn't be answering any of the CFTC's questions. With the BBA's hometown regulator in its corner, Ewan and his colleagues breathed a sigh of relief.

• • • •

A month later, on October 10, Ewan and Miles Storey at Barclays got on the phone. Markets were closed for Columbus Day in the United States. "That just gives us more time for more banks to fail," Storey joked.

Ewan wasn't as jovial. A few days earlier, someone had called him to complain about the inaccuracy of the Libor submissions made by a German bank, WestLB—the same company that employed Darrell Read's buddy as a Libor submitter. Ewan phoned the bank and relayed the complaint. The next day, WestLB boosted its submission. "Between us, I was horrified at the ease with which I did shift the Libors," he told Storey. "You can see exactly when it happened." Was this a sign of just how arbitrary banks' submissions really were and how easy it would be for someone to call in a favor and get a bank to change its data?

Later that month, the BBA held a meeting with representatives from some of the world's biggest banks to discuss the CFTC investigation. Executives at the American giants—Citigroup, Bank of America, and J.P. Morgan—grumbled about the CFTC's vague requests for reams of detailed information. They were reminded that the CFTC had limited powers to tell banks what to do. Some of the banks, though, remained antsy. Barclays had a policy of generally destroying audio recordings of phone calls involving bank employees after a year or so, but it hadn't adhered to its own policy. Its army of compliance officials and lawyers soon discovered that tens of thousands of the audio files still existed—worrisome, indeed.

A week later, the FSA finally got around to asking the BBA to provide the CFTC with some rudimentary information. There was no deadline.

. . . .

On the evening of November 4, a senior official at the Bank of England, Paul Fisher, shot off a personal note to Ewan. It had been a long day at the central bank, with a global crisis raging. Fisher's job included keeping tabs on the foreign-exchange market, which, thanks to the violent financial turbulence, had suddenly become a full-time occupation. But Fisher was preoccupied with an unrelated problem. He had read a Goldman Sachs research note earlier that day about Libor. Fisher was no expert on the benchmark, but he knew its definition: It was the rate at which banks thought they could *borrow* money from each other. The Goldman report had gotten the definition wrong, describing Libor as the rate at which banks *loaned* money to each other. When Fisher noticed the error, it got him thinking: How widespread was the confusion? Libor was an integral part of the world's financial plumbing, so how could the great Goldman Sachs misunderstand what the rate was supposed to be measuring? Fisher tried to find the definition of Libor on the BBA's website. When he finally tracked it down, he told Ewan, the definition seemed to be "ambiguous to say the least." Out of curiosity, he checked Wikipedia's description of Libor; it included the same mistake that Goldman had made.

"If Goldmans can get it wrong, maybe there's a complete lack of public understanding?" Fisher wrote to Ewan. "If so, I would start by putting the official definition in pride of place on the BBA website. And then get someone's son or daughter to edit Wikipedia." A week later, someone corrected Wikipedia's definition. It was perhaps the only time that the BBA actually addressed a grievance about Libor.

CHAPTER 10

Entre Nous

Hayes was back in Las Vegas, this time with Tighe. It was December 31, 2008. The couple had flown in from Los Angeles, where they'd spent a few days touristing around Beverly Hills and Hollywood after Christmas. (One of the first things Hayes did was track down Rod Stewart's bronze star on Hollywood Boulevard's "Walk of Fame.") They had stayed at the Beverly Wilshire, one of Los Angeles's finest hotels. One day, Hayes wanted to check out Venice Beach, the bohemian boardwalk neighborhood crowded with body builders and peddlers of drug paraphernalia. He asked the hotel concierge where to catch a bus to get there. The stiffly dressed concierge looked at him like he was crazy. Perhaps he'd be more comfortable taking advantage of the complimentary car service that the hotel offered for its customers' pleasure? So Hayes and Tighe were chauffeured to the dingy beach in a silver Rolls-Royce.

In Vegas, they stayed at the Four Seasons. They had New Year's Eve plans to meet some friends for dinner and drinks at a swanky club overlooking the Strip, but that afternoon Hayes began behaving weirdly, even for him. He was rude to the hotel staff. He shouted at Tighe. Miffed, she went out for drinks without him. They reconnected at the club, packed with revelers in sequined dresses and party hats. Hayes was still agitated, alternating between sulking to himself, snapping at waiters, and being gruff with their friends. Tighe was familiar with this mood; she had dubbed it his "grumpy zombie" state. She and one of her friends went off on their own for a while so that she could vent about Hayes. When she returned, she gave him an ultimatum: "If you don't start behaving, you'll be spending New Year's Eve alone." Hayes pulled himself together, but Tighe could tell he remained anxious.

As midnight approached, Hayes, sweaty and shifting from foot to foot, shoved a glass of champagne into Tighe's hand. He took her by the arm and half-dragged her to a large window with a panoramic view of the Strip. Fireworks exploded, and suddenly the night sky was just as colorful as the boulevard below, illuminated with blinking lights from casinos and electronic billboards. Hayes pulled an engagement ring out of his pocket and thrust it into Tighe's palm. It was platinum with a massive, round-cut diamond. There was no speech, no taking a knee. "Will you marry me?" he asked. Tighe cried and said yes. Relieved, Hayes apologized for his bad behavior all evening. "I was so nervous," he explained. She embraced him. The year was only a few minutes old, but already 2009 was off to a promising start.

· · · ·

The end of 2008 hadn't been bad, either. Hayes had stitched together an impressive string of winning trades. Some of them— Hayes estimated they accounted for perhaps $2 million to $5 million of his profits that year—stemmed from the Libor-moving efforts he deployed with his colleagues, rivals, and brokers. Hayes wasn't the only one playing with the rate, but the relentless pressure he applied—and the leverage he enjoyed with the brokers and fellow traders as a giant market maker—made him a standout. As always, Hayes didn't spend much time thinking about whether what he was doing was right or wrong. Those weren't values he assigned to his job. His sole criterion was whether what he was doing was making money.

And he was doing that in spades. His final tally for the year: about $89 million in profits for UBS, a home run even in calm markets. If normal investment banking pay standards applied, Hayes was headed for a multimillion-dollar bonus early in 2009, especially when coupled with the prior year's promotion and promised payout of $2.5 million.

While Hayes was soaring, Read was finally stepping aside. "Adios, mate," he e-mailed Goodman on December 10. "Thanks for giving me a job and a start on the road to a life of no sleep and too much alcohol." He apologized for constantly interrupting Goodman's early-morning train rides with Libor requests. As a postscript, he told Goodman where Hayes wanted Libor to move over the next few weeks: "Nudge nudge!"

Hayes bought Read a walking stick as a sarcastic retirement gift; Read thanked him, saying it would come in handy as he strolled the beaches of the Bay of Plenty. The broker expressed his affection for the trader he'd spent every day over the past several years talking to. Hayes replied with uncharacteristic warmth. "Words cannot adequately express how much I have enjoyed working with you over the years, you have seen me grow from a trainee to a grumpy old git, but as the market evolved I feel we have both learnt together and that always gave us a real edge in the market as we thought along the same lines," he wrote. "This year has been the pinnacle of my career and you played a huge part in it. In short you are irreplaceable and I am gutted that you are going."

Read was not quite done, though. Despite having retired days earlier, he texted Goodman on December 29 to ask about the direction of interest rates.

Goodman responded a few minutes later: "Request from M'lord: Get a life."

"Understood," Read texted. "Over and out!"

. . . .

Hayes's banner year was well known in Tokyo, and it didn't take long in 2009 for the job offers to start arriving. Deutsche Bank and Morgan Stanley put out feelers in February, then Barclays joined the fray. Even Goldman, which Hayes had spurned the prior year, was back to wooing him. Hayes didn't rebuff the offers. UBS, like many other large, risk-loving investment banks, was suffering gargantuan losses that had necessitated a $54 billion government bailout. In late February, after the bank lost another $9 billion, its CEO, Marcel Rohner, was removed. His replacement was a forty-year banking veteran named Oswald Grübel, who previously had run crosstown rival Credit Suisse. One of his first moves was to dock just about everyone's pay. Large bonuses were off the table. Pieri summoned Hayes into his office and delivered the bad news: Rather than the award of at least $2.5 million that he'd been expecting, UBS would only be paying him $250,000. "UBS shafted me," he told a friend.

So as he had the prior year, Hayes told Pieri, who in turn told his bosses, about the suitors. A few days later, Carsten Kengeter— the co-head of UBS's large investment banking division, a tall, well-built German with a passion for extreme skiing and yoga—called

Hayes and tried to extinguish his interest in the other banks. He promised that UBS would look out for Hayes and that he would check the feasibility of making another ironclad bonus guarantee. Hayes and Pieri asked Kengeter to speak to Tighe, who was pushing hard for Hayes to test the waters with other banks. "I think getting his fiancée around is key," Pieri said. Kengeter never called her. Tighe remained convinced that Hayes should be entertaining the rival offers.

The wooing lasted all spring. Hayes wasn't especially keen on working for any of these other banks, but he knew it was in his interest to keep flirting. Pieri and Kengeter engaged in a full-court press to prevent him from defecting, with Kengeter placing regular reassuring phone calls. It was unusual for an executive of Kengeter's seniority—only a rung or two below the CEO of the entire company—to be so involved in retaining a midlevel trader, but it reflected Hayes's importance to UBS. And that importance only seemed to be growing. Hayes was off to a smoking start in 2009.

• • • •

Day after day, week after week, Farr and his colleagues planted Hayes's Libor-moving requests with a small cluster of interest-rate traders around London. It wasn't hard; all Farr had to do was drop it into conversations he was supposed to be having anyway. In fact, it was a good way to force himself to be in regular communication with traders at big banks.

The bigger challenge for Farr—who happened to be in physical therapy after the latest in a series of recent motorcycle crashes—and his colleagues was figuring out how to execute the sham switch trades that Hayes continued to deliver as thanks. Finding Hayes a trading partner was key, and that task was getting harder. Multiple traders rebuffed the RP Martin brokers, including J.P. Morgan's Stuart Wiley, who now told Farr that "we can't do switches anymore."

So it fell to Danziger, who was increasingly disgusted with the situation at RBS. The bank, recently nationalized by the British government, wasn't paying anyone bonuses. "I don't give a fuck around here at the moment, so whenever you want to do it, I'll always do it," he told Aaron. Danziger figured the switch trades were a good way to make up for some of the lost largesse—this way at least the brokers would lavish him with meals, booze, and weekend getaways.

Hayes left the details of these trades to a London colleague named Simon Oddie, who had a specific way he wanted the transactions structured. It was no secret that they were happening, but, all the same, it was in everyone's best interest not to be too blatant about them. After all, even though UBS was getting what it paid for in the form of help with Libor, the only purpose of the trades was to pay fees to RP Martin. The trick, Oddie told Farr, was to make sure the two trades were separated by at least a half hour or so. "I thought it would raise less questions than if I did them at the same time," Oddie explained. "It's just a case so it doesn't flag up anything."

"I understand fully, mate," Farr confirmed.

A couple of weeks later, on Valentine's Day, the broker crashed his motorcycle yet again. This time his beloved Ducati got mangled. Farr was shaken up and bruised. "You should stop riding those death traps," Hayes suggested. It was the rare request from Hayes that Farr wasn't inclined to honor.

. . . .

In February 2009, Alexis Stenfors set out on a vacation with his wife, Maria, daughters and in-laws to India—his first break from work in nearly eighteen months. He was coming off an awesome year, having raked in about $120 million in profits for Merrill Lynch—largely a reflection of placing bets that anticipated the financial crisis. But Stenfors knew his career as a trader was nearing an end. Part of it was the relentless stress of day after day of high-stakes trading. He had developed a painful infection in his chest that his doctors attributed to stress. His right forearm and wrist, severely strained from his constant use of a keyboard and phone, had to be wrapped in an elaborate brace. Stenfors spent most of his waking hours in pain. And his year was off to a bad start: The financial industry was rebounding from the depths of the crisis, and Stenfors's bearish bets were no longer looking so wise.

But there was something else, and it was far from a minor concern. On the more-than-eight-hour flight to India, Stenfors was finally honest with himself: He had been engaged in an elaborate scam at Merrill Lynch. Every day, he had to attach values to his massive portfolio of investments and lately he'd been assigning bogus numbers that made it look like he was enjoying considerably more success than he really was. At first, he'd regarded this as a temporary fix—it only had to keep his managers off his back until his fortunes improved. But his fortunes hadn't improved; his losses only deepened. By the time he boarded the plane, his little fib had grown into a nine-figure monstrosity. The anxiety was gnawing at him. Still, he did nothing. On his second morning in India, though, Stenfors called a colleague back in London to check on his portfolio. The response was alarming: Merrill Lynch officials were digging through his books, apparently alerted to anomalies. Stenfors spent a day weighing his options. He decided that he had no choice. He told Maria that he'd been "mismarking" his books. She didn't know what that meant, so he explained that it was the equivalent of hiding a big loss in a drawer. Then he phoned his boss, who was skiing in Switzerland. "I have something I need to tell you," Stenfors began. Then he admitted everything.

Stenfors had hoped that the act of confessing would feel like a weight lifting off his shoulders. It didn't. He just felt guilty. After a few days of further reflection, and an eerie silence from the folks in London, Stenfors thought maybe he should get a lawyer. He got in touch with one through a mutual acquaintance; the lawyer instructed him to immediately return to London. It was starting to dawn on Stenfors that this might be more serious than he'd initially assumed. So he said goodbye to his family, which was about to visit the Taj Mahal, and flew to London.

After a couple days of legal meetings, there didn't seem to be anything more to do. He figured he might as well rejoin his family, so back he went to India. Meanwhile, his Merrill Lynch managers scrambled to assess the damage. It was considerable—he was sitting on more than $400 million in losses. Notified by Merrill, the FSA opened an investigation.

Shortly after Stenfors and his family returned from their vacation, Merrill suspended him; he'd be fired a few months later. Merrill publicly described the problem as "an irregularity."

The muffled description didn't stop Stenfors becoming an instant pariah. A Finnish newspaper attacked its native son for helping cause the global financial crisis—a considerable exaggeration. Photographers gathered outside the family's home. His landlord refused to refund the security deposit on his apartment, arguing that his wife had suffered severe emotional distress due to their tenant's newfound notoriety. (The landlord eventually agreed to refund half the deposit.)

Farr broke the news to Hayes. "Got any jobs going?? Cause I'll need one. Fucking Alexis has been sacked," he said. "The guy is a lovely bloke and doesn't deserve the sh-- he is getting," Farr continued, for once censoring his language. "I don't believe for a minute that he is doing anything illegal."

"He is a scapegoat," Hayes agreed. Then he and Farr got back to plotting how to push Libor higher.

• • • •

Hayes received a steady stream of visitors that spring. One was the Citigroup researcher Scott Peng, who had heard of a prolific, brilliant trader in Tokyo and wanted to meet him. The two sat down at a sushi restaurant—obviously not Hayes's choice—and chatted about the markets. The subject of Libor manipulation didn't come up.

Amid a mid-March heat wave in Tokyo, Farr arrived. Hayes volunteered Alykulov to serve as his tour guide, taking him on a boat ride and to Tokyo's biggest video game arcade. "Got yourself a good one there, mate," Farr told Hayes after meeting Tighe for the first time, "a top bird."

Tighe thought Farr seemed like a genuine guy—it would be hard to fake his sloppy attire and casual demeanor—but in general her fiancé's brokers struck her as an insincere, cloying bunch. Once, when she went out to one of Tokyo's many expat bars, a bunch of brokers lined up to talk to her, literally standing in a queue, patiently awaiting the chance to buy her a drink and pay their respects. She felt like the wife of a Mafia don.

That was awkward, but it was nothing compared to the embarrassment that Hayes sometimes caused. Once, Tighe's boss, a partner at Herbert Smith, hosted a barbecue for his team at his Tokyo apartment. Tighe and Hayes showed up toting two bottles of expensive wine as a gift. Hayes looked forward to drinking them, but when he handed the bottles to the host, they were placed on his already-ample wine rack. He and Tighe were directed to a small bar area where some other wine bottles were already uncorked. Hayes, who was learning all he could about wine in preparation for his wedding, could tell that the open bottles were considerably cheaper than the two he had brought. Within earshot of the host, he declared that he thought it was inappropriate to accept expensive bottles of wine and then to serve a cheap alternative. Mortified, Tighe told her fiancé to shut his mouth. Later, Hayes wandered outside to the patio, impressed by this rare luxury in a Tokyo apartment. Tighe's boss, now manning the grill, mentioned that he was really enjoying the barbecue. Hayes responded that he could understand that sentiment: The low cost of the wine and food that he was serving, compared to the benefits that the party would have in terms of motivating his team, meant the event was a good investment. Tighe, standing nearby, groaned.

A few weeks after Farr left, Tighe's sister, Emma, arrived for an eight-day visit. Emma, who taught chemistry and biology to high school students, thought Hayes was awfully odd. She noticed that he sometimes went up to objects and sniffed them like an animal. One evening, the sisters stopped by a small bar called Magumbos, a popular spot for the city's rowdy Western brokers and traders, featuring a bell that customers could ring when they bought cheap shots of liquor for the other customers. It was around 10 P.M. on a weeknight, so Hayes had long since retired. A man seated next to Emma and Sarah seemed to be listening in on their conversation, conspicuous partly because he was drunk and partly because half his face appeared slack, like he had some sort of muscular problem. It was Roger Darin. He and Tighe had never met, but he somehow had discerned that this was his nemesis's fiancée. Interrupting, Darin told Tighe that he hated Hayes, and, checking out Emma, he added: "It looks like he's gone for the wrong sister."

• • • •

Read had spent the past few months living in a small house across the street from the beach in Tauranga. Notwithstanding a problematic neighbor, the setup seemed idyllic. But his boys didn't like it there, and Joanna felt even more isolated than she already had. Read eventually caved, and as long as he was moving back to Wellington, he figured he might as well work. He'd been missing the buzz of the markets, and opportunity beckoned. Executives at a variety of brokerages were begging Read to return to the industry; ICAP in particular thought it was sacrificing huge amounts of potential revenue by not having a broker in place with a good relationship with Hayes. In late March, Read had exploratory conversations with ICAP, Tullett Prebon, and BGC. He only had one client, but it was a client that everyone was itching to land. Eventually, lured by a doubled pay package, Read decided to come back to the ICAP family.

If Read's unretirement wasn't enough to lift Hayes's spirits, the trader's performance in the first four months of 2009 should have done the trick. By May he was up $105 million—and only a small fraction, perhaps 5 percent, was due to his Libor-massaging efforts. This was the kind of torrid showing that could have a real impact on UBS's overall financial results. Hayes endured bad days, even a couple of bad weeks, but the good times far outnumbered the bad ones. Sitting all day in front of his towering bank of computer screens, his back and eyes and arms aching, Hayes had become perhaps the biggest player in the Tokyo market. He had honed his computer models so well that on the vast majority of transactions he executed, he notched a small profit. And with the tens of thousands of trades he was doing, those small profits quickly piled up.

· · · ·

Guillaume Adolph grew up in the Bordeaux region of France. He was short, chubby, and pale-skinned and frequently ducked out of the office for cigarette breaks. He had been a successful trader in London for Italy's UniCredit Bank, but that was the minor leagues of investment banking. In 2006, Merrill Lynch poached him. For a couple of years, Adolph worked near Stenfors in Merrill's London offices. The two didn't get along well. Adolph was prickly and ill-tempered. His already thick French accent seemed to grow thicker on the frequent occasions when he was angry or agitated. Shortly before his wedding in April 2008, after losing tens of millions of dollars in a matter of a week or two, Adolph was fired. In a vivid illustration of how Wall Street traders rolled the dice with other people's money, rarely facing personal consequences when their gambles went awry, Adolph was hired as a trader in Deutsche Bank's huge London office barely two months later. In addition to trading Japanese interest-rate derivatives, he was promptly put in charge of the bank's yen Libor submissions. His boss was David Nicholls, the manager who had insisted to John Ewan that Libor was impossible to manipulate.

A couple of years earlier, at the ICAP Christmas dinner, Stenfors had pointed Adolph out to Hayes from across the crowded room, but the two had never met. Still, a relationship developed. It started off casually, with Hayes and Adolph chatting electronically via their computer terminals. (Hayes struggled to pronounce or spell the Frenchman's name, so he decided to call him "Gollum," a nod to the famous Tolkien character.) At the time, Adolph was a big interest-rate derivatives trader, not as big as Hayes, but big enough that it was inevitable that the two regularly were on the opposing sides of trades. That meant it could be mutually beneficial to know each other, if for no other reason than to make sure the brokers who served as middlemen weren't pulling the wool over either of their eyes. And, of course, Gollum was responsible for Deutsche Bank's yen Libor submissions. He often told Hayes that he was setting Libor based in part on where he needed the benchmark to move to benefit his trades—the kind of power Hayes, who had to rely on Darin, could only dream of.

By August 2008, Hayes and Adolph were doing enough business together that Hayes thought it was time to take the relationship to the next level. "Look, I appreciate the business and the calls," he said. "We should try to share info where possible. Also let me know if you need fixes one way or the other."

"Sure," Adolph said.

The partnership—an "alliance," Hayes called it—meant that the two traders would cooperate when possible on the levels and directions of their banks' Libor submissions. Striking such a deal with a competitor was uncharacteristic of Hayes. Of course, he lodged plenty of requests for favors from rivals, but those weren't part of long-term agreements. Indeed, he tended to view his rivals as enemies, worthy of clobbering with golf clubs. And Hayes knew that teaming up with a rival trader to share information and nudge Libor in helpful directions bordered on collusion. But when he mentioned the arrangement to Pieri, his boss seemed unbothered.

The relationship soon proved lucrative. At 10 A.M. on May 13, 2009, in London, Adolph sent Hayes a heads-up message that his Deutsche Bank colleague planned to lower the bank's U.S. dollar Libor submission by twenty basis points in about an hour. That was a massive move—usually, a shift of a single basis point would be considered significant—and it promised to knock the overall Libor average lower. "Entre nous," the Frenchman whispered.

Hayes rushed to Pieri's office, interrupted a meeting, and told his boss what he'd just learned. Pieri asked what he thought they should do. Hayes suggested loading up on a derivative that would gain value if U.S. dollar Libor plunged. Pieri agreed, and Hayes executed the trade. When the BBA published the daily Libor figures ninety minutes later, the average had indeed dipped. Hayes's trade scored an instant $1.25 million profit for UBS. Pieri congratulated him on his latest coup—never mind its questionable provenance.

So big was Deutsche Bank's move that it caught the attention of the normally somnambulant BBA. Ewan asked Thomson Reuters, which collected the data on the BBA's behalf, to phone Deutsche Bank to make sure the data hadn't been entered incorrectly. Maybe the bank meant to reduce its submission by two basis points, not twenty? Nope. "That's what we want to put in," Deutsche Bank's submitter confirmed.

Then Ewan's phone started ringing with complaints from other banks. The huge cut had left Deutsche Bank's Libor data lower than those of its peers. The matter was discussed at the next meeting of the Libor oversight panel. The FXMMC instructed Ewan to pay Deutsche Bank a visit, so he did, marching over to its tan, brick building. In a meeting room decorated with what looked like expensive modern artwork, a Deutsche Bank employee insisted that the submission reflected the bank's true borrowing costs. Ewan reported back to the FXMMC, which decided that nothing improper had occurred. That was the end of the matter. It would prove to be the only time the oversight committee ever investigated a bank's Libor submission.

CHAPTER 11

Gods of the Sea

By the summer of 2009, the financial system had bounced back from its near-death experience. The recovery created a puzzling situation. Many of the world's leading banks were now partly owned by taxpayers, owing to massive government bailouts. The economies of much of the Western world remained mired in deep recessions, thanks in no small part to their banks' misadventures. Corporate chieftains were paying lip service, if nothing else, to the idea of humility and remorse, and indeed some banks had become more conservative. (In June 2009, for example, Royal Bank of Scotland emptied out big parts of its investment bank. Among the casualties was Hayes's mentor Brent Davies, who was let go after a two-decade career there. The large, charismatic Davies—who years earlier had warned Hayes to "never trust a broker"—quickly landed a job as a broker at ICAP, where his responsibilities included winning business from his former colleagues and rivals.)

At the same time, though, markets were surging, powered by the release of pent-up demand among companies and rich individuals. That was translating into fat profits for Wall Street banks and their traders. So, despite all the rhetoric about the financial crisis meaning "the end of Wall Street," Wall Street was on a tear, and many traders had regained their swagger. Deepening the paradox, it was actually in the best interests of the banks' new government owners for their wards to return to profitability, since that would enable the governments to sell their stakes in the banks at a profit, helping quiet public fury over the unpopular bailouts. And the best way to get the banks back to their normal profitable ways, at least according to the bankers themselves, was to unleash the creative, aggressive, risk-taking genius of their traders and investment bankers.

Hayes had just returned from a weeklong vacation in Thailand. He'd been there once before, with Ainsworth. This time he took Tighe to a different tropical island, Koh Samui. They stayed at the Four Seasons, which had become the only hotel chain that the obsession-prone Hayes was willing to spend money on. Once again, Hayes had refused to wear sunscreen, and this time his burns were so severe that he became ill. The rest of the vacation was spent with Tighe nursing him back to health while he fretted about turbulence in the markets.

Back in Tokyo, he called Farr. The broker had previously volunteered to pay for a chunk of the vacation. Hayes felt a bit guilty about it, but not so guilty that he didn't accept the offer. "I'll just give you my bill for my hotel room, if that's alright," he said. "The thing is, mate, it's in Thai baht." No problem, Farr assured him. RP Martin would just convert the figure into pounds and deposit the money into Hayes's personal bank account. "I appreciate that," Hayes said sheepishly. "The thing is, it's about 5,000 bucks, mate." Farr was unruffled. He had already checked with his boss Cliff King about covering part of Hayes's trip. The money was transferred.

Hayes, of course, didn't need help with the hotel bill, but he nonetheless was grateful for the friendly gesture. He suggested to Farr that he reciprocate via a big switch trade—yielding far more in commissions than RP Martin had paid to cover the hotel. It was mission accomplished for Farr.

In late June, Hayes asked Wiley to get his J.P. Morgan colleagues to bump six-month Libor higher. "It would probably suit me as well, but our guys seem to be very by-the-book," Wiley said. "If I ask them, they'd almost [move it in the opposite direction] out of spite." Still, Wiley got on the phone with his Libor-submitting colleague, who, sure enough, refused to help. Wiley told Hayes.

"They sound like pricks," Hayes declared in an instant message from his Bloomberg terminal.

Hayes's obnoxiousness was nothing new, but the "pricks" remark nonetheless irritated Wiley, and so he called Wilkinson—with whom Wiley had previously plotted to move Libor in helpful directions. Now Wiley relayed a badly distorted version of what had just happened. "Tommy Hayes" wanted Libor moved, Wiley said, "which I had no intention of doing. But of course I don't want to piss him off, so I sort of went for a bit of pretense." He said he had told Hayes he would check with his guys, but never actually did anything.

"Oh mate, that's so illegal, it's ridiculous," Wilkinson sympathized, laughing.

Continued Wiley: "So I came back with a Bloomberg saying I spoke to my guys . . . and he sends an e-mail back saying, 'your guys are pricks.'"

"Fucking hell," Wilkinson responded. "He's out of control, isn't he? Now you know what we're dealing with."

"He's got to be careful phoning up banks," Wiley said.

"You just don't do that."

"He'll get in all sorts of trouble."

Now it was Wilkinson's turn to bend the truth. "Well, he sort of tries it around here," he said, "but we said, 'mate, look, if you've got any views on Libor, we'll listen to them, but that's as far as it goes.'" Wilkinson, laughing louder now, mimicked Hayes's requests to ICAP. "Aye aye, shepherd's pie," he giggled, recycling the old yarn about the out-of-control Hayes. "Get in the bath!"

"I don't want to piss him off by saying that I'm not going to do anything at all, but I'm just pretending to," Wiley lied again.

"Mate, absolutely, yeah, I think you've made the right call," Wilkinson agreed. "Just fucking leave it be. Put the onus on someone else."

• • • •

Noel Cryan was in South Africa, having followed Britain's national rugby team, the Lions, there for a tournament. The trip wasn't going quite as planned. For starters, his traveling companion's hotel room was robbed. And Hayes was driving Cryan crazy. This was nothing new; Cryan was accustomed to Hayes's antics. Most of the time, he managed to turn the other cheek. (There were exceptions. After one tirade, Cryan had threatened to come to Tokyo and kill Hayes. The broker smashed the phone down, kicked his chair onto its side, and stomped out of the building.) In this case, Cryan had warned Hayes he was going on vacation beforehand, but the message didn't seem to have registered. Hayes called Tullett looking for the broker. When told that Cryan was in South Africa, Hayes exploded: "He's a fucking lazy crit. He's never in work, that boy. He's had more holidays this year than I've had in the last three years." Hayes called Cryan on his cell phone, too, warning that he might sever his relationship with Tullett. The rant lasted almost ten minutes.

"Mate, I'm in fucking South Africa," Cryan responded. "What the fuck do you want me to do?"

Once Cryan was back in London, Hayes teased him about the hotel room getting burgled. Cryan, trying to make conversation, said that things had been quiet lately, depriving him of brokerage revenue. He wasn't asking for charity, but just like that Hayes volunteered a switch trade to help him out. After assailing Cryan a few days earlier, now Hayes acted as though they were friends. Cryan happily accepted the offer, and Hayes, true to his word, arranged a lucrative switch trade. Danziger—who recently had run up such a huge tab on a night out with Cryan that Tullett's normally laissez-faire bean counters had taken notice—took the other side of the transaction as a way to say thanks.

These quid pro quos had become an established pattern for Danziger. In June, after an afternoon and evening of drinking, Danziger and Lee Aaron decided to go to a club, Mahiki, along with several other brokers and traders. The tropical-themed nightspot—frequented by celebrities and located amid the hedge funds and Ferrari showrooms of London's Mayfair neighborhood—had a pair of wooden, Pacific island statuettes guarding its main entrance, along with a few black-shirted bouncers. Aaron was outrageously drunk when he arrived, and Danziger "was fucking out of his head," Aaron reported the next day. The bouncers wouldn't let the inebriated group in unless they forked over a fee to access a VIP area. They paid. Inside, Danziger and Aaron started guzzling £250 bottles of vodka. By the end of the night, they had run up a £2,200 tab. Aaron knew that was too much to charge on RP Martin's account, at least without prior approval, so he pleaded to Danziger for help. But the RBS trader didn't want to split the bill. He had a better idea. "Just put a switch through," he drunkenly proposed. Aaron agreed.

The next day at 6:30 A.M., after a few hours of sleep, Aaron was at work. He was still a bit drunk, his voice hoarse. He phoned RBS. "Danziger owes me a little switchy today," he told the guy who answered the phone. "Is he in?"

"Don't actually see him" was the response.

"There's number one rule, if you go drinking, make sure you get in," Aaron slurred. "That is the only rule. . . . It doesn't matter if you go out drinking till four o'clock in the morning. Make it home, make it into work, and then people will send you home if you look like shit. But at least make the effort to make it in. That's the only rule."

"Yeah, I know," the RBS guy said.

Eventually Danziger showed up and a 100 billion yen switch trade got done. It netted RP Martin nearly £20,000 (about $33,000) in commissions—almost ten times the size of the Mahiki bill.*

The combination of a fierce hangover and the £20,000 windfall had Aaron in a loopy mood, and he spent most of the rest of the day telling jokes. "Did I tell you that fucking one-liner?" he asked a colleague. "'She's about as useful as Anne Frank's drum kit.' That fucking line is great." Aaron's colleague didn't get it, possibly because it was out of context—Aaron wasn't using it to refer to anyone in particular. "Well, she had to be quiet, didn't she?" he explained. "So a fucking drum kit is fucking useless. She was hiding in the wall, wasn't she?"

A few days later, Danziger pinged Aaron with a nonalcoholic request: "Low Libors again please."

"Gotcha," Aaron replied.

---

* When Aaron submitted the Mahiki receipt for reimbursement, he made up a client. He didn't want Danziger's name involved.

• • • •

One day in June, Hayes got an e-mail from Neil Archer, an impos-
ing bald Australian who worked as a recruiter for a number of big
banks. He was reaching out on behalf of Citigroup. The New York
bank had just hired a refugee from Lehman Brothers, a star trader
named Chris Cecere. Citigroup sent him to Tokyo to build up the
bank's interest-rates trading business. Cecere had consulted with
Archer, and the pair drew up a short list of Tokyo's best rates traders. Hayes was at the top. Archer asked Hayes if he'd be interested
in a meeting. Sure, he said.

Hayes and Cecere met at the Maduro Bar in the Grand Hyatt
hotel in Roppongi. It was afternoon, and the dark, wood-paneled
jazz bar, which featured live music in the evenings, was mostly
empty. Hayes ordered a very expensive glass of orange juice. Cecere
drank a beer. Unlike when he was feted by Goldman, Hayes felt
comfortable around Cecere. They both dressed haphazardly, showing up at the swank bar in jeans and sneakers. The curly-haired
Cecere sported a bushy, unkempt beard, making his thin face look
fuller than it really was. Five years older than Hayes, Cecere was
brainy without being saddled with social awkwardness. He spoke
in rapid-fire bursts and exuded nervous energy. They each could
tell that the other was a savvy trader, and Hayes later reported to
Tighe that Cecere was probably "the smartest guy I've ever met."
The day after their hotel meeting, Hayes sent a follow-up note to
thank Cecere for his time and to signal that he was open to further
discussions.

At the next meeting, the CEO of Citigroup's Japanese investment banking business, Brian Mccappin, came along. So did
Tighe. They met in the top-floor bar of another hotel, with sweeping views of Tokyo's skyline. Mccappin, an easygoing, karaoke-

loving Brit, quickly determined that Tighe was the key decision maker—and that she liked to drink. Downing glass after glass of expensive wine on Citigroup's tab, Tighe did most of the talking at the meeting. Hayes didn't say much and then after a while abruptly ended the meeting, declaring that he had made other plans.

Hayes and Tighe were both enthusiastic about him joining Citigroup, especially after Cecere introduced his wife, Megan, a pretty American with brown hair and hazel eyes. The two couples got along well. Hayes and Tighe liked the idea of him working for a U.S. bank; that would make it easier for them to one day move to New York. Plus, Hayes had come to distrust UBS after it failed to live up to its compensation promises. It didn't hurt that Citigroup was offering a $3 million cash signing bonus, on top of a generous salary and the expectation of an additional year-end bonus.

It was a ton of money, but Hayes, partly because of his UBS experience, fretted. Citigroup had become the poster boy for an out-of-control banking industry. Through a flurry of aggressive acquisitions, its voracious architect, Sandy Weill, had built the company from a small commercial lender in Baltimore into one of the world's biggest financial supermarkets, offering everything from checking accounts to derivatives, with the primary goal of pushing the bank's share price ever higher. (Weill was famous for interrupting meetings to check Citigroup's stock.) Even as the financial crisis got under way, Citigroup had kept gorging on risky investments until, on the cusp of collapse, it had to be rescued, twice, by the U.S. government, which pumped $45 billion into the bank. An outside monitor had been appointed to reform Citigroup's pay practices; unsurprisingly, the government wasn't wild about the idea of its dependent continuing to lavish employees with huge paychecks. But the bank assured Hayes that the promised paycheck wouldn't present a problem—the government restrictions only applied to the bank's top executives, not rank-and-file employees. (The loop-hole was opened in response to pressure from Citigroup brass, who warned their government overseers that clamping down on big pay packages lower down the food chain would put the bank in an un-tenable competitive position. That wouldn't be in anyone's interest, right?)

When UBS learned that Hayes was again talking with a rival, the bank scrambled to retain him. By then Hayes was up nearly $150 million—and the year was only half over Pieri wrote a de-tailed, five-point e-mail to his higher-ups in Zurich and London listing all of Hayes's attributes. One of them was his "strong con-nections" with Libor setters, which Pieri described as "invaluable." Plus, he was an "excellent risk manager. . . . It's not just the money he can make, it's the money he will save UBS (and has done) in times of crisis," Pieri gushed. "During Lehman, we excelled, whilst other banks lost."

Kengeter got back on the phone to plead with Hayes. Another top executive, a silver-haired Brit named Alex Wilmot-Sitwell, called Hayes from London to sing the trader's praises. Hayes's squawk box was bleating with trading opportunities, and he told Wilmot-Sitwell that he had to run. "You go make your money, that's far more important," Wilmot-Sitwell said.

. . . .

Tighe pushed her fiancé to accept Citigroup's offer. Hayes, how-ever, still felt the tug of loyalty to UBS—not to mention the fear of leaving the comfort of a familiar institution. He turned to Read for counsel. His main advice: If he was seriously considering staying at UBS, make sure he got any commitment for more money etched in stone. "It needs to be in writing and checked by a decent lawyer,"

Read said. Hayes's problem was that, in some situations, he just wasn't good at saying no—an odd characteristic for someone with a well-deserved reputation for being blunt to the point of rudeness. "If I say no to the CEO of the investment bank [Kengeter], that I don't trust his word, then I am looking like a disloyal employee," Hayes reasoned.

"You have two years of broken promises," Read said. "You are not going to risk getting mugged again. The buck stops somewhere at UBS and that person needs to put numbers down in writing."

"I wish you could be my agent and just do the negotiating for me," Hayes mused. Read joked that he'd be happy to do it—for a fee.

While Hayes was a rainmaker, he had made enemies with Darin and others at the bank who resented his pit-bull style and, Hayes suspected, envied his success. Some executives thought it would be best for UBS if Hayes just left. When Darin's boss, Yvan Ducrot, saw the e-mail with Pieri's glowing endorsement, he forwarded it to Darin and Holger Seger. "Could you please give me some balancing points against this bullshit," Ducrot asked.

Darin was happy to help. He responded that colleagues perceived Hayes as an "immature, explosive person regularly losing his temper." He said other banks and brokers were aware of—and often joked about—Hayes's behavior. What's more, his efforts to get his pals in London to goose Libor were well known. "I find it embarrassing when he calls up his mates to ask for favours on high/low fixings," wrote Darin, who of course had been using his power as UBS's yen Libor submitter to benefit his own trading positions. "It makes UBS appear to manipulate others to suit our position; what's the legal risk of UBS asking others to move their fixing?"

Seger was the manager who, years earlier, had pushed Andrew Smith and his rate-submitting crew in Zurich to collaborate more with the bank's swaps traders. "If you want to know the reputation he has in London, let me know," Seger wrote Ducrot. "But trust me, you won't like the sound of it."

The anti-Hayes forces, though, were severely outgunned. With Kengeter and Wilmot-Sitwell on board, UBS agreed to fork over a $500,000 retention payment to Hayes. Kengeter promised him he was looking at a year-end bonus in excess of $3 million. "We agreed he would turn off Citi," Kengeter triumphantly reported to Pieri and others. "I told him . . . that he should get on with making money so I can pay him more."

And, enticing Hayes even further, Darin received a promotion that felt more like a sidelining: He was sent back to Zurich and stripped of his responsibilities as a Libor and Tibor submitter. Those duties would now fall to Hayes's team.

Darin, about to lose his last scrap of leverage over Hayes, figured he might as well make the most of his final days. He knew that Hayes needed Tibor higher, so he decided to lower UBS's submission. The next day, Darin's last in the Tokyo office, Pieri walked over to his desk and asked him to stop playing games. Tibor needed to go up, or at least not go down again. Darin smirked. It was clear to Pieri that Darin had been acting "spitefully" and that he was planning to do it again. Indeed, Darin lowered UBS's Tibor submission. Hayes and Read were chatting when they noticed. "Roger's parting gift," Hayes grumbled. "He tried to screw my position. Next week we have control."

. . . .

That summer in London, UBS's Koutsogiannis, aka Pete the Greek, was finally getting nervous about all the Libor machinations. One day in late June, he messaged a colleague: "JUST BE

CAREFUL DUDE." It wasn't clear exactly what Pete was referring to, and perhaps that was deliberate. But it became obvious when his colleague responded: "I agree we shouldn't have been talking about putting fixings for our positions on public chat. Just wanted to get some transparency though." Their consternation was a sign that word of the CFTC investigation was slowly trickling down through the ranks at UBS and other banks. Like a radar detector on a seemingly deserted stretch of highway, banks' compliance departments were starting to sound the alarm about cops lurking up ahead.

Nobody told Hayes. He had a huge set of trades dependent on Libor rising in mid-July and then falling afterward, and he acted accordingly. The day after Pete the Greek's warning, Guillaume Adolph sent Hayes a message asking for his cell phone number. Hayes provided it, and the Deutsche Bank trader promptly called. Adolph noted their mutual desire to keep six-month Libor as high as possible. He suggested they act together to lift their submissions over the next two weeks, and then lower them later, to suit both of their interests. Hayes, pacing in a small conference room just off UBS's trading floor, agreed. Then his phone died. When he returned to his desk, he realized he wasn't entirely sure what he had just agreed to, thanks to the scratchy cell phone connection and Adolph's heavy accent. He figured he'd just double-check with Adolph that he had understood correctly. So he typed the plan into an instant message.

"Basically I will help you in two weeks time," he wrote to Adolph. "But for the next two weeks, I really, really need you to put six-month higher." After July 14, "I need six-month to crash off, like you."

"Perfect," Adolph confirmed. "That is no problem for me."

Still, Hayes wanted to triple-check that nothing had been lost in translation. He had a ton riding on Libor going higher. "But please move six-month up on Monday," he emphasized.

"Understood." When Hayes kept repeating himself, Adolph drew a line: "OK enough." Hayes still didn't stop. Six minutes later, he was still hammering in the same message. "Enough enough," Adolph demanded.

A few hours later, Hayes figured it would be prudent to provide Adolph a final reminder. "Please make sure you put the six-month up for me," he said.

"Oof," Adolph responded, as if he'd been punched in the gut. "Enough enough."

"I'll shut up now," Hayes said.

Hayes's agreement with Adolph marked the start of what would be his most frenzied effort to get Libor to swing in favorable directions. Over the next few weeks, he bounced from broker to broker, and via them from bank to bank—HSBC, Société Générale, Deutsche Bank—until he ultimately got most of what he wanted. Libor climbed higher, then declined, partly due to luck and partly due to banks honoring his requests.

. . . .

Read showed up in Tokyo for one of his periodic visits to see his lone client. Night after night, he and Hayes went out, accompanied by a local broker named Anthony Hayes. He was nicknamed "Abbo," derogatory slang for "Aboriginal." (The moniker was the result of an incident when the young Australian broker, working at the time in ICAP's Sydney offices, didn't show up for work. It turned out he had decided, without bothering to inform his colleagues, to try his hand at cattle ranching. Not long after his "walkabout," Abbo returned to work at ICAP as if nothing had happened.) Abbo was hulking and while his head was bald, his body was covered with a thick layer of dark hair—no secret to anyone in Tokyo given his tendency to strip naked when drunk. The trio feasted on ribs at Tony Roma's, watched cricket, and hung out at Hayes's local pub. Hayes was comfortable at the Windsor, but it wasn't very exciting for his friends, so one night the three went out looking for something more rambunctious. After several hours of preliminary boozing, around midnight they ended up at Magumbos, the same bar where Tighe and her sister had bumped into Darin a few months earlier. They were drunk, one of them in particular. "Abbo was off his nut," Read recounted. The bar was crowded, and when Abbo vomited, he soaked numerous customers.

When Hayes shared his plans to work with Deutsche Bank and HSBC to massage Libor, Read warned that the three banks shouldn't move their data all at once. "It will look very fishy," he said. "I'd be very careful how you play it" or risk "people questioning you. . . . Don't want you getting into shit."

Hayes was nonchalant. "Don't worry, will stagger the drops . . . us, then Deutsche, then HSBC, then us, then Deutsche, then HSBC," he explained.

Read gave a thumbs-up: "Great, the plan is hatched and sounds sensible."

Read met Alykulov for the first time on the Tokyo trip. The pair had chatted occasionally over the years, but never face-to-face. Now Read happily dispensed detailed advice to the young trader. "You should do just fine," Read said, impressed with his aptitude.

"Yes, unless Tomster makes veins pop up in my head," Alykulov said, before dubbing him "Tomster the Ripper." Alykulov had come to wonder if the volatile Hayes perhaps suffered from some sort of dual-personality disorder.

"Has he left you alone today?" Read asked.

"Mate."

"I take it no then :-)"

Just that morning, Alykulov explained, he had run a trading idea past Hayes, who "told me it was a stupid idea and I should go and die."

"Glad it's not just us he's like that with," Read said. "Tell him to fuck off now and then, usually does the trick."

One warm day in early August, Read and Alykulov were bantering back and forth. Markets were drowsy. Their conversation meandered, turning philosophical. Have you seen the movie *Troy?* Alykulov asked. Read said he had watched the Brad Pitt epic a couple of times. "In one scene," Alykulov said, "young Paris tells his brother that gods must have blessed them with good winds. Remember what Hector replies?" Read couldn't recall the specific scene.

Alykulov paraphrased the line: "Gods of the sea can bless you in the morning and curse you in the afternoon."

"Too true, mate," Read agreed.

• • • •

Hayes was on a globe-hopping work trip, hitting Hong Kong and Singapore before heading to London. Such was his renown in the market that the visit to London triggered gossip among traders that he had returned for good. His next stop was Zurich, to be followed by a vacation in the Avignon region of France with his family, then back to London for a few days before finally returning to Tokyo. His three-week visit to Zurich was mainly to talk to UBS's computer programmers about improving the bank's trading models; the Excel spreadsheets he had built in Tokyo had worked as advertised and now UBS wanted to spread them throughout the organization. But Hayes had another reason for wanting to go to Zurich: He had continued to talk with Cecere and the Citigroup guys. Still on the fence, he hoped that visiting the UBS mother ship might help him make up his mind.

Before he arrived, Hayes was included on an e-mail chain that should have worried him. UBS executives wanted to hold a meeting about their Libor and Tibor settings in Tokyo. "There is increased scrutiny of how fixings are being done," a bank executive, Yugo Matsumoto, wrote to Hayes, Pieri, and others. "As a result we need to be sure internally that our fixing process is robust and explainable . . . [and that] we are above reproach." Hayes wrote back saying he was confused about the purpose of the meeting. Matsumoto told him not to worry—just explain how the process works and everything would be fine. Hayes accepted that, and moved on.

Later, ensconced at UBS's offices in the pastureland outside Zurich, Hayes shot off a casual e-mail to Pieri about his efforts to get Libor moved. The plan was nothing unusual, but in Tokyo, Hayes and Pieri communicated in person, not over e-mail. Hayes was outside getting some fresh air when his cell phone rang. Pieri asked if Hayes was in the office; Hayes said no. "Don't ever send me an e-mail like that again," Pieri snarled. "I could lose my job over that." Stunned, Hayes promised not to put it in writing again.*

Hayes had never before been to UBS's Zurich offices, and he was shocked by the different culture there. It wasn't just the pastoral setting. Hayes ate in a luxurious corporate dining room where waiters served three-course lunches paired with wine. It was a throwback to a bygone era, one in which well-appointed, sit-down

---

* When Hayes returned to Tokyo a few weeks later, Pieri apologized for the outburst. He said he had overreacted to the mounting concern inside UBS about the U.S. investigations into the dollar version of Libor. "The message I got was not to stop doing it, it was to stop e-mailing about it," Hayes would say.

meals, often enjoyed in private clubs and always featuring generous servings of wine and brandy, were deeply embedded in the fabric of banking. The custom struck Hayes—accustomed to wolfing down lunch at his desk, if he ate at all—as over-the-top, especially for a bank struggling to stay afloat in the aftermath of a financial crisis. (The opulence was especially aggravating because UBS at the time was trying to phase out his housing allowance in Tokyo.) More personally, some of the Zurich traders treated him like an outcast, presumably a product of his frosty relationship with Ducrot and Darin's team. Back in Tokyo in late August, he told Tighe he'd felt like a leper, not a star, and for days he ranted about how UBS wasn't looking out for him, even though he was devoting his life to the firm.

As if sensing the shifting dynamics, Citigroup delivered a sweetened offer. To Tighe, the decision seemed easy: Go to Citigroup. But Hayes agonized. He kept waking his fiancée in the middle of the night to tell her about nightmares he was having about betraying Pieri. At lunchtime one day, he showed up unannounced at Tighe's law firm. As they walked in circles around the building's small internal courtyard, Hayes proclaimed, "I don't think I can do it."

"That doesn't make any sense," Tighe said, exasperated. "You're supposed to be the logical one!" Finally she gave him an order: Either accept Citigroup's offer or stop whining about how UBS was mistreating him.

That did it. Hayes handed in his resignation to UBS on September 3. Pieri refused to accept it and sent him home for the next two days. Then he trudged over to Alykulov, put his hands on the youngster's shoulders, and instructed him to stop building up positions in any trades that involved Hayes; Alykulov quickly figured out what had happened. (Brokers were told Hayes was out sick.)

The Swiss bank made a last-ditch effort to keep him. UBS executives noted that Hayes had raked in another $20 million since the $500,000 retention payment in June—bringing his total earnings for the bank to about $280 million over a three-year period. But it was too late—Hayes had already signed a contract with Citigroup, giving him an annual salary of 23.9 million yen (about $240,000) and an up-front cash signing bonus of 292 million yen ($2.9 million), plus a guaranteed 188 million yen ($1.9 million) to compensate for future payments he was forfeiting by leaving UBS.

Hayes left with plenty of trepidation. Some of his interactions with brokers made him nervous, especially those involving switch trades. And then there was the collusive arrangement with Adolph. Now his phone, e-mail, and instant-message records were sitting at a bank that presumably was furious with him for defecting. Hayes wondered whether that could come back to bite him.

As Hayes left, UBS shifted responsibility for handling Libor submissions away from traders and clarified that such submissions should no longer be based on factors like trading positions or brokers. In fact, some at UBS doubted whether it made sense for the bank to even remain involved with Libor. Recent public scrutiny "leads to a higher regulatory risk and reputation risk and we believe it would be worth for senior management to consider the ongoing benefit of being a Libor contributor bank," read an internal memo written two weeks before Hayes left. The qualms would prove prescient, but they went unheeded.

Word of Hayes's defection quickly spread. "This will be a hit to morale and we run a risk that other members of the team may be vulnerable," a morose Pieri warned colleagues. Another UBS executive informed colleagues that they would need to rein in their expectations for the performance of Hayes's former rates trading team. "Previously we would be trying to make $125m+ with Tom in the seat," the executive wrote. The new forecast was for roughly $60 million.

To comply with the terms of his contract at UBS, Hayes had to take a few months off before he was allowed to start at Citigroup. Such mandatory breaks were known in the industry as "gardening leave," because they gave transitioning employees time to putter around in their gardens. Hayes wasn't much of a gardener. But he had plenty of other business to attend to.

CHAPTER 12

In the Flag Room

In March 2009, six months before Hayes signed his contract with Citigroup, a letter postmarked Washington arrived at the bank's Canary Wharf skyscraper in London. The letter was from the CFTC, and it posed a series of rudimentary questions: How did Libor work? How did banks figure out the data they submitted every day? Who exactly came up with the estimates? Could someone please explain the whole process? It was a remarkable series of questions for an agency whose investigators had spent much of the past year looking into the benchmark. Somehow, the CFTC still lacked a basic understanding of how banks set Libor.

Citigroup was inclined to be helpful. After all, having doled out $45 billion in taxpayer aid, the U.S. government controlled 36 percent of the company. And the CFTC, for years an afterthought among Washington's regulatory apparatus, seemed destined for more power with a Democrat, Barack Obama, now in the White House.

The CFTC's request for information wound its way through Citigroup's byzantine organization before finally landing on the desk of Andrew Thursfield—the very man who had repeatedly insisted that Libor was as robust as could be. The Brit had spent his entire career working in the bowels of Citigroup, which he joined as a trainee in 1988. His job at the moment was running the bank's treasury desk in London. His team, squished into a corner of a vast trading floor on the second floor of the Canary Wharf tower, was responsible for figuring out how money should be most efficiently allocated and transmitted among the bank's appendages in more than one hundred countries, arranging for one Citigroup unit to transfer money to another. In essence, it acted as a bank within the bank. Thursfield also continued to manage the bank's Libor submissions, and as Citigroup's representative on the FXMMC that oversaw the rate, he was well situated to help the CFTC with its queries.

In retrospect, the manipulation at the heart of the Libor scandal was hard to miss. But, at least to outsiders, it wasn't so obvious at the time. The organizations closest to Libor, namely the BBA and the banks, had done everything in their power to hide the rate's deep problems. The daily moves in Libor were not so massive as to suggest tampering. They also were not consistently in one direction; some days traders yanked it higher, other days they shoved it lower. The definition of Libor, and the way that definition was interpreted, was fuzzy—not to mention the fact that banks didn't have rules about how their employees should set the rate and no regulator was responsible for overseeing it. And recognizing the bogus switch trades was nearly impossible to outsiders, given the tens of thousands of transactions taking place every day. Deliberately or not, Hayes and others had taken advantage of those circumstances and, absent ironclad evidence of wrongdoing, they were a bit like athletes whose performance notably improves even as they age. Are their skills the result of harder work, greater luck, or something illicit? And unlike athletes, traders' feats didn't take place on a field and weren't televised. They were hidden deep inside vast financial institutions.

Thursfield was supposed to help the CFTC explore those inner recesses. He crafted an eighteen-page PowerPoint slide show, defining Libor and detailing the legitimate sources of information banks looked to as they came up with their Libor estimates each day. One section walked the CFTC officials through "a typical day" for an interest-rate trader, the type of person who not only was involved in the Libor-setting process but also tended to have lots to gain or lose based on the outcome.

In another slide, Thursfield took a computer screenshot that showed where several brokerage firms—ICAP, Tullett Prebon, and Tradition—were estimating, or "suggesting," Libor would land on a random day. He noted in the presentation that such broker run-throughs were a source of "market color" that Citigroup sometimes relied on to decide on its Libor submissions.

That was an understatement. One of the bank's Libor submitters, Laurence Porter, often called a buddy at ICAP and asked him where yen Libor was likely to end up; he then used that figure as the basis for Citigroup's submission. The forty-three-year-old Porter had been involved with Libor since the 1990s, and he was still in charge when he met Burak Celtik, a graduate trainee cycling through various departments. Porter took Celtik under his wing. By 2008 he had handed over many of his Libor-submitting duties, including the yen version, to his mentee. One of his first instructions was for Celtik to get signed up for Colin Goodman's run-throughs. The inexperienced Celtik—whose name was pronounced CHEL-tick, even though everyone in London insisted on pronouncing it like the Boston basketball team—promptly started copying the run-throughs verbatim, errors and all. To anyone paying attention—and not many people were—it was an unequivocal sign of Libor's malleability.

There was another feature of the Libor-submitting process that Thursfield didn't mention to the CFTC: Banks were taking into account their trading positions when deciding where to pin Libor. Thursfield knew this was happening. For example, in September 2007, he had multiple conversations with a Citigroup manager named Scott Bere, who asked Thursfield to push Libor lower. The e-mails made clear that the bank's trading positions were one of the factors they used to determine their data. Thursfield promised Bere that he'd pressure brokers accordingly.* Now, two years later, Thursfield didn't see a need to trouble the CFTC with such technicalities.

. . . .

Short and skinny with a long, pointy nose, Gary Gensler grew up in a working-class neighborhood in Baltimore. His father, Sam, was the son of Eastern European immigrants and founded a company that supplied cigarette dispensers and pinball machines to Baltimore's plentiful bars. Sometimes Gensler and his identical twin, Robert, accompanied their father on sales and maintenance calls. They also tagged along when Sam, a steadfast Democrat, drove up to Annapolis to lobby state legislators about regulations related to the vending machine industry. It was Gensler's first taste of politics, and he liked it.

The Gensler twins were determined to escape the blue-collar world. They were both math whizzes and attended the University

---

* Thursfield would later say he didn't realize that Bere wanted Libor moved to benefit the bank's trading positions.

of Pennsylvania together. Gary was the coxswain on the crew team, a role that required him to get his weight down to a rail-thin 112 pounds—which he did, quickly, a sign of the almost reckless intensity and commitment that would mark his career to come. After graduating, he joined Goldman Sachs at age twenty-one and shot up through the ranks. At thirty, he became the firm's youngest-ever partner. A Goldman partnership was one of the most coveted distinctions on all of Wall Street—something that people typically spent decades striving for and often failing to achieve—not to mention the ticket to vast riches. Gensler had managed it without seeming to break a sweat. His brother followed a similar path to wealth, becoming a portfolio manager at T. Rowe Price, the giant mutual fund company headquartered in Baltimore. Soon he emerged as a star stock-picker, someone who seemed to have an innate knack for buying shares before they gained value and dumping them before they cratered. He became a frequent talking head on business news channels. Sometimes when Robert appeared on CNBC, his twin's colleagues would wonder what on earth Gary was doing on TV blabbing about the shares of some random company.

After eighteen years at Goldman, Gensler was set for life, with a reported net worth of about $60 million. He left to pursue a career in public service—a proud if arguably self-serving tradition among partners at the Wall Street firm. Another Goldman executive, Robert Rubin, had been tapped by Bill Clinton to become the U.S. Treasury secretary, and Gensler moved to Washington to work for him as an undersecretary. Rubin presided over an unprecedented period of economic growth—and, with the White House's support, the dismantling of much of the bank-regulatory apparatus that had been erected to prevent a repeat of the Great Depression. Gensler was an enthusiastic advocate of loosening what the Clinton Democrats—along with much of the Republican Party—argued was an antiquated, counterproductive system of overseeing things like derivatives and the energy markets. Those who interfered with their antiregulatory campaign—such as Brooksley Born, the CFTC chairman who thought her regulatory agency should actually do some regulating—were sidelined or forced out. When Republicans took over Washington in the 2000s, Gensler found ways to keep his public profile alive, writing a book about the danger of falling for the allure of star mutual fund managers. (He and Robert appeared on public television to debate the topic.) In his spare time, Gensler climbed mountains and ran several marathons, as well as a fifty-miler when he turned fifty.

In 2008, Gensler took advantage of the connections he'd forged at Goldman and in Washington and acted as the Obama campaign's unofficial liaison to Wall Street. It wasn't exactly an awe-inspiring position. Once, he gathered the CEOs of several big banks in a private room at the Willard hotel, across the street from the Treasury Department and a stone's throw from the White House, to explain to them why supporting Obama was in their best interests. Lloyd Blankfein, who as Goldman's CEO was the unofficial King of Wall Street, showed up a little early. As soon as Gensler arrived, Blankfein walked up to say hello—and goodbye. "I don't think I will be able to stick around," he said. Gensler, sensitive to his standing with powerful people, took it as a slight.

Obama soon rewarded Gensler for his support, nominating him to become the chairman of the CFTC—the same role that Born had stepped down from a decade earlier after pressure from Treasury officials including Gensler. By now Rubin's breed of Wall Street–loving Democrats had fallen out of favor amid a financial crisis. Gensler's nomination encountered stiff resistance from liberal senators. "At this moment in our history, we need an independent leader who will help create a new culture in the financial marketplace and move us away from the greed, recklessness, and illegal behavior which has caused so much harm to our economy," Senator Bernie Sanders said as he announced his intention to block Gensler's appointment.

Gensler, fifty-one at the time, knew what he had to do: Cleanse himself of his now-toxic centrist credentials. He launched an offensive to convince his doubters that, if confirmed, he would embrace a tough-on-Wall-Street approach, transforming the sleepy CFTC into a force to be reckoned with. He wowed one critic at a big public-interest group by conceding that he had erred in the past with his laissez-faire views—a rare acknowledgment of screwing up from a public official. The about-face worked. The Senate voted to confirm Gensler as CFTC chairman, and he started the job on May 26, 2009.

. . . .

Thomas Youle and his fellow graduate student Illenin Kondo had spent the day and now much of the night in a cramped office they shared at the University of Minnesota, where they were both pursuing doctorates in industrial organization, a branch of economics. All day they had been sifting through financial data in between bantering about economics and current events. Now the two night owls walked home to the house they shared in Dinkytown, across the Mississippi River from the economics department. Youle loved walking over the 10th Avenue Bridge, inspired by the wide river and the wider sky. In the winter, when the temperature sometimes dipped to minus 40 degrees, Youle would still trudge across, sometimes moving backward to shield his thin, boyish face from the bitter wind. On this May night, the dark brown river was barely visible, though Youle could hear it churning below.

Like Gensler a Maryland native and math whiz, Youle had always wanted to be a professor. But now that he was on that career path, he was struggling mightily to choose a topic for his doctoral thesis, a subject to which he would devote the next couple of years—if not more—of his life researching. His initial idea had been to look at competition in the Texas electricity markets. His thesis adviser, an economist named Patrick Bajari, told him that sounded dull. How about pursuing something related to banking? The industry was in the throes of a nasty crisis—surely there were sexy topics to explore. So Youle, not knowing where to begin, embarked on a needle-in-a-haystack search for a topic. Every federally regulated bank periodically has to fill out something known as a "call report," jammed with heaps of granular data about all aspects of its balance sheet. The call reports were publicly available, but finding anything in them was next to impossible for a layperson. Youle found a way to download, in bulk, every big bank's data. He spent the next several months aimlessly wandering through the numbers. When he occasionally encountered something that sounded interesting, he bounced it off another grad student, Connan Snider, a couple of years ahead of him. Snider wasn't shy about telling Youle that his ideas were lame, which they generally were. Youle did, however, unearth some interesting nuggets. For example, he learned that some of the biggest American banks, such as Citigroup and J.P. Morgan Chase, were stuffed with trillions and trillions of dollars of derivatives linked to interest rates, particularly Libor. Youle socked that knowledge away and kept hunting.

As Youle and Kondo walked across the bridge, their conversation turned to Libor. The apparent problems with the rate—the fact that banks seemed to be deliberately understating their borrowing costs—had been in the news, and one of Bajari's colleagues had pursued preliminary research into the area. Suddenly, in Youle's mind, something clicked. It was so simple: Libor was set by banks that—he knew from the call reports—were sitting on mountains of derivatives that hinged on Libor. Was it possible that what everyone had assumed was the reason for the skewing—banks' efforts to trick the public into thinking their funding costs were lower, and the institutions were healthier, than they really were—was only part of the story?

The next day, Youle told Snider about his eureka moment. Could this work as a thesis topic? For once, Snider smiled. "Now *that* is a good idea!" he exclaimed. The two started brainstorming about statistical methods he could use to prove that banks were messing with Libor to benefit their portfolios of interest-rate derivatives. The more they talked, the more excited they became. Snider offered to work with Youle on the project; Youle said yes. Then they explained their idea to Bajari. He, too, was pumped. It meshed nicely with his area of expertise: ways to prove whether firms were operating collusively.

Now the question became how to go about proving their hypothesis. Snider and Youle spent an afternoon toying around with a primitive game-theory model. Then they looked at alternative data sources on banks' borrowing costs to gauge Libor's accuracy—similar to the methodology that Mollenkamp and Whitehouse had used in their *Journal* piece a year earlier. Over the following weeks, they dug through research about how different prices for medical care altered consumers' behavior, creating a phenomenon known as bunching in which people clustered around certain price points. Drawing on that research, they devised several categories for Libor submissions: highest, lowest, and a few middle tiers. Youle spent some time working in the offices of the Federal Reserve Bank of Minneapolis, which was equipped with a nearly magical tool: a Bloomberg computer terminal crammed with just about every bit of financial data imaginable. After he downloaded a couple of years' worth of Libor submissions for dozens of banks, across a half-dozen currencies and many different time periods, Youle and Snider laboriously entered the data into a spreadsheet and then divided the submissions into the high, low, and middle categories. If nothing weird was going on, they figured, the submissions should have been evenly spread, more or less, across all the categories.

But when they plotted the data on a chart, the submissions appeared clustered around the fringes of the highest and lowest categories. Because of the way Libor was calculated—with the highest and lowest submissions thrown out, and the rest averaged—banks that wanted to move the rate would have had to aim for the highest or lowest possible levels without being knocked out of the average. When the two students looked at the chart, the bunching phenomenon jumped out at them.

This, they realized, wasn't the behavior of banks trying to mask their rising borrowing costs by submitting artificially low Libor data. It was the behavior of banks trying to push the benchmark in very specific directions.

"Holy shit, this is great!" Bajari blurted when Youle and Snider briefed him. He instructed them to write a paper that could be published quickly—hardly the norm in an academic field where peer-reviewed articles can languish for years. "People are going to steal this idea," he warned. His students thought Bajari seemed to be thinking more like a scoop-hungry journalist than a perfectionist academic.

About six months later (quick in academia), after countless all-nighters and considerable hounding from the impatient Bajari, Youle and Snider completed a draft of their article. It ran thirty pages, including several pages of charts attached at the end, and was titled: "Does the Libor reflect banks' borrowing costs?" They noted the consensus view—held by everyone from the *Journal* to the CFTC—that Libor manipulation appeared to be motivated by lowballing. Their research, they wrote, "points to a more fundamental source, namely that bank portfolio exposure to the Libor give them incentives to push the rate in a direction favorable to these positions." The technical language masked the importance of what they had found.

They submitted the paper to a bunch of academic journals. An editor at the *Journal of Finance,* the field's foremost publication, was among those who shot it down. "This is ridiculous," the editor huffed. "Even if it's true, who would care?"

Nobody would publish it.

· · · ·

Gensler hit the CFTC like a hurricane. He was brilliant, and he knew it, accustomed to always being the smartest guy in the room. And he was blunt, sometimes brutally so. He could be intimidating, partly because of his demeanor (anyone who interpreted his tendency to preside over meetings while slouched in a chair with his loafers off as a sign he was laid-back was in for an unpleasant surprise) and partly because of the sheer weight of financial expertise he was carrying around in his brain. "I don't think you know what you're doing" was a common Gensler refrain if he took issue with an employee's work. His no-holds-barred approach might work on a Goldman Sachs trading floor, but it was jarring inside a staid government agency staffed by not-very-well-paid civil servants. He sowed discord with some of his fellow commissioners, threatening to plant negative stories about them in the media if they didn't vote the way he wanted them to.

Gensler also had a softer side. His wife, Francesca Danieli, an artist, had died of breast cancer in 2006 at age fifty-two, and the widower was deeply devoted to his three daughters. He maintained his home in Baltimore and commuted to Washington every day, taking the 7 A.M. train there and the 7 P.M. one home. If his youngest daughter needed help with her homework, Gensler would pack his briefcase and catch an earlier train home. After the girls went to bed, he would pick up where he'd left off at the office. Colleagues routinely fielded his phone calls after 11 P.M.

Many employees gradually warmed to Gensler, even if they detested his pit-bull personality. Sure, he was tough, but his goal of trying to empower what had been a federal backwater was worthy. While many regulatory agencies had relied on narrow, conservative interpretations of their responsibilities in order to avoid wading into controversial territory, Gensler encouraged staff to search widely for new areas in which they could assert their authority. One day that spring, Stephen Obie briefed Gensler on the cases that the enforcement division was working on. Included in the rundown was the Libor investigation. Gensler liked what he heard.

. . . .

In an office park adjacent to San Francisco International Airport, two attorneys, Joseph Cotchett and Nanci Nishimura, had been toiling on a lawsuit against some of the world's biggest banks. Brash, cocky, and hard of hearing, with his thinning white hair combed straight back, Cotchett had been a Special Forces paratrooper after he graduated from college with an engineering degree in 1960. Then he became a lawyer—a flamboyant one. He dressed in gaudy suits. He once showed up in a London criminal court as a spectator and loudly critiqued the prosecutor's tactics, earning a stern rebuke from the white-wigged judge. His drink of choice was red wine, with several ice cubes sloshing around in the glass. His decaying marriage had become fodder for Bay Area tabloids, which regaled readers with rumors about Cotchett's alleged proclivity for parading around his house naked in the presence of his teenage daughters. (Cotchett denied those allegations.) But he was one of the country's best-known trial lawyers, a heavyweight Democratic donor who had taken cases to the Supreme Court. Cotchett and Nishimura had spent years consumed with their case against banks. It claimed that U.S. towns and cities, including Los Angeles, had bought derivatives designed to protect them against big swings in interest rates but that banks had engaged in anticompetitive practices to steer municipalities to derivatives that—no surprise—benefited those banks (or their employees or friends). Cotchett was enraged by the manner in which the banks had exploited unsophisticated customers, but it also made his mouth water: His firm pocketed a boatload of fees when lawsuits like this won in court or, as more often happened, yielded giant settlements with deep-pocketed defendants eager to avoid the time-consuming and potentially embarrassing discovery process.

In scouring clients' derivatives contracts as part of that lawsuit, Nishimura had repeatedly encountered Libor (it was embedded in many of the derivatives). Now, in spring 2009, she started seeing Libor pop up in occasional stories in the financial media. The government was clearly sniffing around, and Nishimura had a pleasing thought: If Libor was manipulated, up or down, it almost certainly had an impact on her municipal clients. Some of them had derivatives that were supposed to pay out if Libor moved higher; others had the opposite positions. Either way, this looked like easy money. "This could be a huge case," she told Cotchett, who didn't disagree. Nishimura started canvassing clients to see if they'd be interested in exploring a class-action lawsuit against the banks for manipulating Libor. It wasn't a hard sell. The deepening recession had caused tax revenues to dry up all over the country, and cities and public entities, like the University of California system, were eager to find ways to refill their coffers. Going after the banks seemed more than fair, considering the disproportionate role they'd played in capsizing the American economy.

The city of Houston, already a plaintiff in the derivatives case, was one of the first to sign up to join a Libor suit; its mayor issued a press release declaring that it wasn't a question of whether the city was owed money by the banks for stiffing them on Libor, but how much the city was due. Louisiana's attorney general invited Nishimura to make a presentation to state officials. She flew to New Orleans, where a lawyer picked her up at the airport and drove her the seventy miles to Baton Rouge. As they passed beat-up pickup trucks with gun racks and Confederate flag bumper stickers, the petite, well-dressed Asian-American woman felt out of place. But by the time Nishimura's escort led her into Louisiana's thirty-four-story art deco capitol building, she had managed to calm her nerves. She addressed a roomful of angry, and surprisingly smart, finance officials from around the state. They told her that many struggling parishes had purchased derivatives that, for one reason or another, weren't delivering the anticipated financial rewards. Few of the officials had read the contracts' details. Most didn't know what Libor was. A few assumed it was an official interest rate set by a British government agency. None of them had heard of the BBA.

. . . .

Once a year, many of the world's leading financial regulators gathered at a sprawling estate in the English countryside. About two hours by car outside London, Wiston House was built in the late sixteenth century on a property that spanned six thousand acres of rolling hills and farmland. The majestic stone mansion was straight out of *Downton Abbey*. Wiston House now served as an elaborate conference center, and a British government agency charged with organizing meetings to enhance global unity was one of the main outfits that used the space. Among its events was the annual regulatory shindig.

Gretchen Lowe was unhappy when she arrived. Back in Washington, her bosses, McGonagle and Obie, had been growing antsy. The Libor investigation appeared dormant. Part of the problem was the vague, open-ended questions the CFTC had sent out to banks and the BBA. Plus, the initial round of queries was voluntary—was it really a surprise that few banks had bothered to respond? But an equally severe problem was that the FSA seemed to be taking its sweet time forwarding the Americans' requests for information to London-headquartered institutions. That was playing right into the hands of the industry, which was hoping the CFTC would find something better to do with its time. The FSA's apathetic attitude seemed to border on passive-aggressive.

At Wiston House, Lowe bumped into FSA enforcement honcho Margaret Cole. Lowe pulled her aside and, doing her best to remain diplomatic, explained that the CFTC was treating the case as one of its highest priorities. She confided that the newly arrived Gensler was heaping pressure on his staff to find ways to overcome the agency's weak reputation. Lowe told Cole that she hoped the FSA would take the inquiries seriously. At the end of the chat, Lowe was left wondering whether Cole cared.

. . . .

Hayes, in addition to having neither tucked in his shirt nor shaved, was damp when he arrived at Citigroup's London headquarters on a Thursday in October 2009. The driving rain had rendered umbrellas useless, and he was running late. That's what a month of gardening leave will do to you, he had thought to himself when he realized that he had misremembered the start time of the day's first meeting.

Citigroup wasn't his employer yet. He technically remained on UBS's payroll, and he wasn't supposed to be doing any work—certainly not interacting with his new company—until his compulsory three-month hiatus ran its course. The only reason he was even at Citigroup's offices that morning was that he happened to be in London. Back in Tokyo, Hayes's eyesight had been bothering him for a while. Now that he had a few months off, he checked himself into London's Moorfields Eye Hospital for laser surgery. He also was starting to scout for houses that he and Tighe potentially could buy in his hometown of Winchester. When he'd mentioned to his soon-to-be Citigroup colleagues that he'd be in England, they suggested he stop by for a visit. So here, a bit soaked, he was.

Hayes was escorted across the bank's sprawling second-floor trading room, buzzing with more than five hundred traders and salesmen, each with as many as eight computer monitors, multiple phones, and squawk boxes. He felt at home. In a far corner, Hayes reached his destination: the small group of interest-rate traders and Libor submitters led by Andrew Thursfield. By now it was nearly 10 A.M., half an hour after Hayes was scheduled to meet with Citigroup's fastidious Libor man. "Oh yeah, sorry I'm late," Hayes said nonchalantly. "I thought it started at ten o'clock." Thursfield noticed that the disheveled trader was carrying a printout of his schedule that clearly listed the appointment time as nine thirty.

Thursfield didn't even understand why he was supposed to

meet this guy. Hayes wasn't based in London. He wouldn't be working in Thursfield's section of the bank. He wasn't even employed by Citigroup yet. Thursfield introduced himself, explaining that, among other things, his desk's duties included submitting Citigroup's Libor data. Hayes didn't miss a beat: "Great, you can help us out with Libor," he said. Thursfield looked taken aback but didn't say anything. Hayes thought he seemed a bit stuck-up. The pair walked up and down rows of surrounding desks, with Thursfield introducing him to traders and Hayes making snide comments about the bank's antiquated phone systems. When they circled back to Thursfield's desk, Hayes launched into a monologue about his dominant position in the Japanese market, where he said he was responsible for 40 percent of all interest-rates trades, and his strong relationships with Libor submitters and traders at other banks. He talked about how he routinely asked them to move their submissions to suit his trading positions. He mentioned, a couple of times, the killing that UBS had made after Gollum alerted him to Deutsche Bank's plans to slash its Libor submission.

Thursfield was stunned. Of course, he knew a lot of this was happening in the market. But especially lately, with U.S. regulators showing a keen interest in Libor, he figured all banks, not just Citigroup, were trying to steer clear of such machinations. He, for one, was trying to preside over a squeaky-clean process. His team, in particular Laurence Porter, canvassed other parts of the bank and various market participants to try to ascertain exactly what it was costing Citigroup to borrow money from other banks. Sometimes Porter came up with bad information, but at least he was diligent. And in any case, Hayes's boastfulness offended Thursfield. It seemed impolitic to talk so openly about the dirty business of moving Libor to benefit your bank's trading positions.

The next day, Thursfield and another executive, Steve Compton, spoke on the phone. Compton asked what he had thought of Hayes. Thursfield paused, considering how to word his response. Normally, he would try to adhere to British etiquette and cushion any caustic comments with understatement.* But he had found Hayes too objectionable to be polite. He was "unimpressive" and "ultra-arrogant," Thursfield replied, describing how he openly talked about getting information from other traders. Compton asked if he got the impression that Hayes planned to continue such practices at Citigroup. Absolutely, Thursfield said, appalled. "I mean, we just paid another $75,000 bill to the lawyer this week for the work they're doing on the CFTC investigation. So, that side of things, I mean it obviously happens, and you know it's all subtleties about it." Based on his short visit with Hayes, subtlety didn't seem to be his strong suit.

"I'm a bit nervous about anyone that kind of really touts the fact so openly that they are sort of 40 percent of the market," Compton agreed. "I don't think it's ever a good thing to be 40 percent of the market."

But there wasn't much either man could do about it. Chris Cecere, who had hired Hayes, had some formidable allies inside the bank. He'd been recruited by a fellow Lehman Brothers veteran named Andrew Morton, who had wisely resigned from the Wall Street firm a week before it filed for bankruptcy protection. Now Morton was Citigroup's head of interest-rate trading—a powerful role, multiple rungs above Thursfield. (Morton, one of those who interviewed Hayes before Citigroup signed him, was a minor legend on Wall Street. As an academic in the 1980s,

---

* Years later, Thursfield would employ textbook restraint when he said of Hayes: "It would be fair to say that I did not form a high opinion of this individual."

he had helped devise a model to value obscure interest-rate derivatives. The system was widely adopted by bank traders and came to be known as the Heath-Jarrow-Morton framework.) At Citigroup, Morton's mandate was to revitalize what had been a key profit engine in its investment banking division. And the way to do that, at least as far as he was concerned, was to pump lots of money into hiring hotshot traders with hearty appetites for risk. There was no way Thursfield was about to pick a fight with Morton or one of his lieutenants to protest them hiring Hayes.

But Thursfield had other weapons in his arsenal—namely, letting everyone know just how much he disliked the new trader. Later that day, in a phone call with a Citigroup trader in New York named Mark Smith, Thursfield derided Hayes as an "absolute idiot." When Smith countered that he'd heard good things about him, Thursfield went on a tirade. "He came across as a total wide boy," he said, using British slang that loosely translates as a sleazy wheeler-dealer. "He was basically saying he made half his money just on finding out what Deutsche were doing on their fixings 'cause it was his best mate around there. And he was quite open about that."

"Sounds a bit risky," Smith said, "given we're being investigated."

"I find it amazing that if he was being that blatant, whether it be by phone or by e-mail or anything, that it's not gonna get picked up," Thursfield ranted. Surely, he said, "UBS will be supplying information to the CFTC."

It didn't improve Thursfield's mood that a rumor was circulating that the bailed-out bank had agreed to pay Hayes an astronomical bonus. The figure Thursfield had heard was $6 million. "He is probably telling everyone," Smith grumbled.

· · · ·

While Hayes was rubbing people the wrong way at Citigroup, Obie was also in London. He was there for a regulatory conference being held in the luxurious Royal Garden Hotel in Kensington. On the conference's first day, he was a speaker on a panel with his former boss at the CFTC, Gregory Mocek. Bespectacled and balding, with a penetrating blue-eyed stare, Mocek had run the agency's enforcement division during the Bush administration, the period in which Obie pursued some of his career-defining energy cases. The Louisiana native, a passionate duck hunter, was now in private practice in Washington, tasked with helping clients defuse CFTC investigations. One of his marquee clients was Barclays.

That evening, Mocek and Obie caught up over drinks. They met in a private lounge at the Grosvenor House hotel, across the street from Hyde Park and a short walk from the conference venue. Mocek, exhausted, stretched out on an overstuffed red sofa. He had a surprising message: Barclays wanted to meet with Obie as soon as possible. Obie couldn't help feeling suspicious—after all, most banks had been doing everything possible to avoid assisting the CFTC. Why did Barclays suddenly perceive it as beneficial to change tack? Mocek explained that the bank had stumbled upon some important new Libor evidence.

A day or two later, Obie showed up at the FSA's headquarters, considered neutral ground, to meet with Mocek and the Barclays officials. In a large, glass-walled room, Mocek explained that the bank had been sifting through more than 22 million e-mail records, audio files, and other documents, in the process racking up tens of millions of dollars of legal and other fees (a number that, presumably to Mocek's delight, was growing by the day). Mocek fiddled with a computer, and then the scratchy sound of two men with thick British accents played over the room's speaker system. The voices, Mocek explained, belonged to a Barclays trader and his manager; the recording was from the previous fall, at the peak of the financial crisis. The two men were debating whether to move Libor lower to avoid unwanted public scrutiny. The trader, who was in charge of the bank's Libor submissions, resisted, fearing such a move would breach BBA rules. His manager said they didn't have a choice—the order to reduce Libor was coming straight from executives at the bank, who in turn had received the instructions from someone senior at the Bank of England. This was a bombshell: Not only were bankers on tape talking about gaming their Libor data, but they were doing so at the behest of a central banker! As the recordings played, Obie's adrenaline surged. Then Mocek showed some follow-up e-mails that the unhappy Libor submitter had sent to his manager and the bank's compliance department, in which he reiterated how uncomfortable he was with the orders he was receiving. Barclays promised to provide all the material in duplicate to any regulator who wanted it. Finally, Obie thought, a breakthrough!

That evening, he and Cole met for a previously scheduled dinner at a riverside restaurant with views of Tower Bridge and the City's distinctly shaped skyscrapers, their lights twinkling in the damp night. The two regulators discussed the stunning materials Barclays had just disclosed. Cole's skepticism about the Libor investigation seemed to have faded. Obie managed to suppress a glib smile.

· · · ·

Back in Washington, Obie received a package containing a compact disk with the audio files and other materials that Mocek had disclosed in London. By now, bits of evidence had been trickling in for a few months from banks that seemed to be hoping that they could get the CFTC off their backs by providing convoluted spreadsheets and copies of mostly innocuous e-mails and internal chat sessions. Occasionally, the team stumbled across something shiny, such as a trader making a potentially incriminating remark. Then Lowe and her teammates would start searching for that trader's name in other places. Most of the time, though, they found nothing.

The Barclays package was different. Toting the CD, Obie raced up to Gensler's suite, two floors above the enforcement staff's seventh-floor warren. "I've got something you need to see," he told Gensler. The agency chief didn't use a computer, so they walked out to his assistant's desk. Obie ducked behind the desk, slid the CD into the computer, then double-clicked one of the audio files. The scratchy sound of cockney-accented bankers filled the windowless foyer.

At first, Gensler didn't say anything, processing what he had just heard. Then he asked: "If a central bank official is directing this, is it illegal?"

"That would be a creative defense," Obie replied. He was surprised by Gensler's muted reaction. He didn't really know what he'd expected—it's not as if the no-nonsense multimillionaire was going to start jumping up and down in excitement. But Gensler soon became more enthusiastic. At the next meeting of the agency's five commissioners, Obie played a few of the Barclays recordings, not just the one with the Bank of England reference but also other snippets of banter, cursing, and bluster. As he did so, Gensler kept interrupting. "Wait, listen to this part!" he blurted before especially juicy bits. The recordings had their intended effect: When Obie finished, the room was silent except for the soft hum of a ventilation system and the sound of one commissioner chuckling in disbelief.

• • • •

Hayes whiled away the remainder of his gardening leave in Tokyo. He caught up on British TV programs and made lots of sausages. He slept in. He paid frequent visits to a local bowling alley, where he and Nigel Delmar tried to improve their mediocre games. He celebrated his thirtieth birthday in October at a party Tighe threw at a fancy Mediterranean restaurant called Cicada. Cecere and his wife came; Brian Mccappin, eager to impress his new hire, made an appearance. Hayes immersed himself in planning his wedding, scheduled for September 2010.

And he contacted Read with an unusual request. He planned to be in London for the holidays and was looking for a nice place to take Tighe and a group of ten friends out to dinner on New Year's Eve. The catch: He didn't want to pay. He bluntly asked Read if ICAP would foot the bill. This took chutzpah. Following Hayes's departure, UBS had frozen its fixed-fee arrangement with the brokerage. And since he wouldn't be trading for the next few months, ICAP wasn't making money off him. But Hayes told Read that the whole tab wouldn't be much more than £1,000. Read pulled some strings and made it happen. The soon-to-be millionaire would get his free meal.

• • • •

Ever since working on the energy cases earlier in the decade, Obie had been dying to land another investigation that would allow him to harness the fearsome power of the Justice Department and its investigative arm, the FBI. Now he called a longtime acquaintance, Robertson Park, in the Justice Department division that pursued fraud cases.

Park, tall and gregarious with a thick gray beard, was at his desk on the third floor of the Bond Building, a 108-year-old relic a block away from the White House, when his phone rang. Obie told him he had something special for him to hear. Park looked out his window at a construction site, surely the lustrous new home of an expensive law firm or lobbying shop. Over the phone, he heard typing and then muffled static and then the voices of the Barclays traders. "Oh my God," Park said when the recording ended. He didn't know much about the Libor investigation, but he could tell this was extraordinary. Obie filled him in on the backstory, noting the parallels to the energy cases they had worked on together.

Park didn't require much persuading. By now, more than a year after the onset of the worst crisis since the Great Depression, the public was yearning for someone, anyone, to be held accountable. No executives on Wall Street—or any other major financial center, for that matter—had faced jail time for their roles torpedoing the world's economies. In fact, some of the dethroned bank CEOs had walked away from their crippled institutions with immense personal fortunes. To anyone who had lost his home or been chased down by bill collectors, it was offensive, and public outrage was increasingly aimed at government authorities who didn't seem to be doing much to identify, much less prosecute, the crisis's villains.

Part of the problem was Justice's aversion to indicting big companies. In 2002, the department had filed criminal obstruction-of-justice charges against Arthur Andersen, which had been Enron's auditor and had destroyed thousands of documents as the Houston energy company collapsed in a massive accounting fraud. The case against Andersen was meant to showcase the Bush administration's seriousness in its crackdown against corporate crime, but the presumption at the time was that the giant accounting firm would strike a deal to avoid the case actually ending up in court. Instead, the ninety-year-old firm decided to roll the dice by going to trial. After a six-week trial and ten days of deliberations, the jury delivered its verdict: guilty. Andersen, already severely wounded by the loss of important clients and employees, now unraveled entirely. More than twenty thousand employees lost their jobs.[*]

The destruction of a major company caused prosecutors to become painfully conscious about the possible consequences of charging a firm whose business hinged on public confidence. The Bush administration quickly changed tack to focus on rehabilitating the cultures of wayward companies rather than punishing them for wrongdoing. The banking industry deftly exploited this new stance, repeatedly pointing out that tens of thousands of jobs were on the line. The scare tactics were effective; with a few small exceptions, neither banks nor their executives got charged. "In reaching every charging decision, we must take into account the effect of an indictment on innocent employees and shareholders," Lanny Breuer, the assistant U.S. attorney general, would tell a gathering of New York lawyers. Obama's attorney general, Eric Holder, later echoed that sentiment, prompting congressional critics to print Monopoly-style cards bearing the image of a winged Rich Uncle Pennybags escaping from a cage, along with the message: "Your bank has been deemed 'too big to jail' by the U.S. Department of Justice."

By 2010, newspaper opinion pages were beginning to brim with unfavorable comparisons to the reckoning that took place after the Depression, when a Senate panel named and shamed the

---

[*] The U.S. Supreme Court overturned the conviction in 2005.

industry's leaders. Even after the much smaller savings-and-loan crisis of the 1980s, more than eight hundred bank officials had ended up behind bars. The harsh comparisons weren't entirely fair—just because Wall Street fat cats were despised didn't mean they had committed any crimes. In fact, the nation's banking laws had been sufficiently watered down during decades of deregulatory zeal that much of what the bankers had done was perfectly legal. And building criminal cases was difficult. Many senior bankers had used layers of managers to insulate themselves from the potentially incriminating process of sending e-mails or having recorded phone calls about sensitive topics. The one thing worse than not going after any banks, some prosecutors believed, was going after a big bank and losing.

Fair or not, the public attacks resonated in the upper echelons of the Obama administration. Inside the Bond Building, they stung the longtime prosecutors who wanted nothing more than to build a big case that would generate banner headlines and quench the public's thirst for justice.

Until now, Park hadn't ever paid attention to Libor. Now he started spotting references to it everywhere—in the business section of newspapers, in online advertisements, even in personal loan documents. It was one of those things that could make you feel the fool: Here was this number that was connected to so much, and yet it had remained hidden in plain sight.

Park went to his boss, Denis McInerney, who had been hired earlier that year by Breuer to run Justice's fraud division. The white-haired McInerney had been a longtime prosecutor in New York and in the federal Whitewater investigation against the Clintons; as a defense lawyer, he'd represented Arthur Andersen in its obstruction-of-justice case. One of the reasons Breuer had hired him was to pursue more financial crime cases. "Denis, this is important," Park told him, before explaining what he'd heard from Obie. The two men summoned a team of fraud investigators from their unit and invited the CFTC over to the Bond Building to strategize. The gathering was held in a dilapidated and claustrophobic conference room nicknamed the Flag Room. It was ringed with banners from different branches of the U.S. military and the seals from the government investigative agencies, such as the CFTC, that Justice tended to partner with; low ceiling panels had been removed in a few places to allow flagpoles to poke through. An ancient TV-VCR combo was mounted on the wall. The chairs surrounding the conference table were in various states of disrepair and uncomfortable to sit in. None of that mattered when Obie, once again, played the Barclays recordings. Their significance was clear to everyone in the hushed room. This was the whale they'd been hunting for—a winnable case against the big, rich banks.

. . . .

Before officially joining Citigroup, Hayes paid a couple clandestine visits to the bank's Tokyo offices in the Shin-Marunouchi Building—a newly constructed skyscraper that housed hundreds of shops and gourmet restaurants—to check out its technology and how traders' desks were set up. He asked for several modifications to his eighth-floor workspace and to the computers that he'd be running. The bigger priority, though, was getting Citigroup to join the group of banks that helped set Tibor. Aside from the yen version of Libor, this was the most popular instrument for Japanese interest-rate derivatives to be linked to. The Tibor panel consisted of seventeen banks, and joining the group would provide Hayes and his new colleagues with a clearer understanding of the benchmark's movements—and, more important, it would enable Citigroup to influence those movements. After talking to Hayes, Cecere e-mailed several colleagues, including Andrew Morton, to ask about the process for getting Citigroup on the panel. "For obvious reasons this is important to the bank and to trading," he wrote. Morton and other executives authorized Cecere to apply to join. They wouldn't learn for a couple of months whether the Japanese Bankers Association, which administered the benchmark, approved the application.

On December 3, Hayes showed up for his first day of work. That morning, Citigroup wired £1,967,250 ($3.2 million) into his personal bank account.

· · · ·

As word spread of the slam-dunk Barclays evidence, more regulators jumped on the bandwagon, including the FSA, which overcame nearly two years of skepticism and launched its own investigation in the spring of 2010. The U.S. Securities and Exchange Commission also asked banks to hand over reams of data and internal documents. UBS had somewhat successfully stiff-armed the CFTC, and it tried to deflect the SEC to British and Swiss regulators. But the SEC investigators had less patience than Gensler's crew, and, after meeting a bunch of UBS employees, they bluntly accused the bankers of being obstructive.* In the meantime, UBS assured the SEC that nothing seemed to be wrong with Libor.

That spring, the CFTC demanded that UBS hire an outside law firm to accelerate its slow-moving internal review. The scope of the agency's investigation remained limited; it was only looking at

---

* Pete the Greek went straight to the BBA and told Ewan about the meeting. Pete's theory—which the credulous Ewan apparently bought—was that the SEC wanted to undermine Libor's legitimacy so that it could create its own competing interest-rate benchmark.

potential issues with the U.S. dollar version of Libor in 2007 and 2008. Yet UBS, even after grudgingly hiring the law firm of Allen & Overy, continued to drag its feet.

A month or two later, an increasingly frustrated Obie was in London and decided to pay a surprise visit to Switzerland. Finma, as the Swiss regulator was known, had repeatedly cited local bank secrecy laws as a reason that, alas, UBS wouldn't be able to hand over extensive documents or otherwise cooperate much with the Americans. The CFTC wouldn't pay for a direct plane ticket to Bern, where Finma was based, so Obie flew to Munich, where he had a thirteen-hour layover before his short connecting flight. By the time he arrived a day later, he was exhausted and angry. He read his Finma counterparts the riot act. The Finma officials, speaking with thick Swiss-German accents, assured Obie that they would try to speed things up.

Dealing with Citigroup proved easier. In March 2010, the SEC and CFTC sent a round of subpoenas to the bank and some employees. Peng, who by then had left for a job at Credit Suisse, also was asked to speak to the investigators. He spent a whole day at the SEC's New York offices explaining how Libor worked and how he had stumbled onto the benchmark's problems nearly two years earlier. "What should we be looking for?" an agent asked him—suggesting, to Peng's dismay, that the regulators remained clueless.

Another subpoena landed on Thursfield's desk in London, nearly a year after he delivered his slide presentation, and Citigroup's lawyers told the government they would do anything they could to help. Hayes by then had been working at the bank, albeit half a world away, for a few months.

And then there was the BBA. On a Friday morning early in the summer of 2010, a half-dozen men in suits and with American accents showed up at the group's headquarters. They were from the

CFTC and the SEC, joined by a lone Brit from the FSA. Knight had taken the day off, not an uncommon occurrence for her on a summer Friday. "Is John Ewan here?" one visitor asked. Ewan stood up, looking frightened. The men ushered him into a meeting room, where they remained for more than five hours. On their way out late that afternoon, the investigators unplugged two of the BBA's computers and lugged them to a car waiting outside.

CHAPTER 13

A Slap on the Wrist

"Who manipulates yen Libor?" Guillaume Adolph asked Mirhat Alykulov one day in late September 2009, a few days after Hayes left UBS for the last time. "I have a bad feeling somebody is." Coming from Adolph, it was a bizarre question, apparently intended to somehow manipulate or extract information from Alykulov. With Hayes's departure, the Kazakh had been elevated a rung or two at UBS and now was interacting directly with more brokers and rival traders, such as Gollum.

"Sometimes Citi and Chase are fucking around," Alykulov said, playing dumb. "Can't stand them moving it up and down."

"Bullshit," the fiery Frenchman responded.

"What's bullshit?"

"Tom was setting the Libors he wanted."

"Nah," Alykulov said, "our guys in Zurich don't even wanna talk to us on Libors." The lies zipped back and forth between the two competitors.

It wasn't Alykulov's only relationship built on a dishonest

foundation. Read dished out advice to the newly mentor-less trader about what he could do to nudge Libor in helpful directions. "Mirhat, you realise that you have the ability to influence the three-month fix," he pointed out on one occasion. Alykulov thanked him.

Read, however, was running out of steam. He and Joanna had bought a dilapidated villa that they planned to renovate—a "hovel," Read called it. The coming year, Read would collect roughly $1 million in salary and bonus, but to save money, he planned to do some of the home improvement work himself. When not with hammer and paintbrush, he hoped to spend time watching the local Wellington soccer team, which was suddenly winning games thanks to the import of an aging star from England. It was time to wash his hands of Alykulov.

"You have been a pleasure to talk to for these past few months but the more I have thought about it, the more I think that you talking directly to [ICAP's Japanese affiliate] will work out best for UBS," Read e-mailed. "Tom will be under intense pressure to 'produce' early on and, as a result, he will be even more unreasonable than normal . . . lucky me!"

Alykulov, however, wasn't quite ready to let Read go. Over Christmas, he repeatedly complained to Read that his ICAP colleagues in London weren't doing enough to knock six-month Libor lower. Read e-mailed Wilkinson about the earful he was getting. (Wilkinson, coming off his best year ever, was due to collect nearly $2 million in salary and bonus.) Alykulov and Hayes, Read explained, were both under the false impression that Goodman "talks individually to his banks and exerts his views in that way." Read had spent years cultivating the illusion that Goodman was doing more than he really was; he didn't want Wilkinson to shatter it with some offhand comment.

· · · ·

It didn't take long for Hayes to figure out that Citigroup's culture was different from UBS's. Sure, on the face of it, there were some striking similarities. Over the years, through countless acquisitions orchestrated by hard-charging CEOs, both had been transformed into earth-spanning behemoths that, depending on your perspective, epitomized either the tremendous potential of the new era of financial globalization or the perils of the deregulatory fever that had swept the Western world. In the years before the crisis, both had gone on reckless benders, top executives at both banks seeming to possess uncannily bad timing, crowding into markets just before they imploded. Their respective CEOs, Charles Prince at Citigroup and Marcel Rohner at UBS, both had paid for the resulting calamities with their jobs. And, of course, both banks had received massive government bailouts and become international symbols of greed, mismanagement, and scandal.

But there were big differences, too. Every bank Hayes had worked for during his eight-year career was from a different nation—and only one, RBS, was from his home country. Now he was working with lots of loud, brash Americans. Hayes had been known for his intermittent outbursts, but Citigroup's trading floor in Tokyo was of another volume altogether. Employees frequently used the "hoot and holler" system that allowed them to talk into their phone line and have their voice blasted out of every trader's speaker system; that system had existed at UBS, too, but it was rarely used. Even the Brits at Citigroup, like Mccappin, were on the wild side. "I was in the office till 5 A.M.," the CEO moaned to Hayes one morning. Hayes asked why. Mccappin clarified that the Office was the name of a Tokyo nightclub. It was a far cry from UBS's relatively staid culture.

Cecere was the brashest of the bunch. He loved going out, twisting his colleagues' arms to have another drink and then another. He seemed to draw energy from social situations. Somehow all the partying didn't come at the expense of him working hard. Within days of Hayes joining, Cecere was trying to figure out how to help his newest employee move Libor and Tibor. If Citigroup's application to join the Tibor committee was accepted, the bank's first submission could have a big impact, potentially influencing other banks. Hayes asked Cecere to identify the employees who'd be responsible for Tibor and to set up a meeting. Cecere did so, and he also asked a Tokyo teammate, a Malaysian named Stantley Tan, who was in charge of the cash desk in Japan, to figure out who Citigroup's relevant Libor submitters were in London. Tan reported back that it was Thursfield's group, which also included Laurence Porter and the green-behind-the-ears Burak Celtik.

Cecere dispatched Tan to see how amenable Thursfield's crew would be to helping. The initial signals seemed good, Tan reported. As a test, Cecere asked Tan to complain to London that its most recent yen Libor submission was too high. After Tan relayed the message via e-mail, Cecere forwarded the exchange to Andrew Morton. "I've taken over global coordination of doing this properly," he wrote. The hand-in-glove collaboration between traders and Libor submitters would have been the envy of banks like UBS, which had spent years trying to foster such cooperation.

Tan, though, had misread the mood in London. Porter was unsettled by his e-mail and mentioned it to Thursfield. It seemed to Thursfield, who had spent considerable time over the past year dealing with queries from regulators, that while such behavior might have been acceptable in the past, his Tokyo colleagues weren't behaving as if a major government investigation was under way. This was the latest ill wind to blow from Japan, after Hayes's disagreeable visit a couple of months earlier. So Thursfield typed out a long, carefully worded response, a polite but firm reminder that Citigroup's Libor submissions were not subject to debate. "The rules surrounding rate setting are strict," he wrote to Cecere and others. "Any recommendations or suggestions as to where rates should be set have to be disregarded." Just to cover all his bases, Thursfield checked Citigroup's Libor submissions and was relieved to see they hadn't moved; Celtik apparently had disregarded Tan's request. Nonetheless, he took Celtik and Porter aside and told them not to tolerate any interference from Tokyo. Then Thursfield forwarded the whole e-mail chain to one of the bank's compliance officials.

Cecere passed the exchange to Hayes, who hadn't been included on Thursfield's missive. If Hayes bothered to scroll through the long sequence of e-mails, it didn't influence his behavior. A few days later, Hayes decided to visit London early in 2010 to attempt to build a personal relationship with Thursfield's squad. "I think we need good dialogue with the cash desk, they can be invaluable to us," he wrote to Cecere and a London-based colleague, Hayato Hoshino, who was assigned to work with Hayes. "If we know ahead of time [where Libor is going] we can position and scalp the market." Hoshino had moved to London from Tokyo just a few months earlier, and spoke broken English. His shy, diminutive personality earned him the nickname "Little Hoshino," and his relatively modest $91,000 salary made him all the more eager to impress Hayes and learn how to become a star. Hayes suggested that he and Hoshino try to curry favor with the cash guys by taking them out to a fancy dinner. Despite sitting nearby, Hoshino had never actually met Thursfield's crew. He got to work planning a get-together.

. . . .

One day in mid-December, Hayes was sitting at his desk, trying to get his Excel spreadsheets to interact properly with Citigroup's computer systems, when an interesting e-mail landed in his inbox. A member of Citigroup's financial research team in Tokyo recently had met with senior officials at the Bank of Japan. The central bankers had been surprisingly candid, and the researcher had gleaned valuable clues about the Bank of Japan's thinking on the direction of interest rates and its plans for upcoming bond auctions. Given the central bank's enormous power over rates, the exclusive information would be valuable to just about any trader with a stake in short-term fluctuations in rates or the yen's value relative to other currencies. For that reason, the report was confidential and not supposed to be shared outside Citigroup.

Hayes skimmed the document. There wasn't much he could actually do with it. He wouldn't be trading for nearly two months, and by then, the research would be obsolete. It would be a shame, though, to let such useful information go to waste, so, disregarding instructions, he decided to send the report to Adolph. After all, he still owed Gollum a favor for the precious advance notice he'd given on Deutsche Bank's Libor plans earlier in the year. "Have some yen info you maybe interested in," Hayes typed into a chat session that morning. "Will you promise not to forward, reproduce, etc.?"

Adolph swore not to, "on my son head." Hayes pasted the full report into the chat room. Then they discussed the possible implications of what the central bankers were saying. They agreed it was likely to push Libor and Tibor slightly lower. The report was one variable—an important one—for Adolph to consider as he tinkered with his derivatives portfolio that day.

"Anyway that's as a favor," Hayes concluded.

"Nobody apart from me will hear anything," Adolph vowed.

. . . .

In January, Hayes flew to London, the first stop on another of his world tours and his first as a Citigroup employee. He had meetings lined up with clients and a variety of bank personnel, but the most important item on his agenda was the meal with Thursfield's team. Hoshino had tried to organize a dinner, but Porter suggested lunch instead, which he figured would be less formal and shorter. As it was, Thursfield was out of town, so it was just Porter and Celtik joining Hayes and Hoshino. That was fine with Hayes, who, despite being bad at reading people, could tell he hadn't made a great impression on Thursfield back in October.

Hoshino booked a table at Roka, a loud, trendy Japanese restaurant across the street from Citigroup's skyscraper—exactly the kind of scene that Hayes hated. After ordering wine for the table, he got things started by casually explaining that from time to time he and Hoshino planned to ping Celtik with suggestions about where they thought yen Libor should be set, based on what they were seeing in the Tokyo market. Hayes characterized it as normal behavior, not a big deal—it was how things had worked during his days at UBS and other banks before that, he said. Porter emphasized that everything should be couched in the language of "market color," as opposed to Hayes saying he wanted Libor up or down to suit his portfolio of derivatives, and he cautioned that his team was under clear orders to keep Citigroup's Libor submissions in line with its competitors. Hoshino hardly spoke. At the end of the meal, Hayes picked up the tab and left with a good feeling.*

His next stop was New York, where he visited the bank's headquarters and sat down with some big clients, including the hedge fund run by the legendary investor George Soros. He also traveled to lower Manhattan to meet officials at the Federal Reserve Bank of New York—a meeting arranged by Citigroup and eagerly accepted by the Fed, which was always looking for insight into the inner workings of overseas financial markets. The secretive central bank, based in a fortresslike stone compound just off Wall Street, was one of the primary guardians of the U.S. financial markets. (It was the Fed whose officials two years earlier had heard warnings from Barclays about traders manipulating Libor.) Hayes was thrilled to have the chance to compare notes about what he was seeing in Tokyo's markets and to grill the officials about the direction of U.S. interest rates. The whole trip was exhilarating—but also exhausting. Hayes had to meet firms that specialized in Japanese trading and therefore operated during Asian market hours at night; once done, he would retreat to his Waldorf-Astoria hotel room to watch *Seinfeld* reruns.

Back in Tokyo, one of Mccappin's deputies received an unsettling phone call from an acquaintance at UBS who was no fan of Hayes. The UBS man told him that Hayes had a reputation for trying to skew Libor. Citigroup should watch out, he warned. The deputy informed Mccappin of the conversation. Mccappin— possibly suspicious of the UBS source's motives, given Hayes's controversial reputation inside his former employer—brushed off the concern. He wasn't about to let some vague innuendo tarnish his

---

* Porter would later claim that he began the lunch by warning that Citigroup wouldn't base its Libor submissions on Hayes's trading positions.

new star—a man he had just lavished with praise during a raucous ski weekend in the mountains of Karuizawa.[*]

Cecere, meanwhile, received some good news: Citigroup's application to join the Tibor panel had been accepted by the Japanese Bankers Association. Citigroup would join the committee in April. It "makes us more relevant," Cecere boasted to Morton and Mccappin.

"Just remember all the issues involved," Morton responded. Citigroup, after all, had been fielding increasingly frequent government inquiries about Libor.

Cecere and Morton were tight, two Americans sharing the swashbuckling Lehman ethos. They looked down on some of their new colleagues. Once, after going to dinner with Citigroup's top executive in Asia, Stephen Bird, Cecere described the meal to Morton. Bird, a Scotsman, was gunning to become Citigroup's overall CEO, and Cecere noted that he didn't seem interested in getting his hands dirty with nitty-gritty operational details.

"I find it very hard to take seriously someone with that much of a Scottish accent," Morton remarked.

"It's very difficult," Cecere agreed.

"It's like, you know, you expect him to be a paperboy or something like that," Morton chuckled. "Come on now, lose the fucking Scottish accent to take him seriously."

Cecere heeded Morton's be-careful message about Libor. Ten days later, he sent a note to Stantley Tan saying they needed to figure out how they were going to coordinate their rate submissions with London. "No need for any e-mails on this, but I think we should speak in person," he wrote. A couple of months later, he asked Tan to work with London to keep Libor steady, noting that his team had

---

[*] Citigroup denies that Mccappin received such a warning.

a lot of money riding on the outcome. Then he added: "But I mean if you can't, you can't, so please don't feel pressure from me."

. . . .

Hayes started trading in February. Right off the bat, his temper flared. His first day, infuriated by things not going his way, he informed first one broker, then another, that he was severing his relationships with them—a temporary move known as "pulling his line"—as punishment for their perceived ineptitude. Within hours, he'd pulled his lines with ICAP, RP Martin, and Tullett Prebon. He reinstated one of the lines that afternoon, only to revoke it later that day. (The episode would go down in brokerage industry lore as one of the era's epic tantrums.)

Notwithstanding his fierce mood, Hayes's return came none too soon for his brokers. He was such a big player in Tokyo that traders expected him to inject new life into what recently had been moribund markets. That, of course, was good news for brokers whose profits were directly linked to the amount of business traders were doing.

Farr was among those happiest to have Hayes back, but he wasn't having much luck fulfilling his client's Libor requests. When he called Luke Madden, an HSBC trader, in February, Farr got a discouraging response. "He fucking said to me not to ask him again," the broker recounted to Hayes. "They've all got right fucking funny on it recently." Here was one more sign that the Libor-skewing game was nearing its end.

Read, too, was dying to get back to work. His do-it-yourself home renovation had turned into a nightmare. "Think of a number, double it, and then add a bit more," he said of the spiraling costs. Adding to his stress, his mother had been staying with him and Joanna the past three weeks. Dealing with Hayes promised to cause more heartburn—indeed, it didn't take long before a perceived screwup prompted Hayes to threaten to sever Citigroup's entire relationship with ICAP—but Cecere had negotiated a fixed-fee arrangement, similar to the one with UBS. It made a certain amount of abuse worthwhile.

Hayes now had two reliable contacts at ICAP. Brent Davies was getting accustomed to his new career as a broker. It was less lucrative than being a trader, but that wasn't the end of the world. "I've always been poor and content, like a Buddhist monk," he told Hayes.

"I know the more money I have seems to make me no happier," Hayes replied—a confounding sentiment for someone who'd long complained about his compensation and had finally become a millionaire.

In early March, it was crunch time for one of Hayes's first big batches of trades at Citigroup, and he badly needed Libor lower. He enlisted Farr, Read, and Davies, the latter with the express intent of working over their former RBS colleague, a Libor submitter named Paul White, to get the bank to knock down its submission. "Can I pick your brain?" Davies messaged White a little while later. "We have a mutual friend who'd love to see [Libor] go down."

"Haha TH by chance," White replied.

"Shhh."

"Hehehe, mine should remain flat, always suits me if anything to go lower."

"Gotcha, thanks, and, if you could see your way to a small drop there might be a steak in it for ya, haha," Davies coaxed.

"Noted ;-)" White confirmed.

And so it went, next verse, same as the first. Hayes's Citigroup colleagues also lent a hand. Hoshino was dispatched to Celtik's desk, and Hayes and Cecere regularly gathered in a conference room with the Tibor submitters and badgered them to move the bank's data to suit their trading positions. Occasionally, when the cash desk colleagues in Tokyo were being stubborn, Mccappin pitched in with a phone call or a meeting; as CEO, he was well situated to push them to comply with Hayes and Cecere's Tibor wishes. Sometimes, Mccappin placed the call with Hayes standing in his corner office, admiring its splendid views of Tokyo's Imperial Palace and its surrounding gardens, just so the trader would know the CEO really was doing his part.[*]

As always, no one seemed concerned about the effects of skewing the rate on people outside the bank. But even the normally oblivious Hayes was growing nervous about how this might look. "Make sure not to put it in writing," he noted to Hoshino after asking him to push the London guys to get Libor lower.[†]

Citigroup's submission declined. On a conference call with Porter the next day, Hayes thanked him for his help. "No worries," Porter responded.

"I might occasionally ask Hoshino to pop over" with more requests, Hayes said.

"We won't look at individual positions or anything like that," Porter answered carefully, "but, you know, often it's just a case of drawing our attention to a trend in the market that might not have moved, and we'll look at it and if it feels appropriate, then obviously we'll reflect it in the market."

In other words, Hayes interpreted, don't be too blatant. "That's perfect, that's really great," he said. "I appreciate that."

"No worries," Porter repeated.

---

[*] Citigroup denies that Mccappin made such requests.

[†] Hayes would later claim that he simply thought it would be more effective if Hoshino casually approached the London colleagues in person, and that's why he told him not to put it in writing.

. . . .

In his nine-year career as a trader, Hayes had earned several million dollars for himself and several hundred million dollars for his employers. Now 2010 was off to a great start. By early April, after two months of trading, he had hauled in about $50 million for Citigroup. He was thirty years old, engaged to a woman he loved, living in a spacious three-bedroom, three-bathroom apartment with a large balcony overlooking the fancy Roppongi neighborhood. (Citigroup paid the monthly rent of roughly $7,500.) With his huge signing bonus, Hayes was officially a high roller—not that you could usually tell. He still preferred hanging out at the Windsor or at home. Orange juice and hot chocolate remained his beverages of choice. If he needed to drink beer for some reason, he diluted it with a sugary soft drink. When Tighe went on a work trip early that year, Hayes's idea of a big night was inviting Nigel Delmar over to watch *American Idol.*

Hayes was happier than he'd ever been.

. . . .

A month later, he and Tighe headed off on a vacation to Lang-kawi, a Malaysian archipelago. By then, Hayes was up $40 million for the year—in other words, he'd lost $10 million over the past month. And world events didn't cooperate with their holiday plans. Greece was buckling under a heavy load of debts, and nasty rumors—of the country ditching the common European currency or of the eurozone unraveling altogether—were ricocheting around Wall Street. Because of the euro's role as a benchmark against other currencies, the fears and fluctuations wrought havoc with Hayes's portfolios. He spent his first days in Malaysia glued to his Black-Berry, tortured that he was away from the office, trying to keep up with how his trades were weathering the turmoil. The answer: not well. But plenty of other people also were losing money. It wasn't cause for particular alarm.

Then, around two thirty in the afternoon of May 6 in New York, stock markets started nosediving. The Dow Jones Industrial Average plunged nearly 1,000 points within a few minutes, one of the largest drops ever. At first, market watchers stared at their screens, thinking they were witnessing the onset of another global stock market collapse. Then, just as quickly, the markets recovered most of their losses. The momentary event was soon dubbed the "flash crash."* Despite the rebound, markets remained volatile; Hayes's trading book yo-yoed up and down as much as $15 million a day.

The couple remained in Malaysia, but any hopes for a relaxing vacation were dashed. When Hayes had to pee, he insisted that Tighe sit in front of the TV and shout if anything happened in the markets while he was relieving himself. One night, they went out to dinner. At the restaurant, Hayes hardly spoke to Tighe—he was cemented to his phone, checking the market and repeatedly calling Cecere in Tokyo. Afterward, they retreated to their luxurious room at the Four Seasons, where Hayes flipped on CNBC for his nighttime markets vigil. The next morning, he asked her why they hadn't gone out to dinner the previous night. He had completely forgotten.

---

* Years later, regulators would still be searching for a convincing explanation for what caused the plunge. American authorities would criminally charge a socially awkward math whiz named Navinder Sarao as a primary culprit. Trading out of his family's modest London home, Sarao had been using algorithms to simulate bids and offers—a strategy that prosecutors would allege had helped trigger the crash.

. . . .

By the time the vacation was over, Hayes's portfolio had gone from being up $40 million for the year to being $20 million in the red. He returned to Tokyo in a nasty mood. He had always taken losses personally, and this was pure carnage, the worst he'd ever suffered. He struggled to hold back tears as he explained the losses to his bosses, first Mccappin, then Cecere, then Morton. None of them were worried. "Win some and lose some," Cecere said.

More losses loomed. Two of Hayes's Citigroup colleagues soon quit for jobs at Deutsche Bank. Their defections would have been unremarkable, except that early in the morning before they handed in their resignations, while their colleagues slept, the two traders came into the office, accessed a shared computer drive, and printed out reams of data about Hayes's trading portfolio. They didn't much like Hayes, whose arrival at Citigroup had marginalized them. Because his positions were so big, there was no way that a single trader or even a single bank could move the markets against him. But if a bunch of banks joined forces, it was different—and that, it appeared, was what the two traders had in mind.

Hayes soon noticed that Deutsche Bank established five trading positions that seemed specifically tailored to go against five of his own biggest gambles. It would have been a very odd coincidence, and he alerted Cecere. Citigroup examined internal surveillance videos and logs of activity on its printers, which confirmed Hayes's suspicions. The two traders remained on the bank's payroll during their gardening leave, and when confronted they insisted they had shredded the documents just after printing them. The explanation didn't make sense—why had they printed the materials in the first place? Before long, Hayes's trading positions became common knowledge across Tokyo. Rival banks started to attack.

This was hardly an unprecedented phenomenon—and it made Hayes's willingness to talk openly to rivals and brokers about his trading positions especially tough to comprehend. Back in the late 1990s, Long-Term Capital Management, at the time the world's largest hedge fund, unraveled in the space of six late-summer weeks partly because Wall Street banks like Goldman Sachs had gleaned valuable information about what assets it was holding. (Hayes was familiar with this tale, having read *When Genius Failed*, the definitive account of the fund's collapse.) Banks had a number of potential reasons to try to undermine a rival trader's wagers. One was simply malice: Long-Term Capital, like Hayes, had rubbed a lot of people the wrong way through its arrogance when it was swimming in money, and schadenfreude is a powerful force on Wall Street. But there was a more practical motivation as well: Struggling traders were likely to have to dump their positions in a hurry, leading the prices of whatever assets they were selling to tumble. Hence, it was common for traders to amass positions that would gain value as those bets unraveled—a strategy that tended to accelerate the selloff, worsening the troubled trader's woes.

This was the position Hayes now found himself in. And as his losses grew, he dug himself into a deeper hole. For the past month, he had been in a bizarre dance with Alykulov. They were no longer colleagues, but they remained pals. At least that's how Hayes saw it. He'd always been a tough boss to Alykulov—and not a very good one, by his own estimation—but he respected and liked his former underling. Now he wanted to explore hiring Alykulov at Citigroup. (He also was interested in working with him to make sure Libor moved in mutually beneficial directions.) One day in late April, he invited Alykulov out for a beer. Alykulov already had plans that night but suggested Sunday or Monday evenings instead. But that wouldn't work for Hayes. "Sunday night I get sex," he explained. "I only get it once a week so reluctant to go out that night." He was serious.

"Haha," Alykulov responded. "That's sacred then." They settled on a weekday lunch instead and had a long chat—all about Libor and Hayes's trading strategies. Alykulov the next day was departing for a vacation in Bolivia, but he didn't even mention the plans to Hayes, who refused to talk about anything other than interest rates.

Afterward, Hayes suffered a bout of anxiety. He checked with Alykulov to confirm that their talk was secret and that he wouldn't tell his UBS colleagues what Hayes was up to in the market. The material "is for you only," he said. Alykulov agreed.

But Alykulov didn't see Hayes as a friend; this was all business. And business meant their interests diverged. After Hayes had defected, Pieri and others at UBS became terrified that Hayes would use his inside knowledge of UBS against the bank. That was what gardening leave was supposed to protect against, but Hayes's former colleagues rightly surmised that he was unlikely to adhere to the strictest interpretation of the three-month cooling-off period. By the time Hayes started racking up profits at Citigroup, Pieri and his colleagues were obsessing about their former star. Pieri's fears turned out to be unfounded—Hayes stuck to his word not to attack the positions he'd amassed at UBS—but in the industry's no-honor-among-thieves culture, it's easy to see why Pieri was nervous. He urged Alykulov to try to pry information out of Hayes. If nothing else, that would allow UBS to piggyback on his trades, position its own portfolio against his, or simply get out of his way.

On May 14, Hayes invited Alykulov out again. Alykulov balked, partly because he already had dinner plans. "Look," Hayes began, "I spent a long time training you. I hope that I was OK to you. . . . I think that we either take the view that we work together like I do with Deutsche, or we go our separate ways. Together I think it benefits you and me. But I need to trust you and vice versa. I will leave it up to you."

"I do look up to you since you trained me," Alykulov said, and grudgingly agreed to stop by the Windsor after his dinner.

Hayes said he'd be there around 9 P.M. "You need to decide whether you want us to stay in touch like I do with Gollum at Deutsche," he reiterated. "Or we just shake hands and go separate ways." After twelve minutes, and no response from Alykulov, Hayes was nervous. Had he pressed too hard? Come on too strong? "Is that ok? Are we meeting later?" Nine more minutes passed. No response. "Yes/no?" Hayes pleaded, like an anxious teenager waiting to see if a crush will return his phone call. Almost an hour later, Alykulov put Hayes out of his misery. He confirmed he would come to the Windsor. Hayes breathed a sigh of relief. He shouldn't have.

A week later, Pieri, Yugo Matsumoto, and Naomichi Tamura were once again fretting about Hayes, trying to figure out his positions in the turbulent market. The three managers exchanged their theories. Then Alykulov chimed in: Hayes has a position that profits if U.S. dollar Libor rises.

"Oh really?" Tamura asked.

"Wow," Pieri said, impressed with the youngster's scoop. They all scrambled to assess what that meant for their portfolios and the broader market. Then Pieri asked how Alykulov knew.

"He told me," Alykulov explained. Hayes had indeed trained Alykulov well: It was every man for himself. Hayes wouldn't learn of the betrayal for years.

. . . .

Buckling under heavy losses, Hayes redoubled his efforts to get Libor moved in helpful directions—sometimes in a manner that bordered on recklessness, deluging his contacts with requests, even when they'd already indicated that they couldn't help. It was hard to tell if Hayes simply couldn't take a clue or didn't care what they said; in any case, the barrage continued, to his Citigroup colleagues, to his brokers, to his competitors.

All the e-mail traffic was making Cecere squirm. He told Hayes and Hoshino to stop communicating in writing—in the future, he instructed, talk about Libor via cell phones, "so nothing is lost in translation over e-mail." (Citigroup didn't record cell phone calls.) Hoshino interpreted that order, coming from a manager, to be as good as condoning the Libor-moving requests.

One day in June, Mccappin and Andrew Morton had a phone call about some of the problems they were having in the trading business—problems that, in no small part, were caused by Hayes's struggles. Morton mentioned that various government authorities were delving into Libor; subpoenas had started to fly. It was the first Mccappin had heard of the investigations, and he was alarmed, especially because he had noticed that the pace and intensity of requests from Hayes and Cecere seemed to have been increasing of late. He informed Cecere about the government scrutiny and told him that he and Hayes should no longer communicate directly with Stantley Tan and his cash desk colleagues. Instead, the requests should be routed through Mccappin.

That week, Kii Ko, one of the Citigroup employees responsible for Tibor submissions, happened to have a brief conversation with Mccappin. Ko said that Hayes and Cecere in the past had told the cash desk not to lower Tibor, even though the submitters thought that's what should happen based on Citigroup's borrowing costs. Now the same thing was happening again. Tan, who was Ko's boss, had a similar chat with Mccappin. The problem, Tan had told Mccappin, was that Hayes's team kept flip-flopping on what they wanted—a reflection of Hayes's trading positions changing from day to day. It made Citigroup look stupid to keep reversing the direction of its submissions. Mccappin was "very clear" about the problem, Tan told Ko afterward. So Mccappin now found himself in the middle of an awkward tug-of-war between different factions of Citigroup Japan.

With his colleagues less inclined to help, Hayes tried Gollum. The Deutsche Bank trader was having a middling year and had relinquished responsibility for the bank's yen Libor submissions. (Hayes was under the false impression that he still retained some influence over the rate.) Adolph, however, had gotten wind of the government investigations. So when Hayes started pestering him for help getting Libor moved—the same type of request he'd lodged many times before—Adolph shot him down.

"Enough," he said, cutting him off.

Hayes kept going, detailing what he was looking for.

"I have no influence or control nor [do] I want to be involved," Adolph said.

Hayes was confused. "Sure thing," he said, trying to defuse the awkward situation. "Well how are you doing anyway." Later, as he deconstructed the conversation, he figured maybe Adolph had been brusque because of the tough year he was having. Or maybe it was that he was no longer in charge of yen Libor? Then an un-settling thought crossed his mind: It was almost as if Adolph was worried that someone might read through their chats in the future.

· · · ·

When Hayes left UBS, Pieri had taken it as a personal betrayal. He had stuck his neck out, over and over again, for his star, extract-ing rare concessions from top UBS brass—and Hayes still quit. It made Pieri look bad. The anger festered. By summer, Pieri was out for blood.

Hayes "is so stubborn and thinks he is bigger than the market," Pieri gossiped to a Credit Suisse trader named Paul Ellis, as the two marveled about the size of Hayes's trading portfolio. "I had to rein him in all the time when he was here"—that was a lie; in fact, UBS had encouraged him to pile on riskier trades. "I knew that when I hired him and prevented it, and told him he was at risk of blowing up when he left." Pieri hinted to Ellis that Hayes was circumventing Citigroup's risk management systems. "It would be interesting if someone were to drop an anonymous line to their market risk guys," he said.

Ellis then cited a market rumor about one of Hayes's specific trading positions. "I can confirm he had that position," Pieri responded. If his losses kept piling up, he continued, "Tom will end up the fall guy . . . as Chris [Cecere] is Andrew [Morton]'s mate. These are reckless Lehmans guys managing the place. . . . Chris is way over his head and his boss Andrew has no idea how to run a business. They bought the racehorse but don't have a good jockey." Over lunch later that month, Pieri explained to Ellis how Hayes used brokers at ICAP and elsewhere to move Libor in favorable directions.

Hayes and Cecere had picked up inklings that Pieri was among the leaders of an anti-Hayes bandwagon. Cecere, for example, had noticed Pieri trading in a bizarre fashion that made it seem like he was simply trying to damage Hayes's positions, not make money for himself, but he hadn't really believed that was happening. It would be an irrational way for an executive at a major bank to act—his compensation was tied to his trading desk's profits, not a rival bank's performance. Hayes, meanwhile, had finally come to the conclusion that he probably shouldn't be placing his trust in Alykulov, given his connection to Pieri. But neither Hayes nor Cecere realized the severity of the situation until June 28, when Cecere went out for drinks at a crowded Tokyo bar. In a city with more than 13 million inhabitants, he ended up seated at a wooden table right next to Pieri and another UBS trader. The two UBS men were sipping white wine and talking shop. They didn't seem to recognize Cecere. So he sat there, nursing his drink and eavesdropping. At one point, he pulled out his phone and surreptitiously snapped a grainy photo of the two men.

"The ONLY thing he [Pieri] spoke about was screwing Tom and Citibank," Cecere wrote later that night in an incredulous e-mail to Morton and Mccappin. He attached the photo as proof. "His end game is to inflict pain and not make money. He sounded like a raving zealot who'd lost the plot. . . . Given his trades in the last day and a half, he's now spending money to have a go at Tom/us. Not that it really matters, but this is what we are dealing with."

. . . .

Three days earlier, Hayes had set in motion a chain of events that would inflict far more damage than anything Pieri could do. It was the last Friday in June, sunny, warm, and clear in both Tokyo and London. Hayes was still losing money. Growing desperate, he had convinced himself that, if his next batch of trades didn't pay off, it would cost him his job. That afternoon, talking to Hoshino on his cell phone, he asked him to lean on Celtik to increase Citigroup's submissions by 0.01 percentage points on Monday and Tuesday.

Hoshino tentatively walked over to Celtik's desk. "Here's a message from Tom," he said quietly. "It would be good for us if Libor went up by one basis point." Celtik told him to stop—they couldn't be talking about this kind of stuff. Trying to drive his point home, he claimed that some Barclays traders recently had been arrested for just this sort of behavior.*

Hoshino shuffled away, rattled. He called Hayes and told him what had happened. "Oh, okay," Hayes replied, unperturbed. When Hoshino relayed what Celtik had said about the Barclays traders, Hayes brushed it off. The two of them hadn't actually been asking Celtik to *move* Libor, he explained—they had simply been stating aloud what would *please* them. Hoshino didn't buy the tortured distinction.

Celtik told Porter about the conversation with Hoshino. Porter told him to tell Thursfield. Thursfield told his boss, Compton, as well as Matt Jerman, a senior executive. Jerman told Morton, who said he would inform the bank's compliance department.

By the following Monday, nobody from compliance had called, so Thursfield took it upon himself to phone one of the bank's compliance officers and tell him everything. Knowing what it knew about the U.S. government's escalating investigations, the bank didn't really have a choice: Within days, Citigroup launched an internal review into the matter.

．．．．

Unaware that the compliance department had been alerted, Hayes kept pushing traders and brokers to nudge Libor up or down. But it was getting harder. Farr sent an apologetic e-mail to let him know that Luke Madden at HSBC had texted him—not for the first time—"asking me not to mention Libors again." Then Hayes asked Hoshino to call him. Hoshino had been sufficiently frightened by the prior week's incident that he rang Hayes on his work

---

* No Barclays traders had been arrested. It's unclear what Celtik was referring to.

line, not his cell phone, figuring Hayes wouldn't talk about Libor on the recorded line. He was wrong; without hesitation, Hayes asked Hoshino to go back to Celtik. Hoshino hung up and called Hayes back on his cell phone. "I don't want to do it," he said. Why was Hayes having such trouble getting the message?

In the middle of the day on July 6, Hoshino was summoned into a meeting room. A phalanx of compliance officials was waiting for him. Terrified, he stammered through the interview, repeatedly failing to remember recent events surrounding his and Hayes's Libor requests. The Citigroup investigators perceived him as uncooperative. Hoshino didn't tell his Tokyo colleagues about the meeting.

About a week later, though, Cecere detected that something was amiss—maybe Hoshino had been scolded, and that's why he was no longer cooperating. Cecere called Morton to figure out what was going on. Morton said the London Libor submitters had complained to compliance.

"Those fucking cunts!" Cecere exploded. "What is wrong with them? Pardon my language, but that drives me fucking mental. Pick up a phone and have a word with me."

Morton tried to calm him down, to no avail. "What the fuck kind of bank is this?" Cecere sputtered. "Turn your own people in instead of just picking up a phone and saying, 'Look, this is really not comfortable. Please stop it.' Like that's all you have to say, and it's done." But of course it hadn't been done, until now.

· · · ·

One morning that month, Citigroup traders in London arrived to find neatly printed documents placed on their desks overnight. The message spelled out, in detail, the acceptable procedures surrounding the Libor submission process. In Tokyo that day, all of Citigroup's traders were called into a meeting room to hear a similar message. A bunch of executives, including Mccappin, were piped into the meeting via speakerphone. From this point forward, no traders were allowed to speak to the cash desks. Any exceptions had to be authorized by the compliance department. The rules were now crystal clear, even to Hayes.

· · · ·

On a Sunday evening in July, Cecere called Hayes on his cell phone. "I need to speak to you," he said. They decided to meet at the Windsor. The two sat in the deserted pub, as they had a dozen times in the past, a beer per banker, although Hayes hardly touched his. Then Cecere got to the point: "Tomorrow these lawyers are coming in to do this investigation into Libor."

"Why?" Hayes asked. Cecere said someone in London had gotten uncomfortable. Hayes asked whether he needed to worry. No, Cecere said. He told Hayes to distance himself from whatever it was that Hoshino had done to kick up this whole storm. As for the broader question about whether he had been asking the London crew to move Libor, Hayes should just explain that this is the way things worked in the market. They hadn't done anything wrong—or, if they had, just about everyone was guilty.

Lawyers from a high-priced law firm, Cleary Gottlieb, flew from New York to interview Hayes. They invited him into one of the bank's finely furnished conference rooms, a few floors below where Hayes worked, that Citigroup generally used to impress clients. The lawyers were armed with reams of internal documents. Hayes tried to follow Cecere's advice. The lawyers presented him with e-mails and chat transcripts showing his dialogue with

Hoshino; Hayes's spin was that he was only asking him to provide general market commentary to the London team. He told the investigators that he had no idea what Hoshino had actually said that so inflamed Celtik and Thursfield. But every time he opened his mouth, Hayes could tell the lawyers thought he was lying—which, of course, he was. They kept asking questions that led him to contradict his previous answers. They seemed especially exercised about a phone call where Hayes told Hoshino to grab a reluctant Celtik on his way to the toilet to press him for Libor help. They also made a big deal about how Hayes, in his first days on the job, had encouraged Hoshino to butter up the submitters.

That night, Hayes went home and told Tighe what had happened. "These lawyers came to interview me today," he said. Tighe instantly knew this wasn't good. Did they interview anyone else? she asked. No, just me, Hayes replied. By the end, Hayes told her, it had seemed more like an interrogation than an interview. "They had me saying left was right, and right was left," he recounted. "I didn't really know what I was saying."

A few days later, Hayes turned to Mccappin for advice. The CEO assured him he had nothing to worry about. After all, the fact that Hayes remained in his job and continued to trade was evidence that this wasn't a big deal. If they really thought he'd done something wrong, surely they would have suspended him. Mccappin repeated Cecere's advice to point the finger at Hoshino.

Tighe, a lawyer herself, wasn't so sanguine. The fact that the attorneys, including high-ranking partners, had flown from New York did not suggest that Citigroup viewed this as a minor problem. She asked Cecere out for a drink. They met at the Windsor. "Give it to me straight," she said. "What's going on?"

"Nothing," Cecere replied. "There might be a slap on the wrist." He smacked his expensive wristwatch for emphasis. Tighe didn't think Cecere was lying, but she wasn't sure he knew what he was talking about, either. At home, she sat down with her fiancé for a serious conversation. It was time, she told him, to hire a lawyer. He needed someone to sit in the room with him during these meetings, someone equipped to square off against Cleary Gottlieb's attorneys. Hayes insisted that wasn't necessary. He told her that he could trust Cecere and Mccappin, and if they said everything would be all right, everything would be all right. There was, he proclaimed, no need to waste money on a lawyer. Tighe shouted at him that he was being unbelievably naïve—but Hayes had the final word.

In August, Hayes departed for his bachelor party—a *stag do,* in British parlance—in southwestern Ireland. The rolling bright green countryside was a refreshing break from Tokyo. Hayes and a dozen-strong group, led by his childhood friend Charlie and his brother and stepbrothers, stayed in a local university's dorms; Hayes thought the stark, bare rooms looked like jail cells. Rounding out the entourage were a few of Hayes's brokers: Noel Cryan, Nigel Delmar, and Danny Brand. The dynamic was strange. Cryan and Delmar had never gotten along, and Cryan thought it was weird that he was there at all. Cryan knew that if Hayes were ever to leave the industry, they'd never speak again. He wasn't so sure Hayes viewed their relationship similarly; it was sad that he viewed Cryan as one of his closest pals. But it certainly wasn't in Cryan's interest to correct that misperception.

The group planned to go sea fishing. But the night before, after hitting up a bar, the guys stayed out late at a local casino, and Charlie blew all the money to charter the boat on losing hands of poker. Hayes had to pay for the outing himself; he caught a large cod. The next morning, the jet-lagged groom-to-be found himself awake while his friends remained passed out after another late night at a club. Hayes called Mccappin to ask about the latest status of Citigroup's internal investigation. Mccappin waved off the query. "Why aren't you drunk?" he asked, recommending pints of Guinness as a good antidote to Hayes's early-morning sobriety. Hayes returned to Tokyo without a hard sense—or any sense at all—of what was happening with Cleary Gottlieb's own fishing expedition.

By the end of the month, Hayes had spent what seemed like an eternity—at least eight hours, by his count—over the course of three or four meetings with the lawyers. Wanting to show that he was being helpful and had nothing to hide, he had agreed to hand over his personal cell phone records—a surprisingly complicated task that entailed him and Tighe going to a cell phone store and explaining in broken Japanese that they needed a printout listing all his calls and texts. He told Farr to stop communicating with him about Libor in writing. Tighe once again ordered him to get a lawyer. Hayes once again refused. And once again, they fought. This time, though, Tighe issued an ultimatum: He could either hire a lawyer or write a formal letter to Citigroup documenting his concerns about the investigation. At least that would create a contemporaneous record of his grievances. If Hayes wouldn't do one of those two things, Tighe said, she would stop talking to him.

The threat worked, although Tighe had to do the work herself. She had quit her job and was preparing to head back to London in early September; she expected to return to Japan after the wedding and honeymoon and spend the following year as a full-time student mastering Japanese. Taking a break from wedding planning, she drafted two lawyerly e-mails for Hayes to send to Cecere asserting that he hadn't broken any rules. Tighe labored over the correspondence, printing out and revising drafts. She authorized Hayes to make minor tweaks but insisted that he let her review them before they were sent. On the back of one copy, she scribbled notes detailing the choreography of the first dance at their wedding, as planned by their dance instructor: foxtrot, promenade, waltz, swing, marching for four counts.

The first missive, sent August 20, protested that Hayes was being treated like a suspect. "I have felt as though perhaps I am being accused of doing something wrong, although frankly I am not sure whether that is the case or not and, if it is the case, I am not sure exactly what I am being accused of," he wrote. Cecere promised to forward the note up the chain of command. The second e-mail, sent nine days later, protested that Hayes hadn't received a response to his first letter. And he complained that a Citigroup employee had come to collect information from him under false pretenses, claiming it was needed for auditors, not the lawyers. "I am now considering making a formal complaint since it appears that my previous e-mail has fallen on deaf ears," Hayes wrote.

Though he didn't mention it in his notes, Hayes had noticed that he was no longer able to access certain websites at work and couldn't e-mail attachments to people outside Citigroup. He told himself it probably was just a glitch in the system.

. . . .

Around 11 A.M. on September 6, Hayes was at his desk trading. It was a hot day, with temperatures in the low 90s, and a stiff wind didn't do much to cool the broiling city. Hayes was sitting at his desk in an ill-fitting Tullett Prebon polo shirt when Mccappin's assistant, Kevin Green, tapped him on his shoulder. "Can I have a word with you?" he asked, beckoning. Hayes grumbled that he didn't want to leave his desk, but reluctantly got up. He figured it was yet another interview with the lawyers, and he started walking to the elevators so he could go down to the same conference room they'd been using. Green instead directed him into an austere, windowless meeting room on the eighth floor. Hayes still thought it was a normal interview—after all, only minutes earlier, he'd been placing bets with Citigroup's money.

As soon as he entered the meeting room, though, he realized this was something different. Mccappin was there. So was Morton, who had flown in from London. A couple of lawyers and human resources officials were crowded in, too. Hayes's adrenaline pumped.

Mccappin got things started. This was a formal meeting, not a debating forum, he declared. Citigroup had completed its internal investigation and concluded that Hayes had attempted to manipulate Libor and Tibor. He might have violated multiple Japanese laws in the process. All of this was grounds for Citigroup to fire Hayes, Mccappin said—and that was what the bank intended to do. An HR official handed Hayes a typed letter, signed by Mccappin. "Such conduct is in clear violation of provisions of the Citi Code of Conduct, resulting in the potential for serious regulatory or reputational harm to . . . the entire Citigroup organization," Mccappin read aloud, without looking up. "Moreover, we regret that you did not cooperate fully with Citigroup's internal investigation into your conduct. The foregoing constitutes clear grounds for punitive termination."

Hayes struggled to comprehend the words. A dreamlike haze seemed to cloud the room. Was this really happening? Someone asked Hayes to sign the letter. He refused. "It's ironic," he said angrily, "because Brian was doing the exact same thing."

"But he didn't have any trading positions," a lawyer responded.

Hayes asked for a severance payment. The executives exchanged glances and whispered to each other. Hayes was escorted to a tiny room with nothing but a table and a phone. They told him to wait there. Left alone, he called Cecere, who didn't answer. Then he phoned Tighe. She was in the middle of getting a massage. "Look, I've been fired," he announced.

"Oh shit," she said. "I'll come home."

The meeting reconvened; Hayes's request for severance was turned down. But he was allowed to keep his signing bonus, as well as another $2.4 million he'd collected in the ensuing ten months. And the bank promised not to tell any prospective employers in the future about the circumstances in which he'd left. Hayes considered that to be a victory. Pushing for more, he told the group that nobody had ever explained to him the rules he was now accused of violating. He said he wanted to invoke a whistle-blower's clause in his contract to point the finger at senior management: Cecere and Mccappin knew what was happening and participated, Hayes threatened to sue. The meeting ended, about forty-five minutes after Green had tapped him on the shoulder. Now Green ushered Hayes down the hall. He asked what Hayes wanted to take from the office. Just his two lucky pandas, he said. Anything else? Green asked. "A noose," Hayes responded. Then Green marched him out of the building.

· · · ·

Hayes went home and slumped onto the sofa. He was in a state of shock. "I can't believe it," he told Tighe over and over. He alternated between holding his face in his hands and raking both hands through his hair, sending flakes of dandruff into the air. Tighe wasn't so surprised by the situation. She had seen this, or something like this, coming weeks ago.

Hayes called Farr on his cell phone. The broker was stunned when he heard what had happened. Hayes told him that during the hours of interviews, the lawyers had played tapes of some of his phone calls with Farr about Libor. This, Hayes said, was a big part of why he'd been fired. Terrified and confused, Farr decided not to tell his RP Martin managers.

Rumors about Hayes's abrupt departure began to circulate. The prevailing wisdom was that he'd been fired for losing a lot of money. "Can't say I am too surprised. Shame though," an ICAP executive e-mailed Wilkinson. But others were closer to the real reason. Pete the Greek and Sascha Prinz were among those trying to figure out what happened. Prinz by now was at Bank of America. Pete the Greek was still looking to escape UBS and was pressing Prinz to get him an interview. "You heard about Tom Hayes?" Prinz asked.

"Yeah, sacked for cause. Pretty nasty."

"Supposedly he tried to influence New York guys in setting Libor, and they have that on tape," Prinz gossiped.

"That is ugly," Pete the Greek said.

Elsewhere, traders and managers wondered why Hayes had been fired for doing what so many others also were doing. "Of course [he] requested that submissions be favorable to his position, [but Citigroup] evidently took a hard line with him for some reason," a puzzled Deutsche Bank trader e-mailed his managers.

• • • •

Morton and other Citigroup executives needed to figure out how to explain Hayes's disappearance to the outside world. Eventually they settled on cryptic, imprecise language: "Tom breached the internal rules at Citi for the management of his positions" and "left the firm yesterday." If pressed for more details, employees could respond: "He attempted to manipulate daily markings on his positions"—which wasn't true. A memo cautioned against linking his departure to Libor. "Never talk about Libor fixing," it said. "If we talk about his wrongdoing on fixing of [yen] Libor, most customers would think Citi committed a violation.'

Clients were also to be told that the damage would be limited because, with Hayes's three-week wedding and honeymoon approaching, he had already exited many of his positions in advance. That was not altogether convincing, and in fact Hayes's investments proved painful to unwind, in part because they were so well known across Tokyo's trading community. Citigroup officials later estimated they incurred about $50 million in losses.

• • • •

Hayes and Tighe flew back to England together, in synch with her previously planned departure, but a week earlier than he'd planned to travel. He was still working the angles, looking for new jobs. Adolph had sent him a commiserating text message when he heard about the firing, noting that he had endured a similar experience at Merrill Lynch back in April 2008: "You got fired just before your wedding, just like me." He then helped arrange a job interview for Hayes at Deutsche Bank's London office. But when Hayes checked in at the reception desk, word came down that he was not to enter the building. A Deutsche Bank executive, Mark Lewis, instead met Hayes at a nearby restaurant. He brought Adolph along. Hayes and Adolph, despite their long history, had never actually met. Hayes was left with the impression that Deutsche Bank was interested in hiring him, but the process would need to work its way through the bank's internal bureaucracy.

Stress was causing Hayes to act even more strangely than usual. A day or two before the wedding, Sandy drove her son to Tighe's parents' house. Tighe and her mother, Karen, invited the two in for lunch. Hayes answered on his mother's behalf: "Oh no, Karen, don't worry about that. Mum was just saying to me in the car, 'Oh God, I don't have to go in for food with them, do I?'"

The Tighe women looked at each other, stunned. Hayes stood there grinning.

"I didn't mean it like that, I really didn't," Sandy stammered. "It's just that I've already eaten."

Nobody was offended, Karen assured Sandy, who didn't look like she believed it. Afterward, Tighe told her fiancé why what he'd just done was inappropriate. Hayes responded with a bout of hysterical laughter.

Tighe was devastated by Hayes's firing. She had been eagerly anticipating returning to Tokyo as a full-time student. That door now had slammed shut. "I am home but very depressed," she wrote to one of her Japanese friends, who had asked whether she should wear Western or Japanese garb to the wedding. "I can't really be bothered to even think about the wedding. I can't get my mind off the fact that I am being forced to leave Japan." She and Hayes had been talking about starting a family of their own. That idea, too, was shunted to the back burner. "I feel very unsettled about what has happened and I guess I am going to have to go back to work if he can't get a job. Sigh," she wrote to Cecere's wife, Megan. "I only just quit!"

The wedding took place in the English countryside on the third anniversary of Hayes and Tighe meeting at the InterContinental swimming pool. Hayes had picked the date; Tighe considered that to be probably the most romantic thing he'd ever done. The venue was a Four Seasons hotel in an old Georgian manor house surrounded by rolling farmland, near where Tighe grew up. Tuxedoed waiters served cocktails and hors d'oeuvres in a courtyard where wild rabbits hopped. Hayes wore a formal British morning suit. (At Tighe's insistence, he stopped wearing his golden QPR pinky ring in advance of the wedding.) Tighe was in a body-hugging, strapless white dress with her back exposed. Custom-made diamond jewelry sparkled on her neck and ears. Hayes had invited several former colleagues. Cecere couldn't make it, but a bunch of brokers—Brent Davies, Noel Cryan, Darrell Read, and others—and their wives were there. Cryan and Read huddled in a corner, gossiping about Hayes's firing and wondering what the full story was. Despite the careful choreography and dancing lessons, Hayes botched the second promenade of their first dance. As the party wound down, Hayes wrapped his arm around his wife, and they watched as more than $10,000 of fireworks exploded in the night sky. Hayes had booked the second-nicest suite at the hotel; the king of Thailand was occupying the best rooms.

Afterward, they flew to the Maldives for their honeymoon. They stayed in a villa on stilts in the Indian Ocean. The weather was awful. They huddled together inside, listening to rain and waves lash the house.

PART III

The Second Scam

CHAPTER 14

He's the One

David Meister came from a family of engineers, and for many years he was inclined to honor that heritage. He went to the University of Delaware and earned a degree in chemical engineering. Meister cherished the certainty behind the finite, controllable science and math. But he soon recognized another certainty, which was that chemical engineering wasn't sexy. Meister's attention strayed. He kept reading news stories about the era's fearless prosecutors, who were cracking down on the New York Mafia's five families and the likes of Ivan Boesky and Michael Milken, the financiers who would go to jail for crimes related to insider trading. Meister was inspired—and, if he was honest about it, lured by the flame of publicity. Abandoning engineering, he enrolled in law school.

After graduating, Meister landed a job at a firm where he defended accused financial criminals for a few years. Then, eager to round out his résumé, he became a federal prosecutor in the U.S. Attorney's Office in Manhattan. He worked under John Carroll, one of the lawyers who had prosecuted Milken back when Meister was in college. The experience cemented the new prosecutor's interest in financial crime, which he found more subtle and complicated than open-and-shut Mafia cases. And his engineering background gave him an added advantage: He wasn't afraid of numbers.

Meister soon returned to private practice, following Carroll to Skadden, Arps, Slate, Meagher & Flom, one of Wall Street's most powerful legal outfits. There, Meister became rich. But by 2010 he was itching for a new challenge. He had plenty of money, but he was nearly fifty years old and wanted to make sure he left his mark somewhere. Maybe he could try another stint working for the government?

As it happened, Gary Gensler was in the market for someone to run the CFTC's enforcement division. He had grown sick of Obie, who he felt wasn't paying enough attention to headline-grabbing cases. Meister didn't know much about the CFTC. But the world of former federal prosecutors—the world in which Gensler was searching for his top cop—was small and tight-knit. He wanted an aggressive and ambitious individual who would take an expansive view of what constituted the agency's powers and would bring new urgency to the job. Before long, word reached Gensler that Meister was on the market. Then word traveled back to Meister to gauge his interest. He was intrigued and, after meeting the impressive Gensler, decided to take the job, splitting his time between CFTC headquarters and the agency's New York offices, two blocks from where the twin towers once stood.

When Meister arrived in early 2011, the Libor investigation was one of the agency's top priorities. But it wasn't moving fast. No longer was the FSA the main impediment—slowly but surely, information was starting to trickle across the Atlantic. The bigger problem was of the CFTC's own making: Its investigators may have been enthusiastic, but they didn't seem to be acting with much urgency. Meister was by nature impatient. He thought government bureaucracies tended to waste time on investigations. It wasn't that no progress had been made, but the Libor investigation was mired in a never-ending cycle of data mining. Each time McGonagle, Lowe, and their small band of investigators found a piece of potential evidence, they socked it away, and then the search resumed. The way Meister saw it, the agency already had the goods—not just in the form of cold, hard data, but also the juicy phone calls and electronic messages in which Barclays employees talked about their manipulative schemes. All this additional forensic work struck him as unnecessary.

Meister wasn't the only one to reach that conclusion. On the CFTC's ninth floor, some of the commissioners had come to view McGonagle, Lowe, and Obie as talented, dogged investigators who were unable to close the deal. They seemed too cautious, a tendency that had been reinforced by the agency's historical culture. The consensus was that they weren't the right people to be running a major federal investigation.

Meister drew up plans to revamp the CFTC's strategy. Then a bombshell from Tokyo detonated.

. . . .

After salvaging their rain-drenched honeymoon with a shopping spree in Dubai, Hayes and Tighe returned to Japan to pack their belongings. They had a small farewell party at the Windsor. Hayes—feeling nostalgic and recognizing that this was the end of an era for him—sought to patch things up with some former colleagues. "Despite the end, I had a good time here and wanted to say thanks for bringing me over a few years ago," he e-mailed Pieri. It was a generous—arguably naïve—gesture, considering that Hayes by now knew about Pieri's elaborate efforts to destroy him. Pieri responded a few hours later congratulating Hayes on his wedding and updating him on Donna giving birth to their second child, a boy. Pieri suggested that they grab beers in London at some point to reminisce about the crazy events of recent months.

"It's not the same without you in the team for sure," Pieri wrote. "I will remember those years with fond memories."

Then Hayes and Tighe departed Japan for the last time. Hayes left behind a large unpaid tax bill stemming from the millions he'd collected from Citigroup that year.

At Citigroup, Mccappin grew increasingly worried about his vulnerability to the expanding investigations. He wrote himself, for posterity, a long e-mail with bullet points on what he knew, and when, about Libor. "Daily submissions would try to be biased to the lower side," he said without mentioning that the strategy was crafted at least in part with specific trading positions in mind. Mccappin didn't see anything wrong with this: "I know we have now heard this (everywhere) but I was genuinely not aware of any formal policy/guideline on these matters."

With Hayes out, Read called it quits, too—just as he had said he would years earlier. But a few months into his second retirement, he got a phone call from the head of ICAP's Wellington outpost. The office was suddenly doing a brisk business in New Zealand bonds and other products; would Read be interested in coming back? Bored at home, he took the bait and returned. It wasn't the same without Hayes around. Now he had multiple clients, none of whom he knew well. The screaming was gone, but so was much of the fun.

At RP Martin, despite the loss of a second crucial client, spirits remained high. Caplin, feeling generous, doled out a round of bonuses to the yen-derivatives squad in late September. Farr pocketed the equivalent of $31,000. Lee Aaron got a five-year contract extension and a $16,000 bonus. The cash-strapped Gilmour also collected $16,000.

Citigroup's compliance and HR departments concluded that Hoshino had just been following Hayes and Cecere's orders and that while the impressionable young man hadn't acted as he should have, he had learned his lesson. He certainly was contrite. His punishment was a written warning—essentially a second chance.

As for Cecere, he handed in his resignation shortly after Hayes was terminated. It was voluntary, but Citigroup had told him he might be fired if he didn't step down on his own. His cell phone and e-mail were quickly disconnected. Always the salesman, Cecere described his resignation to Hayes as an act of protest—he said he did it "in disgust." Cecere wasn't terribly worried about the future: He was already in talks to join a huge international hedge fund, Brevan Howard, as a trader in its Geneva headquarters.

Before leaving Tokyo, Cecere had one last thing he wanted to do: take a shot at Pieri, whom he had come to loathe ever since spying on his conversation in the bar. Cecere called a friend at UBS and told him exactly why Hayes had been fired. Was UBS aware, Cecere asked, that Hayes and Pieri had been doing the same thing during their time together? Given the escalating nature of the government investigations, he suggested, perhaps it would be in the Swiss bank's interests to take a look at Pieri's and Hayes's records. The message was passed up the chain of command at UBS and, miraculously enough, it wasn't shunted aside. Instead, the bank decided that someone needed to trawl through Hayes's communications to see what they contained—exactly the sequence of events that had worried Hayes back when he had left UBS a year earlier. Who would handle this distasteful task? Not, it turned out, the compliance department or the bank's legal team or the outside law firm, Allen & Overy, that the CFTC had forced

315

UBS to hire. UBS instead told Pieri to investigate himself and his former underling.

Pieri decided it would be simplest to focus solely on Hayes's communications with Alykulov. He quickly reported that, lo and behold, Hayes and his mentee had been trying to move the bank's Libor submissions to benefit their trading portfolios.

That was enough to prompt UBS to take things more seriously. Pieri was relieved of his investigative responsibilities in favor of a major U.S. law firm, Gibson, Dunn & Crutcher. It didn't take long for the attorneys to grasp the depth of the problem: It wasn't just a couple of Tokyo traders freelancing as Libor manipulators. The wrongdoing was institutional, stretching from Tokyo to Singapore to London to Zurich, and involving not just low- and mid-level traders but also their managers, their managers' managers, and even some high-ranking executives who either knew what was going on or should have. And it involved numerous banks and brokerages—a systemic racket.

Gary Spratling, a mustachioed partner from Gibson Dunn's San Francisco office, delivered the bad news to UBS executives: If the bank didn't play its hand right, it was headed for billions of dollars in financial penalties, or worse. After all, prosecutors in the United States seemed to be dying to give the public what it wanted by filing criminal charges against a major bank. But Spratling—a master tactician and a specialist in antitrust law—had an idea. Antitrust laws in many countries included provisions granting immunity or leniency to those who were first to report problems. (In the United States, antitrust regulators even give partial amnesty to the second company to tattle.) If UBS raced to the authorities in the United States and elsewhere before anyone else did, and not only confessed its own sins but also promised to help build cases against its rivals, it might win leniency. Spratling made it clear that there didn't seem to be other good options.

So, starting in December, UBS and its lawyers embarked on a worldwide damage-control tour, meeting at least a dozen anti-trust authorities and banking regulators in Switzerland, England, the United States, Japan, the European Union, even Canada. At each stop, the bank owned up to what it had found—what looked like an industry-wide effort to skew yen Libor and other iterations of the benchmark—and supplemented its admissions with a sampling of the e-mails, chat sessions, and recorded phone calls that the internal investigators had unearthed so far. The bank offered to provide extensive cooperation, including by serving up UBS employees as witnesses and countless gigabytes of electronic evidence, in exchange for full or partial immunity.

It was a seminal moment for investigators. Here was one of the world's biggest banks, delivering what looked like a ready-made case on a silver platter. Until now, the Libor inquiries had focused mainly on two things: the practice of lowballing and the idea that individual traders at a handful of banks like Barclays were doing bad things in isolation. The investigations had been confined to a narrow time period—2007 and 2008—and only the U.S. dollar flavor of Libor. Now it was clear that the suspect activity occurred over a much longer period and in multiple Libor varietals. And, most important, it looked like there was a network of collusive behavior. That meant the scandal was much bigger than a random, haphazard attempt at manipulation, and it demolished banks' claims that this was the work of just a few bad apples.

Spratling had reason to be optimistic about his plan. One reason was that he knew how the system worked. Before joining Gibson Dunn, he had spent twenty-eight years working in the

Justice Department, rising to become a deputy assistant attorney general in charge of prosecuting international cartels—precisely the type of case that UBS was now owning up to being part of. Thanks to his long government career, Spratling had fostered some useful relationships. One of those was with his former subordinate, Scott Hammond, who by 2011 was the top criminal prosecutor in Justice's antitrust division. Hammond had helped devise the leniency program for self-reporters that Spratling now hoped to take advantage of. The two men remained close.

Spratling's strategy worked even better than he reasonably could have hoped. Antitrust authorities in Washington, Brussels, and Bern tentatively accepted the bank's deal and offered it at least partial immunity. But the bigger victory, the more stunning one, was that UBS somehow ended up in a position to set the course of the unfolding investigations. As part of its agreements to cooperate, UBS volunteered to handle the massive task of sifting through millions of pages of records and interviewing witnesses. That appealed to the regulators, who were constrained by tight budgets and busy schedules and didn't want to squander scarce resources on a wild-goose chase. But it also meant that crucial work—the act of laying the first bricks in the investigative foundation—was outsourced to a very biased party. UBS and its high-priced hired guns would now be the ones determining which evidence and witnesses showed up on regulators' and prosecutors' radar screens. If UBS didn't discover certain evidence, or decided for whatever reason not to share it with the authorities—well, it would probably never come to light.

So, before sending out subpoenas to UBS to ascertain the potential roles played by its senior executives in the scandal, the CFTC asked Gibson Dunn how to frame the legal documents. The law firm insisted that the subpoenas' scope be narrowed to only look at formal boardroom minutes and other official company documents, not e-mails, chat transcripts, phone calls, or handwritten notes—and the CFTC agreed, bowing to the firm's assertion that anything wider would be unmanageable. When Gibson Dunn reported that UBS had destroyed all of the recordings of employee phone calls in Tokyo, there was nothing much that investigators could do. Nor did they complain about the fact that UBS had blacked out the identities of certain people, presumably executives, included on various internal e-mail chains that the bank handed over. And they had to trust Gibson Dunn's matter-of-fact determination that eight million of the documents that UBS had initially flagged as relevant to the investigation simply wouldn't be available to U.S. or British regulators because they were housed on the bank's Swiss computers and therefore fell under the country's stringent bank secrecy laws.

This was a fantastic turn for UBS, which could now attempt to confine the investigation to an isolated group of wayward employees who no longer worked for the bank or at least already had been suspended. Sure, mistakes were made, but the guilty parties had been cleared out and the bank had come clean. Even better, UBS could steer the investigators away from the corner offices. And so, when the CFTC asked Gibson Dunn to come up with a list of individuals who should be on the subpoenas that the agency was preparing to send to UBS—names that would determine the search terms that the bank used to sieve through millions of pieces of internal communications—one was especially prominent: Tom Hayes.

. . . .

After leaving Tokyo, Hayes and Tighe flew to Barbados. The newlyweds stayed at Sandy Lane, a luxury beachfront resort frequented by celebrities. After the trauma of the past few months, and the washed-out honeymoon, they felt they deserved the sunny break—although it was marred by a blowout fight after Hayes, who uncharacteristically had consumed multiple boozy drinks, caused a scene accosting a retired Scottish soccer star, Gordon Strachan, whom he spotted at a gala dinner. Back in England, they moved into a large apartment in a converted sugar warehouse in an increasingly gentrified London neighborhood. It was just down a busy street from where Tighe had lived before she moved to Tokyo. The flat in Sugar House was much nicer than anywhere she'd lived on her own, though, decked out with polished wood and with a well-dressed doorman standing sentry downstairs.

Hoping to return to the banking industry, Hayes got to work looking for a new job. Around the turn of the year, he went with Read and another former colleague to watch a cricket match in Sydney with tickets paid for by ICAP. The excursion had been lined up before Hayes was fired, but he regarded it as a good omen that the tickets hadn't been revoked—he wasn't *that* toxic. Once back from Australia, he started dialing up his old industry contacts to see if there were any nibbles. The first, in early 2011, came from Bank of America. After cleaning up the mess left by its hasty Merrill Lynch acquisition, the North Carolina–based bank was back in expansion mode. In January, Bank of America flew Hayes in for two days of interviews in its new skyscraper in midtown Manhattan. As a reference, he listed Cecere, who had told him he'd be happy to help. In late March, Hayes e-mailed Citigroup's HR woman in Tokyo—the same one who participated in his firing—and told her that she would be hearing soon from "my future employer for a reference." (The HR woman said Citigroup would confirm Hayes's dates of employment and wouldn't say anything else.) Hayes and Tighe confidently prepared to move to New York, but when a Bank of America executive happened to mention the plan to one of Hayes's former bosses at UBS, the job disappeared.

Deutsche Bank seemed to have gotten cold feet, too. A second interview was canceled. "You weren't careful enough," Mark Lewis explained. Hayes e-mailed him a few more times, hoping something had changed. Lewis didn't respond.

Hayes wasn't stupid. He could see what this meant: His financial career was over. It was a sad, sobering moment. But life went on. Hayes had never learned to drive. Before moving to Tokyo, he had taken lessons, but he spent most of the time sitting in the passenger seat, explaining his tortured love life to the bemused driving instructor. In 2011, at age thirty-one, he decided it was time to get a license. Despite taking lessons, he flunked the test. On his second attempt, after committing the entire British highway code to memory, he passed. Having transferred his obsession with all things Porsche to one of its German rivals, he celebrated by buying a dark gray Mercedes SL500 convertible, a blue four-door Mercedes AMG sedan, a dark blue Mercedes minivan, and a black Mercedes 4x4. He gave a Mercedes coupe to his younger brother, Robin, a grade school teacher who had been driving a beat-up Volkswagen. Robin appreciated the gesture, although he was self-conscious driving the flashy £60,000 car through his school's working-class neighborhood.

That fall, Hayes enrolled in a one-year MBA program at Hult International Business School in London. He recognized that one of his weaknesses, after a career as a solitary trader, was working with others. In fact, that had been a weakness going back to his adolescent days. "I've got to learn how to be a normal individual," he thought, "rather than just some guy who just does what the hell he wants whenever he wants." He aced most of his classes, putting him on track to finish second in his class of aspiring business leaders.

••••

Even before UBS came clean, the CFTC and some Justice Department officials had heard the name Tom Hayes. He'd appeared in snippets of conversations that UBS previously had handed over as part of its simulation of cooperation, and he also had scattered cameos in chat transcripts that one or two other banks had produced for the agencies. But he hadn't been a central figure. Then, in January 2011, when UBS lawyers showed up at the CFTC offices, Meister scanned through some of the materials the bank was disclosing. Hayes was all over the documents. He came across as a typical Wall Street guy: arrogant and angry, a bit of a bully. Meister imagined him living large, partying into the wee hours at raucous Tokyo nightclubs. It would feel good, he thought, to nail this guy.

Obie—who with Meister's arrival had been demoted to running the enforcement department in the CFTC's New York office—had his doubts. Sure, Hayes looked like the most enthusiastic and skilled practitioner of Libor manipulation in Tokyo, but Obie recognized that this man was a bit weird. He seemed to exhibit hallmark traits of someone with Asperger's syndrome—obsessiveness, naïveté, obliviousness to social niceties, an inability to see things from other people's perspectives. All of that, Obie felt, made Tom Hayes a good target to try to flip; he probably would have plenty of dirt to dish on his superiors, and—emotionally removed—less loyalty to anyone but himself.

Meister, however, was in a hurry. He wanted the first batch of Libor cases to reach fruition by early 2012. It was an ambitious deadline, but it would be a huge achievement to mark the end of his first year at the CFTC. Plus, it would help pacify the impatient and micromanaging Gensler, who wanted regular, sometimes daily, updates on the investigation's progress.

· · · ·

Around the same time as the CFTC visit, UBS and its squadron of lawyers showed up at Justice's antitrust office, which sat in the department's main headquarters on Pennsylvania Avenue in Washington. But neither the bank nor the antitrust bureau alerted the fraud team in the nearby Bond Building, and William Stellmach was furious when he found out. Doughy-faced and nebbishy, his pleated pants hiked up higher than was fashionable, Stellmach had joined Justice's fraud division in July 2010. His nerdy appearance belied his tough pedigree. He had spent the prior several years as a federal prosecutor in New York. When he arrived in Washington for the new job, he was thrust into Justice's nascent Libor investigation. Stellmach, along with his colleagues Robertson Park and Denis McInerney, had begun to see the case as the vehicle for sating the public hunger for Wall Street prosecutions. The trick was to find some individual bankers who could be served as red meat.

There was a history of tension between Justice's fraud and antitrust sections—generally friendly competition, but sometimes not-so-friendly clashes over jurisdiction. With UBS's visit to antitrust, Stellmach perceived Spratling and the bank as trying to spark an internal Justice turf war aimed at getting the antitrust team—led by Hammond—to grant immunity and leaving the fraud section out in the cold. Stellmach complained to Spratling, who denied that was his goal.

One morning in early spring, trying to make peace, Spratling's team returned to Justice, but this time to the Bond Building for a belated presentation to Stellmach and his fraud colleagues. The gathering was held in a well-appointed conference room on the fourth floor, designed as a venue for greeting foreign dignitaries—a far cry from the dingy Flag Room. No sooner had the session begun than a squabble broke out. Spratling was under the impression that his pals in antitrust had given assurances that, thanks to the bank's cooperation, nobody at Justice would file charges against UBS or its employees. That's not how Stellmach and Park saw it. A grant of immunity from antitrust covered only that section's investigation, they explained; it didn't bind the fraud division. It was inevitable that someone was going to get charged—after all, one of the main points of the Libor investigation was to prove that U.S. prosecutors could finally nail someone. And, based on what the prosecutors had been picking up from their counterparts at other agencies, UBS and its former employees were starting to look like the most promising targets.

Spratling, trying to convince the prosecutors not to charge either his client or its current employees, volunteered to bring UBS employees to Washington to serve as Justice's guide dogs. He also walked the lawyers through hundreds of pages of evidence. UBS had certainly done its homework, matching up internal communications and Hayes's requests to brokers with actual movements in UBS's Libor submissions and occasional fluctuations in the benchmark itself. They weren't huge moves—only a couple of basis points in one direction or another. And it wasn't possible to definitively prove causation; it was conceivable that UBS's submissions might have moved without Hayes's pressure. (Another drawback: It involved a Japanese, not an American, interest rate, which meant it had less impact on, and therefore less cachet with, the U.S. public.) But for the first time, Stellmach and Park thought they were looking at evidence of real manipulation—the type of stuff that could actually hold up in court and that might have affected the wide range of institutions and individuals that had purchased derivatives to protect themselves from volatile interest rates. The damage to one person's credit card bill might have been negligible, but when you added up all of those credit cards, all of those car loans, all of those mortgages—well, it didn't look quite so minor. And the blatant nature of the e-mails and chat snippets resolved any lingering doubts about whether the evidence could be open to a more innocent, benign interpretation.

Hayes, in the course of that hours-long gathering, emerged as the obvious target. "He's the one," Park told colleagues afterward. That was just as UBS wanted it. In subsequent meetings, witnesses provided by UBS would describe Hayes—slim and not quite six feet tall—as large and physically intimidating. The shepherd's pie anecdote resurfaced, casting Hayes as potentially violent. He was beginning to resemble a bogeyman. Nothing had been formalized, but in their heads, Stellmach and Park finally had their man.

. . . .

On the afternoon of Friday, March 11, 2011, a violent earthquake rumbled up from more than fifteen miles beneath the surface of the ocean off Japan's northeastern coast. It shook buildings all over the country, but the worst damage came from the sea. The shifting underwater plates unleashed a tsunami of biblical proportions, with a wall of water thirty feet high bulldozing Japan's coastal prefectures. It ruptured a nuclear power plant. More than sixteen thousand people would perish.

In Tokyo, Alykulov felt the quake and its aftershocks and then watched, awestruck, as news reports showed the extent of the damage caused by the tsunami. He decided it was time to get out of town. A few months earlier, UBS had suspended him from his job. He was still getting paid—that way the bank could ensure that he and others in similar situations would cooperate with the Americans—but his career prospects were in doubt. It was a jarring, embarrassing turn for someone who not long ago had thought he had a bright future as a trader. After a few glum days, he started trying to figure out what to do with his life. As a first step, he went back to Kazakhstan. Then he decided to learn yet another language. He set off for Spain, keeping in close touch all the while with the Washington criminal defense attorney—a tall, buzz-cut trial lawyer named Nate Muyskens—that UBS had hired to represent him. Muyskens told him he was eventually going to need to come to Washington to meet with FBI agents and Justice prosecutors. So after Alykulov returned to Tokyo from Spain just in time for the earthquake, he packed his bags and, without telling anyone, got on a plane to Washington. It was all such a blur that he forgot to bring a suit. On the car ride into town from Dulles International Airport, Alykulov stopped at a department store and dropped $500 on a new suit so that he could look presentable when he showed up at the Bond Building. He charged it to UBS—after all, this trip was on behalf of his employer.

By the time he arrived in Washington, Alykulov had worked himself into a lather, convinced that this trip would culminate with him in a jail cell. The easygoing Muyskens, whose clients ranged from bank traders to Justin Bieber, told him to chill—all he had to do was cooperate, he explained, and Justice would promise not to prosecute him. But Alykulov wasn't wild about that idea. He knew Hayes by now was one of the main targets. Alykulov didn't much like Hayes, but he knew his former boss regarded him as a friend, and the thought of knifing someone in that situation made him a little queasy. Plus, he was genuinely fond of Tighe. When the time came for their appointment at the Bond Building, Muyskens had to physically push Alykulov out the door to walk the few blocks down New York Avenue. Even when he got there, Alykulov seemed to have trouble explaining what he'd actually done wrong. Gradually, though, he overcame his compunctions—he told himself that he had an obligation to UBS and its thousands of employees to help resolve this mess—and spent dozens of hours serving as a much-needed Sherpa for the prosecutors and FBI agents.

When you got down to it, everyone who had been part of the effort to manipulate Libor—Hayes, Pieri, Farr, Read, Alykulov, Goodman, Cecere, and on and on, even UBS itself—was a trader, no matter their particular place in the market. Hayes had been odd and abusive, but it had been worth tolerating because everyone was getting paid well. Morals were never part of the equation. Feeling sorry for the loser on the other side of your winning trade was career poison. And so now, too, it was time to trade, to come out ahead, to find the weak one—the muppet—and grind him into dust. There was no need for a group meeting, a halftime huddle: Those who had worked with Hayes knew that just as he'd been the key to the vault, he was now the key to a very different door. If someone was going down, UBS had to make sure it was Tom Hayes. And if Tom Hayes was going down, everyone who had worked with him had to do whatever he could to make sure Hayes fell alone. The good thing was that there was at least a little truth in the lie: Hayes had, in fact, been central to much of the Libor-skewing effort. But no orchestra is made up of a single musician.

Hayes, Alykulov told the Justice investigators, had orchestrated the whole thing. What about current UBS employees and executives? Alykulov downplayed their involvement. Hayes, he made clear, was the mastermind.

. . . .

Back in London, Tighe was a couple of months pregnant; the baby was due in October. Between severe morning sickness and doctors' appointments and her decision that they needed to move—the Sugar House flat wasn't child-friendly, nor was the surrounding urban grit—their lives were hectic but on track. They started shopping for a house in London's exurbs.

One day in March, Hayes received a Facebook message from Alykulov: "We need to talk." He said the Justice Department wanted to speak with him and that he wanted to get Hayes's advice on what to do. Hayes still hadn't spoken to any regulators, and he was eager for any scraps of information he could pick up about the course of the U.S. investigations. He sent Alykulov his cell phone number. A couple of days later, on a mild, damp afternoon, Hayes and Tighe were in the prenatal wing of London's University College Hospital, a sleek, modern building with green-tinted windows. They were there for Tighe's twelve-week scan, a crucial exam that would show if the fetus had any serious abnormalities or health problems. As a midwife moved an ultrasound wand over Tighe's growing midsection, Hayes's cell phone rang with a call from a number he didn't recognize and that didn't appear to be from England or Japan. While Tighe lay there, anxious, Hayes stood up, walked out of the room, and answered the phone.

It was Alykulov, who said he was calling from Kazakhstan— hence the long, strange phone number on Hayes's screen. As Muyskens had promised, Alykulov had been granted a nonprosecution agreement that stated that Justice wouldn't go after him as long as he cooperated fully. The FBI agents initially had tried to convince Alykulov that they hadn't been able to track down Hayes's phone number. He'd be doing everyone a big favor by reaching out to his former boss over Facebook to establish contact, the investigators said; the sooner they got in touch with Hayes, the better it would be for him. One thing led to another, and on this day, Alykulov was sitting in his lawyer's office in Washington. FBI agents had devised an elaborate system to make it look like the call was coming from Alykulov's native country. Audio of the call was being recorded and piped live into a room at the Bond Building, where prosecutors and FBI agents sat around a conference table listening. They had prepared a list of questions for Alykulov to ask Hayes, hoping to get his former mentor to acknowledge that what he'd been doing was wrong or to make some other sort of incriminating statement—perhaps encouraging Alykulov to lie or destroy evidence.

Alykulov—trying to fight back a debilitating sense of anxiety and betrayal—started the call by repeating what he'd said in the Facebook message: Justice wanted to schedule an interview. "Should I talk to them? What should I tell them?'

"The U.S. Department of Justice, mate, you know, they're like . . . the dudes who, you know . . . put people in jail," Hayes answered. "Why the hell would you want to talk to them?"

Her ultrasound finished, Tighe walked into the prenatal wing's waiting room, its walls covered with posters featuring cherubic babies and signs barring phone calls. Hayes was pacing and talking on his cell. Tighe could tell from his expression—his whole face was screwed up in a confused, agitated look—that something strange was going on.

Alykulov had just mentioned that he had printed out e-mails in which Hayes had asked his subordinate to help move Libor. "What should I do with them?" he asked.

"Why are you printing e-mails?" Hayes asked, furrowing his brow.

Tighe started listening carefully to his end of the conversation.

They were clearly talking about Libor and the Justice Department. She motioned for him to get off the phone; when that failed, she whispered, urgently, for him to tell Alykulov not to destroy evidence or to lie. If this was a trap, she didn't want her naïve husband stumbling right into it. Hayes complied, then asked Alykulov whether the Justice Department wanted to talk to him. Alykulov, his adrenaline surging, said he didn't know. Hayes, growing apprehensive about Alykulov's carefully worded queries and nervous tone, asked whether he was recording the call.

"I did this, too," Alykulov said. "Why would I record it?"

With Hayes still on the phone, Tighe took an elevator downstairs to collect the test results that would show whether the fetus was at risk of Down syndrome. She couldn't believe she was going through this alone. The results showed virtually no risk of the syndrome. Angry despite the good news, she rode the elevator back up and found Hayes still on the phone. He was in the process of telling Alykulov to just blame his managers. "That's what I'm going to do," Hayes said.

At the Bond Building, FBI agents thought that Hayes's suggestion that Alykulov shouldn't talk to the investigators might be enough for an obstruction-of-justice charge. A couple of days later, though, they decided to take another shot, hoping for cleaner evidence. Hayes was finishing up lunch at the Cuckfield pub in East London with his stepbrother Ben O'Leary, who worked at a nearby hospital, when his phone rang. The Cuckfield, housed in a nineteenth-century stone inn, had a beer garden in the back, and Hayes stood there in the early-afternoon sunshine. Alykulov asked what struck him as a series of leading questions. "Should I tell them about your friend at RBS?" Alykulov wondered.

"Brent? What's he got to do with it?" Hayes asked.

"Should I tell them about your friend at Deutsche?"

"Well, I wouldn't mention it," Hayes said, "but if they ask, you should tell them." In any case, he added, everything was done in writing, so it wasn't much of a secret.

. . . .

In 1986, in response to what became known as the Roskill Report, the British Parliament created the Serious Fraud Office, consolidating what had been a national patchwork of antifraud forces into one central government body. The report, named for the senior judge who helmed a special committee, had found that "[t]he public no longer believes that the legal system in England and Wales is capable of bringing the perpetrators of serious frauds expeditiously and effectively to book" and that "the overwhelming weight of the evidence laid before us suggests that the public is right. In relation to such crimes, and to the skillful and determined criminals who commit them, the present legal system is archaic, cumbersome and unreliable." The newly launched SFO's mandate was to investigate and prosecute complex, large-scale fraud and corruption cases—attacking the stock swindlers, bribery schemes, and manipulative practices that were rife in the City at the same time that Margaret Thatcher's government was encouraging middle-class people to invest their savings in the market. Housed in a run-down office building on an out of-the-way street north of the City, the SFO got off to a fast start; its probe into the 1991 collapse of the Bank of Credit and Commerce International resulted in the convictions of several bank executives. But by the 2000s, the agency's statistics were looking soft: Each year, it prosecuted perhaps two dozen individuals, most of them relatively small-time offenders, notwithstanding the agency's goal of going after only the highest-level criminals. The agency was dogged by internal scandals, doling out lucrative severance packages to ousted employees and spending a small fortune for its chief executive to travel back and forth between London and her home in England's Lake District.

Perhaps worst of all, high-profile investigations faltered in sometimes spectacular fashion. In 2006, for example, facing intense diplomatic and political pressure not to offend an important British ally, the agency abandoned its investigation into whether British arms manufacturer BAE Systems had bribed Saudi Arabian officials for lucrative military contracts. (The continued investigation "would have been devastating for our relationship with an important country," Prime Minister Tony Blair explained.) And at dawn one morning in March 2011, the SFO and police forces raided a series of residences and arrested two well-known property tycoons, the brothers Robert and Vincent Tchenguiz. The arrests, part of an investigation into the collapsed Icelandic bank Kaupthing, were probably the SFO's highest-profile actions ever—and they quickly became its biggest embarrassment. The SFO eventually dropped the case, admitting it had misinterpreted evidence involving the Tchenguiz brothers. For its troubles, the agency became known in some quarters as the Seriously Flawed Office, and the government drew up plans to strip it of much of its funding.

Despite its woeful reputation, if you worked for an entity that was pursuing fraud investigations involving British culprits or victims, the SFO was a crucial way station: Protocol dictated that you at least check in with the agency. So in May 2011, two months after the Tchenguiz arrests, an official at the United Kingdom's antitrust enforcer, the Office of Fair Trading, contacted the SFO. The antitrust agency had been looking into Libor manipulation since the prior December, when UBS had showed up, out of the blue, to turn itself in. Over the next several months, UBS employees had provided testimony and evidence to help the OFT build a case—similar to the processes going on in other world capitals. Now, the OFT wondered, would the SFO be interested in joining forces to bring the investigation across the finish line? Following a preliminary phone call, the OFT mailed over a dossier of evidence, forming what it thought was the backbone of a promising fraud case—exactly the type of investigation the SFO was designed to tackle and one in which much of the investigative legwork already had been completed. The SFO took the matter to its executive board. The response eventually came back: "At this time the SFO cannot commit to using their resources on this case." Its tail between its legs, the underfunded agency was trying to reorient itself toward simpler cases.

Robertson Park at the Justice Department had a similar conversation with the SFO that spring. He informed his London counterpart that Washington had in its sights a British citizen who looked increasingly like the ringleader of the Libor scandal. Would the SFO care to get involved? No thanks, came the immediate response. Park hung up, puzzled by the agency's indifference. Shouldn't they be clamoring for a piece of the action?

. . . .

On May 9, Terry Farr was invited into a meeting room at RP Martin. Only a few weeks earlier, he had called Hayes to check in, and the pair made plans to catch up over beers. But when the appointed date came, Hayes backed out; he had a doctor's appointment. They rescheduled. The next time, Farr had to cancel when a client asked to get drinks. They never managed to meet up. It was too bad, because Farr had been eager to hear more about how Hayes had handled Citigroup's internal investigation. As word of Hayes's downfall and the intensifying government investigations had spread, RP Martin had opened its own review into the matter. Mustard's hated compliance squad dubbed it Project Green and, with the help of outside lawyers, collected volumes of chat transcripts, e-mails, and recordings of phone calls. When Farr arrived at the meeting that May morning, he was asked to describe his twelve-year employment history at RP Martin. He told the lawyers about how he'd first met Hayes, who was looking for a junior broker to mold. Farr downplayed the importance of the relationship. They only met every eighteen months or so in Tokyo, he said. He didn't mention that they'd spoken every day for years. Then the meeting was over—there was nothing more to it. Jim Gilmour was brought into a similar meeting the same day, with the same result: nothing.

Two months later, in mid-July, Farr was called in for another meeting. This time he was briefed on the broadening scope of the brokerage's internal investigation, which was examining possible violations of antitrust and other laws. Farr was informed that RP Martin had been contacted by the CFTC, the European Commission, and Canadian regulators. The firm's internal searches had turned up an overwhelming amount of material that was of interest to the regulators and that Farr hadn't bothered to mention in his previous meeting. RP Martin's lawyers laid out two options: He could switch into another job—something far away from the yen desk—or he could be suspended but still collect paychecks. Neither option sounded disastrous. Farr decided to go on paid leave. Then, for the next six months, nothing seemed to happen.

. . . .

A few other dominoes began to fall. At RBS, Paul White and Neil Danziger were suspended after the company turned up troves of embarrassing—and potentially incriminating—communications in an internal investigation that it named Project Zen.

An investigation got under way at ICAP, too. In September, Wilkinson was on vacation when Frits Vogels, the manager in London, called. He told Wilkinson to cut his vacation short and get back to meet with the firm's lawyers.

Around that time, violent riots were engulfing large swaths of London. Protesters vented their rage about police abuses by torching and looting businesses. "I can't believe it," Read e-mailed Wilkinson. "I'm here in Wellington looking at London burning."

"The end is nigh," Wilkinson responded. The men wouldn't speak again for years.

• • • •

Kweku Adoboli, who attended the University of Nottingham at the same time as Hayes and then joined UBS as a summer intern, had climbed through the bank's ranks. Despite starting in the unglamorous "back office," where he earned a paltry £33,000 salary (roughly $60,000), the cheerful and charismatic Ghana native had managed to scratch his way up to an actual trading job in London. By 2010, the thirty-year-old had been promoted to the rank of director, his salary had jumped to £110,000, and he was on track to pocket a handsome £250,000 bonus. But the next summer, his career started to unravel. Every trade he executed, every market prediction he made, turned out dead wrong. His weren't the only positions that were curdling; his entire team was losing money. Rather than wave a white flag, Adoboli concocted an elaborate cheating scheme. He took advantage of UBS's rickety compliance and risk management systems and entered fake offsetting trades into the bank's computer systems to conceal the fact that his risk levels were soaring to out-of-control heights. At first, the ploy worked: It bought him and his colleagues some time, and they managed to make up most of the money they'd been hemorrhaging. But then the bleeding resumed, and this time there was nothing Adoboli could do to stanch it. By August they were staring at a $3 billion loss. "We need a miracle," he posted on Facebook.

The miracle never came. On a Monday afternoon, he gathered his team at a bar across the street from UBS's offices and told them he was prepared to take the fall. He went home and e-mailed his bosses, confessing what he'd done. Then he returned to the office and explained the mechanics of his scheme. Late that night, UBS called the police, who came to arrest him and hauled him off to prison. UBS announced a few days later that Adoboli's trading had cost the bank $2.3 billion. The next week, as questions swirled about how UBS management possibly could have failed to notice such massive and problematic trading, the bank's CEO, Oswald Grübel, handed in his resignation. For a second time, UBS got to work arming investigators with evidence against an employee, casting him as a lone, rogue operator inside an otherwise law-abiding company.

At his trial, Adoboli pleaded not guilty to the criminal charges of fraud. In a drab brick courthouse on the south bank of the River Thames, the prosecution painted him as a greedy, reckless fraudster whose selfish actions had cost UBS shareholders billions of dollars. Adoboli's defense was that he was a scapegoat for the bank's out-of-control, risk-crazed culture. He had learned everything he knew from UBS—including the ways to navigate around the bank's haphazard internal checks and balances—and everyone knew exactly what he was doing. Indeed, other UBS employees had referred openly in e-mails and electronic chats to his fraudulent strategy. Some colleagues had participated. The jury didn't buy it. He was convicted and sentenced to seven years in prison.

. . . .

With Tighe's due date only a few weeks out, Hayes continued his tradition of attending every Queens Park Rangers game, home and away. She had been frustrated with Hayes's conduct throughout her pregnancy. He hadn't been very sympathetic when she was largely bedridden in the first trimester, and now he wasn't showing any indications of adapting to their soon-to-change life. Was he oblivious or did he not care?

Baby Joshua arrived shortly after 11 P.M. on October 7, 2011. The lovestruck parents nicknamed their cuddly newborn "Mr. Marsupial," which was eventually shortened to "Mr. Sups" and, finally, "Supy." Hayes dressed Joshua in soccer gear. "QPR fan, just like Daddy," Tighe captioned a photo on Facebook when the baby was two weeks old. That was sweet, but the exhausted Tighe was less pleased when, two weeks later, Hayes announced that he was going on a road trip to watch QPR play. "You just don't get it!" she shouted.

And yet, by and large, everything seemed normal. They socialized with Hayes's business school classmates. To accommodate their expanding family, in December they bought a large house on a quiet road in the village of Woldingham, a thirty-minute train ride from central London. The seven-bedroom Old Rectory was their dream home, spacious yet homey with raw wood floors (except in the bathrooms, whose tiles were heated). The huge kitchen—equipped with top-of-the-line appliances, a wine refrigerator, and an island countertop made of volcano granite—opened into a dining room with sweeping views of the countryside. They paid the £1.2 million (nearly $2 million) price in cash, using a chunk of Hayes's Citigroup signing bonus. Before they moved in, they started a major renovation project, building a new three-story wing and redoing much of the house's electrical wiring. They paid using some of the £960,000 in profits that Hayes recently had racked up trading currencies and stock indexes through an online brokerage account. Hayes, for all his sins, remained a prodigious trader, by all accounts one of the best at his craft on the planet. He found his success gratifying, proof to himself that his investing savvy wasn't contingent on him sitting on a noisy bank trading floor; he could do it just as well from the comfort of his own home.

On December 16, Japan's Financial Services Agency issued a pair of two-page press releases announcing the filing of "administrative actions" against UBS and Citigroup for trying to manipulate yen Libor and Tibor. These were the first times a regulator had disciplined a bank for skewing an interest-rate benchmark, the inaugural fruits of UBS's global confessional circuit a year earlier. But while the Japanese orders were a milestone, they weren't much to behold and therefore attracted little media attention. The regulator didn't impose any financial penalties—UBS and Citigroup just had to stop trading certain derivatives for slightly less than two weeks. The actions didn't name any individuals. The UBS order referred anonymously to Hayes. The Citigroup document only referred to a character identified as "Trader B," who along with "Director A" engaged in what the regulator described as "seriously unjust and malicious" behavior. Hayes was Trader B, and Cecere was Director A. Mccappin, referred to simply as "the CEO," was accused of having "overlooked these actions" despite knowing about them.

Hayes and Cecere drew solace from the fact that nobody from the Japanese regulator or the banks had contacted them as part of the investigation. And they hadn't been publicly named. Still blissfully unaware of the intensifying U.S. and British investigations, the two men figured this was the end of the matter.

CHAPTER 15

Spiders

Andrew Smith was in Portsmouth when his cell phone rang. He was on England's windy southern coast with his wife, Christy, who was about to give birth to triplets. On the line was a colleague in UBS's offices out by the Zurich airport. Several years earlier, Smith had worked there as a low-level, and largely unsupervised, trader responsible for some of the bank's Libor submissions. Now, in May 2012, he was based in UBS's London office.

Smith's colleague was calling to give him a heads-up: UBS's human resources department would be sending him a written warning about his role in *l'affaire Libor*. A few months earlier, Smith had been hauled into an interview with the bank's HR and compliance people, who had grilled him about whether he'd ever moved Libor up or down to accommodate requests from traders. The answer, of course, was yes: Everyone had been doing the same thing. It was the first moment Smith deduced that perhaps he'd done something borderline or even wrong. Ever since, he'd been wondering if another shoe would drop. Now, with impeccably bad timing, here it was.

A day or two later, Christy gave birth, and word came from his boss that a bunch of his colleagues who had been involved with Libor had just been told they were losing their jobs—UBS's latest attempt to convince prosecutors that any wrongdoing was perpetrated by a cluster of *former* employees. The good news was that Smith wasn't among those getting a pink slip. He was just getting a warning letter. "Congratulations," his boss said.

Pieri and Alykulov didn't fare so well. Both had been suspended more than a year earlier and had held out hope that they could salvage their finance careers. Alykulov was doing everything he could to impress American prosecutors while simultaneously looking for new jobs in Tokyo—he and his lawyer could see the writing on the wall. Pieri was less farsighted. Around the time he was put on paid leave, he moved to Hong Kong, expecting brighter career prospects in UBS's offices there, away from his tarnished Tokyo reputation. He waited around in Hong Kong, collecting paychecks, submitting to interviews with UBS lawyers, and wondering when the bank would end his suspension. It never did. In May, UBS informed him and Alykulov—and more than a dozen others—that they could either resign voluntarily or be fired. That was an easy choice: Resigning didn't leave a blemish on your employment records. As a parting blow, the bank demanded that Pieri relinquish some of the UBS shares that he'd been given as part of his prior compensation.

Smith's triplets were a few days old when he received the anticipated warning letter. The bank told him he had to sign it that very afternoon. His punishment was that his bonus, due to be paid out the next day, would be docked by a certain percentage—but the letter didn't specify the percentage, and Smith never found out what his bonus would have been otherwise. That wasn't the only thing that confused him. The letter said the warning was based on the bank's Libor investigation and Smith's "behavior at that time," but it didn't state what he had actually done wrong. Smith was left to ruminate about the possibilities. Maybe it was something dumb he'd said in a chat? Was it the fact that he'd complied with his colleagues' requests? He wasn't really sure, and he didn't really care. His family had just expanded by three people, and he wanted to put the whole episode behind him. He signed the letter.

．．．．

Now the game was truly afoot. At ICAP, two senior managers told Wilkinson in January that the FSA had decided that it was no longer appropriate for him to keep coming in to the office;* he would be suspended. Wilkinson's employees took him out for pizza to commiserate.

Wilkinson had plenty of company. The prior September, ICAP's general counsel informed Read that he was being suspended. That wasn't so bad; Read just relaxed at home in New Zealand and did nothing. Goodman and Brent Davies also were put on paid leave.

That spring, Wilkinson was in London to see his tailor, and he and a former colleague caught up over coffee. The colleague said he'd been interviewed by the Justice Department. Wilkinson heard through the grapevine that Justice also had interrogated another former ICAP broker—someone who had hardly ever interacted with Hayes. Now *that* was alarming. Increasingly troubled, the brash, hedonistic Danny the Animal started going to a shrink to talk about the investigation. Goodman also was in rough shape.

---

* The FSA would later tell Wilkinson that his bosses had been lying—the agency had nothing to do with his suspension.

A psychiatrist diagnosed him with "a major depressive disorder," put him on antidepressants, and enrolled him in individual and group therapy sessions. Over beers with a former colleague one afternoon, he sat in the pub sobbing.

After belatedly joining the investigation, the FSA was now an enthusiastic participant. In addition to reviewing reams of evidence that it had collected from banks and brokerages, it was interviewing their past and present employees. And while the FSA was lagging behind its American competitors in terms of the physical evidence it had gathered, here it possessed an advantage: Most of the suspects in the case were British citizens who had worked in London and currently resided on British soil. The FSA, therefore, had a much easier time tapping this human intelligence. How valuable it would turn out to be remained an open question.

That spring, Farr and his lawyers arrived at the agency's headquarters to be interviewed. Greeted in the FSA's lobby by an enormous sculpture of an owl bearing its razor-sharp talons, the visitors were given name tags and escorted up a spiral staircase to an interview room. The FSA had the right to compel people to honestly answer questions or be held in contempt of court, though that information couldn't be used against that person in a criminal court, unless it proved to be false or misleading. Farr, who'd been ordered to appear, wasn't happy to be there. He intended to be polite, but he had no interest in helping the FSA build cases against him or his colleagues.

The interview got under way with an FSA agent asking Farr how often he carried out Hayes's requests for him to talk with traders and other brokers. "I would regularly say to him I would, but it was sales talk and bravado," he replied. "I didn't always ask people. I just said I would."

Farr further explained that his band of brokers had a communal Bloomberg account—in Farr's name and situated at his desk, but his colleagues also used it. So, really, Farr now told the investigators, it was basically impossible to say if anything that had been written in his name was actually written by him. Farr said he had an awful memory so, as much as he would love to help, he just couldn't be sure about what he'd written.

Trying to resolve this uncertainty, the FSA pointed Farr to a Bloomberg chat with Hayes in which Farr's son Sam was a topic of discussion. "I just wondered if that made it more or less likely that it was you who was making these entries?" an FSA investigator wondered.

"It could have been me," Farr said.

"I think the bottom line is, did you have a teenage son at that time?" the agent asked.

"I do have a teenage son."

"Did you at the time?"

"Yeah, well, he's not a teenager anymore, but I did have a teenage son at the time." For a moment, that seemed to settle the matter. "But the guys who I work with all know I have a teenage son as well," Farr added. "I'm not denying this is me. . . . I said I just can't recall that it was me."

Another investigator, Patrick Meaney, was losing patience. "But the point is the other guys on the desk are not going to sit there and pretend to be you and pretend that they're talking about your teenage son."

"Why aren't they?" Farr asked.

"Because what's the point? What would be the point of doing that?"

"Well, they may do," Farr said, then started to mumble about their possible motivations.

One of Farr's lawyers, Shah Qureshi, stepped in. "I don't think

Terry, with respect, was suggesting that anyone was trying to pretend to be him. I think his point is that others did use that line."

"We seem to be having a great deal of problem getting you to acknowledge that, and I'm wondering why that is the case," Meaney said.

"I'm not denying it's me," Farr said. "I said it's likely me." It was 5 P.M., and the interview was brought to an end for the day.

When the process resumed the next morning, Farr still was playing games. The investigators were getting frustrated. He said he didn't know what the word *counterintuitive* meant. He said he wasn't misleading Hayes, then later acknowledged that perhaps he'd "told him the odd white lie on occasions." He said, over and over, that he didn't remember things that he'd spent hours chatting about. He said that, to the extent that he had seemed to agree to do anything untoward, he often misspoke in chats.

When the interview turned to the switch trades, Farr claimed that they weren't tied to attempts to get Libor moved in helpful directions. Instead, they were Hayes's way of thanking Farr for the "bespoke services"—prices, information, market intelligence, trades—that he was providing. On another occasion, Farr insisted that he had no idea what Hayes was referring to when he thanked Farr for his help and Farr promised to keep helping.

"Your answer is not credible," Meaney snapped.

• • • •

Early in 2012, Hayes's name started surfacing in the media. The first reference was a *Wall Street Journal* article on February 7. Awkwardly headlined "Rate Probe Keys on Traders," it reported that U.S. authorities were investigating a number of traders and that, at the center, was a British man named Thomas Hayes. The story, which ran on the cover of the *Journal*'s Money & Investing section, seemed to be based on reporters figuring out the identities of the anonymous individuals mentioned in the Japanese regulator's reports a couple of months earlier. (The story also mentioned Cecere and Mccappin.) Soon other news organizations followed up with their own reports.

Hayes had been in talks with Hult about joining the business school as a teacher to lecture students about how finance worked in the real world. The media attention led Hult to revoke the offer. Hayes panicked. He told Tighe that maybe he should just kill himself. It was the first time he'd said anything like that. He didn't seem serious, but Tighe was alarmed.

Notwithstanding mounting evidence to the contrary, Hayes still insisted he didn't need a lawyer. So he was surprised to hear that Brent Davies had hired one. When he asked whether Davies thought he should find one, too, Davies didn't hesitate: yes. Hayes's father, a reader of the business press, saw his son mentioned and also urged him to lawyer up. Hayes ignored both of them. But Tighe put her foot down. At first, he argued, again, that since he'd done nothing wrong he didn't need a lawyer. The disagreement escalated into yet another shouting match, and this time Tighe prevailed. Yet when Hayes contacted one law firm after another, none would represent him. The problem wasn't that he was an unattractive client—quite the contrary. But most of London's prestigious law firms already had been retained by other individuals and institutions ensnared in the expanding Libor investigation.

Eventually, in March, he settled on a small firm called Fulcrum Chambers. The lawyers and their new client sat down in the Victorian brick building where they had a suite and went through his situation in detail. It was a remarkably upbeat gathering—the first indication of what would become a surreal and disastrous legal relationship. The fact that his name had been mentioned in newspapers as a key figure perversely struck Hayes as encouraging, and his lawyers didn't disagree. "The press exposure on me is a positive sign," he asserted. "The stuff that's not in the press is the stuff you need to worry about. People aren't going to leak info on me if it would jeopardize a massive investigation. People are more willing to speak if they're not scared." For a man as logically minded as Hayes, it was bizarre reasoning.

The Fulcrum team discussed the possibility of Hayes suing Citigroup for wrongful termination. "They will have to pay for mistreating you," a Fulcrum lawyer, David Williams, intoned. Another, Ivan Pearce, warned him against speaking to the press. "The information you have is powerful," Pearce explained. "Leaking anything would weaken that power."

Hayes asked about the odds that he would be charged by and then extradited to the United States, which he knew from Alykulov was conducting a criminal investigation. This, he acknowledged, was the only thing that really frightened him. American courtrooms were notoriously inhospitable places for white-collar defendants, thanks in part to U.S. prosecutors' ability to strong-arm witnesses into testifying in exchange for lighter penalties. (British prosecutors lacked such plea-bargaining powers.) And prison sentences in the United States tended to be far longer—not to mention less pleasant, given the violent conditions in many American prisons—than those imposed by British courts. Williams estimated that the chances of him facing U.S. criminal charges were "10 percent or less." The Justice Department didn't have an interest in getting into an extradition fight with the United Kingdom, he said. "You're not that important to them," Pearce added.[*]

---

[*] Williams added a caveat: "Strange things do happen."

The lawyers suggested that Hayes get in touch with Cecere to see about coordinating their legal strategies. So Hayes and Tighe flew to Geneva, where Cecere had begun to work at Brevan Howard. It was a nice reunion, the women discussing motherhood, the men speculating about the direction of the government investigations. Cecere didn't seem worried, but he soon started telling acquaintances that—to his great surprise—his former employee apparently had constructed a "spider network" to execute his nefarious Libor scheme. It was an apt handle: With strands stretching across the globe, the web trapped the naïve and unsuspecting. Cecere, too, was trying to cast all the blame on Hayes, even though this web was in fact shared by many spiders—Cecere among them.

. . . .

For a few weeks that spring, the financial world's attention was consumed by another scandal in London. A trader in J.P. Morgan's London office, Bruno Iksil, had amassed huge positions in an exotic class of derivatives called credit default swap indexes. Before long, his bets grew so big that he was controlling a substantial slice of the market and had acquired a nickname: the London Whale. As Hayes had learned, size is a mixed blessing, and when markets turned against Iksil, competitors smelled blood and attacked. Things quickly careened out of control—soon Iksil's team was sitting on losses of more than $2 billion.

When the media caught a whiff of what was happening—a story made infinitely sexier by Iksil's nickname and J.P. Morgan's reputation for having survived the financial crisis unscathed—the bank's overconfident CEO, Jamie Dimon, dismissed the whole saga as "a tempest in a teapot." But losses kept growing, eventually exceeding $6 billion. Regulators and prosecutors started investigating. Soon they zeroed in on Iksil's underling and his manager as the primary culprits; both would be criminally charged. The high-ranking brass who'd thrilled to the profits Iksil generated, as well as the senior executive who supervised the disastrous investment strategy, were not prosecuted.

. . . .

In early May, Read flew in from New Zealand to sit down with the FSA. He had been on paid leave from ICAP for eight months now, spending time with his family and volunteering at a Presbyterian retirement home, where he tended its gardens and to its frail patients. The meeting room was crowded: There were four FSA investigators, a CFTC official who had traveled from Washington (a second CFTC investigator joined over the phone), and four of Read's own lawyers. The tone quickly grew testy. Meaney asked Read about Goodman's daily run-throughs, with their column of "suggested" Libor data. Why, he asked, was Goodman suggesting where banks set Libor? Read said it was more a prediction, a forecast, than an instruction. "But why isn't it called 'predicted Libors' if that's the case?" Meaney pushed.

"'Suggested' and 'predicted,' don't you think it's the same word?" Read said.

"No."

"You don't? . . . 'I *suggest* these are the Libors,' 'I *predict* these are the Libors.' It's the same thing, isn't it?"

"No."

"We'll agree to disagree," Read announced.

"I think in common English understanding, the word 'suggest' and the word 'predict' are actually quite different," Meaney said.

"Well," Read concluded, "I think you're being very pedantic."

A couple of hours later, Read tried to explain why there seemed to be so much evidence indicating that he and Hayes were working together to try to influence Goodman's run-throughs. "We'll take credit for things we don't do. Of course, it's just a broker's way," Read told the investigators. "If he says, you know, 'I like these high,' and they go up, then of course I mention it: 'Oh, it's probably down to us, I would imagine, Tom.' You drip-feed these things into people's psyches." Read argued that it was virtually impossible that ICAP had any sway over banks' Libor submissions. "We can't influence that. What we can do is try and take the credit for stuff."

"Does that seem a little bit dishonest to you?" an FSA investigator, Harsh Trivedi, asked at another point.

"No, it's not dishonest," Read said. "Why is it dishonest?"

"You're telling Tom you're doing something that now you're saying you didn't do," Trivedi explained. Meaney chimed in: "Wasn't it also highly risky? In the sense that Tom Hayes was your only client and so you couldn't afford to lose Tom Hayes as a client and so, if you had been essentially misleading him over a long period of time . . . and he had found that out, what would his reaction have been?"

"Well, it's, you know, there's no way he can find out if we're doing something or we're not doing something," Read replied. "I'm not that fussed, to be honest. I didn't go to New Zealand to work, and it wouldn't bother me one way or the other."

"Do you routinely mislead your clients?" Meaney asked.

"No."

Would Hayes "be surprised to learn that you were passing him misinformation over all this time?" a CFTC official asked.

"How am I passing misinformation?" Read asked, tying himself in a knot.

Why didn't Read alert his compliance department to what Hayes was seeking? "Well, why should I?" Read responded. "I think banks do things that are inappropriate every day. . . . Why should I pick up on them? It's not up to me. I'm not a regulator."

"No," Trivedi snapped, "you're not a regulator. And if inappropriate activity is brought to you, you don't have an obligation to escalate it, is your proposition?"

Precisely, Read agreed. "I think if brokers brought everything to you then the brokers would end up having no clients . . . and therefore there'd be no broker jobs." With that, one of Read's lawyers suggested that perhaps it was time for a short break.

．．．．

Six days later, it was Wilkinson's turn. He'd been preparing for weeks for this interview, sifting through the documents that had been handed over to regulators, who shared them with Wilkinson's lawyers so their client could familiarize himself. When the day came, he and three lawyers were met by four FSA agents and a CFTC investigator.

Wilkinson's hope, encouraged by his lawyers, was that a can-do, cooperative attitude would score him points. When Wilkinson started referring to his colleagues by their nicknames, his lawyer, Matthew Frankland, politely interrupted. "I'm conscious that it's second nature to you, but bearing in mind the FSA may not know who Junior, Lord Bailiff, Clumpy, Rodders, Hair, Lurch, and Noggin the Nog are."

"We know who most of those are," Meaney said.

"Because we can probably give you a crib sheet if it's helpful," Frankland offered.

"Yep, I'm here to help," Wilkinson seconded. At times, he

seemed to be introducing new elements of complexity, just so he could help the FSA interviewers wade through them. Acronyms tumbled out of his mouth. What did his clients trade? Not just instruments linked to Libor and Tibor. There was Z-Tibor. There were JGBs, which trade on TSE. There are BLAHs. What are those? Well, Wilkinson explained, "a BLAH is an IMM Z-Tibor forward rate agreement on a single period swap against an IMM overnight index swap for the same period."

"Yeah," said Trivedi.

There was more. "There's also JLOs," which were similar to BLAHs. "What else did we trade? Butterflies, we do Butterflies in swaps. Do you understand what Butterflies are?'

"No."

Butterflies are a complex type of derivative: three swaps bundled into one, Wilkinson explained, unleashing a tsunami of numbers and other details. "They're quite lively," he added.

To avoid getting the investigators' hopes up too much, Wilkinson let them know early on that he had "a dreadful memory. I go home at night, and the next day I forget what I was doing the day before." It was a convenient flaw when being asked to recall potentially illegal things he'd participated in. But one thing Wilkinson had no trouble remembering was that Hayes was a nightmare. Here, the broker said, was a guy who deserved to be punished. He trotted out the notorious story about the shepherd's pie; the FSA eagerly lapped it up, with one official noting earnestly that the fresh-out-of-the-oven pie must have been dangerously hot.

"Yeah, so that's the guy we're dealing with really," Wilkinson agreed. He went on to regale the investigators with tales—possibly exaggerated—about Hayes's unparalleled clout in the markets, how he was "a force of nature" not to be reckoned with, how he seemed imbued with nearly magical powers.

Wilkinson had a harder time pinning everything on Hayes when he was confronted with evidence pertaining to Read and Goodman. But Wilkinson insisted it was all an act, including those times when Wilkinson himself asked Goodman to comply with Hayes's wishes. And even if Goodman *was* sending out skewed data, why would any bank listen to him? "We're a lowly broker. We just shout a price and buy them a beer. In the hierarchy of things, why would they listen to Colin?" But, of course, some banks *did* use the run-throughs to set their own Libor submissions, and Goodman *did* occasionally change his run-throughs in accordance with Hayes's requests.

Confronted with e-mail traffic in which he told Read that he would "bully" a colleague into changing the run-throughs, Wilkinson insisted that he didn't remember the incident and that in any case, he certainly didn't bully anyone. Then why had he told Read that he had? "I often spun stuff, exaggerated stuff with him," Wilkinson said.

"Are you putting a spin on us?" Trivedi asked.

"No. It's a bit different spinning a colleague than spinning, you know, a compelled interview in front of the FSA and the CFTC. If I was to spin or blag a client to get a trade done or to appease a colleague, it's a hell of a lot different than sitting here telling you guys a load of bollocks." That day's interview ended after about six and a half hours. The FSA thanked Wilkinson for his time. "My pleasure," he said.

· · · ·

That spring, Goodman was hanging out in a pub. He'd had quite a bit to drink and found himself talking to a fellow broker. His name was Spencer—Goodman didn't catch his last name—and he worked at RP Martin. Goodman mentioned that he was "on extended holiday."

"Oh, why is that?" Spencer asked.

"I'm just on extended holiday," Goodman answered.

The cryptic response was enough of a clue for Spencer to figure out who he was. "Okay, you're involved in that, are you?" Spencer, it turned out, had some familiarity with the Libor investigation. He mentioned that RP Martin possessed an audio recording of Hayes shouting at Farr to get Libor down. Even in pubs, it turned out, Goodman couldn't escape the scandal.*

A couple of months later, he was ushered into an FSA interview room crowded with FSA and CFTC investigators, as well as four of Goodman's own lawyers. Goodman remained emotionally frail. His psychiatrist had warned him about the perils of undergoing intense questioning; he was liable to make mistakes or just fall apart. They took lots of breaks, generally at the broker's request, but even lunch—which the FSA had wheeled into the meeting room—was eaten under watchful eyes.

That morning, the FSA handed Goodman a small stack of spreadsheets and charts. Investigators had examined his daily "Suggested Libors" in 2007, 2008, and 2009 and compared them to what various banks actually submitted. It was clear that a number of banks had repeatedly mimicked his suggestions up to four decimal places. Goodman said he had occasionally suspected as much. "I just looked at certain banks when I'd think, 'Oh, maybe . . .'" But he said he didn't realize how many banks were frequently doing it.

---

* The same was true at home. One day, he was setting up an old iPhone for his son and encountered a cache of years-old materials: photos, e-mails, text messages. Dozens of the texts were with Read. Goodman alerted his lawyers, who passed the messages on to the FSA. They would become crucial pieces of evidence against the two men.

Instead of suggesting that Goodman was being dishonest, as the investigators sometimes did with Read and Wilkinson, Meaney took a softer approach. "At this point, I would remind you how important it is in this interview to be full and frank in your answers," he said before asking Goodman for the real reason he was getting an extra monthly payment on behalf of UBS. Goodman acknowledged that it was partly for his help with Libor—but he denied that it was anything improper. "If Darrell asked me to do something, I did what I thought the market was going to do and I generally ignored him," he said. ("I can see it looks ridiculous," he acknowledged.) Even on occasions when Goodman had seemed to engage, he claimed that it was all a ruse to get Read off his back. "Unfortunately, I avoid confrontation," Goodman confessed. "I tend to put my head in the sand."

The interview adjourned around 5 P.M. That night, Goodman's mother-in-law fell down the stairs. She broke two ribs and her arm, and her body was covered in pitch-black bruises. Blood clots formed in her broken arm. The doctors thought they might need to amputate it, but she was too weak. They put her chances at survival at one in ten. Goodman's wife was already trying to be strong for her beleaguered husband—and now this. Goodman told the FSA the next morning that he wanted to get the interview done with. "Do you feel that you're capable of giving evidence today, notwithstanding all the other personal issues?" an investigator asked.

"Yeah, yeah, fine," Goodman said.

The questioning didn't get too aggressive, and the interview broke for lunch at 12:33 P.M. Shortly thereafter, Goodman got a phone call. His mother-in-law was dead.

••••

Gary Gensler knew this would be a big day. It was a pleasant early-summer morning in Washington, and he had arrived at work early. Around 8:15 A.M., he phoned the Treasury Department, trying to reach Tim Geithner. The Treasury secretary—who in a different job four years earlier had pestered the Bank of England's Mervyn King about the problems with Libor—wasn't around, so Gensler spoke to one of his deputies. He wanted to give Treasury advance notice: In approximately fifteen minutes, the CFTC would be issuing a press release that had the potential to rattle investors and move markets. He thought Geithner should know beforehand.

The CFTC's June 27 announcement was indeed a doozy. Barclays had agreed to settle charges—not just with the CFTC but also with the Justice Department and the FSA—that it had tried to manipulate Libor. The bank's lawyers and executives had figured they'd derive an advantage from being the first institution to resolve the accusations. They were braced for a media and public lashing, but they figured it would quickly subside. Surely, the public would realize that it reflected Barclays's extraordinary cooperation with the authorities.

As part of the settlement, in which Barclays agreed to pay about $450 million in penalties, it admitted that its employees and executives had engaged in a long-running scheme to skew Libor for the bank's own benefit. Each regulator released dozens of pages of documents detailing the bank's misdeeds, including quotes from the damning phone calls and chat transcripts that had mesmerized investigators for the past two years. Now, for the first time, the public was given a taste of what the Libor scandal entailed. Lowballing—the practice of banks understating their true borrowing costs in an effort to appear healthier than they really were—was indeed widespread, and the settlement documents contained a tantalizing nugget: Unnamed members of Barclays's "senior management" were directly involved in the efforts.[*] Soon the race was on among journalists to identify those executives.

Just as Gensler and his colleagues had hoped, the settlement hit all the right notes: bankers behaving badly, a mysterious but powerful interest rate, the obligatory champagne references, a whiff of executive suite complicity. The settlement dominated newspaper headlines and TV news shows. Even the comedian Jon Stewart weighed in, gleefully informing his late-night viewers that Libor was a "mythical half wild boar, half lion." In Britain's House of Commons, David Cameron, the Conservative prime minister and longtime friend of ICAP's Michael Spencer, denounced the "probably illegal activity." Hayes angrily watched on TV as the Labour Party leader Ed Miliband—a family acquaintance thanks to his mother's years of work for Gordon Brown—denounced Cameron for not taking a harder line against Libor manipulators. "Whenever these scandals happen, he has failed to act and he stands up for the wrong sorts of people," Miliband declared. A few days later, another Labour leader, Ed Balls, said: "The reason why people are so angry is they think when people avoid their taxes or cheat on benefits they get sentences in jail. But when bankers do massive multimillion- or billion-pound frauds, there aren't criminal prosecutions."

The uproar grew even louder when it became clear that the "senior management" that had ordered the lowballing was none

---

[*] Barclays's lawyers successfully negotiated to keep any clues about the executives' identities out of the settlement documents.

other than the bank's CEO, Bob Diamond, and his top deputy, Jerry del Missier. Within days, Mervyn King demanded that Barclays remove Diamond, whose brash American tendencies had long offended the central bank governor's sense of propriety. King soon got his way; del Missier also resigned. But instead of defusing the scandal, the departures fueled it. For the first time in years, senior bank executives had paid a personal price for misconduct that occurred on their watch. Suddenly Libor seemed to be the vehicle with which authorities could exact vengeance on an industry that for too long had acted with impunity.

Parliament convened hearings and set up a committee to investigate misconduct in the banking industry and what could be done about it. One of the things, it was quickly decided, was to pass a law that officially made it illegal to manipulate benchmarks like Libor. Up until now, the rates hadn't been subject to any regulation or legal or government oversight; clearly, if lawmakers wanted to shout about the criminal actions of bankers, it would help for the actions to formally be classified as crimes.

A few days later, bowing to political pressure, the Serious Fraud Office issued a one-line press release: Its new director, David Green, "has today decided formally to accept the Libor matter for investigation."

Angela Knight canceled the summer parties the BBA had planned to throw for bankers and members of Parliament. She apologized for the short notice, but noted, "this is not the time for such an event to take place."

. . . .

Beyond lowballing, there was another element of the scandal that, until the Barclays settlement, hadn't been on many people's radar:

the massaging of Libor to benefit banks' trading portfolios. And as the days passed, people started paying more attention to this new flavor of manipulation.

Hayes had carefully read the Barclays documents. He came away feeling reassured. "Thankfully my name seems to have been forgotten!" he e-mailed his stepfather. "I may escape by virtue of the fact that my stuff all took place in Japan with Yen interest rates, luckily I don't trade dollars. If mum is worried please reassure her as the press are sensationalising it all as usual!"

That month, a confident Hayes decided the time was right to launch a new company. Some of his university friends were looking for money to launch a software programming business in their native Bulgaria. Hayes agreed to provide about £150,000, enough to hire about a dozen people temporarily, and to file the legal paperwork himself. The launch of the company, Title X Technology, seemed like a big step toward rebooting his life.

. . . .

A jowly former prosecutor with an unsettling penchant for, midconversation, snapping photos of whomever he was talking to, the new SFO director, David Green, was hanging his credibility on the success of the Libor investigation. The Treasury had agreed to provide an extra £3 million to bankroll the case, and the SFO had assigned a couple dozen people to it.

But Green remained cognizant of his agency's limited resources, and he was nervous about getting outgunned by the Americans. The SFO team was led by Damian Holling, who had joined the SFO in 2009 after years working as a Hong Kong police officer focused on financial crime. Tall, slim, and with receding black hair, Holling had immediately focused the agency's investigation on what had been going on in UBS's Tokyo office—after all, practically everyone in the legal community knew that the Swiss bank was, under its own ground rules regarding the flow of information, willing to help anyone who asked. The SFO quickly sent out notices to Hayes's former employers, as well as RP Martin and ICAP, demanding that they hand over relevant documentation. That same month, the United States formally requested permission, which it needed to seek under a treaty between the two countries, to interview a number of British suspects in the Libor case. At the SFO's behest, the United Kingdom stalled on approving the application.

Hayes's lawyers, meanwhile, started prepping their client for what to expect. Unlike in the United States, where an arrest is often an immediate precursor to being charged, British authorities arrest suspects as part of the evidence-gathering process, often at an early stage of the investigation. Hayes's lawyers said it was most likely that the SFO would just call to schedule an interview, but they couldn't rule out Hayes's house being raided and him being hauled off to jail for the day.

Spooked, Hayes called his old Tullett broker Noel Cryan. "Have you heard anything?" he asked. "Apparently I'm being investigated."

"Mate, yeah," Cryan said. "I mean, obviously the rumors are rife." Cryan mentioned that British regulators had been searching through the brokerage's e-mails.

"I think they're building a case and I could get a knock at the door any morning," Hayes said. He added: "Can we meet up?"

Cryan paused. He had never liked Hayes much, and now, he knew, the guy was toxic. "To be quite honest, I'm not going to meet you, no." Then he added: "I'd rather you didn't call me either because I'm not comfortable with it."

• • • •

In early December, despite feeling put off by the British government's foot-dragging with Justice's interview requests, McInerney placed a courtesy call to the SFO in the interests of transatlantic harmony. He gave Green a heads-up that Justice planned to file criminal charges against Hayes and another person on December 12. (That other person was Roger Darin. Though the two men loathed each other, the United States had collected gobs of evidence that showed them working together to move UBS's Libor submissions. Justice concluded it was important to charge more than one person in order to show that this was a conspiracy, not just a lone bad guy.) The charges would be filed under seal, before being unveiled roughly a week later, McInerney explained.

"OK, fine, thank you," replied Green. Unless the SFO moved swiftly, it was about to lose one of the investigation's easiest targets—someone who also happened to be a British citizen—to the Americans.

CHAPTER 16

A Crook of the First Order

Hayes, Tighe, and Joshua had finally moved out of the child-unfriendly Sugar House apartment over the summer. But the renovations of the Old Rectory were dragging on longer than expected, so they had temporarily relocated to Tighe's parents' home. Finally, in early December, the Old Rectory was ready to be occupied, more or less. Construction debris still littered the property, and some work was still under way, but it was better than living out of suitcases and feeling like nomads. Movers unloaded scores of boxes into various rooms, and over the next week, the couple got to work unpacking.

The night of December 10 was freezing, with temperatures dropping into the mid-20s—unusually cold for southern England. A thin layer of snow dusted the ground outside the Old Rectory. A little before 7 A.M. the following day, Tighe was starting her morning routine; there really was no hurry, as neither she nor her husband, who remained in bed, had jobs to go to. Just then, a loud banging on the front door startled them both. Hayes assumed it was construction workers showing up for work early. He got out of bed and looked out the second-floor window. It was still dark outside—the sun wouldn't rise for another hour—but his curving gravel driveway was ablaze with floodlights. The snow and ice sparkled.

Tighe, maneuvering around the unpacked boxes in the foyer, made her way to the door. A crowd of uniformed and plainclothes police officers entered. Hayes padded downstairs in his underwear. An officer presented a warrant for his arrest, saying he was accused of manipulating Libor. The officer pronounced it "lee-bore."

Hayes couldn't help himself. "You mean LIE-bore?" he blurted, correcting the officer's pronunciation. Tighe commanded him to return upstairs and get dressed. The police permitted him to eat a piece of toast and drink a cup of tea before they drove him the twenty traffic-choked miles into central London. Their destination was the Bishopsgate Police Station, a stout cement building directly across the street from the RBS offices where Hayes had started his banking career more than a decade earlier. In a custody suite while he was waiting to be booked, he was with two other arrestees: One, in handcuffs, was suspected of sexual assault. The other, slim and with short, graying hair, turned out to be Gilmour, who, along with Farr, had been picked up at his Essex home in a similar raid early that morning. Hayes had never before seen Gilmour, although he'd occasionally communicated with him in electronic chats, and had always pictured him as being fat and pink-faced, like Wilkinson. The surprise allowed for a moment of distraction, but not much more.

Hayes was escorted to a small cell, where he was left alone. There was a metal toilet and a bed with a thin mattress. Weak

winter light filtered in through a small window Hayes kept pressing a button on the wall, summoning an officer and asking for cups
of tea. He spent the day pacing back and forth.

Back at the Old Rectory, Tighe called her husband's lawyers.
Then she phoned Emma, who by then was at the school where she
taught. When Tighe told her sister what had happened, Emma
was floored. She had no idea things were so serious; ever since
Hayes had been fired, the couple had downplayed the severity of
the situation. The police who had remained after Hayes was taken
away spent the next nine hours rifling through unpacked boxes
and photo albums and carting away computers, Hayes's phone,
and other electronic devices. Trying to avoid scaring her fourteen-
month-old son, Tighe managed to maintain her composure.

Hayes's attorney Lydia Jonson arrived at the police station early
that afternoon. She advised him not to answer any of the SFO's
questions.

At 5:30 P.M., Hayes was escorted into Interview Room 3 at
the police station. Gilmour had already been brought into another
room nearby and informed that he was suspected of conspiring
with Hayes and Farr. He spent nearly three hours walking a pair
of SFO investigators through eighty-five pages of evidence they'd
gathered—e-mails, chat transcripts, phone recordings. Gilmour
did his best to be helpful and insisted, over and over again, that he
had just been doing his job. (Farr had declined to answer any of the
questions during his three-hour interrogation.)

Two SFO investigators plopped an accordion file filled with
112 pages of documents on a metal table in front of Hayes. They
explained that he had been arrested because he was suspected of
conspiring with his RP Martin brokers to manipulate yen Libor.
Jonson read aloud a brief statement saying that Hayes didn't wish
to comment at this stage, and then the agents outlined their case

against Hayes. They quoted from electronic chat transcripts. They showed his trading records. They played recordings of him on the phone with other traders and brokers, the conversations peppered with what an SFO agent named Matt Ball apologetically described as "quite industrial language." Each piece of evidence was followed by questions, and each time, adhering to Jonson's advice, Hayes replied: "No comment." The process ground on for hours. Hayes struggled to contain his frustration. "Still got another bloody 75 pages of this, yeah?" he remarked at one point.

"We'll get through it as quickly as we can," answered the tall, lumbering Ball, who had worked at the agency as an investigator for the past decade.

"You're going to need a full day," Hayes muttered. The interrogation wrapped up around 8:30 P.M. He was offered one last chance to speak before being released on bail, with his passport held in escrow. "Not at this stage," he said. "I'm biting my tongue."

• • • •

The SFO issued a press release that morning announcing that it had arrested three British men as part of the Libor investigation—the first arrests, anywhere in the world, connected to the long-running case. The agency didn't identify the men, but it listed their ages and the counties in which they'd been arrested. It didn't take long for the media to figure out—and then publish—their names.

Inside the Justice Department headquarters and the Bond Building, word traveled fast about the SFO's arrest of Hayes. The reaction was swift and unanimous: outrage. The British agency clearly was trying to mark its territory. It was all the more galling because Justice not only had done much of the legwork on the investigation but also had tipped off Green about the U.S.'s impending charges—which seemed to be the only thing that motivated the arrest. The consequences were significant: If Hayes was under criminal investigation in England, the likelihood of a British court agreeing to extradite him to the United States to face a similar case was small. And with his passport having been seized, there was no chance Hayes could come to the United States and cooperate with the prosecutors on his own volition. Just like that, their lead suspect—someone whom the fraud section and FBI had spent nearly two years building a case against, collecting evidence, interviewing witnesses, even placing entrapping phone calls—had essentially vanished.

McInerney left Green a blistering voice mail complaining about the SFO swooping in to steal Justice's primary target. Green never called back. The U.S. State Department was enlisted to lodge a formal protest with the British cabinet secretary responsible for diplomatic affairs.

The next day, the fraud section filed its criminal charges against Tom Alexander William Hayes—as well as his old nemesis, Darin—under seal in a Manhattan court. The still-secret complaint included a long affidavit by an FBI special agent summarizing the evidence and attesting to the defendants' alleged wrongdoing. Near the end, it quoted Hayes telling Alykulov not to talk to the feds.

• • • •

Hayes was confident that his arrest was just a big misunderstanding. (Always superstitious, he blamed it on the mysterious disappearance of a lucky T-shirt emblazoned with the words *Destined for Glory* and the QPR logo.) Tighe, uncharacteristically, was similarly sanguine. Everything would be cleared up, they told themselves, once Hayes presented his side of the story. Sure, the things he was accused of doing might look bad to an untrained eye, but there were legitimate explanations. Everyone in the industry was doing more or less the same thing. Hayes was following orders. His bosses knew what he was up to. They didn't object; in fact, they were doing it, too.

The day after the arrest, Tighe discovered a small round hole in the ceiling of the master bedroom. And she noticed that their baby monitor had started producing lots of noisy feedback. Hayes went out and bought a disposable phone. From his yard, he called Jonson and told her that he was going to scour the house for electronic bugs and destroy any he found. Don't do anything of the sort, Jonson warned. (It turned out that one of her colleagues, when he arrived at the Old Rectory following Hayes's arrest, had spotted a police officer placing what he thought might have been a bug on one of their Mercedes cars.) She told him and Tighe not to talk about the case on the phone or in the house or car. At Jonson's suggestion, they paid a former British intelligence officer £3,500 to sweep the house for eavesdropping devices. He blasted classical music to trigger sound-activated devices while he walked from room to room, scanning the house with eavesdropping detection equipment. The search came up empty. Hayes, feeling better, mugged for a goofy photo wearing the ex-spy's headphones and other equipment.

The relative calm was reinforced a few days later. Hayes had hired a hotshot attorney to represent him in the United States: Steven Tyrrell, who was McInerney's predecessor as the chief of Justice's fraud section and now was a high-priced criminal defense lawyer. Tyrrell set up a meeting with his former colleagues, whom he described as his "old friends." On the night of December 18, he reported back to Hayes and Jonson with good news. The U.S. prosecutors were furious with the SFO for not giving them a heads-up on Hayes's arrest. But, Tyrrell said, he "would be very surprised" if Justice was poised to take action against Hayes. It "just doesn't seem that they would be at a point where they would be ready."

. . . .

The next day, Hayes and Tighe stayed home working on his defense. They went through all the questions the SFO had asked him at the police station, which provided a helpful glimpse of the case prosecutors were assembling. Sitting together at the kitchen table, the couple pulled together answers and explanations to each query. Then, in early afternoon, big news landed: UBS had agreed to pay an enormous $1.5 billion to settle the Libor manipulation case. The deal—which made UBS the second bank, following Barclays, to resolve the investigation—was the product of weeks of frenzied negotiations between the Swiss bank and U.S. and British authorities, who wanted to announce a settlement before the Christmas holidays. UBS's punishment was more than three times larger than the one imposed on Barclays, and the bank's Japanese subsidiary had agreed to plead guilty to criminal charges. That represented a minor breakthrough for American prosecutors, who had managed to overcome some of their fears of charging a company—albeit only a very small part of a very large company that wasn't based in the United States.

UBS's spin doctors described the episode as the work of a few bad apples, not the latest devastating indictment of the entire company's practices and culture. In a briefing session with journalists before the deal was even announced, a senior executive branded

Hayes as the entire Libor scandal's "evil mastermind." It was just UBS's bad luck to have hired such a criminal genius.

When the settlement was announced, Tighe shifted gears. She printed out a copy of the documents detailing the U.S. and British governments' cases against the Swiss bank. With Joshua balanced on her lap, she went through the files, marking them up with a yellow highlighter. She was relieved. They made it clear that Libor-rigging was widespread. Her husband wasn't even named. The reports from various regulators were sprinkled with vague references to the involvement of unnamed higher-ups at UBS. It seemed like a get-out-of-jail-free card for her husband. After all, who could blame Hayes for doing something that everyone, including his superiors, knew about? For a few happy hours, the family's crisis seemed to be easing. She and her husband had no idea that UBS was already presenting Hayes as a master con man who manipulated not only the market but also his own innocent employer.

That evening, Tighe was in their shiny new kitchen preparing a joint of roasted lamb for dinner. Hayes sat in what he had already designated as his favorite chair, in the breakfast nook just off the kitchen, puttering on his Apple laptop. A news alert popped up. He clicked the link. A video of the U.S. attorney general at a press conference in Washington started playing. Hayes watched for a few moments, a horrified lump rising in his throat.

"Sarah, I've been charged by the U.S.," he announced.

It didn't compute. "What did you say?" she asked. "What did you say?" she asked again, her voice rising to a shriek. "What did you say?"

"I've been charged by the U.S.," he finally repeated. His face went gray. His eye started twitching.

Tighe's legs wobbled. Then she vomited.

. . . .

Late that afternoon, Roger Darin was at home in a Zurich suburb when his phone rang. On the line was Bruce Baird, his UBS-appointed lawyer in Washington. Baird was best known for his time as a federal prosecutor in New York, when he led the criminal prosecution of Michael Milken. He subsequently became a white-collar defense attorney. Baird had known that Darin was in legal jeopardy in the Libor case, because Justice had refused to grant him immunity; in fact, the investigators hadn't even interviewed him. That couldn't be a good sign. But Baird had doubted his client would actually be charged anytime soon, at least not without someone placing a courtesy call to the well-connected lawyer. But when Baird tuned in to Justice's press conference, he heard the prosecutors announcing that they were charging two men: Hayes and Darin. Baird was stunned and angry. He took a deep breath and called his client, bracing for an awful reaction. To the lawyer's surprise, though, Darin's response was muted. He seemed to take it in stride. Perhaps, Baird figured, it was just his unemotional Swiss-German nature? Or maybe he was in a state of shock. Baird had learned over the years that it was nearly impossible to predict how people would react to horrible news. And this certainly was horrible news.

. . . .

The next day, Hayes traipsed into London for a noon meeting with his lawyers. A soft rain was falling. The American charges called for an immediate pivot in the team's legal strategy. Notwithstanding the SFO's arrest, the United States planned to seek Hayes's extradition in January. The top priority became avoiding being shipped off to the United States, where he figured he would inevitably be convicted and spend decades rotting in a violent prison, thousands of miles from his family. Now, his lawyers told him, the key was to lay the groundwork for being charged by the SFO before he could be extradited to the United States; under British double jeopardy rules, that would largely take extradition off the table.

Already that morning, Pearce had called Ball at the SFO. He said the Hayes camp was eager to set up a meeting as soon as possible to discuss the possibility of cooperating. "We don't want there to be a tug-of-war over Tom," Pearce said, adding that he agreed with the SFO that his client should face the charges against him in London. "SFO want you here and not going anywhere else," Pearce reported to Hayes a few hours later, framing this as "[g]ood news in a bad situation."

. . . .

Despite the criminal charges, the settlement with UBS was not met with relief or acclaim by the public; indeed, it seemed yet another example of a big bank buying an indulgence. In early January, a British parliamentary committee held hearings on the deal. A number of past and present UBS executives were called to testify, and following the playbook, they pointed the finger at one former employee in particular. A British lawmaker, Nigel Lawson, blasted Hayes as "a crook of the first order." A top UBS executive at the hearing, Andrea Orcel, smiled and nodded in agreement. UBS's head of compliance, Andrew Williams, said that "clearly his conduct was reprehensible. I think it's fair to say we were all disgusted by it."

Alex Wilmot-Sitwell, who had helped persuade Hayes not to jump to Goldman back in 2008 and had now become a top executive at Bank of America, was another witness. "I don't recall him," Wilmot-Sitwell said of Hayes. "I never met him." For good measure, he added that he wasn't even sure Hayes worked at UBS at the time that Wilmot-Sitwell was co-head of the investment bank. Hayes watched the testimony on TV, not believing the dissembling he was hearing. Carsten Kengeter—Wilmot-Sitwell's counterpart who had played such an active role convincing Hayes that he was a star and shouldn't defect to a rival—wasn't even summoned to the hearing.

Hayes began to question whether he could trust his lawyers. He certainly didn't trust the SFO, and that left him worried about striking a deal with the agency. "What if the SFO abandon me?" he asked his lawyers. Even his mother seemed to desert him. Sandy had never liked the idea of her son working for a bank, and the current mess, she concluded, was the inevitable outcome of him joining a despicable industry. Sandy was so angry about the shame that Hayes had brought on her family that, one day in early 2013, she refused to babysit Joshua. Her lack of support opened a deep rift within the family. "How can I convince a jury that I'm innocent if my own mum doesn't believe it?" Hayes asked himself. Tighe was irate and would remain so for years. Hayes and Sandy wouldn't speak to each other for the rest of 2013.

One night, unable to sleep, Hayes searched the Internet for Brits who had faced similar situations. He came across David Bermingham, one of the so-called NatWest Three investment bankers who were extradited to face U.S. criminal charges for their roles in the Enron scandal. Hayes e-mailed Bermingham asking if they could talk. Bermingham had been following Hayes's case in the media. He invited Hayes to come out to his home in Oxfordshire, a northern exurb of London.

When they met, Bermingham told Hayes his bizarre tale. After

Enron imploded, he and his two British colleagues had been investigated for personally enriching themselves, to the tune of millions of dollars, in a complex deal with Enron and some of its executives. When the Justice Department charged the bankers in 2002 in Houston, Bermingham's lawyers urged the SFO to investigate and file its own charges against him so he could avoid extradition. The SFO refused, so Bermingham's lawyers sued—perhaps the only time in history that someone had sued a government to force it to file criminal charges against the plaintiff. The ploy failed, although the three former bankers' public images evolved at least slightly from greedy "womanising buccaneers" into victims of America's imperialistic approach to enforcing its laws all over the world. In 2006, they were sent to the United States, where they pleaded guilty and were sent to jail before being shipped back to England to serve the remainder of their thirty-seven-month sentences.

Bermingham—clean-cut and looking every bit the preppy retired investment banker—told Hayes the key was to find a way to defuse the U.S. situation. Otherwise, it could literally ruin his life; the United States would stop at nothing to get its hands on him. "If those charges are out there, you can never leave the country again," he warned.

Driving home, Hayes was struck by the anger still burning in Bermingham's eyes, years later, at having pleaded guilty to a crime he didn't feel guilty of. Nonetheless, his lawyers were hard at work trying to put Hayes on a path to do just that: cooperating with the SFO—and pleading guilty to its anticipated criminal charges—to take U.S. extradition off the table. It was a matter of some urgency. In mid-January, the American embassy in London contacted the SFO to notify it that the United States planned to move forward with an extradition request. In Washington, Tyrrell put out feelers to Justice to see if they'd be interested in having a dialogue with Hayes; maybe they could strike a deal. Justice was at best lukewarm. So at a meeting with the SFO, Hayes's lawyers made their pitch for their client to be admitted into a special cooperation program, normally reserved for members of organized crime, that would ensure he got credit for assisting. "I can imagine he would be quite a useful person," Jonson told them.

The SFO's Stuart Alford agreed that Hayes would be valuable. The agency "is keen to do all it can to look at not the low-lying fruit but to take it beyond that," he said. "Cases can be jumped forward" with help "from the inside."

. . . .

On the morning of January 29, Hayes headed into London to sit down with the SFO, the initial step in becoming a cooperating witness. Hayes's lawyers and the SFO had reached an informal deal: He would plead guilty and agree to testify against his alleged co-conspirators. The agreement unofficially called for a sentence of about twenty months of prison time, although technically that decision would be up to a judge. Hayes's lawyers told him that, if all went well, he'd probably serve less than a year in jail, plus some time with an electronic monitoring device. It didn't sound fun, but it beat the alternative.

First, though, Hayes had to convince the SFO that he would be sufficiently open and honest that his cooperation warranted a deal. It was called a "cleansing interview"—he had to come clean about all his wrongdoing and provide the investigators with an overview of the kind of stuff he could tell them. It was essentially an audition, and it would extend over a couple of grueling days. Jonson had coached him, especially about how to respond to the SFO's inevitable question about whether he had acted dishonestly.

The key was to sound candid, not defensive. During rehearsals, though, Hayes kept veering off onto tangents and struggling to remember exactly what to accept responsibility for. Jonson, desperate to avoid a disaster, e-mailed him a few talking points. "I accept that I was influencing a rate that was intended to be completely independent and devoid of any influence other than that of an independent submitter," the note read. "Clearly I did this to benefit the bank's position."

When Tighe left her husband at the train station that morning, he looked like he was about to cry. "I'm so proud of you," she texted him. He responded that there was nothing to be proud of. On board the train, he looked for the printout of Jonson's talking points. It wasn't in his bag. Panicked, he called Tighe, who had just arrived home. "I don't know how to answer the dishonesty question!" he told her. Tighe ordered him to calm down. She rifled through his papers and found the missing printout. She typed its contents into her phone and e-mailed it to Hayes, who received it just before getting off the train in London.

Inside the SFO's offices, a ring of interview rooms was arranged around a central atrium. To block out noise from the busy street below, the rooms were windowless, creating an intimidating, claustrophobic effect, even for experienced lawyers. With recording equipment switched on, the meeting got under way. Hayes confirmed that he would be willing to testify against his former colleagues. Then came the questions. The first topic concerned whether Hayes had ever previously committed a crime. The answer was surprisingly complicated. Hayes admitted that he'd been busted speeding on multiple occasions and, in order to avoid hefty fines, had taken two speed-awareness classes in a three-year period. That might have violated rules limiting the number of times an individual could escape a penalty, Hayes said. And he admitted that he hadn't paid his taxes when he left Tokyo in 2010. (A few weeks later, he wired money to a friend in Japan, who paid the taxes on his behalf.)

Then Hayes started coming clean about his misadventures in banking. He noted the accusations he'd faced at both RBS and RBC when he left. He admitted that he repeatedly had violated UBS's internal policy governing gifts and expenses. He had taken Tighe out to dinners that cost up to £1,000 and had brokers reimburse him. He hadn't declared the gifts to UBS.

Asked if he admitted having acted dishonestly by manipulating Libor, he answered with one word: "Yes."

"I probably deserve to be sitting here because, you know, I made concerted efforts to influence Libor," he told the SFO in a session a couple of days later. "And, you know, although I was operating within a system, or participating within a system in which it was commonplace, you know, ultimately I was someone who was a serial offender within that. . . . At the end of the day my trading book directly benefited from that, and that directly had some impact on me as an individual both within my seniority within the bank, my standing within the bank, my potential remuneration."

Just like that, Hayes had admitted to being a central part of what looked like a vast criminal conspiracy. He was following his lawyers' advice, but that advice—given to a panicked, desperate man who, it would become clear, hadn't come to terms with what it meant to accept responsibility for his crimes—would later look questionable at best. Now there was no turning back.

It would take nearly two nail-biting months for the SFO to let Hayes know whether he would be admitted into the cooperating witness program. In the meantime, the SFO asked Hayes's lawyers to please not let the Justice Department know that they were talking.

····

After having two of its employees arrested, RP Martin scrambled to circle the wagons—but not around the two suspect brokers. The first step was to fire Farr. His last day was December 31, 2012. He didn't leave empty-handed. On his way out, he was handed a nearly $100,000 termination payment; the remainder of an $88,000 loan from a couple of years earlier also was written off. "I wish you all the very best in the future," the firm's HR manager said in a farewell letter.

Gilmour lasted a bit longer. In mid-June 2013, he was instructed to attend a disciplinary hearing in RP Martin's increasingly busy boardroom. Beforehand, the firm sent him a memory stick containing recordings of phone calls and transcripts of his instant-message chats, as well as a summary of his May 2011 meeting, which Gilmour had signed attesting to its accuracy. In an attached letter, RP Martin's chairman said the hearing would consider "whether, in the light of the attached recordings and transcripts, the information you gave at the meeting on 9 May 2011 was true and accurate." Gilmour's lawyers tried to get the meeting delayed or canceled, citing the ongoing criminal investigation. It didn't work. The meeting took place on June 14, which also turned out to be Gilmour's last day of work. Going forward, he would do occasional work for a friend as a house painter in training.

Then there was Lee Aaron. It had been a miserable year for him. His mother had spent the past twelve months waging a slow, losing battle for her life; she died in February 2013. Between hospice visits, Aaron submitted to interrogations with RP Martin's lawyers. He insisted he hadn't done anything wrong—despite records indicating that he tried to call in Libor-related favors on behalf of his pal Danziger. (The two remained friends. Fired by RBS, Danziger had become a recruiter in the finance industry, and they occasionally met up for beers and to discuss the investigation.) Aaron said that he'd just been telling Danziger "whatever he wanted to hear." And the switch trades? Those were nothing more than a prized customer's way of saying thank you. What about the vast amounts he was spending to entertain Danziger? From 2007 through 2010, the broker had incurred about £180,000 of expenses.

Aaron didn't really see anything wrong with it. Sure, it seemed like a lot, but that was spread over forty-eight months—or, he said, about £2,000 a month. (His math was wrong; it was closer to £4,000.) He guaranteed to the investigators that he had earned far more for the company than he spent on entertainment. His boss, Cliff King, seconded the argument.

But Aaron had been warned about his behavior in the past and now, with regulators breathing down the firm's neck, he was suspended. A month later, he received a letter from RP Martin that accused him of having been "directly or indirectly involved in or connected with or were aware of and failed to raise with management" attempts to manipulate Libor. He resigned, in exchange for RP Martin waiving any contractual restrictions on him joining a rival firm. "In resigning I do not admit the allegations raised against me by the company in its recent disciplinary investigation," he wrote in a July 15 letter.

Aaron by then had lined up a new job as a broker at BGC Partners, which conducted a routine background check. When asked why he left, RP Martin's compliance director responded: "He was suspended in relation to activities linked to the alleged yen Libor manipulation and subsequently resigned." BGC hired him anyway.

. . . .

On March 27, the SFO formally accepted Hayes's application to join the cooperation program. The agency's investigators had high hopes. Hayes had helped them identify dozens of alleged co-conspirators. The plan was for them to be tried in groups of three or four at a time, with Hayes the star witness at each trial. The SFO also envisioned him serving as an expert witness in Libor cases against individuals who weren't part of his network. For the prosecutors, he was a human gold mine. Hayes was relieved to no longer have to worry about being sent off to the United States. It felt a little bit like he'd just been given an antidote after being bit by a poisonous snake.

After he was arrested, Hayes had put an end to his online trading. He had made a bundle of money—more than enough to cover the Old Rectory's renovation—but he knew himself. His life was in too much turmoil at the moment; he wasn't in the right mindset to continue. Still, the prolific volume of his trading had made him a prized customer and, one day early in 2013, an online brokerage firm tried to lure him with a sweet offer: If he opened an account, the firm would match his first £5,000 of profits. Hayes took the bait; he created a new account, deposited about £1 million, and resumed trading, figuring his gains would help pay his soaring legal bills. But after a brief period of making money, his trades started going wrong. He soon lost £100,000. Before long, the account had dwindled to £500,000. Hayes considered cutting his losses, but that wasn't in his DNA. Tighe said that if he thought he could turn things around, he should keep trading. So he did.

One evening in March, Hayes returned from a day of being grilled by the SFO. "It's gone," he informed Tighe. The combination of his trading losses and the lawyers' bills had exhausted the entire £1 million. Hayes sank into a deep depression, the losses cutting to the bone of his self-identity as a skilled trader. He was so out of sorts that he stopped going to QPR matches. He gave his lucky pandas to Joshua and threw away all the polo shirts his brokers had given him over the years—the memories were just too painful.

It seemed like only weeks ago that the couple had been rich. Now they were scrounging for money. They asked Tighe's parents to pay back £5,000 that they'd borrowed. They sold Hayes's Mercedes convertible. Robin returned his Mercedes to Hayes, who sold it, too. (Robin actually was relieved to no longer have the fanciest vehicle in his school's parking lot.) Tighe took out a mortgage on the Old Rectory, a process that required the couple to transfer ownership of the house under her name. Before long, they realized that wasn't enough and started trying to sell their beloved home— only a few months after they'd moved in. Tighe reluctantly decided to go back to work, putting on ice her ambition to have a second child. Shearman & Sterling, the law firm where she'd worked before moving to Tokyo, agreed to take her back. "Re-joining the working population shortly!" she announced on Facebook.

Not much seemed to be going right for the family. A year earlier, Hayes had spotted a small red lump on Tighe's back, under her bra strap. A succession of doctors said it was nothing to worry about. But the lump seemed to be growing. Finally a doctor diagnosed it as cancer—a benign, treatable type of cancer, but cancer nonetheless. One day, Hayes drove Tighe to the hospital to have the lump cauterized. On the way home, on the highway, their car sputtered to a stop. It was out of gas. Hayes was so distracted that he didn't even pull over onto the shoulder. The car just slowed to a halt in the middle of the highway; other vehicles whizzed past, blaring their horns. Tighe was scared. This was their life now: stalled and treacherous.

. . . .

Hayes regularly spent entire days in the SFO's offices giving recorded testimony. By the end, he would log about eighty-two hours of interviews. (The transcripts would run nearly four thousand pages.) To maintain secrecy, and avoid tipping off any of the men whom he was expected to testify against, he signed into the visitors' log in the SFO's lobby each morning using the pseudonym "Stan Bowles," borrowed from a 1970s QPR star.

At first, the interviews were cathartic. Hayes enjoyed talking to a captive audience about markets and trading. He spent much of that spring walking the investigators through his career history and how he made money. He painted detailed portraits of bank trading technology, the mechanics of the derivatives market, how his Excel models worked, how traders and brokers communicated with each other, how traders like him thought and felt. "The first thing you think is, where's the edge, where can I make a bit more money, how can I push the boundaries, maybe, you know, a bit of a grey area, push the edge of the envelope?" he explained. He added: "The point is, you're greedy. You want every little bit of money that you can possibly get because, like I say, that is how you're judged. That's your performance metric."

And then, one by one, Hayes went through all the people he'd worked with over the years, the colleagues and brokers and competitors whom he'd chewed out or begged for favors or bossed around. Any time he was tempted to hold back or spin a conversation in a slightly more favorable light, he remembered what was riding on this process: If the SFO perceived him as being dishonest or uncooperative, the agency could pull the plug on the interviews and throw him to the American wolves. Everything hinged on him convincing the SFO to charge him. And so Hayes sat back and unburdened himself. He repeatedly admitted that he had acted dishonestly to skew Libor. Everyone had.*

When the SFO drew up an early draft of the charges it planned to file against Hayes, each count listed his co-conspirators. Two of the names were especially noteworthy: Carsten Kengeter and Brian Mccappin. When Hayes saw the two men on there, he felt a little better. They were both high-ranking executives, for starters, who unlike Hayes remained employed in the industry. And the fact that the SFO was convinced that senior executives conspired with him seemed to validate his argument that everything he was doing, regardless of its criminality, was condoned by his superiors.

The initial relief of being admitted into the SFO's cooperation program, and the enjoyment he derived from blabbing to the amicable Ball and his SFO teammates, soon gave way to depression and anger. Hayes got heartburn every time he thought about testifying against men like Farr and Read. He couldn't bear the thought of one day having to tell Joshua that he had admitted to being a criminal. He and Tighe both felt he had been railroaded into cooperating, the victim of America's overzealous law enforcement system. And the more he explained his tactics to the SFO, the more he convinced himself that he was innocent—or, at least, no guiltier than anyone else. After all, whose fault was it if he did what he'd been told was okay? How could he be blamed if everyone was doing more or less the same thing? This was just the way the system worked.

He started smoking cigarettes. At home, he spent hours brooding in a cold bath or outside staring at a tree, sometimes in the wee hours of the morning. His sex drive vanished. He stormed around

---

* The SFO team also got ample doses of Hayes's oddball nature. At one point, explaining why he didn't like to manage people, he said: "Mainly because people are variables that don't behave in predictable ways, and, you know, they're difficult to manage And I'd rather manage risk than people."

the kitchen, opening and slamming shut cupboard doors. Sometimes Tighe would wake up in the middle of the night and find her husband staring at her. Other times, he questioned whether his life was worthwhile. "I'll kill myself if you want me to," he offered. "Would it be better for you?" Once he mentioned the possibility of suicide in front of Joshua. Tighe told friends she took the threats seriously, that he needed to be watched all the time. She pushed Hayes to see a therapist or a psychiatrist who could prescribe antidepressants. He refused.

Joshua grew increasingly clingy as the family's stress levels rose. Sometimes he asked why Daddy was so angry or why he had forgotten to feed him or take him to the potty even when he asked again and again. It was becoming clear that Joshua couldn't be left alone with his father—a problem for many reasons, but especially now as Tighe was returning to work. In April, she made the painful decision to take Joshua and move into her parents' house. The marriage seemed to be unraveling.

Tighe checked on Hayes on weekends, and during the week, she dispatched her sister to stop by the Old Rectory. Every day around noon, Emma would stick her head in the door and say hi to her brother-in-law, before getting back in her car and driving away. Nobody said it aloud, but she knew that one of her responsibilities was to make sure Hayes hadn't hurt himself. She had heard him threaten once to throw himself in front of an oncoming subway train, though she grimly figured he was more likely to commit suicide at home. Without telling her sister, Emma researched online how to rescue, or at least detach, someone who had hung himself. When she walked in the door each day, she worried whether she would have to put her new knowledge to use.

All the while, Hayes kept trekking into London to talk to the SFO. On May 21, sitting in one of the closetlike interview rooms, he learned that his so-called friend Read had long been misleading him. An investigator read aloud an e-mail in which Read told Goodman to "never let him know that you send a physical run-through out. I lie about the levels all the time and it makes our life easier." Then the agent handed Hayes a printout of the e-mail to see for himself. "Bloody hell," Hayes stammered. "That's the first time I've seen that." He grasped for possible explanations for the deception. He couldn't believe his own naïveté. "Which shows you actually you think that you know everything that's going on, but quite often you don't," he told the SFO.

The next day, Hayes's interrogators turned to page 146 of a bundle of documents, a numbered to-do list that had been stored on a shared computer drive at UBS, which a number of managers had access to. Hayes had never seen the document before, but as he examined it, he realized that it was essentially an instruction manual for the bank's Libor submitters. It showed that the UBS traders who specialized in interest-rate derivatives linked to euros and dollars were in charge of submitting their own Libor data. They didn't have to go through an intermediary in another department, as Hayes had to do with Darin, in order to tinker with the bank's Libor submissions. But the real revelation was the explicit instruction to the traders about exactly how to take their derivatives positions into account when setting Libor. It was just so flagrant. "It's hilarious," Hayes said. But the humor quickly faded. "You see, this is what winds me up here. Like I'm just like getting hung, drawn and slaughtered by this bank, and then there's this official document for publishing the Libor rates where they're just blatant." Again, everyone was doing it, so why was he being singled out?*

---

* UBS would later say that the instructions didn't represent official company policy and must have been created by a rogue employee.

That evening, Hayes showed up at Tighe's parents' house, so worked up he could barely speak. If UBS was officially trying to manipulate Libor, how could his actions be construed as criminal? he sputtered. Hayes e-mailed his lawyers. He said the new evidence made him wonder if he really should be pleading guilty. In the course of the SFO interviews, "I have seen very little to harm me but a large amount to support what I have told you from the beginning that this was just part of doing my job." After a couple of days with no response, the lawyers proposed meeting to discuss his concerns. Hayes by then had grown discouraged: "I am aware that basically I have little to no option in relation to this."

By June, as the interview process entered its final stage, Hayes's admissions of guilt were growing more equivocal. Asked repeatedly whether he was aware at the time that he was acting dishonestly, he responded: "I was aware of that I was being dishonest, but on a micro scale, on a scale that was not perceptible to people, that was not really influencing the rates, outside of what I would term my permissible range." This was an important concept, at least to Hayes and some of his former colleagues. Their argument was that because each bank's data was supposed to be based on what it thought it would cost to borrow money from another bank on any given day, there was no absolute precise rate, but rather a narrow band of numbers, drawn from a variety of information sources, and somewhere within that band probably lay the truth. But picking a specific figure, down to multiple decimal places, was arbitrary. As long as the Libor submitter chose a data point from within that band, it was hard to argue his numbers were technically wrong—not that this represented much ethical justification for what Hayes and his confederates had been doing.

386

. . . .

Several days later, Hayes and Jonson returned to the Bishopsgate Police Station, this time for him to be formally charged. To their relief, no reporters or photographers were waiting outside. At 8:25 A.M., a police sergeant read aloud the charges against him: eight counts of conspiracy to defraud, involving his time at UBS and Citigroup. (Because Libor manipulation hadn't itself been a crime when Hayes was a trader, the SFO turned to the conspiracy-to-defraud statute, which outlawed entering into agreements with the intent of ripping off another party.)

Hayes and Jonson exited through a back door and decamped to a nearby Starbucks. Hayes blew up, months of frustration boiling over. He berated Jonson about the jail sentence he was likely facing and for allowing him to fall victim to what struck him as a politicized process. (The charges had been filed the day before the parliamentary banking standards commission—convened in the wake of the Barclays settlement a year earlier—was due to release its final report. Among other things, the report recommended stiffened criminal penalties for misconduct. Hayes suspected the timing of his charges was not coincidental.) And to Hayes's disappointment, unlike the SFO's earlier draft document, the actual charges didn't name any of his alleged co-conspirators—only him. Yet the bigger picture was that this was exactly what he had set out to accomplish; now that he had been charged in Britain, the chances of being extradited to the United States receded. He later apologized to Jonson for losing his temper.

Two days later, Hayes was summoned to an arraignment hearing. It was his first public appearance. Not many people knew what he looked like, so the swarm of photographers outside the London courthouse—eager for a shot of the notorious criminal mastermind—snapped photos of all similarly aged men who entered the building. Hayes showed up wearing khakis and a dark blue button-down shirt, untucked. Standing in the glass-enclosed defendants' dock, a staple of British courtrooms, Hayes confirmed his name and address, a new court date was set, and then it was over. It wasn't yet time for him to enter a plea. He and Jonson walked out together. A horde of photographers and camera crews chased them across a busy street.

. . . .

One morning that summer, Tighe woke up and couldn't move her left arm. It was completely frozen. The medical explanation was that calcium deposits in her shoulder joint, built up over many years, had finally reached a tipping point and immobilized her arm. Emma, acting as nurse, thought the real trigger was stress. In any case, how could Tighe juggle a toddler and a job with one arm? She couldn't. She felt she had no choice but to move back in with her husband.

Hayes was overjoyed to have her and Joshua back. But things remained bad. One night, Emma slept over. In the middle of the night, she was awoken by the sound of her sister screaming. She raced to the master bedroom, queasily expecting that Hayes had hurt himself. Tighe told her to go back to bed; she had just had a nightmare. Emma suspected that wasn't the full story. On another summer evening, pacing back and forth in the Old Rectory's open-plan kitchen, Hayes mentioned the idea of driving the car off a cliff—a common refrain for months now. "I'm going to do it," he declared.

Tighe was reaching the end of her tether. "Go on, then," she snapped.

Hayes was starting to entertain a radical idea: pleading not guilty and fighting the British charges. He increasingly wanted his day in court. He wanted to be able to tell his son that, even if he ended up in jail, he had never admitted that he was a criminal. And Tighe had given an ultimatum: Either accept his plight or do something about it. If he remained angry, she would divorce him.

One July night, Hayes couldn't sleep. He eventually quit trying and, starting around 3 A.M., sent a barrage of stream-of-consciousness text messages to an acquaintance:

I feel like I am sleepwalking the path of least resistance. I don't know the odds but I know the truth and I know that I didn't believe what I was doing was dishonest. In some senses I don't care if I get a worse punishment at least I went down fighting. I have never denied doing what I did but how can any sane person really think my actions dishonest in my mind given how open and transparent I was in absolutely every regard? I never sought to hide anything ever, was never told I should not be doing it, was never trained, was directly instructed. So many people got paid from the money I made and I am going to jail, it seems so unjust. I did not do anything for personal enrichment. . . . Yes indirectly I would benefit but this was so minor [in] the greater scheme of how much money I made the bank. In short I am not a rogue operator or bad person, I was a 26 year old in a high pressured job looking to do the best I could and now I have society trying to retrospectively apply some sort of moral code, well why don't they go back to the mid 90's when this start[ed] whilst I was still at school? . . . The public misconception driven by ignorant press and incompetent regulators seeking to deflect from their own short-comings is staggering.

Eight hours later, Jonson met with the SFO investigators again. They were pushing for an ironclad commitment that Hayes would plead guilty. Hayes had told Jonson that he was contemplating fighting the charges. She thought it was an awful idea—he had given eighty-two hours of taped interviews, including countless confessions! "The SFO will crush you," she cautioned. But in the SFO's offices, Jonson deflected the investigators' questions about her client's intentions. "There is a concern about documents we have not seen so far," she warned them. She cited e-mails in which Hayes had been instructed to push Libor up or down—e-mails that her client insisted existed but that apparently hadn't been disclosed to the SFO.

The agency, in its haste to throw together an open-and-shut case, hadn't even asked UBS to hand over all documents. "We didn't want everything in the way the Americans did," one investigator rationalized. "I'm not reading too much into the fact that UBS have withheld material."

· · · ·

In July, the SFO filed criminal charges against Farr and Gilmour. The agency assumed Hayes would plead guilty and testify against all of his co-conspirators—with a witness of his caliber, who in their right mind would fight the charges? And that was good, because aside from its endless interviews with Hayes, the SFO hadn't done a whole lot of investigating over the past year. Not wanting to waste time or money interviewing second-tier witnesses, the agency had even declined offers from lawyers for some of Hayes's former colleagues who were offering to help—part of an effort to ensure that it was the British authorities, not the Americans, who charged their clients.

One of the exceptions was Brent Davies. His life had changed dramatically in the two years since ICAP cut him loose. One day he had been walking down the street in London's suburbs when a film producer for a miniseries about the Vikings spotted him. The hulking, wild-haired Davies looked the part; would he like to be an extra? Why not, Davies figured—it's not like he had a job. So they suited him up in chain mail and a sword; he fit right in. Now Davies was fishing for more acting work. But the formerly gregarious, charismatic man was stressed and miserable. Nonetheless, in July, he managed to tell his story to the SFO, including how he hadn't thought anyone would take his Libor-moving requests seriously. At the half-day interview, the SFO hinted that Hayes was pleading guilty and had agreed to testify against his former brokers.

In August, the SFO started digging into Hayes's assets, not least the Old Rectory, to see if they should be confiscated as the fruits of his crimes. This shouldn't have surprised Hayes, but it tipped him into a wild rage. "They are trying to destroy me, but I'll go down fighting," he fumed to his lawyers.

"If you plead not-guilty, prospects of acquittal are reduced," David Williams cautioned—a bizarre warning, since the chances of acquittal were zero if he pleaded guilty.

"But I get to say my side of the story," Hayes shot back.

"Remember that you are at risk of doubling or tripling your prison sentence," Jonson said.

Hayes countered that, if convicted, he didn't think it was likely he'd end up getting sentenced to more than five years, since "I didn't take any personal benefit from the situation."

For someone who felt such comfort in numbers, he was wildly off—not to mention exercising faulty logic (and incorrectly claiming that he hadn't benefited). Each of the eight counts he was charged with carried a possible sentence of up to ten years in prison. And it hadn't fully dawned on Hayes that he was being cast not only as the Libor ringleader but also as a symbol of the darkest tendencies of the entire banking industry. "You're the scapegoat and so there is a deterrent aspect," Jonson pointed out. Still, Hayes decided, there could be no guilty plea until the SFO took off the table the threat of seizing his family's assets. But the SFO was unlikely to take that off the table until he pleaded guilty. It was a stalemate.

"The trader in me wants to plead guilty," Hayes told an acquaintance in mid-August. "My gut says fight." He went with his gut.

CHAPTER 17

The Unit Cost
of Steak

It was a late-August evening, and the setting summer sun cast long shadows across the winding, tree-lined streets in the small English town of Fleet. Barely a month earlier, Hayes had moved there with his family. They had given up on trying to sell the Old Rectory—buyers were scarce, at least at the price Hayes and Tighe were seeking—and so they had settled for renting it out instead. With that desperately needed income, they moved into a four-bedroom rental house with a small backyard. The house was a short drive from Tighe's parents, so they had easy access to child care when Sarah was at work and Hayes had to meet with his lawyers or appear in court. Hayes also informed their befuddled real estate agent that a key consideration was the house's proximity to a KFC outlet.

Driving home, fried chicken and a Fanta resting on the passenger seat of his remaining Mercedes, Hayes approached a four-way intersection and tapped the brakes. His orange soda teetered, and as he leaned over to prevent it from tumbling to the floor, he took his eyes off the road. The car rolled through a red light. There was a squeal of brakes, then the smash of metal and glass as Hayes's vehicle collided with another car. Hayes was shaken up but not seriously injured; nor was the other driver. (The Mercedes didn't fare so well. Its repair bill would amount to about £15,000.)

Hayes had been struggling lately to remain focused on the task at hand, as unpleasant as it might be, to not let his mind wander to subjects he preferred, like financial markets or QPR's next match or his rapidly cooling dinner. Sometimes, though, when his stress levels rose, the world seemed either to descend into slow motion or to accelerate as if life was being fast-forwarded. It was hard to concentrate at times like that. Now a brief lapse in attention had nearly ended in disaster.

He phoned Tighe from the site of the accident. "I crashed the car," he reported. She was relieved to hear nobody was hurt. But she couldn't shake an unsettling thought: Was it really an accident?

· · · ·

On September 25, 2013, the Justice Department filed felony charges against Goodman, Wilkinson, and Read. Aside from Hayes and Darin, the three former brokers were the first people the U.S. government had charged in its five-year investigation, and a posse of powerful American prosecutors once again took to a podium to denounce their actions. Attorney General Holder accused the men of having "undermined the integrity of the global markets. They were supposed to be honest brokers, but instead, they put their own financial interests ahead of that larger responsibility. And as a result, transactions and financial products around the world were compromised, because they were tied to a rate that was distorted due to the brokers' dishonesty." The charges were filed in a New York court on the same day that ICAP agreed to pay $87 million to settle the U.S. and British Libor investigations. The deal spared ICAP's top executives of criticism, notwithstanding David Casterton's role hammering out the fixed-fee arrangement that authorities now described as corrupt. "I deeply regret and strongly condemn the inexcusable actions of the brokers," Michael Spencer told reporters, emphasizing that the misbehavior had been confined to a few rogue—and former—employees. (In the United Kingdom, Labour lawmakers called for David Cameron's Conservative Party to return the nearly £5 million that Spencer had donated. The party kept the money.)

Like Hayes, the former ICAP brokers now had a powerful incentive to find a way to get the British government to charge them, to reduce the risk of U.S. extradition. And so lawyers for the three men paraded into the SFO's offices to plead with the antifraud agency to prosecute their clients.

The SFO remained in the dark about Hayes's intention to fight the charges. Hayes, out of money, had decided to take advantage of Britain's public defender system, and Fulcrum wasn't eligible to participate in the program.* In any case, his impression was that the small firm wasn't equipped for a major, long-running criminal trial. He set out to find someone to represent him in his still-secret fight against the SFO.

Fat, bearded, and with a mane of long, black hair, George Carter-Stephenson was famous for defending suspects in gruesome, headline-grabbing murder cases. Hayes was drawn to him

---

* Unlike in the United States, where defendants unable to afford their own lawyer are assigned a public defender, in Britain they get to pick a private lawyer who then gets reimbursed through the Legal Aid program.

for several reasons, among them the fact that Carter-Stephenson was willing to accept somewhat less than his usual fee to take his case—a sign, Hayes concluded, that the lawyer was confident of victory and the justness of his cause. Tighe, at least, recognized that it was also conceivable that Carter-Stephenson was eager for the publicity associated with another marquee trial.

Hayes's new legal team told the SFO on October 9 that he would plead not guilty and wouldn't testify as a prosecution witness. Suddenly the backbone of the agency's biggest investigation had turned to mush.

The SFO got to work fulfilling Jonson's prediction from months earlier that the agency would crush Hayes if he fought the charges. For starters, it got a court to slap a restraining order on him, limiting his weekly spending to £250 (less than $400), on the grounds that anything he was spending more than that—especially now that he wasn't paying his own legal fees—could represent an effort to hide or dispose of ill-gotten assets. Then, one October afternoon, SFO officials arrived in the lobby of Shearman & Sterling's offices. A receptionist called Tighe to let her know there were government agents downstairs looking for her. She came down to the lobby and was handed a court order that froze her and Joshua's assets and accused her of trying to hide her husband's criminal proceeds by transferring the Old Rectory ownership to her name. Tighe was mortified. The agents' presence at her work meant she had to explain the embarrassing situation to her boss. As soon as he heard what had happened, Hayes flew into a rage. He regarded the pursuit of his wife and two-year-old son as underhanded and felt that he was being treated like a drug dealer or a terrorist.

In fact, the effort to go after the family's assets was a routine law enforcement tactic. It shouldn't have surprised him that the SFO, spurned by its star witness, was now fighting back. But the restraining order was based on a false premise—that Tighe was hiding assets under her maiden name. In fact, she had always used the name Tighe in professional contexts, and her passport, driver's license, and other official documents were under that name, too. Yes, ownership of the house had been transferred to her. But it wasn't a secret. All the records were public. The judge who signed the asset-freezing order held a new hearing and scolded the SFO for misleading the court. But still, damage had been done.

The agency's next move was to tweak the wording of its charges against Hayes. No longer would he be tried for manipulating Libor "and other interbank offered rates"; now it would just be Libor. The change meant that the British charges didn't fully overlap with the American ones. As a result, Hayes theoretically could be extradited to the United States to face charges of rigging other, non-Libor benchmarks.

The next month, the SFO sent Hayes and his lawyers into a panic when it mentioned in court papers that on top of the collusion and fraud charges that had been public for the past year, the United States also was accusing him of obstruction of justice. That seemed plausible, given what Hayes and his lawyers now knew about his recorded 2011 call with Alykulov. But the SFO eventually acknowledged that it had made a mistake. Hayes saw dirty tricks where in fact there probably was just incompetence—but again, the punch had landed.

· · · ·

For the past couple of years, Tullett Prebon had had its head buried deep in the sand. The firm's longtime CEO, Terry Smith, the son of a truck driver, was convinced that his brokerage had sidestepped the Libor scandal, and he and his deputies basked in schadenfreude as they watched their hated rivals ICAP and RP Martin wriggle in the regulatory crosshairs. But in March 2013, after spending dozens of hours interviewing Hayes, the SFO had decided that Tullett and its brokers might be implicated as well. The agency sent a request to the brokerage for information. Trying to assess the possible damage, the firm set out to interview every employee who had interacted with the now-radioactive Hayes. One of those was the Hong Kong broker Danny Brand, who had bought Hayes the yellow bumblebee socks and had told him he'd been kidnapped when he wasn't at work on time. Brand had been a guest at Hayes's wedding. Now, sitting across the table from a lawyer and compliance official in Tullett's offices, the broker described Hayes as "psychotic" and "an irrational guy at the best of times." Brand said he had never fielded a request to move Libor or participated in a switch trade, but he defended any of his colleagues who had done so by noting that if brokers didn't comply with Hayes's wishes, however unreasonable they might have been, they would have faced serious professional consequences.

Hayes hadn't sought Brand's help with Libor because the broker was based in Hong Kong and therefore lacked the connections with London-based Libor setters enjoyed by other plugged-in brokers—brokers like Noel Cryan. As Tullett plowed through its archive of e-mails and instant messages, Cryan now found himself in an undesirable spotlight. The firm suspended him and then hauled him in for a disciplinary hearing on September 11. Five company officials and outside lawyers crowded into a meeting room. It was the first time Cryan had ever met the head of the brokerage's compliance department.

Cryan argued that he hadn't actually assisted Hayes. He was only creating the illusion of being helpful in order to preserve the lucrative account and to trick Hayes into participating in the switch trades with Danziger. What's more, he said Tullett's upper management—including Angus Wink—knew exactly what was going on with the controversial switches.

A couple of weeks later, Cryan was summoned for another meeting and was handed a three-page letter. Tullett accepted his argument that he hadn't tried to manipulate Libor, but not his claim that senior management knew about the switch trades. It was a convenient interpretation: Tullett bought the portions of Cryan's defense that made it look like Tullett hadn't done anything wrong, but not those that cast aspersions on top executives. (Wink had denied that he knew anything about the switch trades.) "The decision is to terminate your employment with the company with immediate effect for Gross Misconduct," the letter concluded.

In October, Tullett belatedly informed the SFO that it had found recordings that captured Cryan and his colleagues talking with their bosses about the switch trades—just as Cryan had claimed. The firm didn't mention the recordings to Cryan. Tullett had lanced the boil.

· · · ·

The authorities behind the Libor investigation started to cash in on the case's growing cachet.

Gary Gensler rewrote history and credited himself with initiating the CFTC's Libor investigation, telling a *New York Times* columnist in November 2013 that the whole thing started after he read a news story about Libor. "I asked our head of enforcement, 'Should we look into this?'" Gensler claimed, ignoring the fact that the Libor investigation was roughly a year old by the time he joined the CFTC.

Margaret Cole, the FSA enforcer who had seemed lukewarm

about the Libor investigation, jumped to the financial services firm PricewaterhouseCoopers. (Her boss, the FSA's chief executive, leapt to a top job at Barclays, helping the British bank improve its interactions with regulators, and was later knighted.)

In the United States, Stephen Obie secured himself a fat payday at the law firm Jones Day, where his practice involved helping financial institutions navigate the CFTC's rocky regulatory terrain. David Meister—having apparently sated his desire to leave a mark somewhere—returned to Skadden Arps, where his Libor-enhanced credentials added to his résumé (and presumably his paycheck). The same trend took hold among the Justice Department's Libor-busting crew. Robertson Park jumped to the private law firm Murphy & McGonigle, which touted his experiencing bridging the Justice Department–CFTC divide. William Stellmach joined the firm of Willkie Farr & Gallagher, where he helped financial institutions get off the hook in government investigations. And Scott Hammond, who as a top antitrust enforcer had put UBS's law firm, Gibson Dunn, in the driver's seat of the Libor investigation, landed a job in Washington as a partner at . . . Gibson Dunn. There he was reunited with his former boss, Gary Spratling. The law firm issued a press release quoting Spratling: The addition of Hammond "will ensure that Gibson Dunn will continue to be the 'go-to' firm for cartel defense work." Hammond himself was open about the fact that he'd be helping clients deal with antitrust investigations—in other words, outmaneuvering his former government colleagues.

The phenomenon of government officials scoring lucrative jobs at the companies they previously policed was so well established that it had a name: the revolving door. And if everyone was doing it, why shouldn't these guys? Didn't they deserve to enjoy some of the same largesse from putting their unique skills to work? There were no rules prohibiting switching sides, and no matter which direction they looked, they were surrounded by men and women who had enriched themselves by exploiting inefficiencies and loopholes that would be imperceptible to all but the professionally trained eye. So what if their skills were now being used to help powerful institutions avoid the same laws and regulations that they previously had been entrusted to enforce?

••••

On a cool, gray December day almost exactly a year after Hayes had been arrested, he walked into the Southwark Crown Court. The bleak brick building on the banks of the Thames had been the venue, years earlier, of the trial of his former Nottingham classmate Kweku Adoboli. Hayes wore a dark blue shirt and a pair of old black Armani slacks along with his bumblebee socks, which he now believed brought him good luck. Standing in the dock with Farr and Gilmour, he was asked how he wished to plead. "Not guilty," he replied. (Farr and Gilmour also pleaded not guilty.)

Announcing the plea in court—the culmination of months of personal struggle—felt good. Hayes's spirits immediately improved; suddenly the world didn't look like such a hostile place. One afternoon a few days later, he and Tighe were at home watching the World Darts Championship on television. During a break in the action, the camera panned to the audience. It was filled with rowdy, drunk fans, many of them costumed as clowns or rabbits or Star Wars storm troopers. Ladbrokes, a British gambling company that was sponsoring the tournament, had handed out blank signs for people to write on and hold up for the cameras. In black marker, someone had scrawled "Save the ICAP 3"—a reference to Read, Goodman, and Wilkinson. Hayes hit the rewind button on his remote to make sure he hadn't imagined it; sure enough, there it was. He drew solace.

. . . .

To allow Hayes to prepare his defense, the SFO handed over to his team tens of thousands of electronic files—e-mails, chat transcripts, phone calls, interview recordings, trading records, computer screenshots, photos, scanned printouts—that the agency had collected in its investigation. There were scores of gigabytes of data that needed to be read and cataloged. Hayes attacked the new project with the same gusto that he had brought to his job as a trader. He set up shop at his kitchen table and stacked towers of evidence on chairs and alongside salt and pepper shakers and Joshua's placemat. It was solitary work; he sometimes went all day without any human contact. He worked at all hours—not always because he wanted to, but because it beat lying in bed awake, unable to sleep.

Hayes used computer programming skills that he'd learned as a trader to build a vast interactive database in which he kept track of all the exhibits. The database allowed his lawyers to sort the materials by dozens of variables, including the seniority of executives involved in each communication. When that task was complete, he moved on to other information sources. He read through Canadian affidavits. He had German court documents about the firing—and subsequent reinstatement—of several Deutsche Bank employees responsible for submitting Libor data translated into English. He repeatedly instructed his lawyers to submit freedom-of-information requests. A condition of his bail was that he had to stay in England or Wales, so the family took a quick vacation to the Isle of Wight, off England's southern coast. (Hayes's father footed the bill.) Hayes spent the holiday trying to track down Thomas Youle and Connan Snider's paper—which, in the absence of any journals willing to print it, the grad students had self-published online—indicating that Citigroup appeared to be skewing its Libor submissions.

Once Hayes had sifted through all the available evidence, he started the exhaustive task of figuring out how often Goodman's run-throughs actually were beneficial to his trading positions. The answer—unsurprisingly, considering that Read had routinely lied to Hayes—was, not all that often.

Next, Hayes set out to identify who might have been harmed by his manipulative activity. One way to assess this, he figured, was to identify who was on the other side of his trades. By definition, every trade had a winner and a loser, and if Hayes was the beneficiary, who were the victims? This was a herculean task, in part because he had been such a prolific trader. The SFO had provided him with his trading records; there were 45,407 transactions from 2006 through 2010. He went through each one. Of those, about two-thirds, 31,002, involved instruments that were linked to Libor and were relevant to the case. Almost all of those—99.9 percent—were with other banks. The other 43 were with hedge funds and other asset managers. There were no other trading partners—no pension funds or university endowments or municipalities or mom-and-pop investors. In other words, all his trades were with sophisticated institutions; he wasn't deliberately ripping off innocents. Here was a vivid illustration of the closed-loop system that had come to characterize the twenty-first-century financial industry: Banks and other financial institutions trading with each other and nobody else in a self-perpetuating, self-serving cycle.

Of course, that didn't justify Hayes's actions, legally or otherwise. And it conveniently didn't account for those relying on slightly skewed Libor data—basically anyone with a mortgage or loan or hedging instrument whose value was based on the benchmark. It wasn't Hayes's fault alone that states, counties, towns all over the United States—many of them, like Baltimore, slashing school and police budgets to keep afloat amid the recession—had potentially lost millions due to aberrations in Libor. It wasn't Hayes's fault alone that pension funds safeguarding the retirement savings of thousands of cops, firefighters, and teachers might have been stiffed. And it wasn't Hayes's fault alone that other financial institutions—as unsympathetic as they might be, they still managed the investments of millions of individuals and institutions—had ended up on the wrong side of Libor-linked transactions. But Hayes did bear *some* responsibility. And yet those victims didn't factor into his calculus.

. . . .

The list of individuals charged by the U.S. and British governments with crimes related to Libor manipulation continued to grow. In January 2014, the Justice Department filed charges against Paul Robson—aka Pooks—along with two of his former Rabobank colleagues. (Most of the allegations were unrelated to Hayes.) Robson eventually pleaded guilty, becoming the first person to admit to criminality.

Two months later, the SFO charged Read, Wilkinson, and Goodman. It was, perversely, a happy day for the former brokers because it reduced the chances of extradition to the United States. (All three pleaded not guilty.) In October, the SFO charged Noel Cryan, the seventh man in Hayes's alleged ring.[*]

---

[*] The SFO also filed charges against seven former Barclays employees for their alleged roles in

Each time charges were filed, a press conference was convened or a press release issued touting the latest actions as a clear sign of the government's commitment to punishing financial criminals. For the most part, the media played along, and to a certain extent, these creatures of the modern financial system were fair game. They *had* pushed the envelope too far. They *had* gotten rich doing so. They *had* abandoned their moral and ethical compasses. Perhaps they had even broken the law doing so.

And yet even the most vigorous prosecutor would have to admit that these guys had nothing at all to do with the larger financial crisis. They weren't issuing reckless mortgages. They weren't packing those mortgages into toxic securities. They weren't piling on the billions of dollars in borrowed money that would topple some of the world's biggest banks. Meanwhile, the bank executives who had done all those things were sitting pretty. Sure, some of them had lost their jobs, but many had walked away with fortunes worth well into the tens of millions of dollars.

. . . .

In May 2014, Andrew Thursfield and his Citigroup-appointed lawyer showed up at the SFO's offices for two days of interviews. With Hayes no longer a prosecution witness, Thursfield was going to help fill the void, and the SFO wanted to get a feel for its star witness before he appeared in court. "The culture at Citi at the time was far from being dishonest," he assured Matt Ball. Aside from Hayes, "everyone else that I dealt with, and definitely everyone in the Libor process, was totally honest and doing everything to the best of their ability in what were

---

the Libor scandal, although they were unconnected to Hayes.

often difficult conditions." Hayes, he said, was "definitely a bad apple."

But when presented with e-mail after e-mail that seemed to show Thursfield himself taking Libor-moving instructions from traders—in the period before Hayes had arrived at Citigroup—he rattled off excuses. "I have chosen my words poorly here," he said to explain one statement. "This e-mail reflects a poor choice of words on my part," he conceded in relation to another note. "This was a flippant remark of mine," he said about yet another e-mail where he suggested getting Barclays to lower its rates. When shown other e-mails where Citigroup colleagues explained their plans to manipulate Libor, Thursfield insisted he didn't know what they were talking about.

. . . .

The judge assigned to Hayes's case was a former semiprofessional rugby player named Jeremy Cooke. He was a longtime trial lawyer, bespectacled and with bushy eyebrows and brown hair punctuated by white sideburns. He had joined the bench in 2001, the same year he was knighted. A member of a socially conservative Christian lawyers' group, he had ruffled feathers in the past by sentencing a woman to eight years in prison for performing her own late-term abortion.

After months of reviewing evidence and mediating lawyers' pretrial jousting, Cooke was pretty sure Hayes was guilty. Most of the defense's maneuvers to get the case dismissed or delayed or redefined struck him as a waste of time. The trial already had been pushed back to spring 2015, and Cooke was determined to get it wrapped up before the court shut down for that year's August recess.

Carter-Stephenson tried to get the case tossed on an important technicality: Only in the wake of the Barclays settlement had Parliament passed a law officially outlawing the manipulation of benchmarks like Libor, and that didn't apply retroactively. Plus, the conspiracy-to-defraud charges against Hayes hinged on the notion that he had intended to defraud third parties. Well, who exactly were those third parties, and how were they actually defrauded? The SFO hadn't presented evidence that identified victims.

Hayes's lawyers also decided to seek Cooke's recusal, citing comments he'd made in court about the case being "open-and-shut" and his repeated references to Hayes as a "gambler." But in one motion after another, the judge ruled for the Crown (as the prosecution is known in British courts). Cooke, presumably not thrilled by the efforts to oust him, stayed on the case.

. . . .

On an unseasonably warm September afternoon, Farr arrived at Canary Wharf to meet one more time with the regulator that, until recently, had been called the FSA. While the agency occupied the same skyscraper, with the same ferocious owl sculpture guarding the lobby, it had been rechristened the Financial Conduct Authority—part of a government effort to wipe away, once and for all, the old agency's stained reputation. Farr's former employer had undergone changes, too. The Libor investigation had put RP Martin's future in peril; it was sold to its larger rival, BGC. Caplin was removed from power. The FCA fined the former CEO £225,000 and banned him from ever again holding a senior financial job in the United Kingdom, accusing him of presiding over a corrupt, lawless culture. Farr, meanwhile, had sold all but one of his motorcycles, including his two beloved Ducatis. He got a temporary job chopping down trees and selling them at a local market. His life was in turmoil, but at least he had managed to maintain a sense of humor. He joked that his new open-air job was a good use of his "market" skills. To handle some of his legal communications, he registered an e-mail address with the username "terrysinapickle."

Two years earlier, when the FSA last interviewed Farr, he had said he rarely spent time or money entertaining Hayes. But in their subsequent digging, the investigators had found heaps of receipts Farr had submitted for wining and dining his prized client. Why hadn't Farr mentioned these years ago? Well, technically, it was true that he didn't go out much with Hayes. Instead, the trader would send Farr receipts from his nights out in Tokyo or London, and the broker would submit those through RP Martin's expense accounting system and then reimburse Hayes, transferring money directly into his bank account. "We'd give him money back like that," Farr explained.

"And that was common practice for you to do that?" Patrick Meaney asked, stunned by the firm's lackadaisical attitude to what looked like borderline bribery.

"Yes," Farr said. Meaney showed him two receipts from a Four Seasons resort, from Hayes and Tighe's trip to Thailand in May 2009. Then Meaney played a recording of a phone call in which Hayes agreed to take the other side of one of Danziger's switch trades.

"Was this a quid pro quo?" Meaney asked.

"What do you mean, 'pro quo'?"

"That he was giving you something in return. So in return for you paying for his hotel accommodation in Thailand, he's agreeing to do a switch trade for you to give you brokerage?"

"I can't remember actually him saying that, but, I mean, it writes like that there," Farr answered.

. . . .

Through it all, Hayes foraged for different ways to scratch his trader's itch. A friend who worked at an online gambling company had alerted him to a loophole in the fine print of a rival, CaesarsBingo .com. Caesars, like other gambling websites, offered customers an automatic bonus when they deposited money in their accounts. If you deposited $200, you got a $400 bonus—a total of $600 would be in your account. For every dollar you gambled, the odds were that you'd get about 60 cents back. Normally, those would seem like losing odds. But if you gambled the entire $600 at once, you could expect to recoup at least $360—a quick $160 profit above the $200 you'd deposited. If that sounded too good to be true, it usually was: Most gambling sites required that customers place a minimum number of bets, at least a few rounds, with their bonus cash. Through sheer probability, that requirement would ensure that the bonus cash and much of the principal got whittled down. But Caesars had forgotten to require customers to place a minimum number of bets.

So Hayes opened accounts, put money in, received the bonus cash, gambled the whole pot, then withdrew whatever was left— always more than his initial deposit. He scouted the terms of other gambling sites and found a few with similar errors and got to work exploiting those, too. (He gleefully spread the word among friends and family.)

Joshua, meanwhile, had become obsessed with the Disney Pixar film *Cars*. Searching online, Hayes discovered a vigorous market to buy and sell the toy cars associated with the movie. Hayes calculated that he could buy a bunch of the cars in bulk for a price that worked out to less than $1 per car. That bundle would generally include one or two especially sought-after toys that could sometimes fetch more than $20 apiece from avid collectors. He could resell the pricey cars and make all his money back, while keeping all the leftovers. But he overcame his impulse to try to exploit the inefficient market, reminding himself that he had more important, if less enjoyable, things to worry about.

Tighe had concluded that Carter-Stephenson was botching courtroom arguments and feared that he wanted to go to trial mainly to burnish his own reputation; she ultimately convinced her husband to ditch the famous lawyer. His replacement was a slight, mild-mannered barrister named Neil Hawes, who had a background in fraud and finance cases. He lacked Carter-Stephenson's bombast but possessed a quiet, reassuring confidence.

Under Tighe's tutelage, Hayes had made progress at acting more normal. It was hard work; whenever Hayes interacted with other people, including his wife, he had to adhere to rules that he and Tighe had formulated beforehand. (Among them: He needed to ask her each evening how her day had been.) Hayes generally had managed to comply, but it never became automatic. Now, under pressure, he was relapsing. He started pelting acquaintances and strangers alike with information about Libor and why the case against him was a waste of taxpayer money. At dinner parties, he grew agitated as he talked about the injustice of his plight; Tighe's efforts to redirect conversations rarely worked. They eventually stopped going out. Some friends no longer returned their phone calls.

Tighe found it torturous to think about her husband's predicament without a drink in her hand. The recycling bin in their driveway overflowed with wine and beer bottles. (Inside, the kitchen counter was jammed with full wine bottles—a reflection not only of Tighe's prodigious drinking but also of Hayes's penchant for buying in bulk.)

She tried to stage-manage her husband's approaching moment in the spotlight. In the car one morning, the couple discussed how to deal with the fact that, despite all their tribulations, they remained wealthy, especially compared to the jurors, drawn from London's mostly working-class Southwark area, who would be hearing Hayes's case. He kept insisting that he had sacrificed greater riches out of loyalty to UBS; Tighe explained over and over that a jury would not care. He had still earned millions. Nothing was easy: She instructed him to buy a court-appropriate wardrobe; he bought secondhand Armani and Hugo Boss trousers and dress shirts and sweaters on eBay. She persuaded him to get a professional haircut, rather than leaving the task to his mother, in exchange for doing a week of his chores around the house.

Tighe prepped him on how to act during the trial, counseling against his tendency to roll his eyes, and sent him to a personal coach to train him to control his temper, speak slowly, and make eye contact. At a pretrial hearing in April, Cooke ruled that the defense team wouldn't get access to certain additional documents it was seeking. Hayes jumped out of his chair and angrily pointed his finger at the judge. His lawyers struggled to calm him down. Afterward, he went out for fried chicken and a drink with his high school friend David Brown—the same guy who had watched Hayes studying pub slot machines decades earlier. The bar they went to had a two-for-one deal on cocktails. Unable to resist a bargain, Hayes angrily downed one after another. By the time he got home late that night, he was drunkenly ranting about Cooke. He couldn't sleep, so he popped a sleeping pill. It didn't work. He lay awake, slowly sobering up, miserable.

. . . .

Brent Davies had converted his success in the Vikings series to other acting work. His latest job was playing a fighter in the seventh Star Wars movie, *The Force Awakens.* It was being filmed at Pinewood Studios, which occupied a sprawling lot in the middle of a huge park west of London. Between scenes, Davies wandered around in his elaborate costume. Sometimes he called his lawyers and had to be reminded to remove his helmet so they could hear what he was saying. Davies was earning more as an actor than he had as a broker; he was also having more fun. (His lawyers took to joking about whether he'd be allowed to wear chain mail into court.)

After being fired in the summer of 2013, Danny Wilkinson also had found an entertaining diversion, rekindling his career as a DJ. Under the stage name Emperor Constantine, he was part of an electronic group called Hellsinki-V. They scored gigs at trendy clubs and a summer music festival, got a weekly late-night slot on a community radio station, and started producing amateur music videos. Costumed in white lab coats, flimsy 3-D glasses, and bulky headphones, Wilkinson and his bandmates bounced around the stage, waving their arms and dancing, while the audience throbbed along with the music. For some, times were good. Not for Hayes.

· · · ·

One afternoon, a respected London psychologist, Alison Beck, interviewed Hayes at his lawyers' offices. Part of the defense strategy was to argue that Hayes's odd personality helped explain his professional behavior. In the interview, Hayes was his normal, manic self, plowing through minutiae about his old job and the legal case before Beck even had a chance to introduce herself. Listening to Hayes jabbering, Beck quickly concluded that he viewed the world in a very particular and peculiar manner. Human interactions were reduced to digits, with no room for nuance or subtlety. If Hayes trusted someone, for example, he gave that person unconditional, unquestioning loyalty, even if there were obvious reasons to be wary. At one point, Beck asked why he didn't want to testify against his former colleagues. They're my friends, Hayes responded. "Which of them have come out to support you?" she asked. Deep down, Hayes knew she was right. And yet . . .

Beck's diagnosis confirmed what many had informally surmised over the years: Hayes had "a relatively mild form" of Asperger's syndrome. She wrote:

> Mr Hayes does not perceive the world as people without Asperger's Syndrome do. . . . It is consistent with a diagnosis of AS that if manipulation of Libor existed both before and after Mr Hayes' employment in the market, then he is likely to have simply regarded it as acceptable practice. . . . People without AS might recognise the moral grey area of this line of work and might appreciate that excelling in this area would make them vulnerable. . . . [I]n order to function he appears to have needed to believe that his bosses are right because they set the rules. This is a feature of AS. It is also likely to have made him vulnerable to exploitation.

When Hayes heard the diagnosis, he worried that a jury would dismiss it as contrived to help his case—not an unreasonable concern. But a psychiatrist hired by the defense and a psychologist hired by the prosecution arrived at similar diagnoses.[*]

Tighe burst into tears when told about the diagnosis. She had a psychology degree and felt awful that she hadn't identified the con-

---

[*] It fit into a pattern for the Hayes clan. Family members believed that Sandy's father, Peter Hunt—a pioneer in the nascent British computing industry in the 1950s—also had autism.

dition earlier. The signs had been there all along. It wasn't just his "Rain Man" and "Kid Asperger" nicknames. Before showing up at a party, she always had to remind Hayes not to ask people inappropriate things, like how much they earned, or to comment on their weight. His obsession with routine was another: his lucky trousers, socks, pandas, turnstile. These were more than superstitions—they were absolute convictions.

Emotionally spent, Hayes, Tighe, and Joshua spent the long Easter weekend at a nearby Four Seasons, the same hotel where they'd been married. At dinner on Sunday night in the hotel's ballroom, they were escorted to a table near the stage. Tighe pointed out that they were sitting only a few feet away from where they had exchanged their wedding vows more than four years ago. *How their lives had changed since then, for better and for worse!* It was a romantic moment.

Hayes looked up from the menu. He announced that he had made a discovery: The unit cost of steak, as measured by grams of meat, was slightly cheaper if they ordered individual portions instead of a two-person serving. Tighe gaped at him in disbelief.

• • • •

Tighe felt that the whole world had turned against her and her family. One Saturday night in April they attended a friend's wedding in London. Hayes stood around the outskirts of the party, wondering which of the guests realized that he was an accused criminal. Toward the end, Tighe bumped into an ex-boyfriend who mentioned Hayes and his apparent guilt. Tighe leapt to her husband's defense. The disagreement quickly escalated into a loud, drunken fight. Tighe was in a fury. The pair had to be separated forcibly.

As pretrial rulings consistently went against the defense, the trained lawyer in Tighe was coming to terms with the increasing odds that her husband would be convicted. Maybe, she thought to herself, Hayes shouldn't have gone to such lengths to avoid extradition to the United States in the first place. (Fulcrum's advice to cooperate fully, and admit guilt, wasn't looking quite so wise.) She started considering what she would do if her husband was locked up. Feeling betrayed by her country, she scoped out living arrangements and a nursery in Tokyo, where she still had friends. She toyed with a job prospect in Abu Dhabi. She worried that she would skid into a dark, angry depression if she remained in England. Then she reconsidered; she couldn't abandon Hayes.

Increasingly, she was paranoid. One day, she was standing outside her office having a cigarette—a bad habit she had recently resumed in order to deal with the stress. A silver Mercedes stopped at a traffic light. A man in the backseat seemed to be pointing his long-lensed camera right at her. Tighe couldn't quite put her finger on why someone would be photographing her, but she was convinced it was part of a conspiracy. Maybe the SFO was trying to intimidate her?

Hayes chain-smoked. His hair grayed. He had vivid, bizarre dreams. In one, he was running a KFC franchise and showed up to cook himself some fried chicken. At first, he couldn't get the fryers to work. Then customers noticed the restaurant was open and they streamed in. Hayes realized there wasn't any chicken, anywhere. There was only beef stroganoff. He awoke in a panic. In a different nightmare, he flunked professional tests that his rivals passed. Another time, he dreamed that he returned to work and that everything was back to normal. Nobody cared about Libor. This time, he woke to the crushing realization that it was only a dream.

The couple strategized about what they would tell Joshua if Hayes was convicted. They decided on a white lie: Daddy was away at work for the next few years, like a soldier on an overseas assignment. Tighe envisioned a large photo of Hayes hanging in their home. Each night, she and Joshua would wish the portrait good night.

· · · ·

UBS had fired Pete the Greek before he could land a job at a competitor, and things had gone downhill for him from there. As the FCA trawled through internal chats and e-mails from UBS and other banks, the agency encountered the plentiful instances in which he schemed with his colleagues to get Libor adjusted for the benefit of his trading positions. The regulator banned him from performing any influential role in the British financial industry because he "was dishonest and lacked integrity."

Pete the Greek's lawyers appealed the ruling. The FCA had an odd system for handling appeals of this nature: An internal panel called the Regulatory Decisions Committee was empowered to overturn verdicts of the agency's enforcement division if it found that there was compelling evidence that hadn't been properly taken into account. In early April, the committee vacated the FCA's punishment. The crux of the ruling—which was secret due to the confidential nature of the disciplinary process—was that "Mr Koutsogiannis did not behave dishonestly or without integrity in making requests for submissions within what he understood to be an acceptable range."

The FCA recognized the potential import of the ruling on Hayes's defense. A week before the trial was to begin, the agency convened a meeting to decide whether to disclose the ruling to his lawyers. "The sensitivity here is the criminal proceedings and the potential bleed across to other cases," an FCA official told attendees. They decided to withhold judgment for now on whether the Hayes team needed to know.

. . . .

Preparations for the trial went down to the wire. Hayes continued to hunt for witnesses to testify on his behalf. He wondered if Roger Darin might be willing to appear—sure, the men hated each other, but "we now have mutual self-interest," he explained to an acquaintance. "It's like Superman and Lex Luthor teaming up. . . . Sometimes your enemies' enemy is your friend." His lawyers dismissed the idea.

Hayes's team, however, remained convinced that the SFO was engaged in a cover-up by refusing to hand over millions of internal UBS documents that had been dredged up in the Swiss bank's internal investigation. (In fact, the SFO had never actually seen the documents, because UBS and its lawyers successfully argued they were subject to Switzerland's bank secrecy laws.) In court, lawyers debated whether the defense could use Hayes's Asperger's diagnosis to explain why Hayes didn't realize that what he was doing was wrong. The prosecution argued it was irrelevant. Cooke ruled for the prosecution.

That wasn't the only thing upsetting Hayes. He also was frustrated that his lawyers weren't interested in using the spreadsheets he had constructed that showed that his trading partners were almost entirely other banks and that his brokers didn't always adhere to his requests. (His lawyers doubted the spreadsheets would help convince a jury of his innocence.) In court one day, Hayes slipped a memory stick with the spreadsheets to one of Wilkinson's lawyers; someone might as well put all his hard work to use. After all these years, Hayes still hadn't figured out who his friends were.

CHAPTER 18

Charades

Tighe wasn't going to attend most of the trial. She had to work and, in any case, since she was likely to be a witness, British court rules prohibited her from showing up until after she had testified. But Sandy, back on speaking terms with her son, expected to be there every day.[*] She recently had purchased an apartment in London's Maida Vale neighborhood, and Hayes decided to set up shop there for the duration of the trial. That way, he only had to hop on the Tube for a short train ride; he would return to Fleet on the weekends. To get a feel for things, Sandy showed up at the Southwark courthouse the week before the trial was set to begin and sat in on an accused Albanian drug peddler's case. She was the only spectator; jurors stared at her, seeming to wonder what she was doing there.

Hayes and Tighe decided that she would escort him into court the first day—her presence would be soothing and would give the

---

[*] Hayes's father didn't plan to attend. Nick's presence there risked enraging Sandy and, in turn, adding to his son's stress.

photographers outside the courthouse an alternative to the usual fare of Hayes, alone and scowling, as he entered and left pretrial hearings. Hayes planned their itinerary in obsessive detail, allowing nearly two hours of extra time to absorb any unforeseen delays. Things went smoothly until they got in a taxicab outside Waterloo Station. They told the driver where they were going, but he misunderstood and took them to the wrong courthouse. It was only a mile or so away from Southwark, and they were running ridiculously early, but the detour threw Hayes for a loop. His pulse started racing. He broke into a sweat. He clutched a handle inside the cab so hard that his knuckles turned white. "We're not going to make it," he whispered to Tighe, over and over.

As the taxi approached the correct courthouse, it missed the turnoff. On a narrow road clogged with rush-hour traffic, the driver pulled a risky U-turn. A couple hundred yards away from the court, Hayes and Tighe clambered out, relieved that their journey was over. Holding hands in the late-spring sun, they walked the rest of the way. As a crowd of photographers and cameramen trained their lenses on them, a gust of wind lifted Tighe's knee-length turquoise dress. It was more than Hayes could bear. By the time they had made their way inside the courthouse, he was in a full-on panic. He sat in a waiting room, pulling out his hair.

. . . .

Glittering glass-and-steel offices, hotels, and apartment buildings had fast been replacing Southwark's beaten-down buildings. Among these modern arrivals, the Southwark Crown Court stood out as a particular eyesore. The dreary, brown brick structure seemed to have been designed by someone biased against natural illumination. Windows were few and far between, odd architecture for a riverside building overlooking a retired British warship, the City's landmark skyscrapers, and a nearly thousand-year-old fortress, the Tower of London. Upon entering the courthouse, everyone—judges, jurors, lawyers, and certainly defendants—had to pass through a pair of hypersensitive metal detectors. To get to the courtrooms, people had to either navigate two sets of staircases, one of them a fire exit, or rely on small, rickety elevators whose doors had a tendency to crash shut on people's limbs. The occasional mouse scampered along the cafeteria's linoleum floors.

Inside the courtrooms, though, pomp and decorum prevailed. Lawyers authorized to speak in court—barristers—had to wear black cloaks with white neck scarves. On their heads sat light-colored horse-hair wigs—honeycombed on top, tight curls tumbling down the sides, and two tails dangling in the back, cinched off with string. The traditional eighteenth-century attire was even more elaborate for judges, decked out in outfits that resembled Santa costumes: red cloaks with white lining and thick, furry cuffs, red sashes across the chests, and flowing white wigs to top off the ensembles. Not only did everyone stand when the judge entered or exited the courtroom, but anyone who came or went while court was in session was supposed to bow.

Courtroom 2 was a cramped, windowless room with blond wooden benches and harsh fluorescent bulbs embedded in the ceiling. A large metal seal on the wall at the front of the room, behind the judge's raised platform, displayed a lion, a unicorn, a crown, and the monarchy's motto, "Dieu et Mon Droit"—*God and my right*. The prior week, the court clerk had dispensed tickets to the press and public, trying to stave off a mad rush for limited seats, but before the doors opened that morning, a line of spectators snaked into an adjoining hallway. Spin doctors from Citigroup and UBS were there, as were lawyers for UBS, for Hayes's former brokers, and for numerous other parties with interests in the case. Hayes sat in a middle row, biting his fingernails and sipping water from a white plastic cup. (In a rare victory, Hayes's lawyers had argued that their client shouldn't be penned up in the dock; they needed access to him during the proceedings. Cooke assented. The dock, with its two rows of bolted-down purple chairs, was henceforth occupied by journalists.) Sandy—her wispy white hair swept up in a loose bun and a thin, patterned scarf tossed over her left shoulder—sat in the front row of the spectators' box, accompanied by her husband, Tim.

The jury filed in for the first time. Seven men and five women, it was a young, ragtag bunch: Several wore jeans and T-shirts, another a hooded sweatshirt. They carted backpacks, coffees, water bottles, and containers of fruit into the jury box, two elevated rows of chairs and desks perpendicular to the judge and lawyers. Southwark juries, drawn from the area surrounding the courthouse, were notorious among London's bar for being tough for prosecutors; jurors often harbored a distrust of law enforcement authorities. But this would be a fair fight—perhaps the only professionals less favored than such authority figures were bankers like Hayes. Cooke opened the proceedings by informing the jurors that the defendant had been diagnosed with Asperger's syndrome and as a result would have a court-appointed aide, called an intermediary, seated next to him. The aide's role, the judge explained, was to provide Hayes with emotional assistance. The jurors gawked at him like an animal in a zoo.

. . . .

Mukul Chawla was born in Nairobi, Kenya, in 1961, but his parents immigrated with him and his sister to England when they were young, in search of a better education for the children. A lifelong Bruce Springsteen fan, Chawla flirted with a career as a record producer, but it turned out that loving music wasn't a sufficient qualification. He had stints at a tobacco shop and a clothing store before deciding to follow in the footsteps of his father, a lawyer. The elder Chawla, who specialized in property law, was mostly deskbound, and his son was determined to avoid that fate. He wanted to be in a courtroom, not an office. Criminal law beckoned, and a decade into his career as a trial lawyer, Chawla—with an ample belly, bushy black eyebrows, and a lilting baritone voice—was taking on increasingly prominent cases.

In the British legal system, barristers operate out of their own small, private practices and take both defense and prosecution work on a contract basis. Chawla made his name defending a police sergeant accused of unlawfully killing a black paratrooper and by representing one of six men charged with fraud and corruption in connection with a public transportation project. He also prosecuted complex commercial and drug cases for the government. Known for relentless preparation and a knack for winning the confidence of juries with his friendly, low-key demeanor, his peers regarded him as one of London's finest trial lawyers. In July 2012, within a couple of weeks of the SFO deciding to open a criminal investigation into Libor manipulation the agency came to Chawla with perhaps his highest-profile assignment: helping run the case. For the next three years, he had been deeply involved in every aspect of the investigation.

His salt-and-pepper hair peeking out from beneath a blond wig, Chawla stood up in court on the first morning of the trial and began his opening statement. He had written the speech in advance, and now he read it, frequently looking up at the jury, in a soft voice. He introduced himself and his fellow prosecution lawyers and then, to demonstrate that he was a man of fairness, he introduced the defense lawyers, too. This was a simple case, Chawla said, and it was all about greed. Hayes had been motivated by money, pure and simple, and he hadn't let anyone or anything—certainly not the law—stand in his way. At times, Hayes had resorted to threats and bribes, paying out tens of thousands of pounds in corrupt fees to brokers who did his dirty work. The case would drag on for weeks, Chawla warned, and it would involve some pretty complicated financial arcana, but at its heart, it was a fundamental matter of right and wrong. Luckily, the defendant had made things easier: He had confessed to everything, on tape. To demonstrate, Chawla played a snippet of Hayes telling the SFO that he probably deserved to be sitting there. And if that wasn't enough, there were reams of evidence in which Hayes wrote out his instructions to colleagues and brokers. Hayes, Chawla said, had even admitted that his Libor-moving efforts likely netted his employers several million dollars a year of profits—not a lot compared to the star trader's overall haul, but more than enough for him to be guilty of fraud.

Don't be fooled, the prosecutor added. The defense will argue that Hayes wasn't alone in his efforts. That was true—and irrelevant. "Because lots of people are doing it doesn't mean it's not fundamentally dishonest, does it?" he asked. And any argument that the British Bankers' Association's broken processes somehow justified Hayes's behavior would be akin to claiming that burglary was acceptable because someone left a window ajar, he said.

Hayes struggled to contain his emotions. He shook his head. He leaned back in his chair and stared at the ceiling, fists clenched. He scribbled notes. He urgently whispered to his intermediary. He angrily jabbed a finger in Chawla's direction. "Calm down," his aide mouthed.

• • • •

Over the next few weeks, the trial, and Hayes, settled into a rhythm. Court ran from 10 A.M. until an hour-long lunch break began around 1 P.M., then resumed until shortly after 4 P.M. Hayes woke up at 7:30 A.M. and skipped breakfast. On important days, he donned a pair of lucky QPR socks. On the Tube ride to court, he played "Street Fighter" on his iPhone. At the courthouse, he bought a cup of tea from the small coffee shop in the lobby. Then he waited for the day to start, playing sudoku games that he tore out of a newspaper.

During breaks, Hayes and his lawyers huddled in a tiny meeting room across the hall from Courtroom 2. There was barely space for a couple of chairs, a coatrack, and a small table. Neil Hawes and his colleagues would try to soothe their anxious, angry client. In the hallway outside, Chawla, who had quit smoking the year before, could be seen puffing on an electronic cigarette, vapor curling out of his mouth and nostrils.

After court most evenings, Hayes and Sandy walked around a small, hedge-lined park near the Maida Vale flat; she mostly listened as he ranted. She cooked him a healthy dinner with lots of vegetables, he took a shower or bath, then climbed into bed to read or to watch a TV game show called *Love Island*. Then he popped a sleeping pill. Most nights, he tossed and turned.

• • • •

In early June, Hayes's lawyers finally were informed that the FCA appeals committee had invalidated the regulator's punishment against Pete the Greek, concluding that his actions weren't dishonest. At first, the defense team was ecstatic; this was a potentially game-changing piece of evidence. But then Cooke ruled that it wasn't relevant to Hayes's trial because the appeals committee wasn't evaluating Pete the Greek's actions from a criminal law standpoint. The defense wouldn't be permitted to tell the jury about it. The lawyers were crestfallen. Hayes was just furious.

. . . .

There was a consistent pattern when it came to testimony by prosecution witnesses: a remarkable lack of memory when it came to anything that might help Hayes.

As Chawla questioned him, former BBA employee John Ewan claimed he had been completely oblivious to the warning signs that banks were manipulating Libor to benefit their trading positions. He said the first he learned of this despicable practice was when he read the CFTC settlement documents with Barclays in June 2012. "Did you have any suspicion that this type of activity was taking place?" Chawla asked.

"No," Ewan said.

"Could you conceive of this kind of activity taking place?" the prosecutor asked.

"It's not impossible as a thought experiment," Ewan allowed, in a great understatement.

During cross-examination, Hawes went through the BBA's notes from the visits Ewan paid to Libor-submitting banks in 2005 and 2006, showing clearly that one bank after another had voiced concerns about the practices of lowballing and of skewing Libor to benefit trading portfolios. Ewan insisted he hadn't recognized the red flags. When banks raised these concerns, Hawes asked quietly, did Ewan ask for more information?

"I can't recall," Ewan said. "It's ten years ago."

What did the BBA's Libor oversight committee do when it heard concerns like this?

"I don't remember," Ewan said. The real answer, of course, was: nothing.

Hawes asked Ewan about a letter the Chicago Mercantile Exchange had written in 2008, noting that a Libor submitter who inputs data from within a range of feasible numbers "commits no falsehood if she bases her response to the daily Libor survey upon the lowest of those (or the highest, or any other arbitrary selection from among them)." So, Hawes asked, adjusting his thick, black-rimmed spectacles, does that means it's acceptable for banks to set Libor anywhere within a plausible range of numbers?

Ewan considered that for a few moments, shifting in his chair. The courtroom was silent. "That is perfectly consistent with the definition," he finally answered, although he added that "it would be unusual for there to be a notable dispersion between the highest and lowest rates at which a bank could borrow money." Sitting in the back of the courtroom, Hayes pumped his head up and down in a vigorous, victorious motion. It was the most animated he'd been since the trial began.

. . . .

On July 6, the Crown wrapped up its case, a twenty-seven-day onslaught that with breaks had extended over a month and a half. After the jury had been dismissed for the day, Hawes's deputy Christopher Conway prepared Cooke for what to expect when the defense opened its case the following morning. Hayes, Conway warned, would be fragile and if, as expected, he would be testifying for the better part of two weeks, that would put an extraordinary strain on him. The discussions over Hayes's mental state lasted nearly thirty minutes. Hayes sat in the back of the courtroom, listening. "I'm sorry that we're talking about you as if you're not here," Cooke said at one point. Hayes smiled awkwardly.

In the morning, Tighe took a seat in the courtroom, next to Sandy and Tim; Hayes's team had decided not to have her testify after all, so she was free to attend, and she had taken the week off work.

For the first time since the trial began, the courtroom was full. London's legal and financial communities were dying to hear what Hayes had up his sleeve; he must have *something*, given his seemingly crazy decision to fight the charges. Kweku Adoboli, who had just been released early from prison, was among those following the proceedings via Twitter and the media. "I wish him luck," he texted an acquaintance in the courtroom. Hayes, clean-shaven, wore a blue, button-down shirt under a thin, navy blue sweater—and, of course, his lucky QPR socks. Before the judge entered, Hawes crouched in front of his client. "Are you okay?" the lawyer whispered. Hayes nodded. "Are you ready?" He nodded again.

Cooke read a message to the jurors about Hayes's Asperger's diagnosis. Quoting loosely from Alison Beck's report, he explained that "people with Asperger's often don't see shades of grey but often tend to see things in terms of black and white." Hayes has a "pattern of prioritizing patterns and numbers over people" and "doesn't perceive the world as people without Asperger's syndrome do." The judge concluded with a crucial caveat: "You're hearing about Asperger's because it relates to Hayes's presentation as a witness. It's not directly relevant to the case." In other words, the jurors could take his condition into account as it related to any quirks in his testimony, but it shouldn't influence their judgment about his guilt or innocence.

As Cooke spoke, Hayes sat in the back of the courtroom,

chewing on the sleeve of his sweater. Then he marched to the witness stand, walking past Tighe. They shared a smile; her cheeks flushed. Hayes swore to tell the whole truth and nothing but the truth. In his pocket, he carried a folded-up photo of a grinning Joshua lying on a furry white blanket. He planned to pull it out any time his stress levels spiked.

Hawes started the interrogation with a simple question: "Do you accept that you have acted dishonestly?"

"No, I do not accept that," Hayes answered. Things soon got more complicated. His nervousness was obvious. Each time Hawes started to ask a question, Hayes cocked his head slightly to the right and pursed his lips. Sometimes he swiveled to the left, in the direction of Tighe, as if trying to pick up cues from her. He went on tangents. A straightforward question prompted him to rattle off a sequence of data about Japanese interest rates in 2010 and how they tended only to move within a narrow range. "Pause for a moment," Hawes interrupted. "Just slow down." Asked if his requests to other traders and brokers were effective, Hayes said there was no evidence they had been—there might have been correlations, but that's not the same as causation. Then he dived into a scientific explanation about the empirical basis for determining cause and effect with control groups. A question that touched on the Bank of England's efforts to squelch the financial crisis triggered a passionate soliloquy about the central bank's futility. When Hawes mispronounced the name of French bank BNP Paribas, Hayes corrected him. Tighe cringed and shook her head as her husband's focus lapsed.

Then a new problem surfaced. It wasn't just the pressure of trying to keep his facts straight, to not sound too afflicted, to make eye contact with jurors, to not obsess about the fact that his future was hanging in the balance. Hayes's toes had started to tingle. By the time the court broke for lunch, his feet were partly numb. A decade earlier, doctors had wondered about whether similar numbness might be an early sign of multiple sclerosis, but when the feeling faded, the episode had been dismissed as a false alarm. But now, at the worst possible moment, here it was again. Maybe the doctors had been mistaken. Tighe told him it was probably stress related or the result of sitting for a long period in an uncomfortable chair. She didn't entirely believe what she was saying.

That afternoon, Hayes nonetheless hit the crucial points. He introduced the concept of the permissible range and argued that since he was asking for numbers from within that band, he wasn't violating the BBA's definition of Libor. In that case, how could his behavior be construed as dishonest? He also emphasized that Libor was only one part of his overall trading strategy and that, in the middle of the financial crisis, with markets gyrating wildly and banks not lending to each other, the notion that anyone could rig Libor—or that there was even such a thing as an accurate rate— was preposterous.

That night, Hayes couldn't sleep. The case racing through his head, he took a sleeping pill. It didn't work. He swallowed another. Then he started worrying that he was overdosing. The following morning, he was a wired mess. His face was flushed, and his voice had taken on a scratchy tone, as if there was something caught in his throat. Tighe had noticed that sound before, at other times when Hayes was on the brink of unraveling. Now, though, there was nothing she could do. She couldn't even talk to him about the case.

With Hayes on the stand, Hawes walked him through dozens of instances of other UBS employees taking into account their trading positions when they set Libor. Many of the examples predated Hayes's arrival at UBS, and he wasn't a participant in any of the chats and phone calls. Hayes answered calmly and articulately and came off as credible. Previously skeptical journalists in the audience began to wonder whether the case was slipping away from the SFO.

The next day—after a strike by London's Tube workers' union caused the trial to not start until noon and left Hayes fatigued by travel-related stress—Hawes began grilling his client with questions about his communications with the ICAP brokers. Hayes announced that he couldn't believe they were having this conversation without any discussion of whether Goodman actually had adjusted his run-throughs in helpful ways. His own analysis suggested that about half the time the run-throughs weren't beneficial at all. "This lack of analysis, this lack of critical thinking . . . is absolutely typical of how this whole investigation has been carried out, with no reference to numbers," he erupted. Then Hayes took a breath and pulled himself together. His rant was over. "I'm sorry," he said, "what was the question?"

. . . .

In the audience that day were two San Francisco–based lawyers, Joseph Cotchett and Nanci Nishimura. They happened to be in London and figured they would drop by to see the Libor mastermind in person—this was the guy, after all, whose actions were the basis for a series of class-action lawsuits they had filed in 2013 on behalf of several cities, counties, and other public institutions. The litigation was working its way through the federal court system, but it wasn't going as well as Cotchett and Nishimura had hoped. A judge had sided with the defendants—many of the world's biggest banks—and found that the plaintiffs lacked standing to bring the antitrust suit. The lawyers were appealing the ruling, but the situation had left them in grouchy moods, convinced that the judicial system was biased in the banks' favor.

In court that day, Cotchett was wearing a seersucker jacket, a red, white, and blue shirt, and beige cargo pants. He watched as Hawes presented Hayes with what seemed like one leading question after another. "He's sitting up there all arrogant," Cotchett bellowed in the crowded courtroom during a break. "What a disgrace!" He couldn't believe that Chawla hadn't loudly objected to more of Hawes's softball questions.

When Hayes walked past, Cotchett glared at him, contempt burning in his eyes. Tighe, standing nearby, noticed the large, brash American giving her husband a filthy look. The anger, the disgust, on Cotchett's face seemed more severe than anything she'd ever seen from even a prosecutor. Tighe did her best to return the death stare. Cotchett and Nishimura were taken aback by the fearsome look. They didn't know who this tall, blond woman was, but they marveled at the intensity of her stare.

. . . .

The next day, a Friday, Hayes was back on the stand, and Hawes pushed him increasingly hard. This was the final day of the direct examination, and the lawyer wanted to do as much as possible to blunt the lines of attack that he expected Chawla to deploy in what was sure to be a brutal cross-examination. But Hayes was irritated by his lawyer's approach, and his answers took on a snarky, sneering tone. By the afternoon, Hayes was becoming emotional, his voice cracking. At one point he tried to explain that since he was the guy responsible for overseeing all of his team's Libor-dependent trades, he was therefore making requests to benefit everyone's positions, not just his own. "And now I'm wound up sat here. I wasn't operating in a vacuum, though."

"Are you someone who loses your temper?" Hawes asked.

"Yeah, I get frustrated, particularly when I care about things," he said. "I get angry when I feel people aren't doing their jobs properly. I flip out. I have meltdowns. I get insanely angry. I guess I'm trying to communicate and sometimes I find it hard." Hawes asked why Hayes had admitted wrongdoing to the SFO. Hayes recalled his near mental breakdown, how he'd been living day to day, how he'd watched his life falling apart, how he'd panicked and felt like he didn't have a choice. His eyes welled up. The intermediary, sitting next to him on the stand, called for a break. Tighe wiped tears off her face.

When court resumed a few minutes later, Hawes didn't let up. Why didn't Hayes just tell the SFO he didn't do anything wrong? "I knew what I thought and what I wanted to say, but I knew I couldn't say it," he said. He needed to get charged, and to get charged, he needed to admit wrongdoing. "What I wanted to say is, 'I've not done anything, it was just my job, and I'm not dishonest.'" He begged the jury to think about how most people don't show up to work and consider whether what they're doing is honest or dishonest. They just do their jobs.

Hayes bowed his head, his face flushed, his cheeks wet. He dabbed his eyes with a tissue. He kept sobbing on the train ride home. Joshua was sick that weekend. Hayes spent the next two days in bed with his son. Curled up with the boy, he was finally able to sleep.

· · · ·

On Monday morning, Hayes walked into court alone through a drizzle. In the witness box, he propped up the creased photo of Joshua. He was determined to stare at the picture instead of making eye contact with Chawla; that represented his best hope of maintaining his composure.

"Mr. Hayes, do you regard yourself as an honest man?" the prosecutor began.

"Yes."

"Do you think you as a banker"—Hayes interrupted Chawla to clarify that he was a *former* banker—"as a former banker have a different understanding of honesty than other people?" Hayes said he didn't know what other people's understandings of honesty were.

The cat-and-mouse game continued. "Do you think it is right to steal?" Chawla asked, his large left hand supporting his chin and the side of his face. Hayes's mind was in overdrive. He sensed a trap and tried to anticipate what the prosecutor was aiming for, what next question he had in his quiver.

"'Steal' is quite a broad word," he finally answered. "I might steal a cookie from the table when my wife's told me that I'm not meant to take one."

The grilling continued, as did the defendant's evasive maneuvers. "Do you accept that it would be wrong to make money by telling lies?" Chawla asked. "Do you need a rule or a regulation to know when something is honest or dishonest?" Hayes, the prosecutor asserted, was cavalier about the truth. He didn't care about honesty as long as he was getting what he wanted—whether that was making money or being charged by the United Kingdom so that he wouldn't be extradited. Chawla cycled through each of Hayes's admissions to the SFO, followed by a simple question: Was that a lie or was that the truth? Hayes struggled to answer.

"I was not at that time a particularly rational individual," he spat. "I was looking at a world of bad options. . . . My main concern was whether I was going to be put on a plane to the USA in the next seven days."

When Hayes had answered "yes" to the SFO's question about whether he acted dishonestly, Chawla asked, was that dishonest?

"That was false," Hayes conceded.

"Can you not bring yourself to say 'lie'?"

"Well, it was a lie," Hayes finally said. "It's disgusting that I was forced into this situation by the United States government."

Chawla pounced: "Nobody forced you to rig those rates, did they?" Hayes questioned the use of the word *rig.* "Nobody forced you to get brokers to rig rates, did they?" the prosecutor repeated. "Nobody forced you to get other bank traders to rig rates, did they?"

Some of Hayes's answers strained credibility. His prior admission to the SFO that his agreement with Guillaume Adolph was dishonest wasn't what it seemed, he now insisted. He was only trying to tell the SFO that the pact was *more* dishonest than his previous arrangements with others, not that it was actually dishonest. Cooke smirked.

"Was this all a dishonest charade involving you and your lawyer?" Chawla asked.

"This was a means to an end," Hayes answered. "It was me answering questions in a way to optimize my chances of getting charged without regard to my real opinion." Anyway, Hayes ventured, what did Chawla mean by *charade*? "My idea of charades is of a game played at Christmas involving books and films," he deadpanned. Nobody smiled.

. . . .

For such a long, hard-fought trial, there were surprisingly few facts in contention. Everyone agreed that Hayes had peppered dozens of people with hundreds if not thousands of requests to move Libor in advantageous ways. Nobody disputed that Hayes used switch trades to thank the brokers. There was even agreement that Hayes's bosses knew about and condoned what he was doing and that countless other traders were doing more or less the same thing.

The key question was whether Hayes had acted honestly. And his success at establishing that all-important credibility was at best mixed.

"I don't know what the outcome is going to be here," Hayes said in his last words on the stand. "But I know in my heart I did the right thing and I won't have that same life sentence" as if he had pleaded guilty. The judge thanked him. He returned to his seat. Sandy smiled as he walked past.

That night, a Friday, Hayes took a bath, drank a glass of orange juice, and passed out. The trial was nearing an end. He and Tighe knew it might be one of their last weekends as a family for a long time. They spent Saturday at a small music festival near their home. Joshua's preschool friends came for a picnic. Long into the evening, they sat on the village green, the kids playing with dinosaurs and the grown-ups chatting. Hayes seemed content. He managed not to talk much about his ordeal. By the end of the weekend, the last of the numbness in his feet had faded away.

. . . .

The barristers' closing statements followed predictable routes. "This all comes down to honesty," Chawla intoned. "His actions were nothing more and nothing less than dishonest." The prosecutor noted that the disgraced cyclist Lance Armstrong had defended himself by saying his competitors were also doping. "Just because other people are acting dishonestly doesn't give you or other people carte blanche to act in a similar way," Chawla said.

Hawes's main goal was to drape everything the prosecution

had said with a curtain of doubt. Get the jury to go through all the evidence, he figured, and anything could happen. "We are *awash* in evidence," Hawes contended. "Is he so blind, so dishonest, that he simply ignored all these flags that were shown to him? We suggest not." But his delivery—speaking softly, pausing between clauses—was like a lullaby to the jurors who, one by one, seemed to be tuning out. A woman in a black dress decorated with red flowers started to nod off. A juror in the back row leaned his head against the wall and blinked slowly. A third bowed his head and closed his eyes. In the front row, another juror yawned, stretched, and removed his glasses.

. . . .

That evening, Hayes was feeling giddy. For all intents and purposes, the trial was over. Cooke was going to spend the next few days giving the jury detailed instructions about the legal framework for interpreting each piece of evidence. His typed script ran more than two hundred pages. Sitting outside at a pub, smoking cigarettes and drinking beer, Hayes considered the jurors. He was pretty sure he had at least three on his side: Juror 1 (a short man who Hayes decided harbored an antiauthority streak) and Jurors 11 and 12 (who sat next to each other and, Hayes thought, regularly smiled at him). That was enough to guarantee he would either be acquitted or the jury would be hung. Hayes's lawyers also were providing encouragement, perhaps unintentionally. During Chawla's closing statement, Hayes had been grumbling and gesticulating. His lawyers told him to shut up. At one point, they passed him a handwritten note: "You can still lose this." Hayes interpreted that as meaning that he currently was in a position to win.

He and Tighe started envisioning a victory party.

. . . .

The jurors were instructed to use a two-part test to determine whether the agreements Hayes had entered into were fraudulent. The first question was whether a normal, reasonable human would have considered Hayes's actions to be dishonest. If no, then the jury should acquit. If yes, they had to answer a second question: Did Hayes, at the time of his actions, realize that what he was doing was dishonest according to reasonable human standards? If yes, he was guilty. In other words, the jurors needed to put themselves inside Hayes's head back when he was a trader in Tokyo. "You can't open up a person's mind to see what's inside," Cooke observed. The jurors should use common sense, taking into account all the evidence, including Hayes's statements to the SFO and his testimony during the trial. Don't consider sympathy or emotions, the judge said, only the evidence. The jurors left the courtroom hauling armloads of documents and color-coded binders filled with evidence.

Shortly after, Hayes's lawyers met with Cooke in his chambers. He made it clear that, if their client was convicted, he intended to make an example out of him. Hawes broke the news to Hayes and Tighe a few minutes later: He was facing a possible twelve-year prison sentence, worse than the couple had expected. Hayes sat motionless, on the verge of tears. At home that evening, he became manic, talking nonstop, tapping his foot, yanking out his hair. It reminded Tighe of his erratic behavior in the first half of 2013. He will need to be put on suicide watch if he's convicted, Tighe thought to herself.

Day after day, the deliberations dragged on. Time crept by. Chawla's daughter baked chocolate-frosted cupcakes, decorated with tiny silver candies, and the prosecutor brought a Tupperware container of them to court to treat staff and journalists. Ever since his cross-examination, Hayes had been wearing the same outfit every day—his trusty black slacks, a light blue shirt, and a thin blue sweater. (He washed the shirt every evening.) He spent hours pacing in a hallway. At one point, a college friend stopped by to distract him with reminiscences. Another day, a professor whom Hayes had consulted as a possible expert witness hung out on the courthouse's fifth floor with him. Whenever the court's scratchy loudspeakers summoned people back to a courtroom, Tighe's adrenaline surged; she came to dread the sound of static when the system was switched on. Too stressed to eat, they spent their lunch breaks smoking cigarettes by the river, taking in the view of the glistening skyscrapers and the World War II–era gunship the HMS *Belfast* permanently moored on the riverbank. On the way back into court, a swarm of photographers and camera crews filmed them. "Every single time, they do this," Hayes grumbled to Tighe after one smoke break, as a photographer stuck the snout of his camera into his face.

Finally, at 2:35 on the afternoon of August 3, the courthouse speakers squawked with Hayes's name. After a week of deliberations, the jury had reached a verdict.

PART IV

Victory

CHAPTER 19

Within the Ark

For the first time in the trial, Hayes had to go in the dock, accompanied by a guard. With a loud clang, the door was locked behind him. He stood as the jury entered, his heart thumping. The next few moments would determine his fate. He held his breath. "Guilty," the foreman said. Then he said it seven more times. The jury unanimously convicted him on all eight counts. Hayes's face reddened. He shook his head, then sat down and buried his face in his hands. He looked at the jurors, willing them to meet his gaze. None did. Tighe, sitting nearby, looked shell-shocked. Sentencing, Cooke announced, would take place in a half hour.

In the hallway outside, Hayes's family gathered around him. Beth, his half sister, sobbed. Hayes wrapped his arm around her. He removed his watch, wallet, and wedding ring and handed them to Tighe. "Will you wait for me?" he pleaded. She promised she would. She warned him not to do anything stupid. Then he returned to court, dragging a blue-green duffel bag packed with clothes and other belongings. He kissed Tighe.

Cooke, vindicated by the verdict, announced the sentence:

fourteen years. It was one of the longest-ever sentences for a British white-collar criminal, longer even than received by some murderers. Hayes looked terrified. He sat down and ran his hands through his hair. "Fourteen years," he murmured, over and over. The judge read a long statement denouncing him for knowingly committing a crime, for exploiting his subordinates, for pulling out all the stops to manipulate the legal process. Plus, the judge declared, "the conduct involved here must be marked out as dishonest and wrong and a message sent to the world of banking accordingly. The reputation of Libor is important to the City as a financial center and to the banking industry in this country. Probity and honesty are essential, as is trust which is based upon it. The Libor activities, in which you played a leading part, put all that in jeopardy."

Tighe, wide-eyed, gaped at her husband. She didn't cry; plentiful tears would come the next day. "We'll appeal," she mouthed to him. When Cooke finished speaking, Hayes waved goodbye to his wife and mother. He was escorted to the ground floor of the courthouse, where he was locked in a cell with green-painted bars. He felt numb and, for the first time, thoroughly defeated. An hour later, a white van drove him to Wandsworth Prison, a stone fortress built in 1851 and only recently retrofitted to include amenities like in-cell electricity and plumbing. Hayes stared out the van's window, watching people starting their commutes home, wishing that this were only a dream.

· · · ·

The contrast between Hayes's fate and those of his peers was stark. Six of his former brokers were preparing to stand trial, but most of his other colleagues were free—and gainfully employed. Mirhat Alykulov was still in the finance industry in Tokyo, working as a broker. (He partied with his former colleagues, including Paul Ellis, the Credit Suisse trader with whom Pieri had ganged up on Hayes. And he learned to box, participating in a charity tournament alongside the hairy Anthony Hayes, who took the opportunity to temporarily shed the Abbo moniker and be rechristened as the Apeman.) Naomichi Tamura, who over Christmas eight years earlier had instructed Hayes to do all he could to move Libor in a helpful direction, until recently continued to work at UBS. Mike Pieri disappeared to Australia, but remained a free man. Chris Cecere was at a hedge fund. Hayato Hoshino and Andrew Thursfield and Burak Celtik and Laurence Porter all kept working at Citigroup. Holger Seger, who had encouraged Roger Darin and others to collaborate with traders like Hayes, left UBS and eventually landed a job at a small bank in the picturesque Swiss city of Lenzburg. Darin, wanted by the United States, couldn't leave Switzerland without risk of being arrested, but he was ensconced in his native country's financial technology industry.

David Casterton remained a top ICAP executive. In one of his final acts as prime minister in 2016, David Cameron nominated his old pal Michael Spencer to become a member of the House of Lords. (The appointment ended up being blocked.)

And the two executives whose names had appeared on a draft version of Hayes's charges? Well, they were doing better than ever. Carsten Kengeter—who as co-head of UBS's investment bank had pleaded over and over with Hayes to stay, partly because of his priceless connections to Libor setters—was no longer with UBS.[*] Now he was the chief executive of Deutsche Börse, the big German stock exchange. As Hayes's trial got under way, Kengeter unveiled an ambitious expansion plan for the company, including buying

---

[*] Kengeter says he wasn't aware of wrongdoing at UBS.

a large foreign-exchange trading platform, the company's biggest purchase in a decade. Then in March 2016, he announced an even more audacious deal to merge with the London Stock Exchange, one of the world's most prominent markets. Kengeter would be crowned CEO of the sprawling new institution.

Brian Mccappin—who in the most charitable version of events had done nothing to stop Hayes and Cecere from manipulating Libor—never left Citigroup. After Japanese regulators slapped the bank's wrist in late 2011, Citigroup reassigned him to Singapore and then New York. He cycled through some low-profile jobs there. Then, as if by clockwork, when Hayes was locked up, Mccappin was promoted. His new job—head of institutional sales in the foreign-exchange business—sounded obscure, but it represented a ringing public endorsement of a man whose reputation had been badly tarnished. Announcing his promotion, Citigroup described Mccappin as "a valued employee."

Even Angela Knight, who presided over the British Bankers' Association during its inept management of the Libor scandal, landed on her feet. She left the BBA for a job at an association advocating on behalf of the United Kingdom's energy industry. Then, in late 2015, her longtime contacts in the British government decided she was just the person for a plum post advising the chancellor of the Exchequer on how to simplify the country's tax code. A parliamentary committee grudgingly approved her appointment, although it noted it was unimpressed with her tenure at the BBA.

The Bank of England's governor, Mervyn King, retired and in spring 2016 landed a job as a senior adviser at Hayes's former employer, Citigroup. Meanwhile, the central bank plodded along with a years-long effort to come up with ways to delink derivatives from Libor. The idea was that if those ubiquitous financial contracts, representing trillions and trillions of dollars, were no longer tied to an error-prone, theoretical interest rate, well, they would be more reliable. The central bank appointed a veteran of more than twenty years to lead the effort as well as to come up with ways to clean up other markets prone to manipulation. The wiry, floppy-haired man, with a fondness for jogging and golf, had previously done stints at the International Monetary Fund in Washington, during which he'd listened to his nerdy, socially awkward nephew talk excitedly about his interest in becoming a star trader, and as King's private secretary, where he'd helped communicate his boss's laissez-faire attitude about Libor. Since then, the man had climbed the Bank of England's ranks and become its executive director in charge of supervising markets. His name was Chris Salmon. The man responsible for dealing with the Libor scandal's fallout, and for reducing the odds that another scandal took place, was the uncle of the scandal's convicted ringleader.

· · · ·

Banished from the banking industry, Alexis Stenfors had reassessed his life. Within a few months of Merrill Lynch firing him in 2009, he decided to pursue one of his earlier interests: academic research. He enrolled in a University of London Ph.D. program. His research topic was—what else?—Libor manipulation. Eight years earlier, Stenfors had started noticing some fishy stuff going on with the benchmark. Now he had a chance to blow the whistle.

His studies at times were surreal. Once, in a library researching his dissertation, he leafed through a study about rogue traders. In the middle of the paper was a table listing rogue traders dating back to the early 1990s. Near the top of the list, a name leapt out: Alexis Stenfors. Stenfors didn't view himself as a rogue trader; he had just made some mistakes, within a system that more or less encouraged such mistakes. Stenfors typed out a fruitless letter to the journal's publisher protesting his inclusion in the list.

He completed his dissertation, earned his doctorate, and landed a teaching position at the University of Southampton. Eventually he emerged as a sought-after speaker for university students and fellow researchers, a unique pairing of academic expert and industry veteran, of theoretical and real-world experience. Stenfors, more introspective than most, had spent two years regularly visiting a psychotherapist, trying to understand what had motivated him to lie and cheat. Seven years later, he still hadn't figured it out.

Stenfors was glued to the coverage of Hayes's trial. He and his former brokers—these were guys Stenfors knew, guys like him, and now they were staring at years behind bars. At one point, the prosecution questioned Hayes about when he and Farr arranged their first switch trade and were hunting for someone to take the other side. They had turned to Stenfors, who had demurred. Farr had asked Stenfors if the trades seemed dodgy, and he had said yes. Now, in court, the ethical judgment of *Stenfors* was being presented to the jury as a sign that Hayes and Farr knew that what they were doing was improper. It wasn't funny, but Stenfors couldn't help but laugh.

On a drizzly morning in January 2016, Stenfors arrived at a Victorian townhouse in central London to deliver a lecture. His audience was a group of about thirty undergraduate finance students visiting from an Iowa university. Their goateed professor, who in his spare time was trying to launch his own hedge fund, had lined up several guest speakers to give his students a taste of the real world of finance. Most of the students, dressed in tracksuits and college sweatshirts, didn't seem very interested. They sat, sleepy-eyed, at desks under an ornately molded white plaster ceiling. Looking a bit gaunt, Stenfors had dressed up in a suit and tie. He used a laptop to project a slide show titled "Risk Takers, Rogue Traders and Rotten Apples." Stenfors presented himself as a banking industry refugee (although he proudly noted that the prior year, the British regulator had lifted a ban on him working in the industry). He tried to explain what it meant to be a trader. It wasn't all about making money. It was about risk-taking. The adrenaline rush was as much a goal as the fat paycheck. "It's addictive," he noted.

Then he got to his main theme: Rogue traders and other banking miscreants are products of the system. Toss aside everything you've learned about economics, Stenfors advised, the simple, clean world of rational individuals and profit-maximizing institutions. That's not a realistic reflection of the financial industry—*The Hunger Games* is more like it. Everyone is acting to enhance his own interest. When other people are no longer useful, you stab them in the back. "It's not necessarily about money—it's about winning," he explained. Normal systems of morals and ethics don't apply. He recounted how he and his colleagues kept trading as if nothing had happened when the planes hit the twin towers and how traders openly looked down on their lesser colleagues. "You respect fighters. You respect race car drivers. You do *not* respect salespeople. You do *not* respect those who don't take risks." The phenomenon of rogue trading can be understood in part through sociology. "It's a rebellion against institutional controls that deny individuals opportunities for self-actualization," he asserted. In other words, the cutthroat system encouraged amoral, nasty behavior.

It was a stinging critique of the world Stenfors had inhabited and that some of these students presumably planned to enter. His lecture concluded after an hour, and he invited the students to ask questions.

A hand shot up in the front row. It belonged to a spiky-haired,

bespectacled Asian-American. While his classmates hadn't bothered to stifle their yawns as Stenfors spoke, this twenty-one-year-
old had remained attentive, his eyes stuck on the lecturer and his
slide show. Now, called on by Stenfors, he cut right to the chase:
"What can I do to become a trader?"

. . . .

Hayes was transferred from the dungeonlike Wandsworth to
a prison called Lowdham Grange. It was a destination for murderers, drug and weapons traffickers, and violent criminals with
decades-long sentences, but it had a reputation for being relatively
clean and safe. It was situated in the middle of farmland; tractors
were parked around the prison's outskirts, and inside its fifteen-
foot cement walls birds could be heard chirping. Prisoners were
permitted to wear their own clothes and to spend hours roaming
the complex. Hayes's cell was small but cozy, with a metal bed, a
small TV, an electric teakettle, and a metal desk against the wall
below a barred window. Best of all, there was a phone that he could
pay a few pence per minute to use. Each week, he exhausted his
allowance on several-times-a-day phone calls to Tighe.

Hayes drew comfort from the routine of the prison day, with
each activity slotted into a regular time period and little margin for
surprise or disruption. He taught math classes and read books. In
the prison's grand hierarchy of crimes, being a financial crook was
considered much less objectionable than offenses like pedophilia
or violence against women or even selling drugs, and so he didn't
have problems with the other inmates. Some became his friends;
his closest pal was an inmate convicted of murder for bludgeoning
to death his financial adviser. Nicknames were popular in prison,
as they had been in Hayes's previous world. He no longer went by

Rain Man or Tommy Chocolate or Kid Asperger. Now he was the Banker and the Lion of Libor. Inmates crowded into his cell to watch TV segments about him, cheering when pundits questioned the severity of his punishment.

At first, to make the long sentence seem more manageable, Hayes divided each day into 8,640 ten-second increments. Later, tired of that repetition, he split the entirety of his sentence into six-month blocks and then started counting down the hours and days of each slice. Meanwhile, he memorized the prison rulebook. He learned that he was permitted to have a small rug in his cell—a privilege that apparently hadn't been noticed by many other prisoners. When winter came and the temperatures dropped, prisoners padded into his cell, removed their shoes and socks, and luxuriated in his small carpet's softness. Hayes didn't want their company so much as their physical warmth. He figured the exchange of the rug's coziness for their body heat was a fair trade.

On the frequent occasions that he felt his anger boiling up, a fury so intense that it rendered him unable to focus on anything else, he would go to the gym. Before long, he had bulging biceps. When the gym wasn't an option, he would sit down in his cell and whip through a math workbook. The numerical exercises were a source of calming familiarity in his scary new world.

. . . .

Tighe tried to keep her family intact. She told Joshua that Daddy had done something that certain people thought was wrong, even though Mommy and Daddy didn't think it was wrong, and that Daddy now had to go away for a while to sort the mess out. Joshua, the spitting image of his father, took to asking whether Mommy would leave, too. At dinner each night, Tighe called Hayes in his cell and put him on speakerphone so that the family could at least retain a semblance of normalcy. Before bed, Joshua got in the habit of casting a get-Daddy-home magic spell.

The SFO continued to try to confiscate the family's assets. A court eventually ordered Hayes to pay £878,806 (roughly $1.3 million). The Old Rectory went back on the market; a Goldman Sachs banker snapped it up on the cheap.

For months, Hayes, Tighe, and their families clung to the hope of a successful appeal of his conviction and sentence. His lawyers argued that Judge Cooke, who had retired after Hayes's case, had improperly excluded certain evidence, such as Pete the Greek's exoneration by the regulatory committee. And they claimed that the fourteen-year sentence was excessive, especially considering Hayes's diagnosis with Asperger's. An appeals court agreed to hear Hayes's claim and assigned a prestigious three-judge panel—including the highest-ranking member of the English judiciary—to preside. But the judges rejected the effort to get the conviction overturned. They did shave three years off his sentence, which the court said "was longer than was necessary." Hayes and Tighe, however, were crestfallen. They had convinced themselves that perhaps the punishment would be chopped in half.

His landmark victory validated, Chawla headed back to the Southwark courthouse. Hayes's six former brokers—Darrell Read, Colin Goodman, Danny Wilkinson, Terry Farr, Jim Gilmour, and Noel Cryan—were on trial for their alleged roles as Hayes's co-conspirators. The trial took place in the same courtroom where Hayes was tried. The defendants were crammed into the glass-enclosed dock, where a jovial atmosphere prevailed most days. They joked to each other during breaks. Wilkinson's family brought bags of hard candies that Farr, his shirttails dangling, distributed to his fellow defendants. He and Gilmour scooted outside for cigarettes at every opportunity. Cryan spent his spare time eating potato chips and completing newspaper crossword puzzles. Read burned through crime novels.

Chawla projected an air of confidence. Who could fault him, given the comprehensive nature of his victory against Hayes? Much of the evidence that he presented against the brokers was the same that he had deployed against Hayes—the same e-mails, chat transcripts, phone recordings, spreadsheets, and charts. But there were some crucial differences this time. For starters, none of the brokers had ever admitted doing anything wrong, unlike Hayes, who had spent dozens of hours in the SFO's confessional-cum-recording-studio. And the brokers' lawyers were determined to strike a more aggressive, indignant stance than the soft-spoken Hawes had used in the previous trial.

The crux of their defense was that the world the prosecution was describing to the jury—a world in which everyone was expected to play by the rules, where transparency mattered, where honesty and fair dealing were sacrosanct—was a fantasy. The financial industry was not a polite, rules-bound, ethical place; it was a no-holds-barred culture where brokers were actively encouraged to manipulate and lie to their clients. And, the brokers argued, that's exactly what they'd been doing—to Hayes. One after another, they climbed onto the stand and insisted that it was all a ruse—not only their assurances to Hayes that they were doing everything they could to help him, but also the e-mails and instant messages they zinged among each other that appeared to confirm that they were, in fact, trying to help Hayes. It was, they said, nothing more than an elaborate scheme to con the gullible Hayes into handing them his lucrative business.

Why didn't the brokers just say "no thanks" when Hayes sought their help manipulating Libor? Well, they answered, clearly the prosecution didn't understand who Tom Hayes was. He was more than a giant presence in the market. He was an unreasonable, monstrous man. Cryan called him a psycho. Wilkinson gleefully recounted yet one more time the shepherd's-pie-in-the-bath legend. Farr and Read both told the jury about the verbal abuse showered on them by their explosive client. Saying no to this guy was not an attractive option. And it was less bad to lie to Hayes than to actually, God forbid, lie about Libor.

The truth was even more ironic. In maintaining that they had been lying and therefore hadn't acted dishonestly, the brokers appeared to be, well, lying. A rich trove of documentary evidence showed the brokers not only telling Hayes that they were helping him, but also coordinating among themselves and with other traders to carry out Hayes's requests. Of course, there were exceptions—such as when Read counseled his London colleagues not to tell Hayes about Goodman's run-throughs or, if Hayes ever asked, to say that they had spoken to traders at rival banks when in fact they hadn't. But there was little aside from the brokers' testimony on the stand, which appeared to contradict the written record, to substantiate the idea that they hadn't been participating in the scheme alongside Hayes.

The SFO's staff wasn't helping Chawla this time. Under cross-examination, one of the agency's investigators, Paul Chadwick, acknowledged that the SFO had screwed up some of the dates it had included in the charges against Goodman; it turned out he'd been on vacation on those days. Later, Chadwick admitted to Cryan's lawyer that the SFO only got around to interviewing the guys on Tullett's cash desk—whom Cryan would have asked for help on Hayes's behalf, if he did in fact ask anyone for help—after the brokers' trial was already under way. A couple of jurors shook their heads in disbelief.

....

Tighe handed in her resignation at Shearman & Sterling and landed a new job at a smaller law firm nearby, where she figured the workload would be lighter—a crucial concession to her new life as a single parent. (Another law firm refused to hire her because of her husband's crimes.) One morning in January 2016, during a week off between jobs, she took the train into London and headed to the Hatton Garden jewelry district, where Hayes years earlier had purchased their wedding rings. This time, Tighe was getting their valuables—her diamond ring, both of their Rolexes—appraised before they were handed over to the SFO.

Afterward, she decided to stop by the Southwark courthouse to check in on the brokers. A day earlier, the jury had been sent out to deliberate. Now the waiting game had begun, and she knew from experience how tense and miserable that process was. Tighe had been back to the courthouse a couple of times since Hayes's conviction; the SFO's proceedings seeking the confiscation of their assets had occurred just down the hallway from Courtroom 2. Every time she went there, it was like reentering a nightmare. Walking down the same street that she and Hayes had traversed, day after day, holding hands as the photographers tracked them, she would feel a lump rising up in her throat and would stifle a sob. On this January morning, Tighe went looking for Read, whom she still considered a friend. She found him in the cafeteria, reading. They had barely started talking when the courthouse loudspeakers barked, summoning the brokers back to Courtroom 2. After a day of deliberating, the jury had reached its verdict.

The brokers shuffled into the dock. Farr managed a wan smile at his wife, Clare, and son Sam, then buried his head in his hands. Wilkinson had been at home (days earlier, he'd suffered a minor stroke and hadn't returned to court since), pouring himself a glass of wine, when his wife called to say there was a verdict. He had rushed into London wearing an untucked short-sleeved shirt, his face a dark, sweaty red. Gilmour, too, felt beads of sweat forming on his scalp and neck as he waited for the jury to enter. Time seemed to stand still.

Four guards, their keys jingling, entered the dock and locked the door. Tighe took a seat in the courtroom. The jury entered. Wilkinson's mother grabbed Tighe's arm. "My boy," she murmured, over and over.

And then came the verdicts: not guilty. One by one, each broker was acquitted.

With a war cry, Farr tore out of the dock and embraced Clare and Sam, who both were sobbing. "That's four and a half years" of my life, he murmured, choking on tears.

On the way out of the courtroom, two jurors pumped their fists in the direction of the defendants, a motion of solidarity. On the courthouse steps, a juror hugged one of the broker's wives. "Thank you," she whispered.*

. . . .

And so it was. In November 2015, two Rabobank traders, Anthony Allen and Anthony Conti, were tried in federal court in New York for their roles allegedly manipulating Libor. Their colleague—Paul Robson—had testified against them. The trial lasted a few weeks, and the jury eventually convicted the two Brits. Allen was sentenced to two years in prison; Conti's sentence was one year.

But of all the other former traders who would come under the

---

* The Justice Department would later drop its charges against the three former ICAP brokers.

legal microscope—including David Nicholls, the Deutsche Bank manager who'd brushed away suggestions that Libor could be manipulated and who, as of 2016, was under investigation by the Justice Department—none of them were accused of being part of Hayes's vast ring. Tom Hayes had never fit in; now, as always, he was the outsider.

· · · ·

Tighe called Hayes's lawyers and delivered the news. As it happened, they were at Lowdham Grange, about to sit down with her husband. They met in a cubby-size room off the main visitor's area, where tearful wives and squealing children were being reunited, temporarily, with their husbands and fathers. Guests were allowed to buy treats for inmates at a small canteen, and Hayes sipped a bottle of strawberry milk as his lawyers talked him through some paperwork. They didn't tell him of the acquittals until they'd completed all their other business. Hayes was engulfed with emotions when he heard. Here he was, locked up in jail, with most of his worldly possessions being confiscated by the government, and in London his supposed conspirators had just been let off the hook. On the other hand, their acquittals were a token form of vindication; after all, these were many of his alleged confederates. It felt good knowing that the SFO and David Green and Mukul Chawla had suffered an embarrassing defeat. And by not sticking with his original plan to cooperate with the SFO and testify against his former brokers, he had helped these men remain free. "I can look at myself knowing six families are complete, in a small part because of me," Hayes wrote to an acquaintance. He described the brokers, despite their occasional dishonesty, as basically "good guys."

Hayes still didn't grasp what had really happened. These friends who were not friends, these bosses who now claimed not to be bosses, together they had just engineered their greatest trade of all: Hayes for their own freedom. He was the genius, the university man, the millionaire, the star. And he was the fool. Most of them had their money; his would be seized. They had their liberty; he was in prison. Yes, there had been a spider network. Hayes still didn't realize that in the end, he'd been the fly.

The brokers and their families and lawyers decamped to a nautical-themed pub, the Shipwrights Arms, down the street from the courthouse. The mood was giddy. The fastidious, upper-crust barristers shed their wigs and loosened their collars and before long were slurring their words. They gleefully recounted the trial's highlights: how the SFO investigators had looked foolish under cross-examination, how Wilkinson on the stand had angrily denounced the SFO's tactics, the look on Chawla's face as the verdicts were announced. An instant consensus among the lawyers had formed about the trial's crucial turning point. It was when the jurors learned of Hayes's fourteen-year sentence. Surely, the lawyers reasoned, the jurors had rejected the idea of sending these six men to a similar fate.

Cryan had his own theory: The jurors could tell that the defendants were just working-class guys, not dudes who went to exclusive schools and drove fancy cars and quaffed expensive champagnes. He paused, thinking about that for a moment. "We actually did drink quite a lot of champagne," he blurted. "And we'll be drinking more tonight!" He tilted his head back and laughed maniacally.

But the reasons didn't matter. It was finally over. Gilmour, standing alone and looking dazed, fantasized about the vacations he would take once he got his confiscated passport back. Forget about all his other problems, such as his precarious finances. A huge weight had lifted.

Above the pub's blue-painted entrance, a coat of arms displayed the establishment's motto: "Within the Ark, Safe Forever." Not even the fickle gods of the sea, the menacing forces that Alykulov had warned about when he recited Hector's line in the movie *Troy*, could touch these guys now.

Before long, Farr was drunkenly shouting and spilling Guinness on the slick wooden floor. Then Wilkinson waddled in. "Freedom!" he thundered, his arms hoisted above his head in a V. The brokers roared, and someone handed him a pint of beer. The party was just getting started.

The text message I received from Hayes that evening in January 2013 was the start of a years-long relationship. At first, we pinged texts back and forth—him cautiously, me gently trying to pry information out of him or, even better, get him to sit down with me. (During that first exchange of texts, he'd agreed to meet at London's Victoria Station the following morning, but before he could slip out of the house, Tighe got wind of his plan and forbade him from going.) Before long, though, he loosened up. Unbeknownst to his lawyers or Tighe, Hayes began texting me constantly, at all times of day or night, and regularly meeting me at run-down pubs and train station cafes. I typically would buy him a sandwich and an orange juice and then listen as he delivered detailed, stream-of-consciousness explanations about trading, Libor, his former colleagues, the criminal justice system, and, every so often, isolated fragments about his personal life. Aside from a piece of the very first text message he sent—"this goes much much higher than me"—I agreed to treat everything he said as off the record. I could use it as a guide in my reporting but that was all.

After more than a year of this, in which Hayes oscillated between dark depressions and manic overconfidence, I persuaded him to get Tighe to meet me. We sat down alone, in a quiet restaurant on the south side of the Thames. By the end of the evening, we had consumed an unhealthy amount of red wine, and I had gleaned a much fuller picture of Hayes and his environs. Tighe filled out the personal side of her husband, his colleagues, and even their family life in a way that the binary-thinking, mildly autistic Hayes simply wasn't capable of doing. Going forward, I maintained separate relationships with Hayes and Tighe, meeting and corresponding regularly with each individually.

In early 2015, several months before Hayes's trial was scheduled to begin, I asked each of them what I figured was a stupid question: Upon the conclusion of the trial, would they be willing to retroactively put everything they'd told me on the record so that I could tell their story, in full cinematic detail, in the *Wall Street Journal*? I braced for a swift, unequivocal rejection. Instead, they both agreed. Suddenly I had in my possession a trove of thousands of text messages, and rough notes from hours of phone calls and scores of meetings featuring the central figure in a global scandal—a man who, aside from his one text message (which I'd quoted in a February 2013 *Journal* story) and his not-guilty plea, had never uttered a word in public. And from that point on, everything Hayes and Tighe said or did in my presence would be fair game for me to write about once the trial was over. Hayes also provided me with his school and medical records, as well as reports prepared by psychiatrists who interviewed him, and introduced me to a number of family members. The result, in September 2015, was a five-part series in the *Journal* titled "The Unraveling of Tom Hayes."

Meanwhile, I came upon another journalistic gold mine. In the course of its three-year investigation, the Serious Fraud Office had amassed tens of thousands of pieces of evidence: e-mails, electronic chats, text messages, phone call recordings and transcripts, trading documents, personnel records, and voluminous transcripts of interviews the SFO and other regulators had conducted with suspects and witnesses. By then, the antifraud agency had filed charges against Hayes and his six former brokers. Because all seven men were pleading not guilty, their lawyers had received the evidence from the SFO to allow them to prepare for trial. Now I found myself in possession of this hard drive's worth of primary source materials, well over a hundred gigabytes. They included blunt trading room dialogue, captured over instant-message chats and e-mails; recordings of phone calls that traders and brokers placed on their work lines, sometimes to their colleagues, other times to family members; the interviews that brokers and traders gave to authorities, which delved with surprising regularity into the suspects' difficult personal circumstances; and traders' and brokers' personnel records, documenting their compensation, disciplinary histories, and even sick days. I went through every piece of evidence. It was a mind-numbing task—most of what traders talk about, it turns out, is disappointingly dull—but what emerged was a high-definition, unfiltered snapshot of the intersecting careers and lives of the men at the center of the Libor scandal.

This book also is based on scores of interviews I conducted with past and present traders, brokers, and executives and their lawyers; past and present government investigators, prosecutors, and law enforcement authorities; and the litany of other characters—researchers, academics, journalists, lawyers, and others—who populate this book. I gleaned further information from the months of testimony and evidence presented at the trials of Hayes and the former brokers, as well as from the reports and settlement documents of various government panels and enforcement agencies.

I read a number of books—fiction and nonfiction—in preparation for writing *The Spider Network*. I reread some of the classics of the business genre, especially those that Hayes had mentioned to me were influential to him. Those included *Barbarians at the Gate: The Fall of RJR Nabisco* by Bryan Burrough and John Helyar, and *When Genius Failed: The Rise and Fall of Long-Term Capital Man-*

agement by Roger Lowenstein, as well as a smattering of Michael Lewis books. I also read a number of fascinating books related to Asperger's syndrome. They included the sublime *The Curious Incident of the Dog in the Night-Time* by Mark Haddon; *Look Me in the Eye: My Life with Asperger's* by John Elder Robison; and *The Rosie Project* by Graeme Simsion.

In many cases, the dialogue and quotes in this book come directly from phone recordings that I have listened to or transcripts I have read—or conversations, text messages, and scenes that I witnessed or participated in. In other cases, they are from e-mails or other electronic communications that I've reviewed; occasionally, in messages jammed with typos and abbreviations, I have translated them into English and cleaned up punctuation and capitalization. (For example: "gr8" becomes "great," "6m" becomes "six-month," "lbior" becomes "Libor," and so on.) In the case of nondocumentary materials, I have tried to confirm information with at least two sources. When confronted with conflicting evidence or testimony, I have presented what I believe to be the most credible version of events; at times I have noted disagreements in footnotes.

For further information on the provenance of specific items, the Notes section of this book provides a chapter-by-chapter description of where some of the information came from. Because of the repetitive nature of much of the sourcing, as well as the need to maintain some sources' anonymity, the section doesn't individually identify the source of every fact in the book.

Since Hayes was sent to prison, I have stayed in frequent touch with him and Tighe. I've mainly settled for writing him letters, something I hadn't done with any regularity in probably twenty years. (I also visited him.) To my surprise, Hayes, who had such trouble communicating with people in person and seemed painfully out of touch with, even oblivious to, normal human emotions, has proven to be a thoughtful, articulate, even introspective letter writer. His letters come scrawled in ballpoint pens on thin, lined pages (often with footnotes scribbled in the top and bottom margins). They are laden with detailed memories from his life before prison, descriptions of his prison routines and friends, angry rants about what he sees as the injustice of his plight, and admissions that he badly misread situations, over and over and over again. The letters have provided me with another fascinating glimpse inside Hayes's unique mind.

ACKNOWLEDGMENTS

This book never would have happened without the help of a bunch of people. Near the top of that list is, without question, Tom Hayes. Back in 2013, he took a massive—arguably reckless—leap of faith by deciding to open up to a journalist. And then, against the urgings of his lawyers and wife, he doubled and tripled down on that gamble, over and over. I am enormously grateful that he, and eventually Sarah Tighe, came to trust me and put up with my endless questions about their personal and professional lives.

Dozens of other sources—bankers, traders, brokers, investigators, lawyers, prosecutors, journalists, researchers, academics, family members of accused criminals, and even a psychologist or two—were generous with their time as I sought to reconstruct and explain the Libor odyssey. Many of them are characters in the book. Some were more helpful than others; you know who you are, and I thank you.

I never would have dived down the Tom Hayes rabbit hole were it not for my mentor and friend, Bruce Orwall. A few days into 2013, Bruce, the *Wall Street Journal*'s London bureau chief, told me to write a detailed profile of Hayes, who had recently been arrested in Britain and charged in the United States. I resisted, arguing that there was no chance that Hayes or his friends or family would talk to a journalist and that I had better things to do with my time. Bruce insisted. I threw a minor tantrum. Bruce still insisted. I finally relented—and stumbled into what would become the best story of my career. Over the next three years, as my relationship with Hayes progressed, Bruce was by my side every step of the way. He counseled me on how to manage Hayes as a source, no easy feat. He advised me on what stories should be our top priority, and then masterfully edited those pieces. He helped me navigate tricky interactions with the British legal system. And he always forced me to aim higher, deflecting my impatient tendencies and pushing for me to advance things a step or three further than I had initially thought possible. The culmination of this was the *Journal*'s "The Unraveling of Tom Hayes" series. The stories carried my byline, but Bruce made them happen.

I am thankful for the support I've received from the *Journal* throughout this process. I benefited from world-class editing, not just by Bruce but also by one of the *Journal*'s awesome Page One editors, Mitch Pacelle. His fingerprints are all over the book's latter chapters. A cast of at least a dozen—including programming whiz Elliot Bentley and Alex Martin, who came up with the serialization idea—helped "Unraveling" succeed, laying the groundwork for this book. Crucially, the *Journal* was generous with my time. For more than a year, I had the privilege of devoting myself to not a whole lot other than Tom Hayes and Libor. As my manager drily noted in a recent performance review, "the year was something of an indulgence on the part of the *Journal*." Especially at a time when struggling media companies are demanding that journalists churn out more and more, faster and faster, I appreciate that indulgence.

This is my first book, and I didn't know what to expect or how to proceed. My agent, Dan Mandel of Greenburger Associates, was a valuable guide. (Thanks to my *Journal* colleague and friend Liz Rappaport for introducing us.) Dan not only managed to drum up interest in a first-time author's complicated project, but he also pulled off the miraculous feat of keeping me (relatively) calm during the search for a publisher.

I was lucky to end up with Geoff Shandler at Custom House as my editor and publisher. I'd heard horror stories from other fledgling authors about editors who didn't actually edit; one acquaintance had to shell out a five-figure sum to pay an outside editor to improve her manuscript. I was desperate to avoid a situation like that—I knew enough to know that I would desperately need a proactive, engaged editor—and Geoff proved true to his reputation as vigorously hands-on. He marked up each page, often each line, of the manuscript with his trusty red pencil. Then he did it again. (And in some cases, a third or fourth time as well.) It turned out that, despite having written hundreds of thousands of words as a newspaper journalist, I didn't really know how to write a book. Geoff taught me. He also pushed me, hard, to reconsider some of the assumptions I'd made during the reporting process and to not shy away from delving into complex topics. This book is immeasurably better as a result of his tireless, meticulous work.

The entire team at Custom House and William Morrow was a pleasure to work with. Kelly Rudolph in publicity was there from the start with regular suggestions and encouragement. Kyran Cassidy helped bulletproof the book from a legal standpoint. Ploy Siripant designed the delightful cover. Bill Ruoto designed the book's interior. Madeline Jaffe was always available to help—and did so frequently.

At Ebury, which is publishing *The Spider Network* in the United Kingdom and Commonwealth countries, Jamie Joseph was a great partner. He helped me slim down the manuscript and to explain things more clearly. His enthusiasm was valuable during what occasionally felt like a slog. Lucy Oates made things easier. Ebury's marketing guru, Joanna Bennett, helped devise ways to get would-be readers interested. And Martin Soames patiently and thoroughly reviewed the book so that it complied with England's draconian publishing laws.

A number of other people volunteered to provide feedback. Charles Forelle and Justin Scheck, two of the best journalists I've ever worked with, devoted to this book many hours of their personal time that they instead could have spent with their families. They spotted things that didn't make sense and points where my prose turned a shade too purple (as well as a number of mistakes that nobody else had caught), and they suggested ways to simplify the book and eliminate extraneous characters. I am grateful for their support and friendship.

My parents, Peggy and Peter, instilled a love of reading and writing in me at an early age. They also read drafts of this book. My father provided insightful feedback about how to amplify some of the big themes. My mother, who purports to be terrified of numbers and finance, read and re-read the sections on market mechanics and Libor, advising me on ways to make them more comprehensible. My siblings, Nicholas and Liza, and sister-in-law Jordanna served as valuable sounding boards and provided welcome encouragement throughout.

And then there was Kirsten. My lovely wife was an indispensable partner. From the start—a cold, wet Saturday morning in early 2013 when I dragged her, in the first trimester of pregnancy, to visit London's just-opened Shard skyscraper and then spent the entire time exchanging text messages with Hayes—Kirsten not only tolerated my obsession but also encouraged it. Even though she never met Hayes, I felt like she knew him because of how much we discussed him. When I started viewing this as a book, Kirsten was instantly on board. A voracious, sophisticated reader, she plowed through numerous versions of the initial book proposal. She talked sense into me—and gave sage advice—in the project's difficult early stages. She read drafts of the book multiple times, offering innumerable smart suggestions. And on more than one occasion when I felt like I was buckling under pressure, Kirsten stabilized me. She did all of this while handling first one baby boy, then another. I don't know what I would have done without her.

Finally, a special thanks to Henry and Jasper. They didn't directly help on the book—unless you count Henry shuffling pages and scribbling all over the drafts of a few chapters—but their presence in my life is a constant source of inspiration and joy.

PROLOGUE

The description of the ski getaway comes from my interviews with Hayes and another attendee. The description of Mccappin's personal background and musical history comes from interviews with former colleagues as well as a member of Ocean Colour Scene and the band's manager.

CHAPTER 1: WATCHING THE CORONATION

The descriptions of Hayes's family, childhood, and schooling come from my interviews with him and members of his immediate and extended family; his academic records; and reports written by the doctors who examined him and interviewed his mother and wife, leading up to the trial.

The section on Hayes's early professional years is based on my interviews with him and his former colleagues; his UBS personnel files; and descriptions provided by Hayes and others in interviews with the SFO or financial regulators. The descriptions of the old City of London, as well as its modern transformation, are based in part on the excellent *City Lives: The Changing Voices of British Finance* by Cathy Courtney and Paul Thompson (Methuen Publishing, 1996) and on *Other People's Money: Masters of the Universe or Servants of the People?* by John Kay (Profile Books, 2015). Joris Luyendijk's *Swimming with Sharks: My Journey into the World of the Bankers* (Guardian Faber Publishing, 2015) provides other valuable context and anecdotes.

CHAPTER 2: THE HALL OF MIRRORS

The account of Shah Pahlavi's coronation is based on archival *New York Times* stories. Minos Zombanakis's story, and his involvement with the creation of what would become known as Libor, comes in large part from *The Story of Minos Zombanakis: Banking Without Borders* by David Lascelles (Kerkyra Publications, 2011).

Ken Griffin's comment about bets paying off just 52 percent of the time comes from "Citadel's Ken Griffin Leaves 2008 Tumble Far Behind," *Wall Street Journal*, August 3, 2015, by Rob Copeland.

The descriptions of Hayes's time at RBS and his interactions with colleagues there come from my interviews with Hayes; my interviews with other former traders and their lawyers; personnel records; e-mail and chat transcripts; and interviews that a variety of people, including Hayes, gave to regulators.

The history of derivatives, including the section on the IBM swap, is derived largely from Peter L. Bernstein's *Against the Gods: The Remarkable Story of Risk* (John Wiley & Sons, 1998), as well as from *When Genius Failed: The Rise and Fall of Long-Term Capital Management* by Roger Lowenstein (Random House, 2000).

CHAPTER 3: CLASSY PEOPLE

The details about Michael Spencer's childhood and early career are based in large part on this comprehensive profile of him: "MT Interview—Michael Spencer," *Management Today*, January 27, 2005, by Chris Blackhurst, as well as "20 Questions: Michael Spencer," *Financial Times*, April 7, 2011, by Emma Jacobs. The history of Ethiopia comes from *New York Times* archival stories.

The descriptions of what a broker does, the industry's culture, and the personal histories of Hayes's brokers are based on testimony of the six brokers in their 2015 trial, as well as their interviews with regulators; the brokerage's internal disciplinary records; my interviews with the brokers, their lawyers, and former colleagues; reports by law-enforcement and regulatory agencies that punished the brokerage firms; e-mail and chat transcripts; and a series of *Wall Street Journal* stories on the brokerage industry in 2013 and 2014.

The section on Hayes's time at the royal banks of Scotland and then Canada are based on my interviews with Hayes and his former colleagues; various former traders' interviews with regulators and law enforcement; personnel files at both banks as well as at UBS (especially as it relates to the circumstances surrounding Hayes's departure from RBC); and internal chat and e-mail transcripts.

CHAPTER 4: PEAK PERFORMANCE

John Ewan's personal and professional history comes from my interviews with his former colleagues; extensive interviews he gave to regulators and law enforcement; his testimony in the trials of Hayes and the brokers; and personnel records and internal BBA e-mails and phone transcripts. The history of Libor comes from internal BBA materials gathered by regulators as well as interviews and trial testimony by Ewan and Andrew Thursfield. Douglas Keenan described his early run-in with Libor manipulation in his article "My Thwarted Attempt to Tell of Libor Shenanigans," *Financial Times*, July 26, 2012. The account of how Libor ended up in the Chicago Mercantile Exchange's derivatives, and the failed efforts to warn against that, are from this excellent story: "How Gaming Libor Became Business as Usual," Reuters, November 20, 2012, by Carrick Mollenkamp, Jennifer Ablan, and Matthew Goldstein.

The Andrew Smith section is based on former traders' interviews with me and with regulators and internal chat transcripts.

CHAPTER 5: THE LUCKY TURNSTILE

As in prior and future chapters, the accounts of Hayes's personal and professional lives are based on my interviews with him, his friends, colleagues (and their lawyers), and family members; e-mails, electronic chat, and phone recordings; bank personnel records; interviews that Hayes and his former colleagues gave to regulators and law enforcement; information presented in court; and bank and brokerage settlement agreements with regulators and law enforcement. The detail about Hayes bringing a textbook to dinner comes from "Former Deutsche Bank Rate Trader Describes Difficulties in Tokyo's Rates Market," *New York Times,* February 19, 2013, by Hiroku Tabuchi.

CHAPTER 6: THE SYCOPHANTS

The descriptions of Laydon and the pension funds that potentially lost money due to yen Libor manipulation are based partly on lawsuits filed in U.S. federal court by those parties as well as the lawyers who filed the suits and other publicly available information (such as Laydon's LinkedIn page).

As in prior and future chapters, the personal details about the brokers—such as Farr's sexual advice to his son, Gilmour's financial woes, and the Read clan's difficulty adjusting to New Zealand—largely were captured via discussions the brokers had on work e-mail, chats, or phone calls. Other details were disclosed in their trial, in their personnel records obtained by regulators, or in interviews with me.

The background on Alexis Stenfors comes largely from my interviews with him and his wife, as well as lectures he has delivered to students and academic papers he published that discuss his personal background. Broader context, including how other traders and bankers felt around 9/11, comes from Luyendijk's *Swimming with Sharks.*

The scene at the Mayweather-Hatton boxing match is derived from widespread media coverage of the event as well as a video recording of it available on YouTube.

CHAPTER 7: YOUR NAME IN PRINT

The detailed retelling of when Hayes and Tighe met is based on extensive interviews with both parties as well as e-mails they sent at the time they met and Tighe's Facebook page, which I had access to. I also reviewed their personal photos for additional details. Further details come from a psychiatric report produced by Dr. Dere Robertson before Hayes's trial.

I relied on contemporaneous news coverage in the Swiss and American media for the account of the UBS shareholders meeting. The Walsh-Koutsogiannis exchange was conducted over instant messages that were later collected by regulators.

The descriptions of the Hayes family interactions and his introduction to the Tighe clan come from my interviews with members of both families.

CHAPTER 8: A YACHT IN MONACO

The descriptions of the Bali vacation come from interviews with Hayes and Tighe and pictures they took of Hayes's vicious sunburns.

CHAPTER 9: WHAT'S A CABAL?

The descriptions of the states of mind and actions of various BBA officials are based on their e-mail and phone records, contemporaneous BBA documents, interviews they gave to regulators and law enforcement, trial testimony, and my interviews with past and present

BBA officials. The account of the FXMMC meetings comes largely from minutes of those meetings as well as interviews with some participants.

The Scott Peng sections come in large part from interviews with him and former colleagues as well as the reports that he wrote while at Citigroup. Andrew Thursfield's subsequent testimony to the Serious Fraud Office also provided helpful context about the industry reaction to Peng's research.

The account of what went on in the *Wall Street Journal*'s London bureau in 2008—two years before I started working there—comes from interviews with several people who worked there at the time.

The back and forth between Tim Geithner, Mervyn King, and others comes from materials the BBA disclosed to a British parliamentary committee as well as documents published by either the Bank of England or the Federal Reserve. The descriptions of the Bank for International Settlements gathering partly come from Neil Irwin's *The Alchemists: Three Central Bankers and a World on Fire* (Penguin, 2013).

In this and future chapters, the descriptions of the CFTC and Justice Department investigation are based on my interviews with past and present CFTC staff and commissioners, past and present Justice Department officials, and their counterparts at other agencies, such as the FSA.

CHAPTER 10: *ENTRE NOUS*

The description of Carsten Kengeter—yoga lover and extreme skier—comes from this profile: "Ex-banker Carsten Kengeter Moves Fast to Reshape Deutsche Börse," *Financial Times*, February 24, 2016, by Patrick Jenkins.

CHAPTER 11: GODS OF THE SEA

Some of the physical descriptions in this chapter—of Cecere's wife, for example—are based on photos taken of the individuals and that appeared on other people's public Facebook pages.

CHAPTER 12: IN THE FLAG ROOM

The descriptions of Thursfield (and his CFTC presentation) are based largely on his trial testimony and his interviews with the Serious Fraud Office.

The Gary Gensler section is derived partly from my interviews with a wide range of his former colleagues, as well as from other media coverage. Among the most helpful articles was "The Democrats' Stealth Fighter," *Baltimore Sun,* November 3, 2002, by Julie Hirschfield Davis. The description of his ideological about-face came from "Beating the Street," *New Republic,* May 5, 2010, by Noam Scheiber. Several other elements came from "CFTC Chief Gary Gensler Is out to Police Financial Wild West," *USA Today,* November 23, 2009, by Paul Wiseman; "An Ex-Goldman Man Goes After Derivatives," *Time,* April 22, 2010, by Michael Scherer; and "Was Tom Hayes Running the Biggest Financial Conspiracy in History?" *Bloomberg Businessweek,* September 14, 2015, by Liam Vaughan and Gavin Finch.

The section on Thomas Youle and Connan Snider is based on my interviews with them as well as their article, which remained unpublished as of mid-2016. Similarly, the Joseph Cotchett and Nanci Nishimura section is largely based on my interviews with and observations of them as well as "Sealed with a Dis," *San Francisco Weekly,* May 23, 2007, by Will Harper and Mary Spicuzza.

The section on the Justice Department's evolving attitude toward prosecuting big companies is drawn in significant part from *Too Big to Jail: How Prosecutors Compromise with Corporations* by Brandon Garrett (Harvard University Press, 2014).

The descriptions of the subpoenas sent and visits made by regulators are based on public accounts, my interviews with regulators and others present at the visits, and trial testimony.

CHAPTER 13: A SLAP ON THE WRIST

The description of the warning Mccappin received about Hayes comes from a person who was on the call between the UBS and Citigroup officials.

The description of why rivals tend to attack troubled traders is based in part on Lowenstein's *When Genius Failed*.

The comment from the Deutsche Bank trader puzzling over why Hayes was fired comes from Deutsche Bank's 2015 Libor settlement with the U.K. Financial Conduct Authority.

I was given copies of Tighe's e-mails with her friends in advance of her wedding.

CHAPTER 14: HE'S THE ONE

The section on David Meister comes from my interviews with past and present CFTC officials as well as publicly available documents.

The chronology of how UBS came to investigate Libor manipulation is based on my interviews with past and present bank employees, as well as Pieri's interview with Australian regulators. The discussion of Gibson Dunn's role, including regulators' ceding of large chunks of authority to UBS's lawyers, is largely derived from the testimony of Gibson Dunn partner Stephen Sletten as a prosecution witness in Hayes's trial.

Hayes's quotation in his phone call with Alykulov about the dudes who put people in jail is from the Justice Department's charges against him. The rest of the quotations in this section come from Hayes and others with direct knowledge of the calls.

The information about the suspension of RBS traders comes from "Secret Libor Transcripts Expose Trader Rate-Manipulation," Bloomberg News, December 12, 2012, by Liam Vaughan and Gavin Finch.

The section on Kweku Adoboli's downfall comes in large part from "Kweku Adoboli: A Rogue Trader's Tale," *Financial Times,* October 22, 2015, by Lindsay Fortado.

CHAPTER 15: SPIDERS

The Andrew Smith section is based on former traders' interviews with me and with regulators and internal chat transcripts.

The London Whale description is based in part on J.P. Morgan's internal review into the debacle, the results of which were published in January 2013 in a 132-page report.

Colin Goodman explained the circumstances surrounding his mother-in-law's death in detail to regulators.

In this and subsequent chapters, the sections about Hayes's interactions with his lawyers and their interactions with the SFO and Justice Department are derived in part from detailed notes taken by the lawyers as well as my interviews with lawyers and others.

CHAPTER 16: A CROOK OF THE FIRST ORDER

The David Bermingham section is based on my interviews with Bermingham and media coverage of his ordeal starting in 2002.

The draft charges against Hayes, which named Kengeter and Mc-cappin as his co-conspirators, were handed over to Hayes's lawyers, and I saw a copy.

Starting around February 2013 in the chronology, when I began regularly corresponding and meeting with Hayes, I witnessed or had firsthand knowledge of some of the scenes and events, as well as Hayes's deteriorating mental state and erratic behavior. In general, I am the "acquaintance" to whom he spoke or sent text messages. Additional sources include the pretrial reports prepared by a psychologist and a psychiatrist about Hayes's mental health.

CHAPTER 17: THE UNIT COST OF STEAK

The section on the SFO's on-again, off-again efforts to freeze Tighe's assets comes from my interviews with her, Hayes, and lawyers involved in the fight, as well as court documents and other materials filed by Tighe that provide a rough chronology of events.

Gensler's revisionist description of his role in the Libor investigation comes from "The Little Agency That Could," *New York Times,* November 15, 2013, by Joe Nocera.

The description of Hellsinki-V, Danny Wilkinson's electronica group, is based in part on YouTube videos of its festival performances.

An amusing account of Hayes's bingo strategy appeared in the "Caesars Casino Pays Punters in Online Bingo Error," *Guardian,* August 14, 2011, by Rupert Neate. The anonymous twenty-nine-year-old doctor quoted in the story got the tip about the loophole via Hayes.

CHAPTER 18: CHARADES

Some of the biographical items on Mukul Chawla come from the *Times* (London), "Lawyer of the Qeek: Mukul Chawla, QC," September 3, 2015, by Linda Tsang.

Kweku Adoboli texted his acquaintance Lindsay Fortado, a *Financial Times* reporter who was in court and told me about the exchange.

The section on Hayes's numb feet is based partly on Hayes's medical records, which he shared with me.

CHAPTER 19: WITHIN THE ARK

The details about the jurors' actions after the brokers' acquittal come from two sources. The fist pumps were reported by the *Guardian* in the article "Serious Fraud Office Back in the Dock After Libor Acquittals," January 29, 2016, by Graham Ruddick. The juror's hug of a broker's wife was reported in "How Six Brokers Walked Free After Unraveling of U.K. Libor Case," Bloomberg News, February 8, 2016, by Liam Vaughan.

The criminal investigation of David Nichols was reported in "Two Ex-Deutsche Bank Traders Charged by U.S. in Libor Probe," Bloomberg News, June 2, 2016, by Tom Schoenberg.

After the verdicts, I followed the brokers to the Shipwrights Arms, where I witnessed the events that are recounted in the book's final scene.

ABOUT THE AUTHOR

DAVID ENRICH is a veteran writer and editor at the *Wall Street Journal*. He currently is the *Journal*'s Financial Enterprise Editor, heading a team of investigative reporters. He previously served as the *Journal*'s European banking editor, based in London. He has won numerous journalism awards, including the 2016 Gerald Loeb Award for his coverage of Tom Hayes and the Libor scandal. A Massachusetts native and a graduate of Claremont McKenna College in California, he lives in New York with his wife and two sons.